Praise for *The Wizards of Langley*

"Dr. Richelson has assembled a remarkable body of information describing the Directorate of Science and Technology at CIA, based primarily on declassified documents. With his research now available, one can begin to appreciate the extraordinary capability that was created at CIA during the Cold War and the enormous contribution DS&T made to its peaceful outcome. His account accurately portrays the tensions between the Air Force and CIA officers who created these capabilities and Robert McNamara's civilian officials who sought to annex and frustrate them."

—Albert D. Wheelon, Deputy Director for Science and Technology, CIA (1963–1966)

"Instead of cloaks they wear lab coats, and their daggers are laser pointers. They are the men and women of CIA's Directorate of Science and Technology, the little-known organization responsible for pushing the art of spying beyond the edge of reality. In *The Wizards of Langley*, Jeff Richelson takes the reader behind the heavy curtain to show, for the first time, how the wizards perform their magic. It is a unique look into one of the most shadowy areas of espionage by a master of intelligence literature."

—James Bamford, best-selling author of *The Puzzle Palace and Body of Secrets*

"*The Wizards of Langley* is a marvel of balance, new information, and solid research. Richelson rightly focuses on the Division of Science and Technology of the CIA, which played and plays as important a role in enhancing American security as spies—the covert warriors who would be empty-handed had not the wizards provided the tools of the trade. Like his previous books, this one will soon be indispensable."

—Thomas Powers, Author of *The Man Who Kept the Secrets: Richard Helms & the CIA*

"Jeffrey Richelson reads, reads, and reads some more before he writes, and it's paid off, as it has in the past. *The Wizards of Langley* is complete in every way—an inside account of the personalities and policies that drove America's most top-secret operations in the harrowing days of the Cold War."

—Seymour Hersh

THE WIZARDS OF LANGLEY

Inside the CIA's Directorate of Science and Technology

JEFFREY T. RICHELSON

Westview PRESS
A Member of the Perseus Books Group

Westview Press books are available at special discounts for bulk purchases in the United States by corporations, institutions, and other organizations. For more information, please contact the Special Markets Department at the Perseus Books Group, 11 Cambridge Center, Cambridge MA 02142, or call (617) 252-5298.

Published in 2001 in the United States of America by Westview Press, 5500 Central Avenue, Boulder, Colorado 80301-2877, and in the United Kingdom by Westview Press, 12 Hid's Copse Road, Cumnor Hill, Oxford OX2 9JJ

Find us on the World Wide Web at www.westviewpress.com

Library of Congress Cataloging-in-Publication Data
Richelson, Jeffrey T.
The wizards of Langley : inside the CIA's Directorate of Science and Technology / Jeffrey T. Richelson.
p. cm.
Includes bibliographical references and index.
ISBN 0-8133-6699-2
1. United States. Central Intelligence Agency. Directorate of Science and Technology—History. I. Title.

UB251.U5 R53 2001

2001017750

The paper used in this publication meets the requirements of the American National Standard for Permanence of Paper for Printed Library Materials Z39.48-1984.

10 9 8 7 6 5 4 3

If ever legends and stories of American technological genius were deserved and not yet realized, they would be about scientists and engineers, the wizards of CIA and American intelligence who pioneered reconnaissance aircraft like the U-2 and SR-71, photographic satellites from the KH-4 to KH-11, an amazing array of signals intelligence satellites . . . people who worked brilliantly but anonymously to serve their country.

—Robert Gates, November 19, 1999,
at a conference on "U.S. Intelligence and the Cold War."

CONTENTS

PREFACE

To most of the public, reference to the Central Intelligence Agency elicits visions of espionage and covert operations. To the more knowledgeable, the CIA also produces finished intelligence—from the highly controlled *President's Daily Brief* to a multitude of less exclusive intelligence assessments. Far fewer think of the agency in terms of its efforts to exploit science and technology for intelligence purposes. Even an 800-page history of the agency, published in 1986, included only a few references to the agency's Directorate of Science and Technology. Yet, the history of that directorate is a key element in the history of both the CIA and the entire intelligence community.

The directorate has had a dramatic impact on the collection and analysis of intelligence. Several of the most important collection systems the United States operates today are direct descendants of earlier CIA programs. The directorate has designed and operated some of America's most important spy satellites as well as the A-12 (OXCART) and U-2 spy planes, been heavily involved in the collection of signals intelligence (SIGINT), and helped pioneer the technical analysis of foreign missile and space programs. Its satellites and SIGINT activities proved vital in allowing intelligence analysts to assess the capabilities of Soviet missile systems. It is also responsible for a number of scientific advances—including a key component of heart pacemaker technology—that have been made available for medical and other purposes.

Of course, as might be expected of an organization that has been in existence for almost four decades and has tried to operate on the cutting edge, the directorate has not been completely free from folly. Most notably, it funded research in which alleged psychics attempted to report on activities at Soviet military facilities by "viewing" those activities from California. And some of its activities would win no awards from animal welfare leagues. But the directorate's foresight and successes far outdistance its follies and failures.

One element of the directorate's history is the hardware it designed and operated; another is the intelligence it produced through its collection and analysis activities. But at the heart of those activities were individuals—managers, analysts, technicians, and operators. The individuals involved in the directorate's early years overcame a number of obstacles, both bureaucratic and technical, that permitted the directorate to make such a significant contribution to U.S. intelligence capabilities and national security. Others who came along later were instrumental in ensuring that the directorate continued to make key contributions. In each era, a number of those individuals risked their lives in performing their missions.

As part of its celebration of its fiftieth anniversary in 1997, the CIA designated fifty individuals as CIA trailblazers. Included in the list of honorees were four of the seven Deputy Directors for Science and Technology along with numerous directorate employees who made contributions in the areas of signals intelligence, research and development, support to clandestine operations, the design and development of overhead reconnaissance systems, and imagery interpretation. Thus, this book focuses on both the activities and individuals that are crucial elements of the directorate's history.

The Wizards of Langley takes the form of a chronological narrative that traces the evolution of the Directorate of Science and Technology over the almost four decades of its existence. The first chapter covers the period 1947–1961 and tracks the CIA's growing involvement in scientific intelligence analysis as well as the use of technology to collect intelligence. The length of the first chapter is a testament to how deeply involved the agency became in such matters during its first fifteen years. By 1961, the CIA was producing key studies of Soviet and Chinese nuclear weapons programs, operating space and aerial reconnaissance systems, and operating stations along the Soviet periphery to eavesdrop on missile tests.

Chapter 2 focuses on the first attempt, in 1962, to establish a directorate for science and technology, then designated the Deputy Directorate for Research. Each of the subsequent eight chapters focuses on developments during the tenure of a specific Deputy Director for Science and Technology—except that two chapters each are devoted to the tenures of Albert Wheelon (1963–1966) and Carl Duckett (1966–1976). Over the course of Chapters 2 through 10, each aspect of directorate activity—from the development of reconnaissance systems to support to clandestine operations—is covered on two or more occasions.

The final chapter covers the very brief tenures of Gary Smith and (at the time of this writing) his successor, Joanne Isham. It also examines the factors that contributed to the directorate's record of success and what the directorate must do to remain a significant contributor to U.S. intelligence capabilities.

Jeffrey T. Richelson

ACKNOWLEDGMENTS

A variety of sources made this book possible. The reporting of academics, researchers, and journalists on various elements of the CIA's scientific and technical activities provided a foundation on which to build. In addition to their reporting, many also provided advice or passed on material they believed might be helpful. Among the individuals I gladly acknowledge are Matthew Aid, Desmond Ball, Chris Pocock, John Prados, and Robert Windrem. Documents, advice, and assistance were also provided by a number of colleagues at the National Security Archive, including Thomas Blanton, William Burr, Malcolm Byrne, and Michael Evans.

The CIA's Public Affairs Office and Office of the Information and Privacy Coordinator, and the National Reconnaissance Office's FOIA office provided information and documentation that enabled me to go well beyond what had been written before. My thanks go both to the personnel of those offices as well as to others in those organizations who reviewed requested documents for release. CIA releases to the National Archives also proved to be of great value.

I greatly appreciate the willingness of a number of individuals to make time in their schedules to be interviewed, almost all on the record. A list of interviewees I can acknowledge is contained in the Sources section at the end of the book. Special thanks go to Albert "Bud" Wheelon for his willingness to sit for repeated interviews as well as for the hospitality he and his wife, Cicely, showed me. In addition, he, along with Evan Hineman and John McMahon, were kind enough to read a first draft of the manuscript. All errors are, of course, my responsibility.

Finally, I should note that the support of Leo Wiegman at Westview Press proved crucial in turning a proposal into a completed project.

J.T.R.

1

UNEXPECTED MISSIONS

On July 26, 1947, while waiting for Air Force One to fly him to see his dying mother, President Harry S Truman took care of some important government business. By signing the National Security Act, Truman approved creation of a National Security Council (NSC), a unified National Military Establishment under a Secretary of Defense, and a Central Intelligence Agency (CIA). The new agency would report to the President and be headed by the Director of Central Intelligence (DCI).[1]

The CIA replaced the Central Intelligence Group (CIG), which the Secretaries of State, War, and the Navy had established in January 1946 on Truman's orders. The CIG had operated with personnel and facilities borrowed from their departments and was supervised by a National Intelligence Authority (NIA) consisting of the three secretaries and the president's personal representative, Admiral William Leahy. By July 1946, CIG chief Hoyt S. Vandenberg and key White House advisers agreed that the CIG had proved ineffective. An independent agency, explicitly authorized by Congress, and with its own resources, was required.[2]

Heading the new agency was Rear Admiral Roscoe H. Hillenkoetter, who had been the CIG's director since May 1. His appointment interrupted Hillenkoetter's second tour of duty as the naval attaché in Paris. His intelligence experience dated back to World War II, when he served on Admiral Chester Nimitz's staff, with responsibility for intelligence on the Pacific theater. To make a point, Hillenkoetter was fond of quoting Marx, Lenin, and Stalin.[3]

The CIA faced hostility from the military services, whose leaders considered a central intelligence organization a threat to their prerogatives as well as a competitor for resources. A brick building with white Ionic columns on the 2400 block of E Street, N.W., in downtown Washington served as headquarters. Another twenty-five buildings spread across Washington, including temporary wooden structures around the Reflecting Pool in front of the Lincoln Memorial, and by the Tidal Basin, housed other CIA units. According to one account, "the buildings were so rickety that it was not uncommon for safes used to hold classified documents to come crashing down from the upper floors." Whether or not such life-threatening events transpired, there was at least the fear that safes and basic office machinery would suddenly come hurtling through the ceiling.[4]

SCIENTIFIC INTELLIGENCE

The new CIA absorbed a number of CIG components, including the Office of Reports and Estimates (ORE), whose products during 1947 and 1948 included assessments of Soviet foreign and military policy, Soviet weapons, Chinese minorities in Southeast Asia, and the situation in Iran.[5] Scientific studies—on weapons, nuclear energy, medicine, or electronics—were the responsibility of the office's Scientific Branch.

The branch's Nuclear Energy Group had been established on March 28, 1947, when the personnel and files of the Manhattan Engineering District's Foreign Intelligence Section had been transferred to CIG. The group was charged with coordinating and conducting research on foreign nuclear energy developments, as well as determining the information required for solid intelligence analysis.[6] Among those joining the CIG that day in March was Henry S. Lowenhaupt, a Yale University Ph.D. in chemistry, who in 1999 would be named a "trailblazer" by the CIA for his contributions to the field of nuclear intelligence. At that time, Lowenhaupt was still consulting for the agency, having retired in 1990 after forty-three years of service.[7]

But in 1947, and for a number of years afterward, the notion that the CIA should play a significant role in the production of scientific intelligence—particularly as it related to foreign weapons—was not universally shared. The Joint Research and Development Board (JRDB), established by the Secretaries of War and Navy in summer 1946 and chaired by Dr. Vannevar Bush, viewed support from the Scientific Branch as vital.[8] In January 1947, the JRDB concluded an agreement with the CIG that would make the resources of the Scientific Branch "fully available" to the board's chairman.[9]

In October, Dr. Wallace Brode, who had headed the Paris liaison office of the Office of Scientific Research and Development during the war, became head of the Scientific Branch—based on Bush's advice.[10] For the next year, he faced a series of what were, for him, insurmountable obstacles. In December 1947, a senior JRDB official informed Bush that conflict over the size and missions of the CIA had "Dr. Brode completely stymied," and was "blocking his attempts to recruit and organize his staff, and preventing RDB [as JRDB had been renamed] from obtaining any useful intelligence from CIA."[11]

Over the next eleven months, Brode tried to obtain a clear and wide mandate for his organization. Using the guided missile as an example of a modern weapons system that required detailed investigation, he argued that his branch should examine such systems from the basic technology involved through to the beginning of production of operational weapons.[12]

But in October 1948, Bush reported to Defense Secretary James Forrestal that the CIA was highly inefficient, particularly in the scientific intelligence area. Brode lacked resources as well as authority, the latter making it impossible for him to compel the Army, Navy, Atomic Energy Commission (AEC), and other organizations to share information. Brode received little assistance from Hillenkoetter, who had minimal appreciation for the special requirements of scientific intelligence and permitted other agency components to usurp the responsibilities of Brode's branch. Thus, the DCI approved the March 1948 transfer of the Nuclear Energy Group to the Office of Special Operations (OSO), responsible for espionage, an action that violated the 1947 arrangement with Bush's board.[13]

Brode resigned in October for those and other reasons—including Hillenkoetter's failure to support him when his clearance for nuclear data was challenged, as well as the DCI's unwillingness to grant him temporary leave to head the National Bureau of Standards. In a September memo, he had written that the obstacles he was facing could be overcome only by creating an Office of Scientific Intelligence. Not surprisingly, the DCI did not respond.[14]

Although Hillenkoetter felt free to ignore Brode, he could not so easily disregard two key outside reviews. In late 1948, a task force headed by Ferdinand Eberstadt observed that the "failure [to] properly . . . appraise the extent of scientific developments in enemy countries may have more immediate and catastrophic consequences than failure in any other field of intelligence." What was needed was "a central authority responsible for assimilating all information concerning developments in the field of science abroad and competent to estimate the significance of these developments." Such an authority, Eberstadt's group pointed out, would need "access to all available information bearing on the problem" and "must also be able to provide intelligence direction" in the collection of relevant information.[15]

A report prepared for the NSC by future DCI Allen Dulles and two colleagues was also critical of the CIA's scientific intelligence effort. It noted that ORE's Scientific Branch "was expected to become the central group for stimulating and coordinating scientific intelligence. It has not yet filled this role."[16] Dated January 1, 1949, the report had been sent to the White House two weeks earlier. On the last day of 1948, the DCI removed the Scientific Branch from ORE, reattached the Nuclear Energy Group to it, transformed the branch into the Office of Scientific Intelligence (OSI), and designated its chief the Assistant Director for Scientific Intelligence (ADSI). At the same time, OSI was no longer asked to serve as the scientific intelligence adviser to the President or provide intelligence support to the RDB or Atomic Energy Commission.[17]

Heading the new office was Willard Machle, an M.D. and former professor of medicine, who had conducted wartime combat studies, headed the Armored Force Medical Research Laboratory in Kentucky, and been awarded the Legion of Honor for his physiological research. His selection was probably a response to the Eberstadt committee's observations about CIA deficiencies in medical intelligence, particularly with regard to biological warfare and human physiology.[18]

But during the first three quarters of 1949, Machle experienced little more success than Brode, as he and other OSI officials attempted to consolidate the collection and analysis of national scientific intelligence within the CIA. The Office of Naval Intelligence retained primacy in the area of earth sciences data—even though such information was essential for assessing developments not only in undersea warfare but also in guided missile intelligence, areas of considerable importance to national policy.[19]

But Machle was given a golden opportunity in September 1949 when analysis of particles collected by an Air Force weather reconnaissance plane—a method of detection that had been recommended by Henry Lowenhaupt in 1947—led to the inescapable conclusion that the Soviet Union had detonated an atomic device in late August, sixteen months earlier than the CIA had thought possible. Six days after President Truman told the American public about the event, Machle sent Hillenkoetter a memo entitled "Inability of OSI to Accomplish Its Mission." He argued that little had been achieved in correcting the problems cited in the Eberstadt report, "highlighted by the almost total failure of conventional intelligence in estimating Soviet development of an atomic bomb."[20] Machle identified conditions within and outside the CIA that he believed prevented OSI from producing vital intelligence on atomic and biological weapons, aircraft and guided missiles, electronics, medicine, and basic scientific research. Among the problems Machle cited were a lack of CIA authority to coordinate intelligence activities and the failure of intelligence collection offices within the CIA to understand that they existed to serve the intelligence analysts.[21]

A virtually immediate result of Machle's memo was the drafting of Director of Central Intelligence Directive (DCID) 3/3 on "Scientific Intelligence." Written by OSI deputy chief Karl Weber, a Ph.D. in organic chemistry who had joined the agency in 1947, it was approved by Hillenkoetter on October 28. The directive established a Scientific Intelligence Committee (SIC), to be chaired by Machle, that was to coordinate and evaluate the collection and production of national scientific intelligence.[22]

The directive, combined with the belief of Machle and Weber that scientific and technical intelligence included all research and development up to production for operational use, rather predictably resulted in protests from the military services. The CIA was presuming to issue reports on the characteristics and capabilities of foreign weapons systems—a prerogative the military believed to be its exclusively. But the dissatisfaction of the influential RDB with the intelligence it was receiving from the military on just such topics neutralized the services' attack.[23]

Machle, however, would soon leave the scene. He was, according to an official history, "outraged that scientific intelligence should be dependent on clandestine collection by ignorant spooks." When he suspected that the OSO was withholding nuclear-related information required by OSI, he asked members of his nuclear energy branch to exploit their contacts with OSO personnel to obtain that information—a breach of protocol that cost him his job. On March 6, 1950, he was replaced by Dr. Marshall Chadwell from the New York office of the Atomic Energy Commission. Machle, recalls Weber, "had too many corpuscles for people in CIA, particularly the ops [operations] people."[24] Chadwell, in contrast, was a mild-mannered conciliator. And with Chadwell in charge, the military was able to curb and even roll back the authority of OSI.

The generals and admirals were willing to accept SIC jurisdiction over committees on atomic energy, biological and chemical warfare, electronics, and even guided missiles and aircraft. But Chadwell's plan to establish committees on undersea warfare and Army ordnance, which the Navy and Army considered their respective and exclusive jurisdictions, brought a counterattack.[25]

In February 1951, the Army member of the SIC questioned whether it should have any jurisdiction over weapons systems applications—which ultimately led to a decision by DCI Walter Bedell Smith, who had replaced Hillenkoetter in October 1950, to commission a survey of OSI. The survey, by CIA inspector general Stuart Hedden, concluded that the military services had "considerable justification" for their belief that certain areas of science were "their exclusive prerogatives."[26]

When Smith then appointed a committee, with representatives from the military services, Joint Staff, and AEC, to examine the question of scientific intelligence and appointed Loftus Becker as its chair, OSI's position was destined to be weakened further. Although Becker was head of the agency's Deputy Directorate for Intelligence, which Smith had established in January 1952 to unify intelligence analysis, Becker had already expressed his view that the military should be encouraged to expand its work in the scientific intelligence area.[27]*

The report Becker presented to the DCI and the interagency Intelligence Advisory Committee in August 1952 resulted in replacement of Weber's directive. The new directive abolished the SIC and supplanted it with a Scientific Estimates Committee that had no coordination authority, even on paper. It also assigned to the military responsibility for intelligence on weapons systems and military equipment, as well as research and development leading to military systems. OSI was to handle intelligence on the basic sciences, scientific resources, medicine, and "pertinent" applied research and development. The directive did specify that no agency would be considered the final authority in any field, and that any agency could produce internal studies it believed necessary in order to fulfill its responsibilities.[28]

The adoption of the new directive, according to an official history, had a "devastating effect upon the morale of OSI." Becker resented OSI's reaction. On August 21, he met with senior officers and acknowledged the legitimacy of their doubts about the military's competence in the scientific and technical area, but demanded that OSI make a loyal effort to make the directive work. Superior performance, he told them, would lead

---

*In 1952, the CIA consolidated several offices into components for intelligence, operations, and administration—the Deputy Directorates for Intelligence, Plans, and Administration. In 1965, they would become Directorates.

to OSI leadership in the field. The meeting failed to convince OSI's senior members that Becker had known what he was doing when he revoked Weber's directive. But from that time on, OSI devoted less attention and energy to asserting the CIA's role in coordinating scientific intelligence activities and more to developing OSI's capabilities for research in all areas of scientific intelligence, including weapon systems development, "in anticipation of a day when a new DCI and a new DDI [Deputy Director of Intelligence] would value such independent capabilities."[29]

Such a day arrived in early February 1953 when Allen Dulles, who had become deputy DCI in August 1951 after a short stint as operations chief, replaced Smith. In addition, Robert Amory succeeded Becker as head of the agency's intelligence directorate.[30] Two years later OSI's leadership was strengthened when Herbert J. Scoville became head of OSI in August 1955. The forty-year-old Scoville had received a B.S. degree from Yale in 1937, where he had studied chemistry, mathematics, physics, and German. Five years later, he was awarded a Ph.D. in physical chemistry from the University of Rochester. From 1948 until joining the CIA, he had served as the technical director of the Armed Forces Special Weapons Project, which advised the chiefs of the armed services on a variety of nuclear weapons issues.[31]

In 1959, a new DCI directive on the production of scientific and technical intelligence assigned the CIA responsibility for producing such intelligence as a "service of common concern" and "as required to fulfill the statutory responsibilities of the Director of Central Intelligence." The directive also reestablished the Scientific Intelligence Committee, with a mission of fostering coordination.[32]

Amid all the bureaucratic battles, OSI had been actively producing studies and estimates. In 1949, it issued the 64-page single-spaced study "An Estimate of Swedish Capabilities in Science"—a detailed assessment of Swedish scientists, research institutions, and technology programs, including highly classified wind tunnel and pulse-jet engine research. The study concluded that the Soviets would gain a distinct, but small, scientific advantage if it overran Sweden, and recommended "denying" them certain Swedish scientists and research facilities in the case of a Soviet invasion.[33]

That same year, OSI informed the Office of the Secretary of Defense that the Soviets would not invest their scarce resources in developing radiological weapons. Such a program "would interfere with atomic bomb production," OSI stated in a briefing paper. "In addition," OSI concluded, "radiological materials are difficult to handle and disseminate, and their use is relatively ineffective."[34]

Until 1955, when responsibility was transferred to the Joint Atomic Energy Intelligence Committee, chaired by Scoville, OSI was responsible for preparing national intelligence estimates on atomic energy.[35] Its 1954 estimate on the Soviet program reported on the production of uranium, reactor power, and the likely explosive force of Soviet weapons. The study also considered how large the Soviet nuclear stockpile might be in each year through mid-1957, based on alternative assumptions concerning the composition of the warheads and their individual yields.[36]

In 1954, Chadwell and key OSI personnel, along with some consultants, appear to have been called in to aid the CIA's Board of National Estimates in preparing the first full-scale National Intelligence Estimate (NIE) on Soviet guided missiles. The 49-page estimate examined Soviet capabilities to develop all varieties of guided missiles as well as probable Soviet intentions. However, the lack of hard intelligence then available was neatly summarized at the beginning of the estimate: "We have no firm current intelligence on what particular guided missiles the USSR is presently developing or may now have in operational use."[37]

The exercise convinced Dulles that guided missile intelligence had to receive greater attention both within the CIA and across the intelligence community. In late March 1955, the Guided Missiles Branch of OSI's Weapons Division was elevated to division status. (In 1957, a Space Branch was established to monitor Soviet earth satellite, lunar, and interplanetary efforts.)[38]

The nuclear activities of U.S. adversaries and allies, small and large, remained the main focus of OSI's analytical effort. In 1958, OSI began inquiring into Israel's nuclear activities, particularly its production of heavy water and uranium. That same year, the Netherlands nuclear energy program was the subject of a 23-page OSI report, which examined the tiny nation's nuclear research and development program, evaluated its ability to produce plutonium and U-235, and assessed the objective of the program—"the development of economic applications of nuclear energy." A 1959 study of the French nuclear weapons program attempted to assess France's capability to produce fissionable material as well as develop and test nuclear weapons.[39]

In August 1958, the OSI's Charlie Reeves began assembling data on generating stations and transmission lines in the vicinity of known or suspected Soviet atomic energy sites in the Urals, the USSR's most important atomic energy region. Because the production of fissionable materials from a plant was directly proportional to the amount of power consumed, information on power supplied was used to estimate nuclear material production. Starting with a single picture of the Sverdlovsk Central Dispatching Station of the Urals Electric Power System that appeared in the Soviet press, Reeves examined 103 articles in Soviet newspapers and technical journals, 4 reports of visits by delegations, 11 POW returnee reports, approximately 25 local photographs, as well as aerial photography. As a result, in April 1959, Reeves was able to map out the power distribution network in the Urals and determine the approximate power supplied to the U-235 production plant at Verkh Neyvinsk, to the plutonium reactor at Kyshtym, and to the unidentified complex near Nizhnyaya Tura.[40]

MIND CONTROL

After dinner on November 19, 1953, Frank Olson, a scientist with the Army Chemical Corps's Special Operations Division, based at Ft. Detrick, Maryland, shared a drink of Cointreau with several of his colleagues—Cointreau that had been spiked with LSD. Ten days later, Olson jumped to his death. The hallucinogen was added to his drink at the direction of Dr. Sidney Gottlieb, head of the Chemical Division of the Technical Services Staff (TSS) of the Deputy Directorate for Plans (DDP), established in 1952 to consolidate CIA operational activities in one component.[41]

Gottlieb, whose scientific credentials included a Ph.D. in biochemistry from Cal Tech, had joined the CIA two years earlier, at the age of thirty-three. Despite being born with a clubfoot and a stutter, he had become an expert folk dancer and achieved academic success. Along with his wife, he lived on a farm, rose at 5:30 a.m. to milk the goats, drank only goat's milk, made his own cheese, and grew Christmas trees that he sold from a roadside stand.[42]

Although the primary job of the TSS was to devise devices and methods—bugs, recorders, disguised weapons, forged documents, special cameras, and secret writing techniques—Gottlieb did not spike Olson's drink as a prank or out of hostility. He was simply conducting an experiment.

Even before Gottlieb joined the CIA, the agency had already investigated exotic ways in which Soviet agents might affect human behavior. In summer 1949, OSI chief Willard Machle had made a special trip to Western Europe to investigate Soviet interrogation methods. By spring 1950, several CIA branches were considering employing hypnosis for operational use. At that time, Sheffield Edwards, the CIA's director of security, moved to centralize all activity in the behavioral sciences under his control, although OSI continued to provide support to the effort. In April, DCI Roscoe Hillenkoetter approved project BLUEBIRD, whose objectives included "discovering means of conditioning personnel to prevent unauthorized extraction of information from them by known means," and "establishing defensive means for preventing hostile control of Agency personnel." Three months later, a team traveled to Japan to try out behavioral techniques on human subjects. Subsequently, the examination of the possible offensive uses of hypnosis and drugs was added to BLUEBIRD's charter. By December 1950, the BLUEBIRD team had employed drugs to induce a hypnotic-like trance.[43]

Between 1950 and 1952, the responsibility for such activities passed from the Inspection and Security Office to OSI and back to Security, and BLUEBIRD was redesignated ARTICHOKE. One goal of the ARTICHOKE team was to be able to induce amnesia. According to a 1952 agency document, "the greater the amnesia produced, the more effective the results." While Security searched for interrogation aids in the form of a truth drug or hypnotic method, TSS explored a broader topic—the application of chemical and biological techniques to covert operations.[44]

On April 13, 1953, Allen Dulles accepted a suggestion from senior DDP official Richard Helms to establish a program under Gottlieb for "research to develop a capability in the covert use of biological and chemical materials." In addition to giving the United States an offensive capability, such research, Helms wrote, would provide "a thorough knowledge of the enemy's theoretical potential, thus enabling us to defend ourselves against a foe who might not be as restrained in the use of these techniques as we are." The initial budget was $300,000; the program was designated MKULTRA. Use of MKULTRA materials abroad, which began no later than 1953, was designated MKDELTA.[45]

TSS proceeded to investigate the effect of hundreds of drugs, including cocaine, nicotine, and probably hallucinogens such as mescaline. But LSD held the most fascination, in part because only a minute amount could produce a tremendous effect. The CIA wanted to know if the drug could distort a person's loyalty in addition to his sense of reality. Could LSD induce treason as well as hallucinations?[46]

In November 1953, Gottlieb decided to test the drug on a group of scientists from the Army Chemical Corps's Special Operations Division

(SOD), despite two warnings from high-level officials in DDP not to conduct such tests without their approval. There was a certain irony, poetic justice, or cold-bloodedness—depending on one's point of view—in the selection of SOD personnel. Under a program designated MKNAOMI, SOD had been enlisted by Technical Services to produce germ weapons for the CIA's use. The Army scientists had developed darts coated with biological agents and pills containing several different biological agents that could remain potent for weeks or months. SOD also developed a special gun for firing chemical-coated darts to incapacitate guard dogs. Gottlieb later explained that the investigation "was started . . . [at] the height of the Cold War . . . ; with the CIA organizing resources to liberate Eastern Europe by paramilitary means; and with the threat of Soviet aggression very real and tangible."[47]

Olson's death was not a roadblock to Gottlieb's eventual rise to become head of the Technical Services Division (TSD), as TSS would become later in the 1950s. Nor did Olson's suicide, which the CIA secretly concluded was "triggered" by the LSD, end the MKULTRA program. The use of hallucinogens was only one element of MKULTRA; it eventually had 182 subprojects, 33 of which had nothing to do with behavioral modification, toxins, or drugs. Subprojects included electrical brain stimulation and the implanting of electrodes in the brains of several species of animals to enable experimenters to direct the animals by remote control, in the hope they could be further wired and used for eavesdropping. Various elements of MKULTRA would continue until 1963, when the CIA Inspector General discovered the program during an inspection of TSD operations.[48]

OVERFLIGHTS

Seven years to the day after Harry Truman signed legislation establishing the CIA, Dr. James R. Killian Jr., president of the Massachusetts Institute of Technology, received a letter from Truman's successor, Dwight Eisenhower. The president wrote that he understood Killian had been asked by the Office of Defense Mobilization "to direct a study of the country's technological capabilities to meet some of its current problems"—a project that was most directly prompted by a meeting the committee had with Eisenhower in late March. He went on to express his hope that "you will find it possible to free yourself of your many other heavy responsibilities . . . long enough to undertake this important assignment."[49]

Two CIA historians would subsequently write that "when the Central Intelligence Agency came into existence in 1947, no one foresaw that, in less than a decade, it would undertake a major program of overhead reconnaissance, whose principal purpose would be to overfly the Soviet Union."[50] But the assignment Eisenhower asked Killian to undertake would lead to precisely that outcome.

The panel was designated the Technological Capabilities Panel (TCP) and Killian would serve as its chairman. The TCP's Project One focused on offensive capabilities, Project Two on the application of technology to defense, and Project Three on intelligence. The intelligence panel's membership consisted of Edwin Land and Allan Latham Jr. of Polaroid; lens designer James G. Baker and physicist Edward Purcell, both of Harvard; Washington University chemist Joseph W. Kennedy, who had helped isolate plutonium; and John W. Tukey of Princeton and Bell Telephone. Land served as chairman.[51]

The TCP presented its report to Eisenhower on February 14, 1955. "We *must* find ways," it asserted, "to increase the number of hard facts upon which our intelligence estimates are based." The panel recommended "a vigorous program for the extensive use, in many intelligence procedures, of the most advanced knowledge in science and technology." One recommendation involving a specific application of technology had been conveyed to Dulles and Eisenhower several months earlier, and was omitted from the official TCP report due to its sensitivity.[52]

The proposal the panel had made in late October and early November 1954 was that the CIA proceed with a project that had already come to its attention—a specially designed photographic reconnaissance aircraft intended to fly above Soviet radar, fighters, and surface-to-air missiles, a plane that would effectively be invisible and immune to hostile action. In the brief written material transmitted to Dulles, the intelligence panel noted that "for many years it has been clear that aerial photography of Russia would provide direct knowledge of her growth, of new centers of activity in obscure regions, and of military targets."[53]

The plane Land and his colleagues had in mind had been proposed to the Air Force by Clarence "Kelly" Johnson, head of the Lockheed "Skunk Works," who had designed the P-38 fighter-bomber and F-104 Starfighter.[54] But the Air Force was not interested in the specially powered glider, designated the CL-282, which would fly at 70,000 feet, at a speed of 500 knots, to a range of 3,000 nautical miles, with a pilot as the lone crew member. It would carry a special long focal-length camera to photograph objects as small as a man, and bring back images of roads, railroads, industrial plants, nuclear facilities, aircraft, and missile sites within a strip 200 miles wide by 2,500 miles long.[55]

The panel was suggesting that the CIA combine the technological vision of Johnson with the strategic vision of Richard Leghorn, an MIT graduate who had commanded the Army Air Forces' 67th Reconnaissance Group in Europe during World War II. After returning to civilian life, Leghorn began promoting the view, in a variety of venues, that the United States needed to develop a capability for peacetime reconnaissance, which would require high-altitude aircraft with high-resolution cameras.[56]

In a letter to Dulles, Land spelled out a vision for the CIA that went beyond one reconnaissance plane:

> This seems to us the kind of action and technique that is right for the contemporary version of CIA; a modern and scientific way for an Agency that is always supposed to be looking, to do its looking. *Quite strongly, we feel that you must always assert your first right to pioneer in scientific techniques for collecting intelligence. . . . This present opportunity for aerial photography seems to us a fine place to start.*[57] (Emphasis added.)

The letter was an attempt to eliminate the reluctance Dulles had projected when the panel proposed the CL-282 to him in late October 1954. The DCI, faced with the strong advocacy of the project by Killian and other scientific advisers, as well as Eisenhower's desire to go forward, could only accept the inevitable. On November 24, Eisenhower approved a program to build twenty of the spy aircraft for about $35 million and placed the CIA in charge. On December 9, 1954, the CIA and Lockheed signed a contract that allowed work to begin officially on the project, which the CIA code-named AQUATONE. The third key player in the program was the Air Force, which had been enlisted as a cosponsor; it would provide the pilots and train them after their military connection had been suitably obscured.[58]

The CIA official assigned to run the program was Richard Bissell Jr., who had joined the agency that February as a special assistant for planning and coordination and had been briefed on the CL-282 proposal by Land in late August. A graduate of Groton and Yale, he had also studied at the London School of Economics and then taught economics at Yale and MIT. During World War II, he had managed U.S. shipping and then served as deputy director of the Marshall Plan from 1948 to 1951, when he became a staff member of the Ford Foundation. His first contact with the CIA came in late 1953, when he undertook a study of possible U.S. responses to another uprising in East Berlin.[59]

Bissell came to the CIA with a reputation for brilliance. According to former student and Kennedy administration official William P. Bundy, Bissell was "the real mental center and engine room of the Marshall Plan." In his appearances before congressional committees, he inspired sufficient confidence in the value of the revolutionary foreign-aid program for the committees to vote billions of dollars to implement it.[60]

The impression he made on his colleagues in the intelligence world was no different. Robert Amory, whose tenure as DDI overlapped Bissell's years in the agency, remembered him as a "human computer." Arthur Lundahl, the CIA's top photointerpreter for many years, concluded that Bissell "could outwit, outspeak, out-think most of the people around him that I was aware of."[61]

In order to preserve the secrecy that Eisenhower and Dulles insisted on, Bissell suggested locating the project in a "stand-alone" organization, rather than as part of an existing CIA directorate. The resulting Development Projects Staff was the only CIA component with its own communications office and operational cable traffic. Headquarters for the project were also moved to a suite of offices in the Matomic Building at 1717 H Street, in part because of the decrepit condition of the aging office building near E Street where the project began its life.[62]

Bissell's passion for secrecy also extended to his visits to Lockheed. Ben Rich, who succeeded Kelly Johnson as head of the Skunk Works, recalled that "every few weeks I would catch a glimpse of a tall, patrician gentleman dressed improbably in tennis shoes, freshly pressed gray trousers, and a garish big-checked sports jacket. . . . Many months went by before I heard someone refer to him as 'Mr. B.' No one besides Kelly knew his name. 'Mr. B.' was Richard Bissell."[63]

On July 25, 1955, less than eight months after Lockheed had been given official approval to begin the project, Kelly Johnson was ready to deliver the first AQUATONE aircraft to the secret Nevada test site that would subsequently become well-known as Area 51, the world's most famous top-secret base. To hide the aircraft's mission, the plane was put on the Air Force's books as a Utility aircraft. With the U-1 and U-3 designations already taken, it became the U-2.[64]

In the interim, the CIA had beaten back an Air Force attempt to take over the project that it had originally rejected. In March, Air Force chief of staff Nathan Twining proposed that the Strategic Air Command (SAC), headed by Curtis LeMay, run the project once the planes and pilots were ready to fly, but Dulles opposed such an arrangement. The issue was finally resolved, after several months of discussion, by Eisenhower, who wrote that "I want this whole thing to be a civilian operation." He was particularly concerned that "if uniformed personnel of the armed services of the United States fly over Russia, it is an act of war—legally—and I don't want any part of it."[65]

Between April 10 and 14, 1956, U-2s made eight overflights of the United States to test assorted flight and camera systems. Accompanying the heavy camera, which was carried in the equipment (or Q-) bay behind the cockpit, was a mile of ultrathin film, weighing about 300 pounds. On June 20, a U-2 conducted the first operational mission, overflying East Germany and Poland. The plane was ostensibly for weather reconnaissance, belonging to the fictional "1st Weather Reconnaissance Squadron Provisional" at Wiesbaden, Federal Republic of Germany. The actual designation for the unit was Detachment A. An Air Force colonel served as the commanding officer, with a CIA representative serving as his executive officer.[66]

The following day, Eisenhower granted approval to overfly the Soviet Union, although a number of factors, including the weather, delayed the first flight by almost two weeks. On July 2, two U-2s conducted overflights that covered seven East European nations. Then, late on the evening of July 3, Bissell went to AQUATONE headquarters, where he made the "go" decision.[67]

As a result, on July 4, Hervey Stockman took off from Wiesbaden and guided his U-2 over Poznan, Poland, then headed for Belorussia where he turned north toward Leningrad, whose naval shipyards were home to part of the Soviet submarine construction program and were the mission's main target. Also of interest were several major military airfields, coverage of which would permit the CIA to produce an inventory of new Bison heavy bombers. The final leg of the mission took the spy plane over the Soviet Baltic states on its way back to Germany.[68]

The search for Bison bombers was one element of the next day's overflight, which also covered Moscow. Although the city was almost completely blanketed by clouds, the U-2's cameras, equipped with haze filters, produced some usable images of the Soviet capital. More important, the U-2, piloted by Carmen Vito, known as the "Lemon-Drop Kid" due to his habit of carrying a supply of hard lemon candies in his flight suit, brought back pictures of the Fili airframe plant where Bisons were being built, the bomber test facility at Ramenskoye airfield outside of Moscow, the Kaliningrad missile plant, and the Khimki rocket-engine plant.[69]

Another three overflights would be conducted on July 9 and 10, covering much of Eastern Europe, the Ukraine, Belorussia, and the Crimean Peninsula. It came as an unpleasant surprise to the CIA that the Soviets had managed to detect and track the initial intrusions, as illustrated by the attempt of Soviet MiGs to intercept Vito on July 5.[70] On July 10, a Soviet protest note arrived specifying, for the first two missions, the route flown, the depth into Soviet territory the plane penetrated, and the time spent overflying Soviet air space. The note concluded that the "violation of the air frontiers of the Soviet Union by American aircraft cannot be interpreted as other than intentional and conducted for the purposes of reconnaissance." Later that day, presidential aide Brig. Gen. Andrew Goodpaster instructed Bissell, on Eisenhower's orders, to halt all overflights until further notice.[71]

An apparent response to Eisenhower's order was a July 17, 1956, CIA memo that noted "there can be no doubt of the value in terms of our national security of the photographic coverage obtained on 4 July 1956 of five of the seven highest priority targets specified by the USAF." It also suggested that of even greater significance was that "for the first time we are really able to say that we have an understanding of much that was going on in the Soviet Union on 4 July 1956. . . . We now have a cross-section of a part of the entire Soviet way of life for that date." The memo concluded with the observation that "to bar the United States from reaching this understanding through overflights of the critical regions of the Urals and eastward could well be tragic. Five operational missions have already proven that many of our guesses on important subjects can be seriously wrong." To permit such wrong guesses to guide policy would endanger U.S. foreign relations to a much greater extent than carrying out the AQUATONE plan would, the memo asserted.[72]

U-2 overflights of Soviet territory would continue, but sporadically due to Eisenhower's concern about the possible Soviet reaction. The next overflight occurred in late November, and Eisenhower ordered that the plane "stay as close to the border as possible." But by that time, the images from the initial flights had undergone lengthy analysis, and the results led the CIA to conclude that the Air Force claim that the Soviet arsenal contained almost 100 Bison heavy bombers was a significant overestimate.[73]

The missions conducted during the second half of 1957, almost all by aircraft from Detachment B (which would absorb Detachment A in late 1957) at Incrilik Air Base near Adana, Turkey, or Detachment C at Atsugi, Japan, substantially added to the U.S. intelligence community's knowledge of Soviet military forces and industrial capability. During a 23-day period in August, U-2s conducted Operation SOFT TOUCH—seven overflights of the Soviet Union and two of the People's Republic of China.[74]

Targets included the Soviet space launch facility that would become known as Tyuratam; the Semipalatinsk nuclear testing facility; a uranium processing installation at Berezovskiy; and Sary Shagan, where radars were tested against missiles fired from Kapustin Yar, which itself would be photographed in September. In December, Detachment C photographed the ICBM impact site at Klyuchi in the Soviet Far East. Essential to planning the missions targeted on nuclear facilities was the guidance of OSI's Henry Lowenhaupt, who spent much of July 1957 preparing "target briefs, by order of priority, for all atomic targets in the enormous geographical area of central Asia and Siberia."[75]

After 1957, as Eisenhower grew increasingly concerned about the risks involved, overflights of Soviet territory dwindled dramatically—although flights over other areas of the world continued and flights along the Soviet border were authorized. A single overflight was conducted in 1958, and only two took place the following year.[76]

By 1960, the most important national security issue facing the United States was the status of the Soviet Intercontinental Ballistic Missile (ICBM) program. In Senate testimony in January 1960, Dulles painted a less alarmist picture of Soviet ICBM developments than did the Air Force—which resulted in sharp questioning from some legislators. He did not reveal that U-2 imagery had produced no evidence of deployment of the Soviet's SS-6 ICBM outside of the Tyuratam test facility.[77]

Analysts predicted that deployment areas would be located near railroad tracks, given the large size of the missile. A February 2 mission revealed no missile sites, but the Air Force continued to insist that the Soviets had deployed up to 100 missiles. More U-2 flights would be necessary to settle the issue.

Within the CIA there was optimism that such flights, if they entered the Soviet Union in the vicinity of the Soviet-Afghanistan-Pakistan border, could complete their missions unscathed. A March 14 memo noted three penetrations from that area between July 1959 and the February flight that were "accomplished without, to our knowledge, detection by the Soviet Air Defense system." As a result, it was tentatively concluded that "if penetration can be made without detection, there is an excellent chance that the entire mission can be completed without recognition by the air defense system."[78]

And the second U-2 mission of 1960, Operation SQUARE DEAL of April 9, which took off from Peshawar, Pakistan, successfully crisscrossed the railroad network at Sary Shagan. It also photographed Tyuratam, where a new launch area suggested that a new missile was about to appear.[79]

Even before the April 9 mission, Eisenhower had authorized another overflight. On May 1, Francis Gary Powers, the most experienced U-2 pilot with twenty-seven completed missions, including overflights of the Soviet Union and China, departed from Peshawar to carry out Operation GRAND SLAM—the twenty-fourth and most ambitious deep-penetration flight in the U-2 program—which was planned to fly across the Soviet Union from south to north. After overflying Tyuratam, Powers headed for Chelyabinsk, just south of Sverdlovsk. The primary target, Plesetsk, which communications intelligence suggested might be an operational ICBM facility, would come later.[80]

But Powers never made it to Plesetsk. On the morning of May 1, Bob King, Bissell's special assistant, was woken by a phone call from a distressed duty officer repeating the message "Bill Bailey didn't come home." Four and a half hours into the mission, while Powers was above Sverdlovsk, an SA-2 antiaircraft missile had detonated at 70,500 feet and just behind Powers's aircraft, disabling it. During a 1962 debriefing, he recalled feeling a sensation and looking up to see an orange flash and the plane seeming to disintegrate in the air.[81] He ejected, and the Soviet recovery of pilot and plane forced Eisenhower to terminate overflights of the USSR.

In testimony shortly afterward, Dulles told a closed session of the Senate Foreign Relations Committee that the U-2 program had established that the Soviet Union had developed a new medium-range bomber with supersonic capabilities, but "that only a greatly reduced long-range bomber production program is continuing in the Soviet Union." The DCI also noted that the U-2 overflights had produced imagery of a number of long-range bomber airfields and confirmed the location of bases as well as the deployment of bombers. In addition, it provided photographs of the nuclear weapons storage facilities associated with the bombers.[82]

Ground facilities associated with Soviet missile programs had also been a target of U-2 flights. The program also "provided us valuable insight into the problem of Soviet doctrine concerning ICBM deployment," Dulles told his select audience. Aspects of the Soviet atomic energy program that were illuminated by U-2 photography included "the production of fissionable materials, weapons development and test activities," as well as "the location, type, and size of many stockpile sites." In addition, "the Soviet nuclear testing ground has been photographed with extremely interesting results more than once."[83]

Although the May 1 shootdown ended U-2 overflights of the Soviet Union, the CIA still had a valuable asset. In early 1958, a U-2 spotted what the CIA would subsequently conclude was construction of Israel's Dimona nuclear reactor.[84] In August of that year (by which time the program had been renamed CHALICE), in the wake of China's shelling of the Taiwanese-held islands of Quemoy and Matsu, U-2s from Detachment C flew missions over China to monitor People's Liberation Army troop movements—and found no signs of preparation for an invasion.[85]

Still, it was decided that the CIA would "maintain a greatly reduced and redeployed U-2 capability." Approximately half of the CIA's inventory of twelve U-2s would be turned over to the Air Force, and the detachment in Turkey would be closed down. In addition, it was "strongly believed that an appropriate way should be found to use the U-2 to complete the coverage of primary targets in China before air defenses there have been further improved." The project would also receive a new code name—IDEALIST.[86]

U-2s were not the only planes overflying China in the 1950s under the direction of the CIA. In 1954, a small group of CIA and Air Force officers met with Navy officials to arrange for the purchase of seven P-2V7 Neptune maritime patrol aircraft, which had a range of about 4,000 miles. The CIA had chosen the plane because of its capabilities as well as the existence of Navy airfields worldwide. In addition, the small number of CIA Neptunes could easily be hidden in the much larger group of Navy Neptunes deployed throughout the world.[87]

Conversion of the planes from Navy patrol aircraft to CIA covert collectors was conducted first under the designation Project CHERRY (and later WILD CHERRY). The result was seven planes equipped with advanced cameras for low-altitude photography and electronic intelligence (ELINT) gear. The planes were also given a new designation—the RB-69A.[88]

Initial operations with the modified Neptunes began in Europe in 1955 and continued into 1956. Wiesbaden, which became a U-2 base in 1956, received two of the planes, which were often flown by qualified Polish or Czechoslovakian defectors due to their knowledge of the local terrain and East European languages. In addition to flying peripheral missions, the planes were used to overfly parts of the western Soviet Union to collect data on power grids.[89]

In 1957, under a program designated ST/POLLY, RB-69A/Neptunes began flying out of Taiwan and near and into Chinese airspace, primarily to gather electronic intelligence on Chinese radars. The two Wiesbaden-based planes subsequently joined the five originally sent to Taiwan. A crew of twelve was standard for ELINT missions—pilot, copilot, flight engineer, radio operator, and eight ELINT system operators. The crews were handpicked by the Taiwanese Air Force and trained in the United States by the CIA. Missions were launched from Taiwan and, on occasion, South Korea. In addition to the safer peripheral missions were the overflights—which sometimes took the crews to Beijing or Canton, flying below 1,000 feet. The planes were also employed to drop espionage agents, leaflets, and supplies to agents.[90]

BEYOND THE U-2

Richard Bissell and Kelly Johnson had no illusions that the U-2 would be perpetually invulnerable to Soviet countermeasures. All they hoped for was a couple of good years. The Soviet ability to detect and track the plane from the beginning was not expected, but they began thinking about a successor plane long before the May 1, 1960, Powers incident.

In August 1957, the Scientific Engineering Institute (SEI), a Boston-based CIA proprietary that had been working on ways to reduce U-2 vulnerability, began to investigate the possibility of designing an aircraft with a small radar cross-section. SEI soon discovered that supersonic speed dramatically reduced the chance of detection by radar. As a result, the CIA focused on designing a successor to the U-2 that would fly extremely high and fast and would employ radar-absorbing or -deflecting techniques. Both Lockheed and the Convair Division of General Dynamics were informed of the conclusion to guide their research on a possible U-2 successor.[91]

To assist him in evaluating proposals, Bissell once again called on Edwin Land to serve as chairman of an advisory group. Other members included TCP veteran Edward Purcell, Allen F. Donovan of the Cornell Aeronautical Laboratory, and Bissell assistant Eugene P. Kiefer. The group often met in Land's Cambridge office, at times with representatives of Lockheed, Convair, the Air Force, or the Navy attending.[92] In September, the group rejected a Navy-Boeing proposal for a 190-foot-long, hydrogen-powered inflatable aircraft, as well as a Lockheed proposal for a hydrogen-powered aircraft, code-named SUNTAN. Two additional ideas from Kelly Johnson were also rejected—a tailless subsonic aircraft with a very low radar cross-section and a supersonic design designated A-2. The group did approve Convair's continuing to work on a ramjet-powered Mach 4 vehicle, code-named FISH, that would be launched from a specially configured Convair B-58B Hustler bomber.[93]

At a late November 1958 meeting, the panel reviewed the FISH program and Lockheed's newest proposal, the A-3, and agreed that it was feasible to build an aircraft capable of flying fast enough and high enough to make radar detection exceedingly difficult.[94] Eisenhower was already aware of the project via James Killian, who was serving as the first presidential science adviser. The President gave his approval for exploratory work after a December 17 briefing by Dulles and Bissell, with Land and Purcell in attendance. Lockheed and Convair were asked to submit detailed proposals, and they were provided funding for their research. The effort was designated Project GUSTO.[95]

At a July 1959 meeting, the Land panel rejected both the Convair and Lockheed proposals. Convair offered a FISH vehicle that would fly at Mach 4.2 at 90,000 feet, with a range of 3,900 miles. However, the technology of ramjet engines was unproven, and the B-58B had been canceled in June. Meanwhile, the susceptibility of Lockheed's newest proposal, the A-11, to radar detection was considered too great.[96]

The following month, on August 20, the two contractors provided a joint Defense Department–CIA–Air Force selection panel with the specifications for their proposed aircraft. One notable difference was in length, with Lockheed suggesting the 102-foot-long A-12, while Convair's solution, the KINGFISH, was 79.5 feet. Projected speed—Mach 3.2—was identical for both planes. Lockheed's proposal did promise better performance in terms of cruising altitude during the middle and final portions of the flight and range at cruising altitude (3,800 versus 3,400 nautical miles). The A-12 promised to reduce substantially the radar return through an additive in the fuel, which decreased the ability of a radar to detect the afterburner plume. A second novel feature of the design was the plan to use titanium rather than steel in parts of the aircraft in order to reduce its weight.[97]

Some CIA representatives at first favored Convair's KINGFISH design due to its smaller radar cross-section, but they were eventually convinced to side with Lockheed by Air Force members, who had visions of B-58B-like delays and cost overruns. In addition, because of Lockheed's work on the U-2, the company had in place employees with the proper clearances and the security arrangements that would be required for a project that Bissell and Dulles insisted be, if possible, more secret than the U-2.[98]

Because of lingering concern about the A-12's radar cross-section, Lockheed emerged as only the provisional winner—with the requirement that it demonstrate the A-12's reduced vulnerability to radar by January 1, 1960. Project GUSTO was terminated, and Project OXCART was born.[99]

Lockheed's antiradar studies of that summer resulted in the eventual cobralike appearance of the OXCART aircraft. Edward Purcell and John Parangosky, the CIA's program manager for OXCART, had theorized that a continuously curving airframe would be difficult to track with radar because it would present few corner reflectors or sharp angles from which radar pulses could bounce off in the direction of the radar. The studies also resulted in a contract, signed in February 1960, that called for Lockheed to receive $96.6 million in return for twelve aircraft.[100]

Of course, at the time the contract was signed, Gary Powers had yet to be shot down. Whether the project would survive, in a climate where its use over the Soviet Union might be considered too risky, remained to be seen. In late May, Eisenhower told his military aide, Andrew Goodpaster, that he believed the project should go forward on low priority, for Air Force use in time of war. In a memo, Goodpaster noted that Eisenhower "did not think the project should now be pushed at top priority. In fact, they might come to the conclusion that it would be best to get out of it if we could."[101]

CORONA

In early August 1960, the U-2 was no longer flying over the Soviet Union, and the OXCART's future was uncertain. Even if Kelly Johnson delivered the plane promised, it was far from clear that a president would permit it to overfly Soviet airspace. But another CIA-managed project was about to pay huge dividends and revolutionize U.S. intelligence capabilities.

Two and a half years earlier, on February 7, 1958, Killian and Land met with Eisenhower and Goodpaster at the White House to discuss the limited progress the Air Force was making in developing a photographic reconnaissance satellite.[102] The primary objective of the program—first known as the Advanced Reconnaissance System (ARS), then as SENTRY, and finally as SAMOS—was to develop a satellite that would electronically scan the photographs obtained by its cameras and transmit the data back to a ground station, where it would be reconstructed into a picture. A subsidiary objective was to develop a satellite that would return its film back to earth in a canister.[103]

At that meeting, Eisenhower confirmed the decision to assign the CIA responsibility for developing a reconnaissance satellite that could eject its film for recovery on earth. That decision had been prompted by a late October 1957 report from the President's Board of Consultants on Foreign Intelligence Activities (PBCFIA), which stressed the need for an interim photographic reconnaissance system that would be available before either SENTRY or OXCART. Bringing the CIA into the reconnaissance satellite effort had been proposed to General Bernard Schriever, head of the Air Force's Ballistic Missile Division, by Colonel Frederic Oder, head of the SENTRY program. Oder believed that CIA funding would help to accelerate the program. He was also well aware of the CIA–Air Force cooperation in regard to the U-2, inasmuch as Schriever's deputy was Osmond Ritland, Bissell's deputy on the U-2 project.[104]

Not surprisingly, given the success of the U-2, Bissell was assigned to manage the new satellite program, which would soon be designated CORONA, through his Development Projects Staff. Ritland repeated his role as deputy—for the Air Force would remain a key player in the program. Bissell exercised direct control of the program through monthly meetings with contractor representatives.[105] His program staff included U-2 veterans such as Eugene Kiefer, his special assistant for technical analysis, and John Parangosky, who became deputy chief of the CORONA Program Office development staff. Out on the West Coast, Charlie Murphy, a longtime Air Force designee to the CIA, served as Bissell's Field Technical Director at the Lockheed Advanced Projects (AP) facility in Palo Alto, where tests of the cameras and other elements of the payload were conducted.[106]

Five contractors played key roles in the development of CORONA. Itek, a Boston-based company founded by Richard Leghorn, and Fairchild Camera and Instruments were asked to develop camera systems. General Electric and Eastman-Kodak were, respectively, awarded contracts for developing the recovery capsule and supplying the film. The Lockheed corporation would have a dual role—in addition to building the upper stage that would propel the CORONA satellites into orbit, it was given the responsibility for integrating the entire effort.[107]

To provide cover for the launches—the portion of the effort that could not be hidden from public view—the DISCOVERER program was created. Ostensibly a scientific and biomedical research effort that would give some small animals a once-in-a-lifetime joyride into space, it would explain the repeated launches and recovery of payloads from orbit.[108]

As a result, a significant portion of the Air Force's role, such as the procurement of boosters and launches, could be conducted as an overt effort. To carry out those responsibilities, a small program office, originally consisting of four or five people and headed by Lt. Col. Lee Battle, was established at the Ballistic Missile Division headquarters near Los Angeles. Work on the "black" side of the project was handled down the hall.[109]

Early on in the project, Bissell and Ritland made several key decisions concerning the camera and satellite. Originally, the camera to be carried on the first CORONAs, proposed by Fairchild, would remained fixed and scan the earth below as the satellite spun in orbit. In late March or early April 1958, they opted for an Itek design, in which the panoramic camera would scan while the satellite itself remained stable. Fairchild would remain as the camera builder. In addition, they decided that after the Agena second-stage had separated from the Thor rocket booster and carried the payload (consisting of the camera and recovery vehicle) to orbit, it would remain attached. The Agena would ensure that the payload remained stable in orbit, as well as provide power.[110]

On February 28, 1959, a little over a year after the CORONA program started, test launches began from Vandenberg Air Force Base in California. That first launch did not carry a camera, which was just as well, since the Agena rocket failed to reach orbit. Two more camera-less launches, in April and June, also produced failures. In the first instance, the reentry vehicle, instead of landing in the Pacific where it was to be recovered either in the air before final touchdown or from the ocean, landed in the vicinity of Spitzbergen, Norway, near a Soviet mining operation, and was never recovered—at least not by the United States.[111]

The fourth launch, on June 25, was the first to carry a camera, which was subsequently designated KEYHOLE-1 (KH-1). The Itek-designed panoramic camera, manufactured by Fairchild, was capable of scanning 35 degrees in each direction from the line of flight. At the center of its swing, it would point straight down toward the earth.[112]

But that mission proved no more successful than the previous three. The next eight tries, seven of which involved camera-carrying satellites, also resulted in failure of one variety or another. The reentry vehicle would sink or be shot into a higher orbit, or it would fail to detach itself from the spacecraft, or its parachute would not open; other times, the rocket would be destroyed or head for the Pacific Ocean rather than outer space. Failure was constant, even if the cause was not. It was, Bissell recalled, "a most heartbreaking business."[113]

Finally, on August 10, 1960, Navy frogmen recovered the reentry vehicle from DISCOVERER 13 after it had eluded the C-119 aircraft that was supposed to snatch it out of the air. There was no camera on board, but the recovery represented a major step forward for the beleaguered program—a significant enough triumph that James Plummer, Lockheed's CORONA program manager, was thrown into a swimming pool during the resulting celebration.[114] Others were not as elated. The cable from Bissell assistant Eugene Kiefer to Lee Battle read "Congratulations on a random success." Battle was not amused.[115]

But just eight days later, full success arrived. A KH-1-equipped CORONA blasted off and, after some difficulty, attained a 116-by-502-mile orbit, with an inclination of 80 degrees, allowing it to overfly all of the Soviet Union. As it began to pass over Soviet territory, its camera started operating as programmed. Its first photos were of the Mys-Schmidta air base in the Soviet Far East, about 400 miles from Nome, Alaska. On August 19, after seventeen orbits of the earth, which took it over the Soviet Union seven times, the satellite's film-return capsule was ejected and then plucked out of the air off Hawaii as it descended toward the ocean.[116]

PHOTOINTERPRETATION

A few days after the capsule had been recovered and the film processed, Arthur Lundahl, director of the CIA's Photographic Interpretation Center, addressed an auditorium full of his interpreters—the individuals whose skill and special training would begin the process of turning overhead images into intelligence. In the past, after film from U-2 missions was delivered to Washington, Lundahl's photointerpreters were shown a map of the Soviet Union with a squiggly line indicating the route of the U-2. In addition, they viewed blowup photos of particular targets.[117]

The CORONA briefing had a dramatic flair. After the photointerpreters were settled, Lundahl announced that it was "something new and great we've got here." His deputy, Jack Gardner, opened a curtain to show a map of the Soviet Union. Instead of a single line across the map, there were seven vertical stripes emanating from the poles and moving diagonally across the Soviet Union. The interpreters knew the stripes represented the portions of the Soviet Union that had passed under the satellite's cameras. Their immediate reaction was to cheer. After being briefed on what to look for, especially for missile sites at Plesetsk, they began work on OAK-8001, the first photointerpretation report based on satellite photography.[118]

They had an extensive amount of film to study. The first CORONA mission produced coverage of over 1 million square miles—greater than that produced by all of the U-2 overflights over the Soviet Union. There were 1,432 photos, including photos of the Kapustin Yar Missile Test Range, its presumed impact area, SA-2 missile sites, the Sarova Nuclear Weapons Research and Development Center, and several newly discovered airfields.[119] The quality, however, was substantially lower than that achieved by the U-2. The KH-1 camera produced images with a resolution of about 40 feet—sufficient to permit identification of the missile sites, airfields, and facilities, but of little use in producing detailed technical intelligence.[120]

Still, the crude photographs returned by the August 18 mission, along with photos from four additional successful CORONA missions between December 1960 and June 1961, all of which employed the improved KH-2 camera with its 25-foot resolution, enabled Lundahl's photointerpreters to shatter a significant myth—one that had played a major role in the 1960 presidential campaign.[121]

Several years before the campaign, by the time the National Intelligence Estimate (NIE) "Main Trends in Soviet Capabilities and Policies 1957–1962" was completed in November 1957, the Soviets had already tested an ICBM, and it was feared they might have about ten prototype ICBMs for use by 1959. Then, in a December 1958 estimate, the intelligence community stated its belief that the Soviets intended to acquire a sizable ICBM force at the earliest practicable date. The NIE also pointed out the absence of sufficient evidence to judge conclusively the magnitude and pace of the Soviet ICBM program. Indirect evidence, including production capacity and the ability to construct launch facilities, to establish logistic lines, and to train operational units, led to the conclusion that the Soviets "could achieve an operational capability with 500 ICBMs about three years after the first operational date [1959]."[122]

Over the next several years, that judgment was revised downward, in the absence of intelligence to sustain earlier high estimates of the pace of Soviet ICBM deployments. The 1959 NIE suggested that the Soviets might have 140 to 200 ICBMs on launchers by mid-1961, and, speculatively, 250 to 350 by mid-1962 and 350 to 450 by mid-1963. Though smaller than previous estimates, they were consistent with a Soviet missile force that could destroy the vulnerable strategic bomber bases of the Strategic Air Command, particularly since it was believed that improvements in the accuracy and reliability of Soviet ICBMs had sharply reduced the number required to launch an effective attack.[123]

Although such estimates were highly classified, their basic thrust reached the public through key columnists such as Joseph Alsop and prominent politicians such as Senator Stuart Symington (D.–Missouri). The electorate was well aware of Soviet missile tests and even more so of the *Sputnik* and other Soviet space launches. The expectation of a substantial missile gap in the Soviets' favor thus became part of the 1960 election, with Democratic candidate John F. Kennedy lambasting his opponent, Richard Nixon, over the issue.[124]

The NIE for Soviet strategic offensive forces during the period 1960–1965, issued the month after Kennedy's razor-thin victory, reflected different views by various intelligence organizations, but was consistent with the expectation of a significant Soviet advantage in the near future. The Air Force took the most pessimistic view, predicting 200 ICBMs by mid-1961, some 450 by mid-1962, and 700 by mid-1963; the CIA predicted 150, 270, and 400 for the same periods. At the low end were the Air Force's military rivals. The Army and Navy jointly predicted deployments of 50, 125, and 200.[125]

In June 1961, the intelligence community issued a new assessment. It argued that the Soviets might have 50 to 100 operational ICBM launchers and therefore the ability to bring all SAC operational air bases under attack. In any case, the estimate concluded that the Soviets would have 100 to 200 operational launchers within the next year and would almost certainly be able to attack then.[126]

By September 1961, new intelligence had a dramatic impact on the estimates. One item was a top-secret report, "The Soviet ICBM Program," that was based on information from an officer in the Soviet military intelligence service, Lt. Col. Oleg Penkovskiy; this document sharply discounted the near-term missile threat. In addition, electronic monitoring of Soviet missile and space test centers provided data on the types of missiles being developed. The third, and most conclusive, source was CORONA photography.[127]

The estimators noted that through CORONA operations since mid-1960, "our coverage of suspected deployment areas in the USSR has been substantially augmented" and that the photography had "been studied in detail by photo-interpreters with knowledge of US and Soviet missile programs." Analysis revealed that many of the suspected areas did not contain ICBM complexes as of summer 1961. Thus, the NIE, which drew a predictable Air Force dissent, estimated "that the present Soviet ICBM strength is in the range of 10–25 launchers from which missiles can be fired against the US, and that this force level will not increase markedly during the months immediately ahead." The expected number of Soviet ICBMs by mid-1963 was 75 to 125. The Soviets had apparently chosen to deploy only a small number of heavy and cumbersome first-generation SS-6 ICBMs and to concentrate their efforts on a smaller second-generation system for deployment, probably in 1962.[128]

The people who had been members of the CIA's Photographic Interpretation Center when the CORONA program yielded its first imagery were, by September 1961, employees of the National Photographic Interpretation Center (NPIC). NPIC was formally established by National Security Council Intelligence Directive (NSCID, pronounced N-Skid) No. 8 of January 18, 1961.[129] NPIC was to be run by the CIA as a service of common concern for the entire intelligence community—interpreting both aerial and satellite imagery. Its establishment provides another example of how far the CIA had come in employing science and technology in the pursuit of intelligence requirements.

NPIC replaced the PIC and was put under the command of Arthur Lundahl, who already had a long career in the photointerpretation business. At the University of Chicago, he majored in geology. His involvement in aerial photography began during his years as a research assistant, performing geological research in Ontario, Canada. His work required the production of maps based on aerial photography.[130]

Because of his background, Lundahl was requested, as war approached, to help train photointerpreters. After conducting training courses and obtaining his M.S., he joined the Navy and worked on photointerpretation, both in Washington and overseas.[131]

At the end of World War II, he found himself back in Washington, and in 1946 he was asked to help write the charter for the Naval Photographic Interpretation Center. After seven years at the Center, he became convinced that the Navy was "going to go nowhere in photointerpretation as it was then structured." He was also approached by the CIA, which had become aware of a paper he had written—"Consider the Mata Hari with Glass Eyes"—that focused on the potential role of photographic intelligence during the Cold War. His initial reaction was one of skepticism. Years later he recalled telling CIA official Otto Guthe, "I don't know anything about you guys. If you're going to parachute me into Salerno or somewhere, forget it. I'm a scientist." Guthe reassured him that the CIA "was going into the photointerpretation business and they wanted someone to come over and run it who had experience and the right credentials for doing the job. They wanted me to do it."[132]

As a result, Lundahl joined the CIA in early 1953, as head of the Photographic Intelligence Division (PID) of the Office of Research and Reports—with thirteen people and a few hundred square feet of floor space over a Ford dealership, in the Steuart Building, at 5th and K Street, N.W. The operation had the CIA code name HT/AUTOMAT—HT from the initials of security officer Henry Thomas and AUTOMAT because Lundahl conceived of the division as a place where intelligence consumers could come and pick up whatever they needed in terms of interpreted photography. Lundahl recalls that "there was a very narrow front. It was very inconspicuous. It had . . . some funny little sign on the door, and there was some kind of turnstile about 100 feet in from the door and a glass cage where a security guard sat and a dirty little elevator which ran slowly at best. Of course, there was no place to park and no place to eat."[133]

Expansion came a few years later in the wake of the U-2 project, and by 1956, 150 interpreters were occupying 50,000 square feet in the Steuart Building. In August 1958, the PID was merged with the Statistical Branch of the Office of Current Reference and became the Photographic Interpretation Center.[134]

With the initial expansion to 150 personnel came military people detailed from the various armed services. Lundahl sought to make them feel like coproprietors of a national facility, since he felt that if he "had Army, Navy, Air Force, State, NSA, CIA people in there, I would have all the ingredients for nationalization, although this was nowhere in the cards in 1956."[135]

Several years later it was in the cards. In March 1960, defense chief Thomas Gates suggested to Eisenhower the need for a study of the defense intelligence establishment, which he described as a huge conglomerate spending $1.5–2 billion annually. Although Eisenhower reacted favorably to such proposals, the necessary impetus was the shooting down of the U-2 in May.[136]

A May 6 meeting between Allen Dulles, Gates, Budget Bureau chief Maurice Stans, presidential adviser Gordon Gray, and the President's Board of Consultants on Foreign Intelligence Activities resulted in the creation of the Joint Study Group to review various aspects of the U.S. foreign intelligence effort.[137] Recommendations contained in the group's December 15, 1960, report covered all aspects of U.S. intelligence operations—collection, analysis, and the roles of the DCI and the United States Intelligence Board (USIB). Several recommendations were based on the many hours the group spent discussing the problem of processing and interpreting overhead photography. The report noted agreement "in most of the community that a central photographic intelligence center should be established," although it noted that opinions varied as to how much interpretation and analysis should take place at such a center and who should run it. The report recommended that the DCI and Secretary of Defense should determine the details concerning the center's management and that a National Security Council Intelligence Directive should be drafted establishing a National Photographic Interpretation Center.[138]

The question of who would run the center was debated, but not resolved, at three USIB meetings. As a result, the issue was brought up at the January 12, 1961, meeting of the National Security Council. Participants included Eisenhower, Gates, Joint Chiefs of Staff (JCS) Chairman Lyman Leminitzer, Allen Dulles, and presidential science adviser George Kistiakowsky.[139]

The center would be run by either the Department of Defense or the CIA. Gates and Leminitzer argued for Defense because of the military's role in the collection of imagery as well as being the primary intelligence consumer. In addition, Gates argued that although Dulles agreed that Defense should take the lead in the event of war, continuity was required for a proper transition from peacetime to wartime operation. He gave assurances that a Defense-run center would not be removed from Washington and would provide its services to the agencies outside of Defense that required them.[140]

Dulles countered that the PIC was a joint enterprise with 100 Army, 10 Navy, and 7–15 Air Force officers. In addition, the information produced by the center was chiefly military only with regard to targeting, whereas photographic intelligence had tremendous political significance and was a matter of common concern to a number of Washington agencies, including the Department of State. Furthermore, the center had developed a group of career officials who intended to make a career of photographic intelligence. In contrast, military officers were regularly rotated to new jobs. When Gates suggested that if the center was placed under Defense a career staff would be retained, Dulles responded that abandonment of rotation was a new idea for the military.[141]

When Eisenhower expressed his concern that the military had a greater need for timely information than the civilian agencies, Kistiakowsy told him that the CIA center was providing the military with the material it required without delay, that the existing center was "a revolution in photographic techniques," and that the CIA had taken the lead in managing and developing the center. To disturb the arrangement would result in delay and a loss of progress. Instead he suggested expansion of the center.[142]

At least partly on the basis of Kistiakowsy's advice, and partly because he believed Defense had not shown any unhappiness with the current arrangement, Eisenhower decided that the CIA should continue running the interpretation center and that it should be expanded. According to Lundahl, Eisenhower's words were simple: "Well that settles it, Allen . . . Allen Dulles, you're going to run this thing, so carry on."[143]

QUALITY ELINT AND CLANDESTINE COMINT

In late May 1954, while the CIA was in the final stages of preparing for a major covert-action operation designed to remove the leftist president of Guatemala from power, Allen Dulles briefly turned his attention to a very different aspect of the agency's activities. On the twenty-ninth, he approved the CIA's first electronic intelligence (ELINT) program.[144]

The potential value of intercepting and analyzing the signals from radars under development and missiles during flight testing had been recognized by several officers in OSI—particularly James Spears, Ralph Clark, and George Miller. In 1951, OSI had begun building up its expertise in the field as well as giving technical assistance to the British ELINT program. The NSC provided an additional stimulus in 1953, when it assigned the CIA responsibility for evaluating Soviet capabilities for jamming radio signals.[145]

At the time, OSI, which analyzed the material collected, was not the only agency component involved in ELINT. The Deputy Directorate for Plans (DDP) obtained ELINT data through liaison relationships with foreign intelligence services as well as through its own clandestine collection operations. The Office of Communications, a component of the Directorate of Administration, designed and produced equipment for the collection and processing of electronic signals. In October 1953, to evaluate the CIA's activities in the area, an ELINT Task Force was established to review the agency's efforts, which resulted in the plan approved by Dulles. Among its provisions was creation of a CIA ELINT Staff Officer (ESO) to coordinate the agency's ELINT activities, a post held for many years by a member of OSI.[146]

The roles of DDP, OSI, and the Office of Communications remained essentially unchanged throughout the 1950s. But by 1959, there was a substantial expansion of the CIA's ELINT operations, which was facilitated by the National Security Agency's relative lack of interest in the area. NSA had been established in 1952 to perform the national signals intelligence (SIGINT) mission, with power to coordinate the SIGINT activities of the military services. But it was most interested in communications intelligence—obtained by intercepting voice and fax traffic. CIA officials who required ELINT believed NSA slighted the activity in allocation of assets and personnel. In particular, they felt that NSA paid insufficient attention to the collection and analysis of Soviet missile telemetry—which was crucial to estimating Soviet missile developments.[147]

Collecting such signals would require cooperation with countries in close proximity to Soviet testing facilities. On December 8, 1954, a U.S. delegation, led by the CIA's Frank Rowlett, began formal negotiations for a U.S.-Norwegian communications intelligence agreement. Two days later the negotiations concluded successfully. Cooperation involved both COMINT and ELINT, with the CIA funding some of the Norwegian operations. In summer 1955, the Norwegian Defense Intelligence Staff (FO/E) began collecting ELINT from a site at Korpfjell, near Kirkenes and about two miles from the Soviet border. Converting the site to permanent status began in August 1957, and the resulting station, code-named METRO by the Norwegians, began operations in 1958.[148]

METRO's targets included some of the telemetry from Soviet naval missile tests in the far north. In 1958, the Soviets began deploying the SS-N-4 Sark missile on its Golf I submarines. The short-range (350 nautical miles) ballistic missiles carried a single warhead with a yield of 2–3.5

megatons. In 1960, Korpfjell became the responsibility of the newly created Defense Experimental Station Kirkenes, which received its funding from the CIA.[149]

ELINT cooperation with the Norwegians was not restricted to land. In June 1955, the Norwegian sealer *Godoynes* began a 69-day mission in the Barents Sea, code-named SUNSHINE, with the objective of gathering signals from Soviet radars as well as intercepting communications. According to Ernst Jacobsen of the Norwegian Defense Research Establishment, who designed some of the Norwegian monitoring equipment carried by the ship, the vessel was also "bursting at the seams with modern American searching equipment, operated by American specialists." The modern American equipment came from the CIA.[150]

In 1956, the Norwegian intelligence staff concluded an agreement with the shipping company Egerfangst Ltd., whose ships were then employed to collect communications and electronics intelligence in the Barents Sea and along the coastline of the Kola Peninsula. The following year, the former fishing boat *Eger* became the first custom-built ELINT ship. Its transformation was completely paid for by the United States, with the CIA supplying its intercept equipment. The *Eger* then spent several months in the Barents Sea, gathering SIGINT on Soviet naval activities on behalf of the CIA.[151]

Also in the late 1950s, the CIA established a telemetry intercept station in Iran on the southeastern corner of the Caspian Sea. Intelligence analysts within the CIA as well as outside advisers, such as future Secretary of Defense William Perry, then at Sylvania, wondered if the low-powered signals that the Soviet missiles would transmit twenty miles to stations on Soviet territory could also be intercepted 1,000 miles away in Iran. CIA officials gained the Shah's permission for a contingent of technicians to set up antennae in an ancient hunting castle at Beshahr to conduct hearability tests. The tests were to determine how well signals from the Tyuratam test range, which the CIA believed would become a major Soviet test facility, could be intercepted.[152]

In 1958, as part of the "Quality ELINT" program, the CIA made the first significant attempt to measure the power of a radar for intelligence purposes. The targeted radar was the Bar Lock, which had been rapidly and extensively deployed in East Germany and other areas on the Soviet periphery. Intelligence indicated that the new radars were being used to detect and track U-2s penetrating Soviet territory.[153]

Photographs of the Bar Lock indicated that its power output might be sufficiently great to significantly improve Soviet aircraft detection and tracking capabilities. Given the potential threat to U-2 operations, those managing the program pressed for more conclusive intelligence on the Bar Lock's capabilities. Equipment capable of measuring the power output of a radar was installed in a C-119 aircraft. A series of flights followed, the plane flying ostensible supply missions through the air corridors to Berlin, where Bar Lock signals were easily intercepted. Although not all the measurements taken were of high accuracy, the accumulated data did indicate that the power output of Bar Lock was far less than had been determined from photos of it, a conclusion later confirmed by other sources.[154]

The Soviet missile program was one impetus for the CIA's involvement in ELINT, but so too was the Soviet space program. Outer space had become a major battleground in the rivalry between the two superpowers. The Soviets had seized the initiative with the launch of *Sputnik 1* in November 1957 and, in the years following, threatened to embarrass the United States further by sending unmanned spacecraft to photograph and land on the moon, Venus, and Mars.

Rather than wait for the Soviets to announce their missions, accept whatever information they provided, and trust that it was accurate, the CIA wanted the capability of independently monitoring Soviet space efforts. The agency sought to provide advance warning of missions, to determine whether Soviet claims were accurate, and to identify the failures that the Soviets would surely try to conceal.

One target of the CIA's monitoring effort was the first images of the far side of the moon, which *Luna 3* sent back to earth in October 1959. Nicholas Johnson, an American expert on the Soviet space program, assessed the mission as "one of the most astounding technological achievements of any nation, considering the state of the art of the time." The spacecraft developed the pictures on board and then broadcast them to ground stations when its orbit swung closest to earth.[155]

Receiving the broadcast was a matter of employing collection equipment capable of picking up *Luna*'s very weak signal. Deciphering it was dependent on knowing the format in which it had been transmitted. Neither factor was a problem for the Soviet Union, but the task was not so simple for the United States. The effort, according to former CIA official Henry Plaster, involved "special ELINT collection techniques, new approaches to signal analysis, . . . and intelligence interpretation of pictures."[156] The first problem was solved with the cooperation of Sir Bernard Lovell, head of the Jodrell Bank Radio Observatory at the University of Manchester in England. The observatory's 250-foot radio telescope could pick up the weak signals undetectable by standard U.S. ELINT collection facilities—which it did on October 7. Graduate students there, however, in trying to eliminate "noise" from the recorded signal, also obliterated much of the video data. CIA technical analysts had only a single poorly recorded intercept to work with but were able to conclude that the Soviet pictures were authentic.[157]

The CIA also was able to verify Soviet claims that the USSR had developed a radio-television system that allowed continuous monitoring of the dogs carried aboard their *Sputnik 5* and *6* earth-orbiting missions of August 19 and December 1, 1960. The signals were recorded by ELINT sites and OSI analysts were able to transform the *Sputnik 6* signals into pictures, which supported the Soviet claim.[158]

On October 10, 1960, an SS-6 rocket lifted off from Tyuratam, at the instant when the earth's rotation brought it into alignment with a minimum energy path to Mars. Another SS-6 was launched on October 14. The established Soviet practice of launching probes at the precise moment that was optimum for a mission led the CIA to conclude that the launches involved Mars flybys. Intercepted telemetry showed that the loaded upper stages weighed more than thirty tons. Telemetry also told the CIA something that the Soviets, who never announced the missions, did not—that the attempted Mars flybys failed when the third-stage engines ignited and then misfired after burning for only a few seconds. CIA analysts also were able to determine from the very slow acceleration revealed by the telemetry that the vehicles were the most heavily loaded ever launched.[159]

Four months after their Mars failures, the Soviets tried to send two spacecraft on a Venus flyby—*Sputnik 7* on February 4, 1961, and *Venera 1* on February 12. *Sputnik 7* never left earth orbit, but after almost one orbit of the earth, *Venera 1* headed toward Venus. Placing a space probe in a "parking orbit" and then ejecting it toward its target represented another major technical first for the Soviets, who published a description of the launch, orbit, and ejection phases. Their claims proved to be consistent with the data intercepted.[160]

However, neither the CIA nor any other U.S. intelligence organization was able to verify or contradict later bulletins on the mission's progress.

Jodrell Bank again came to the aid of the CIA's ELINT effort, when its radio telescope was employed to track the *Venera 1* spacecraft that the Soviets hoped would reach Venus. Bernard Lovell announced that the spacecraft apparently failed before the end of February, after completing only a small portion of its planned three-month mission. Ironically, when the probe stopped communicating with its Soviet controllers, fifteen days after launch, they had also turned to Lovell for assistance. In mid-May when the probe was to have reached Venus, Jodrell Bank detected possible signals from the vehicle and reported them to Moscow.[161]

The CIA's interception activities in 1959 focused primarily on ELINT, but they also involved interception of communications. This task was performed by perhaps the most secret unit within the very secret Deputy Directorate for Plans—Division D, which was formally a component of the directorate's Foreign Intelligence Staff.[162]

CIA defector Philip Agee reported that by 1964, a Division D contingent had been stationed in the embassy in Montevideo, Uruguay, "for some years." The team used "sophisticated equipment" to "scan frequencies . . . and record radio communications" as part of a program designated ZRBEACH. In addition, Agee claimed that mobile intercept units were stationed as close as possible to encryption machines—particularly those housed in the Soviet embassy—to capture their emanations, which could be employed to decipher the messages.[163]

According to William Martin and Bernon Mitchell, two NSA mathematicians who defected to the Soviet Union in 1960, Division D's mission also included obtaining cryptographic information through more conventional espionage operations. The defectors claimed that Division D bribed a code clerk in Turkey's Washington embassy to supply information that helped NSA read Turkey's coded messages.[164]

EARTHLING

During the 1950s, Pakistan hosted a number of U.S. intelligence operations, some run by the CIA and some by the military, that were designed to collect intelligence about Soviet nuclear, missile, and space activities. Missions to collect debris from Soviet nuclear tests included a stop at Lahore; U-2 flights took off from Peshawar air base; and the U.S. Air Force eavesdropped on the Soviet Union and China from Pakistan.[165]

In March 1961, yet another U.S. intelligence-collection project began operating from Pakistan, in which the CIA was a partner. Rather than relying on aircraft or eavesdropping antennae, the project employed an over-the-horizon (OTH) radar to monitor Soviet missile tests. Such radars use the ionosphere as a reflector for high-frequency radio energy and therefore are not limited to the "line-of-sight" restrictions of conventional ground-based radars. OTH radars promised to provide information on missile and aircraft activity up to 3,100 miles away—by bouncing a radio signal off the ionosphere and onto the target and receiving the reflected signal. The technology had been tested by the CIA, which, along with the Office of Naval Research, shared a U.S.-based radar facility code-named CHAPEL BELL.[166]

Plans for installing an overseas radar were first formulated in 1958. First designated CHAPLAIN, then EARTHLING, the radar was designed primarily for detecting ICBM or satellite launches from the Tyuratam launch site. However, it also proved useful in providing data regarding some Soviet high-altitude atmospheric nuclear tests.[167]

LICENSE TO KILL

Frank Olson's death had been unintended by Sidney Gottlieb, but Gottlieb and TSD did play central roles in CIA plans to assassinate two foreign leaders. In September 1960, Gottlieb prepared an assassination kit, which contained a lethal biological agent, hypodermic needles, rubber gloves, and gauze masks. He then delivered it to Lawrence Devlin, the CIA station chief in Leopodville, who had been ordered to kill Patrice Lumumba, the Congolese nationalist leader then in U.N. custody. A cable from Allen Dulles stated that "we conclude that his removal must be an urgent and prime objective." And Lumumba was killed, but not by the CIA. Devlin never carried out his mission, although he may have been aware of the plans of Belgian agents, who may have actually carried out the murder.[168]

Earlier in the year, Gottlieb had been asked by Richard Bissell, who had become the Deputy Director for Plans in late 1958, to conduct research on assassination techniques. Bissell was particularly interested in the possibility of eliminating Fidel Castro, who like his predecessor was a dictator, but unlike his predecessor was a pro-Soviet dictator.[169]

Bissell's interest continued into the Kennedy administration, fueled by Kennedy's strong desire to eliminate Castro and Soviet influence in Cuba. From 1960 until 1965, there were at least eight plots to end Castro's life. Some of them involved nothing more scientific than a rifle and a bullet.[170] Others plots depended on TSD.

Cornelius Roosevelt, a grandson of President Theodore Roosevelt and the chief of TSD during the fall and early winter of 1960, later told the CIA's Inspector General that methods that had been considered included shellfish toxin administered by a pin, bacterial material in liquid form, bacterial treatment of a cigarette or cigar, and a handkerchief treated with bacteria. His best recollection was that bacteria in liquid form would be the best method, given that Castro frequently drank tea, coffee, or bouillon.[171]

Despite that conclusion, TSD provided botulinum toxin pills to Security Chief Sheffield Edwards in January 1961. However, when Edwards dropped one of the pills into a glass of water, it did not even disintegrate, much less dissolve. In February 1961, TSD delivered a new batch of pills to Edwards, with assurance of their lethality, although it is not clear that this assurance was justified. Edwards then passed them on to mobster Johnny Rosselli in Miami, who had been recruited to serve as the middleman. Later that month, or early the next, Rosselli told the CIA that the pills had been passed on to a man in Castro's entourage who agreed to help kill the dictator, but the man returned them after losing his job and his access to Castro.[172]

Another plot called for James B. Donovan, the lawyer negotiating with Castro for the release of the prisoners taken during the Bay of Pigs invasion, to give scuba-diving enthusiast Castro a wet suit. TSD purchased a suit, then contaminated the breathing apparatus with tuberculosis bacilli and the suit with fungus spores that would cause a chronic skin disease called madura foot.[173] But Donovan gave the Cuban dictator a wet suit on his own, and the CIA destroyed the infected suit.

2

FALSE START

By November 1961, the exploitation of science and technology in pursuit of secret intelligence had become a significant component of CIA activities. While the CORONA and U-2 programs were providing valuable intelligence, the CIA was working on an improved version of CORONA, as well as the successor to the U-2, OXCART. CIA electronic intelligence operations included funding the Kirkenes station in Norway as well as operating the Beshahr station in Iran. The EARTHLING radar in Pakistan was also yielding dividends. In addition, the Office of Scientific Intelligence continued to produce intelligence on a variety of foreign developments, the most important being foreign nuclear and missile programs.

In many ways, it was exactly what James Killian and Edwin Land had in mind when they wrote Allen Dulles in 1954 about the CIA's need to adopt scientific solutions to pierce the Iron Curtain. Dulles had been reluctant to embrace the U-2 program, but he had proved a strong advocate of the CIA's role in such areas—defending the CIA's role in running the U-2 program against Air Force attempts to seize control, opposing attempts to cut the number of CORONA launches, and arguing that the CIA, not the military, should operate the National Photographic Interpretation Center.[1]

But Dulles and, apparently, Bissell were on their way out—both undone by the April 1961 Bay of Pigs fiasco. In the future, historians, commentators, and intelligence officers would debate whether the prime cause for the failure was CIA incompetence or a loss of nerve by President Kennedy. But in 1961, it was Dulles and Bissell who were going to pay the price. Brought in to replace Dulles was John McCone, a staunch Republican, the type often referred to in the press as "rock-ribbed." McCone came to the CIA with impressive credentials in both private industry and government service. Born in 1902 and trained as an engineer, he went on to become executive vice-president of the Consolidated Steel Corporation and then founded his own engineering company, which became a major builder of ships and aircraft during World War II. His government service included stints as the Under Secretary of the Air Force (1950–1951), and Chairman of the Atomic Energy Commission (1958–1960).[2]

Killian and Land, though pleased at the CIA's successes in science and technology, did have some concerns, ones shared by the President's Foreign Intelligence Advisory Board (PFIAB, as the board of consultants had been renamed), which Killian chaired and on which Land served. They would soon bring these to the attention of the new director.

THE NEXT STEP

Killian and Land had concluded that two interrelated problems had developed with the CIA's effort in the science and technology area. The first was Richard Bissell's promotion to the position of Deputy Director for Plans (DDP), which put him in charge of the CIA's espionage and covert-action operations. When Bissell assumed command of the Plans directorate in early 1959, he took the U-2, OXCART, and CORONA programs with him. What had been the stand-alone Development Projects Staff became the Development Projects Division (DPD) of the Plans directorate.[3]

Both Killian and Land looked at science and technology with reverence and as something to be shielded from "contamination" by the "dirty tricks" activities of Plans. Land was particularly upset at the employment of U-2s in the Bay of Pigs disaster. At one of McCone's first meetings with the PFIAB, he discovered that Killian, Land, and others were concerned that the CIA's scientific and technical efforts might be limited by the continuing association with Plans. To protect and strengthen those efforts, they recommended creation of a separate directorate that would focus exclusively on science and technology.[4]

Beyond contamination, they were probably also concerned that with DPD as but one of a number of divisions in Plans, it would not receive the same level of attention from Bissell or his successor as it had in the past—and that the status of its activities would be reduced. They might also have been concerned that the CIA's scientific and technical effort was too scattered and had no single manager: Reconnaissance was the responsibility of DPD; the scientific intelligence and photointerpretation functions were performed within the intelligence directorate; and ELINT operations were conducted by OSI and the administration directorate's Office of Communications. Furthermore, the initially small efforts in each field had grown substantially.[5]

After the meeting, McCone established a three-man working group to review the CIA's organizational structure and activities. CIA Inspector General Lyman Kirkpatrick served as chairman, with PFIAB Secretary Patrick J. Coyne and retired Army General Cortland Schuyler, an adviser to New York Governor Nelson Rockefeller, as the other two committee members. One topic discussed was the suggestion that a research and development directorate be established. As part of their study, they sought comment from all deputy directors. In a still-unreleased January 10 memo on "Technical Intelligence Collection," Bissell expressed adamant opposition to the idea, explaining why he believed the DPD's activities should be managed by his directorate.[6]

At a January 22, 1962, meeting of the PFIAB, McCone told Killian that he planned to establish a deputy directorate for technical collection under which all of the agency's scientific activities would be consolidated. Bissell's opposition to the PFIAB's desire to remove DPD from his control, combined with the fallout from the Bay of Pigs, further strained relations with Killian and Land.[7]

Despite his opposition to a new directorate, Bissell was the leading candidate to become its first head. In fall 1961, McCone and Bissell had agreed that the latter would resign at the end of December. Not long after, McCone's wife died, and McCone asked Bissell to stay on until he determined if he would continue as DCI. When McCone returned to Washington in January, he decided he wanted Bissell to head the new directorate. After receiving approval from Attorney General Robert Kennedy and then President Kennedy, McCone extended an offer.[8]

Since the Kennedy brothers had not changed their mind about the need for Bissell to leave the DDP job, it was a choice between the new directorate or departure. Bissell chose to depart. In a letter to his daughter, he explained that he felt the new position would be a demotion, that it would be very awkward to be cut off from the covert operations he had planned. "I have a horror," he wrote, "of hanging on here to a job that is not at the center of things, as so many people do."[9]

McCone was apparently under the impression in early February that Bissell was seriously considering accepting the position. But in a February 7 letter to the DCI, Bissell wrote, "I have not conveyed to you clearly my feeling with respect to my own future and have allowed a serious misunderstanding to arise." He noted that "you have done me the great honor of urging that I remain . . . as Deputy Director (Research)." Still, he had previously "expressed to you . . . my serious misgivings about the organizational validity of this proposal" as well as his "reluctance, as a matter of personal preference, to assume certain of the responsibilities that would be involved."[10]

Bissell spelled out his objections to the proposed directorate. He questioned the wisdom of transferring the scientific intelligence (OSI) and photointerpretation functions to the new directorate, thus "separating [them] from the other offices under the Deputy Director (Intelligence) that are concerned with the analysis and production of finished intelligence." In addition, although he acknowledged that the DCI might need a policy adviser on signals intelligence issues, he had a "personal distaste for this role." He further explained that if he had a deep interest in the signals intelligence field, he would prefer some operational or managerial position.[11]

Bissell also questioned the idea of splitting the Technical Services Division, placing its research and development activities under the new directorate while leaving support functions with the DDP. He was "inclined to believe that progress in the exploitation of advanced techniques can be accelerated only by forcing a closer integration of developmental and operational activities which will be far easier to accomplish if they remain under common command." As a result, he was not sure if any part of TSD should be transferred to the new directorate.[12]

As for reconnaissance projects such as CORONA, OXCART, and SAMOS, he agreed that "responsibility for these special projects could well be placed elsewhere than in the Clandestine Service and that they would benefit from more top management attention than I have been able to give them for the past several years." However, he questioned whether the CIA could expect to play a significant role in the future.[13]

Even if the agency continued with OXCART and played subsidiary roles in CORONA and SAMOS, the CIA officer in charge of such activities, even if he also was responsible for some portion of TSD and other research and development, would more appropriately be an assistant to the DCI rather than a deputy. That position, Bissell wrote, "would have approximately the same scope as the one I occupied in this Agency in 1958. . . . For me to accept it would mean a long step backward." Shortly afterward, Bissell sent a follow-up letter of resignation, effective February 17.[14]

THE FOURTH DIRECTORATE

Bissell's resignation left McCone needing to find a manager for the CORONA, IDEALIST, and OXCART programs. It also led to renewed pressure from Killian and Land to establish a science and technology directorate removed from covert activities.[15]

On February 14, McCone approved a "headquarters notice" announcing that Richard Helms would replace Bissell as DDP on the seventeenth and that plans were under way to establish a Deputy Directorate for Research and Development. Two days later, another headquarters notice informed readers that effective February 19, the agency would have a Deputy Director for Research (DD/R) at the head of a Deputy Directorate for Research (DDR); that certain functions of the DPD as well other research and development activities would be transferred to the new directorate "in the interest of strengthening the Agency's technical and scientific capabilities"; and that Herbert "Pete" Scoville, longtime head of OSI, would head the new DDR. In late June, Col. Edward Giller, who had been serving as deputy director of TSD, became Scoville's assistant deputy director.[16]

Establishing an organizational structure for the new directorate was a prolonged process, in part because of continued opposition in other segments of the agency. On April 16, the transfer of the reconnaissance activities of the DPD's Special Projects Branch to the DDR was authorized. The branch brought along responsibility for the CORONA, ARGON, IDEALIST, and OXCART programs.[17]

But the "Battle of Charter Ridge," as one Scoville deputy described it, continued into July. An early July memo to Scoville stated that "progress in defining [your] sphere of command and . . . functional responsibilities has been virtually negligible." It suggested that Scoville might consider calling a halt, at least in the short term, to attempts to obtain the transfer of the Technical Services Division and Office of Scientific Intelligence to the new directorate and settle for control of the reconnaissance and ELINT functions.[18]

Finally, in late July, a mission statement for the new organization was issued by Deputy DCI Marshall Carter. The new directorate was not all that had been promised. Its mission was "to conduct in-depth research and development in the scientific and technical fields to support intelligence by advanced technical means." Excluded from its charter were research and development activities to support agent operations, as well as the non-ELINT duties of the Office of Communications.[19]

Carter's memo identified the three offices that would carry out the directorate's responsibilities: The Office of Special Activities (OSA), established near the end of June, would manage the CIA's reconnaissance programs. There would also be an Office of Research and Development (ORD) and an Office of ELINT (OEL), with the latter assuming responsibility for the ELINT activities that had been conducted by OSI and other CIA components.* The Plans directorate retained control over any clandestine agent operations or liaison activities involving ELINT as well as Division D's embassy-based COMINT collection operations.[20]

Two offices that were not assigned to the new directorate, and never would be during Scoville's tenure, were his own Office of Scientific Intelligence and the Plans directorate's Technical Services Division. Scoville had accepted the job on the basis of McCone's promise to transfer the two organizations to the new directorate. But both Ray Cline and Richard Helms objected strenuously.[21]

Cline, an Illinois-born, Harvard-educated veteran of the wartime Office of Strategic Services (OSS), had held both analytical and operational posts in the agency. He joined the Office of Reports and Estimates in 1949, headed the Estimates Staff of the Office of National Estimates (ONE), worked out of the London embassy from 1951 to 1953, transferred from ONE to the Office of Current Intelligence in 1955, and, late in 1957, accepted the position of Station Chief in Taiwan. In March 1962, McCone offered him the position of Deputy Director for Intelligence (DDI), to replace the departing Robert Amory. On April 23, Cline became DDI while disengaging himself from his work overseas.[22]

Cline insisted that OSI remain in his directorate, arguing that removing it would mean "weakening the CIA's analytical voice." He contended that all the analytical units should remain part of the same organization, and that collection and analysis should be handled by distinct components. Richard Helms, the new DDP, felt equally strongly about keeping the essence of TSD, along with some of the directorate's aircraft operations that involved support to covert activities, in his directorate.[23]

There were a number of reasons for Helms's reluctance to part with TSD. A memo noted his "alarm" at any encroachment of his authority to conduct overseas clandestine operations, the concern that the gulf that already existed between those developing agent equipment and those using it would be exacerbated by TSD's transfer out of the operations direc-

*There was some debate about what to call the office. Scoville felt that one proposed title, Office of Electronic Activities, encroached on other people's territory, while others felt that Scoville's suggestion—Office of Electronic Intercept—was too explicit. ("DD/R Staff Minutes 15 June 1962," June 18, 1962, 2000 CIA Release.)

torate, and the aversion of Plans to provide detailed information on clandestine operations to technicians in another directorate.[24]

Of course, as much as Cline and Helms wished to retain control of OSI and TSD, respectively, a mere stroke of a pen by McCone would have effected the transfers. But despite, or perhaps because of, Cline and Helms being McCone appointees, the DCI refused to deliver OSI and TSD to Scoville. Scoville soon discovered that holding McCone to his commitments would be a problem—that the steely-eyed, rock-ribbed Republican was not always as tough as he looked.

ORD

While the OSA and OEL groups were created from existing components of the CIA, the Office of Research and Development (ORD) was a creation of Scoville and his deputy, Air Force Colonel Edward Giller, who also became its first head. They envisioned an office that would look several years into the future, investing in research and development activities that might pay dividends for collectors or analysts in five or ten years.[25] Indeed, failure was part of ORD's mission over the years, not only to find out what would work but also what wouldn't—before another part of the agency poured millions of dollars into a doomed effort.

ORD began work in January 1963 with a staff of three individuals transferred from the technical services division—one person for each of its divisions (Research, Systems, Analysis). The initial focus of the office was to be "research and development . . . to support intelligence collection by advanced technical means." Topics of particular interest identified in ORD's charter were new optical systems leading to improved resolution; use of lasers to permit night photography; chemistry research related to collection concerning biological and chemical warfare activities; and acoustic and seismic research related to missile intelligence.[26]

In addition to research, ORD (through its Systems Division) was to analyze promising ideas falling outside the responsibility of the directorate's overhead and ELINT collection offices and turn them into technical collection systems. The division even fielded collection systems and assumed responsibility for the EARTHLING site in Pakistan.[27]

Part of ORD's initial charter was to assume TSD's main research functions, including in behavioral science, leaving that organization to handle the operational support and related R&D functions that Helms believed must remain in Plans. Thus, ORD took over part of the MKULTRA program. Dr. Stephen Aldrich, a graduate of Amherst and Northwestern Medical School who had served in the agency's Office of Medical Services and OSI's Life Sciences Division, assumed many of the responsibilities that had belonged to Sidney Gottlieb.[28]

With Aldrich directing that portion of ORD's activities, its scientists continued searching for ways of controlling human behavior. The research they inherited from TSD included placing electrodes in the brains of dogs and other animals and then using radio signals to guide them along specific courses. The technical services division also placed electrodes into the brains of cold-blooded animals—apparently snakes. The experiments with dogs were directed at bugging an office, but the experiments with cold-blooded animals may have had a more cold-blooded objective, possibly "executive action-type assassinations."[29]

Creating amnesia remained a major objective of ORD. Advances in brain surgery facilitated far simpler psychosurgery and the possibility that "a precisely located electrode probe could be used to cut the link between past memory and current recall." According to one account, ORD had access to prisoners in at least one American penal institution, and office staffers worked with the Edgewood chemical laboratory to develop a drug that could be used to implant false memories into the mind of an amnesia subject.[30]

ORD also supported work done at the Scientific Engineering Institute (SEI). A group of behavioral and medical scientists was permitted to conduct independent research as long as it met SEI standards. The scientists were available to consult with frequent visitors from Washington. One project apparently involved stimulating the pleasure centers of crows' brains in order to control the birds' behavior.[31]

ELINT

Heading the new Office of ELINT (OEL) was George Miller, who had been serving as head of OSI's electronic intelligence effort. The activities he managed as OEL chief included support to the Norwegian Kirkenes facility, the Norwegian Barents Sea boat operation, the CIA ELINT collectors in Iran, and the "Quality ELINT" program. Support for an Austrian COMINT station, essentially on behalf of NSA, was also a mission of the office.

Collection targets continued to include Soviet space activities as well as early warning radars that were in the developmental stage. On April

26, 1962, the Soviet Union launched *Cosmos 3*, identified only as "a new data transmission system," which was actually a test of a SAMOS-type photographic system (code-named BAIKAL), employing electronic readout to return the data to earth. CIA ELINT specialists attempted to demodulate the signals and similar ones from the *Cosmos* launch of July 28. They were able to establish some of the signal parameters but could not produce identifiable pictures. They did conclude that one or more cameras on board were taking photos, probably of cloud formations, and that the film was developed by an on-board processor. In addition, they determined that the film was being electronically scanned and transmitted to ground-based receivers in the Soviet Union. The effort directed against *Cosmos 9*, launched on September 27, which carried the same type of system as *Cosmos 3,* was more successful. Cloud cover was easily identified in a series of six pictures, and further analysis led to the conclusion that *Cosmos 9* was an experimental weather satellite.[32]

ELINT collection and analysis also focused on two targets that appeared in 1960 U-2 and CORONA photography—a pair of radars the U.S. intelligence community designated Hen House and Hen Roost. Both were located on the western shore of Lake Balkhash in the USSR and looked out from the Sary Shagan antiballistic missile (ABM) test center toward Kapustin Yar, the launch point for ballistic missiles employed in ABM tests. Both facilities were enormous. The Hen House antenna building was over 900 feet long—more than 3 football fields—and nearly 50 feet high. The Hen Roost radar had 2 antennae, a half-mile apart, each over 500 feet long. One antenna was a mere 15 feet tall; the other reached 65 feet.[33]

Radars of this type were just being developed in the United States. Rather than employing traditional radar dishes that were mechanically steered, the face of these phased-array radars consisted of radiating elements. The delay in the signals sent out from those elements meant a beam could be electronically steered to detect incoming objects. But the CIA, the Strategic Air Command, and other elements of the national security establishment needed to know more. They needed information on the system's operating characteristics in order to determine whether the radars could provide the data required by Soviet ABMs to destroy incoming U.S. warheads, and how to neutralize the radars. But electronic monitoring of any activity out of Sary Shagan was virtually impossible at the time. The site was over the horizon from all U.S. ground stations, and the electronic signals emitted by Hen House or Hen Roost would head off into space before they could be intercepted by U.S. antennae.

The first inroad came in late 1962, due to the Soviet decision to renew atmospheric testing of nuclear weapons, testing that involved detonating missile warheads as they approached Sary Shagan. Two missiles were fired sequentially from Kapustin Yar; the warhead of the first was detonated in the atmosphere to determine if the Sary Shagan radars could detect the second missile through the nuclear cloud. The release of such vast amounts of energy can cause radical changes in the radio transmission properties of the surrounding atmosphere. In the highly ionized region created by a nuclear blast, radar waves, which would ordinarily travel straight into space, can be reflected or bent in different directions. On October 28, one of the ABM-related tests at Sary Shagan had just that effect. U.S. ELINT stations in the Middle East, possibly including Beshahr, recorded thirteen new signals, many of which were believed to have originated in the Sary Shagan region.[34]

The signal of greatest interest was originally designated BUEB, which analysis indicated was designed to be used against targets more than 800 miles away. Aircraft flying at the highest altitudes are well below the horizon when they are 300–400 miles from a radar, and they travel rather slowly. Ballistic missiles rise several hundred miles above the earth and approach their target rapidly, making it desirable to detect them as far away as possible. BUEB therefore became a prime candidate to be an ABM radar signal. In addition, each pulse was transmitted at a different frequency, which would be expected from an electronically steered radar beam. One major question remained: Which radar was the United States hearing, Hen House or Hen Roost? It would be a few more years before that question would be settled.[35]

MELODY AND PALLADIUM

Soviet early warning radars were only one focus of the CIA's ELINT effort. Another was the air defense radars that would be crucial to any attempt to detect, track, and destroy U.S. reconnaissance flights that might overfly Soviet territory. That effort had begun in 1959—before the May 1960 U-2 shootdown and while the OXCART program was in its early stages. OXCART staffers wanted to know how widespread the radars were, the extent of territory they covered, the power they radiated, and their sensitivity. While seeking to answer the first question, the ELINT unit of OSI discovered a technique that enabled the Beshahr station in Iran to monitor Soviet missile tracking radars and eliminated the need to rely on chance occurrences such as that of late October 1962.

Gene Poteat, a member of the ELINT staff, joined the CIA after working as an electrical engineer and physicist for Bell Labs, reporting to work in early January 1960. He recalled an occasion at Cape Canaveral in the 1950s when a signal was received from a ground-based radar located 1,000 miles beyond the horizon because the signal had reflected off a Thor IRBM (Intermediate-Range Ballistic Missile) during a test flight. This event led to the suggestion that the phenomenon, which would later become known as "bistatic intercept," could be used to locate high-powered Soviet radars over the horizon from U.S. intercept sites. Instead of pointing ELINT antennae in the direction of possible Soviet radars, the antennae would seek to capture signals reflected off the missiles.[36]

George Miller suggested Poteat try out the idea on two experts from private industry—William Perry of Sylvania and Albert "Bud" Wheelon of TRW. Both men offered moral and technical support. Feasibility studies and engineering calculations followed, which required solving spherical trigonometry equations using slide rules, logarithm tables, and hand-operated mechanical calculators.[37]

Funding came quickly for the program, which Poteat code-named MELODY after one of his favorite sounding words, and the appropriate equipment was installed at the Beshahr site. The MELODY program produced bistatic intercepts of virtually all Soviet ground-based tracking radars, including all of the ABM radars at the Sary Shagan test range.[38]

MELODY also provided new intelligence on the dispersion of Soviet air defense radars, although it did not help OXCART planners to identify all such radars. Determining the range and power of the radars was the objective of the aerial ELINT operations of the Quality ELINT program, but the program also had the more secret element of determining their sensitivity. That element was known by the code word PALLADIUM.

OXCART planners wanted to determine the sensitivity of Soviet radar receivers and the proficiency of their operators. With the help of scientific consultants, Poteat came up with a scheme to electronically generate precisely calibrated false targets and insert them into Soviet radars—deceiving the Soviet radar operators into seeing and tracking ghost aircraft.[39]

The Soviets would expect a radar signal to return after bouncing off an aircraft. The first step in the Quality ELINT deception was to capture the radar's signal and feed it into a "variable delay line" before sending the signal back to the radar. By smoothly varying the length of the delay line, CIA technicians could simulate the notional aircraft's range and speed. The knowledge gained from the Quality ELINT power and coverage measurements enabled program staffers to simulate an aircraft of any radar cross-section—from an invisible stealth airplane to one that would create a large blip on a Soviet radar—and fly it along any path, at any speed and altitude.[40]

The smallest blip would provide a measure of the sensitivity of the radar and the skill of the operators. The key was to find a way of determining which blips the Soviets could see on their radar screens, and which they could not. Poteat and his colleagues considered either monitoring other Soviet radars when a ghost airplane was projected to see if they were switched on in an effort to pick up the imaginary intruder detected by the target radar, or intercepting the pertinent Soviet communications link. With the assistance of NSA, it was possible to intercept and decrypt the relevant communications.[41]

Every PALLADIUM operation involved three teams—a CIA team with equipment to generate ghost aircraft, an NSA team with special COMINT and decryption gear, and a military operational support team. Covert PALLADIUM operations were directed against a variety of Soviet radars around the world using ships and submarines as well as ground bases. The logistics of some operations were particularly difficult. One winter, heavy snows closed all the airports in northern Japan. Because of the small rail tunnels, one CIA officer "spent about three weeks in northern Japan, in the dead of winter, hauling his van of PALLADIUM equipment off trains and trucking and sledding it over the mountains—and putting it back on another train on the other side."[42]

The October 1962 Cuban missile crisis provided an opportunity to measure the sensitivity of the SA-2 radar. During the crisis, a PALLADIUM system was mounted on a destroyer operating out of Key West. The destroyer stayed just out of detection range of a Soviet early warning radar near Havana, and its PALLADIUM transmitting antenna was just above the horizon. The signals from the antenna made it appear that a U.S. fighter plane out of Key West was about to overfly Cuba. Meanwhile, a Navy submarine slipped in near Havana Bay, with instructions to surface just long enough to release a timed series of balloon-borne metalized spheres of different sizes.[43]

Poteat and his colleagues expected the radar to track the false aircraft, while the submarine released the spheres into its "path." They hoped that after the initial detection, the Soviets would turn on the SA-2 target tracking radar in preparation for firing missiles at the aircraft, and then report seeing other targets—the spheres. The size of the smallest spheres detected would establish the smallest radar cross-section that could be detected and tracked.[44]

As Poteat recalled, "We got the answers we went after, but not without excitement and entertainment." In the middle of the operation, Cuban fighter planes began circling over the area where the submarine had surfaced, while another fighter started chasing the ghost aircraft. The PALLADIUM system operated smoothly to keep the ghost aircraft always just out of reach of the Cuban planes. When the Cuban pilot told his controllers that he had the intruding aircraft "in sight" and was about to make a pass and shoot it down, Poteat and the others on the scene simultaneously had the same idea. The technician moved his finger to the switch, Poteat nodded yes, and the technician switched off the PALLADIUM system—causing the ghost aircraft to disappear from the Cuban pilot's radar screen.[45]

The data produced by the PALLADIUM operations, which continued for several years afterward, enabled analysts at OSI and elsewhere to identify which Soviet radars had low power or maintenance problems, which performed below expectations, and where U.S. aircraft might safely penetrate the Soviet border in wartime. OSI analysts also concluded, undoubtedly to the disappointment of the OXCART program office, that Soviet radars could detect and track an OXCART as soon as it came over the horizon.[46]

SPECIAL ACTIVITIES

Of the three groups forming the Directorate of Research, the Office of Special Activities could, during 1962 and 1963, lay claim to conducting the most extensive and important operations. From February 1962 through June 1963, U-2 and CORONA missions yielded significant intelligence on the Soviet Union, China, and a number of other targets.

Nineteen CORONA missions were flown during that time period, all but three of which successfully returned film. There were an additional three successful ARGON mapping missions.[47] Meanwhile, CIA U-2s closely monitored the growing Soviet involvement in Cuba, and U-2s flown by Nationalist Chinese pilots photographed Chinese nuclear facilities. CORONA missions also focused on Chinese nuclear and missile facilities as well as the primary Soviet target.

Cuba, a difficult target for satellites, was frequently overflown by U-2s, as the CIA attempted to determine the nature of the relationship between Fidel Castro's revolutionary regime and the Soviet Union. A particular fear was that the Soviets might be tempted to use an island ninety miles from the United States as a base for offensive weapons. In spring 1962, after receiving reports of increased Soviet activity in Cuba, the CIA requested permission from the NSC Special Group to conduct additional missions. The group authorized an increase of at least two additional flights a month, beginning in May, and NPIC began publishing a *Photographic Evaluation of Information on Cuba* series.[48]

By early August, CIA analysts noted a substantial increase in Soviet arms deliveries to the Castro regime. An early August overflight was conducted too soon to detect the Soviet construction activities then getting under way, but an August 29 mission enabled the CIA to inform President Kennedy of at least eight SA-2 sites in the western half of Cuba. A mission on September 5 provided additional evidence, showing three more SAM (surface-to-air missile) sites as well as a MiG-21 at Santa Clara airfield.[49]

The discovery strengthened John McCone's belief, which was not shared by CIA analysts, including Ray Cline, that the Soviets were deploying Medium-Range Ballistic Missiles (MRBMs) in Cuba. The DCI argued that the only explanation for the extensive deployment of SAM sites was a Soviet desire to hide the missiles from U.S. reconnaissance.[50] Bad weather prevented any missions until September 17, but heavy cloud cover that day prevented the mission from obtaining usable images. Finally, on September 29, an overflight of the Isle of Pines and Bay of Pigs area turned up another SAM site.[51]

In gaining approval for the overflights, the CIA had to face reluctant senior Kennedy administration officials, including Secretary of State Dean Rusk, who feared a shootdown and an international incident. But overflights continued to amass evidence of Soviet SAM deployments, with missions on October 5 and 7 bringing the total of sites discovered to nineteen, although there was still no evidence that offensive missiles had been deployed.[52]

However, the most likely location for the MRBMs was western Cuba, which missions had largely avoided because of the concentration of SAM sites on that part of the island. On October 9, the Special Group met to discuss a recommendation by the Committee on Overhead Reconnaissance (COMOR), an interagency committee responsible for selecting U-2 and

CORONA targets, for a mission over the western part of the island. The committee also recommended that if the overflight did not provoke an SA-2 response, it should be followed by "maximum coverage of the western end of the island by multiple U-2s simultaneously."[53]

McCone brought along Col. Jack C. Ledford, who had become OSA director on September 4. A few months earlier, Ledford had expected that by September he would be assigned to a SAC air base in the Midwest. He had just graduated from the Industrial College of the Armed Forces, when a friend in Air Force personnel called to say he had a good assignment for Ledford in Washington, but the details were highly classified. Ledford, after four years in the area, was looking forward to a change of scenery. But when his friend told him that chief of staff General Curtis LeMay wanted him to take the job, Ledford, who had flown under LeMay in World War II, agreed.[54]

Ledford suspected that Scoville and Giller, both of whom he knew, were instrumental in his selection. At a meeting with the two, they gave him some of the details—additional information would follow if he passed his polygraph exam. When that process was completed, he was officially assigned to an Air Force organization at Bolling Air Force Base in Washington—the 1040th USAF Field Activity Squadron, which served as an administrative office for Air Force personnel assigned to the CIA, NSA, and other intelligence agencies.[55]

At the October 9 meeting, Ledford presented a vulnerability analysis, produced with the help of OSI, concluding that there was a one-in-six chance of losing a U-2. As a result, the Special Group approved a flight over San Cristobal.[56] However, notwithstanding the CIA's role in providing initial evidence of the SAM buildup, the newly approved mission was to be flown instead under SAC auspices. As the Special Group meeting ended, Deputy Secretary of Defense Roswell Gilpatric questioned the plausibility of the CIA's cover story for the missions, which involved alleged flights to Puerto Rico, and argued that it would be better to employ Air Force pilots. In the event of a mishap, officials could claim that a routine Air Force peripheral reconnaissance mission had gone off course. McCone asked Ledford, who agreed that the Air Force had a better cover story but noted that the CIA's U-2s had superior electronic countermeasures and could fly 5,000 feet higher than SAC's; Ledford suggested that the SAC pilots use the CIA's planes. President Kennedy, after meeting with McCone and Gilpatric, approved the mission and the use of Air Force pilots.[57]

On October 11, Department of Defense (DOD), Air Force, and CIA representatives, including Scoville, met to discuss the change in cover stories. The discussion then focused on who would run the next mission. The DOD representatives, who were strongly in favor of Air Force control of the missions, called McCone, who consented. The next day, McCone left for California and did not return until October 14. On October 12, Air Force control became official when President Kennedy transferred "responsibility, to include command and control and operational decisions, with regard to U-2 reconnaissance flights of Cuba" from CIA to Defense. The Air Force then requested the loan of two CIA U-2Cs.[58] The mission flown on October 14 resulted in eight cans of films being delivered to NPIC the next day. The film provided the first hard evidence of the presence of MRBMs and set in motion the Cuban missile crisis, which led to the withdrawal of Soviet missiles from the island.[59]

The transfer of the mission to the Air Force annoyed several CIA officials, both in the short and long term. Lt. Gen. Marshall Carter, the acting DCI, told national security adviser McGeorge Bundy, "I think it's a hell of a way to run a railroad. It's perfectly obviously a geared operation to get SAC in the act." In conversations with senior Air Force and administration officials, Carter argued against the move, pointing out that OSA's operation was up and running and working well. In contrast, the Air Force pilots had no experience with the U-2C. In addition, the Air Force had managed peripheral but not overflight operations. He told Gilpatric, "To put in a brand new green pilot just because he happens to have on a blue suit and to completely disrupt the command and control and communications and ground support system on 72 hours' notice to me doesn't make a God damn bit of sense, Mr. Secretary." But Carter's protestations were to no avail. Even a plea for a gradual transition to Air Force control of the Cuban overflights was rejected—with presidential national security adviser McGeorge Bundy telling Carter that "the whole thing looks to me like two quarreling children."[60]

In addition to monitoring Cuba, U-2s flown by National Chinese pilots, along with CORONA satellites, kept watch on China's emerging nuclear and missile programs. A December 1961 CORONA mission returned the first photos of the Lop Nur nuclear test site. Overhead reconnaissance during the first half of 1963 provided images of the Lanzhou Gaseous Diffusion Plant, a nearby hydroelectric plant, and a nuclear facility at Baotao. The Lanzhou images led analysts to conclude that although the "nearby hydroelectric plant . . . has made some progress, . . . much work remains to be done." Late 1962 CORONA missions provided NPIC's analysts with photographs of a possible uranium mining activity at A-Ko-Su. Earlier in the year, in June, overhead photography of the Shuangchengzi missile test complex showed a large crater about 1,500 yards from one of the launch pads, indicating "one rather spectacular failure."[61]

An even higher intelligence priority than China was, of course, the Soviet Union. Overflights using U-2s were no longer possible, and OXCART was not, in 1962 and 1963, even an option. Until the launch of the Air Force's high-resolution KH-8/GAMBIT satellite in July 1963, CORONA was the sole overhead means of monitoring the testing and deployment of ballistic missiles, the construction of submarines and other naval vessels, the types and locations of air defense missiles and radars, and other key targets.

At least ten CORONA missions between June 1962 and March 1963 provided photographs of the Kapustin Yar and Tyuratam missile test centers, which revealed the major expansion of Tyuratam. Suspected chemical warfare production plants, such as the one at Dzerzhinsk, and facilities probably involved in the testing of solid propellants and related explosives, like the one at Krasnoyarsk, were also frequent targets of CORONA cameras between mid-1962 and mid-1963.[62]

On April 30, 1962, Herbert Scoville could not be found at his desk. He was with several CIA officials in Nevada, at the top-secret Area 51, to witness the first official OXCART flight. Richard Bissell was also there, leading Kelly Johnson to note in his project log "I was very happy to have Dick see this flight, with all that he has contributed to the program."[63] Piloted by Louis Schalk, the unusual-looking plane flew at an altitude of 30,000 feet and a speed of 340 knots—only fractions of what the planes would prove capable of, but it was a start. A May 4 flight that reached Mach 1.1 brought Kelly Johnson a congratulatory telegram from McCone.[64]

But McCone would not remain pleased. Near the end of 1962, flight tests of two A-12s demonstrated the capability to reach 60,000 feet and a speed of Mach 2.16. However, progress was still slow, due to delays in the delivery of engines and the disappointing performance of those that had been delivered. It had become evident that Pratt & Whitney was finding it far more difficult to bring United Aircraft's J-58 engines up to OXCART specifications.[65]

In early December, McCone complained to the president of United Aircraft after learning that there would be another delay in the delivery of engines. As a consequence, "by the end of the year we will have barely enough J-58 engines to support the flight test program adequately." By the end of January 1963, ten engines were available. The first flight with two of them installed occurred January 15.[66]

A few months later, in late May, the project almost was exposed to the public. On a routine training flight, pilot Kenneth Collins' plane stalled and went out of control, due to a faulty air speed indicator, forcing him to eject from the aircraft, which crashed fourteen miles south of Wendover, Utah. Collins was unhurt and the wreckage was recovered in two days, while persons at the crash site were identified and requested to sign secrecy agreements. Two farmers, who arrived near the crash scene in a pickup, were told the plane had been carrying atomic bombs, which discouraged them from getting any closer. The press was given a cover story describing the crashed plane as an unclassified F-105 fighter. All A-12s were grounded for a week, until the cause of the faulty instrument, which was easily correctable, was discovered.[67]

While one component of OSA was wrestling with OXCART's problems, another was concerned with improving space reconnaissance capabilities. The most important aspect of that effort centered around a modification to CORONA, referred to as the CORONA-J or KH-4A. The camera system for CORONA-J, the J-1, was essentially identical to the KH-4 or MURAL camera, with only slightly improved resolution—usually between 9 and 25 feet, although it reached 7 feet at times. The major change involved doubling the size of the film-supply cassette, a change made possible and necessary by the addition of a second reentry vehicle to the spacecraft. KH-4A spacecraft, which began operations in August 1963, eventually carried up to 160 pounds of film, in contrast to the 39 pounds carried in the KH-3 missions. Mission lifetimes grew from a maximum of 7 days for KH-4 missions to up to 15 days for KH-4A missions. The combination of extra film and two recovery capsules increased the frequency with which targets could be photographed during a mission, and increased the probability of finding targets free of cloud cover. A KH-4A mission could produce 18,000,000 square miles of stereo coverage.[68]

During 1962, OSA was also involved in a joint program with the Air Force, designated LANYARD, to develop a satellite intended to provide high-resolution photography of a target located at Tallinn in Estonia. In

1961, KH-4 CORONA photos showed what some analysts feared were antiballistic missiles. The photos were of poor quality, showing roads ending in a circular clearing, like "lollipops in the snow," according to one photointerpreter. NPIC's interpreters concluded that the photos showed construction for the deployment of the SA-5 GAMMON interceptor missile, with three batteries of six launchers arranged around a single engagement radar. The exact purpose of the Tallinn line, as it was called, was to be hotly debated within the intelligence community for years to come.[69]

In an attempt to obtain more detailed images for the interpreters, Scoville approached Under Secretary of the Air Force Joseph V. Charyk, who agreed to pull SAMOS E-5 cameras out of storage and start a crash program to put them into orbit. During 1962, Bob Leeper and Bill Cottrell, Lockheed engineers who worked in the CORONA program, traveled to their company's classified warehouse to examine the cameras. Finding them in good condition, they arranged their transport to Itek in Boston, where they were reconfigured, tested, and shipped back to California to the Lockheed Advanced Projects Facility, where they would become part of the payload. The E-5 camera was redesignated the KH-6, and the hope was for it to produce images with a resolution of 2 feet.[70]

On March 18, 1963, the first LANYARD blasted off from Vandenberg Air Force Base but failed to reach orbit. A May 18, 1963, launch did reach orbit and returned a capsule. Unfortunately, the payload had not been activated, and there were no photographs to settle the debate over Tallinn. Another LANYARD was launched in late July, by which time Scoville was no longer a CIA official.[71]

MEN IN BLUE

On April 25, 1963, Scoville submitted a letter of resignation to McCone, effective June 1 (subsequently extended to June 17). In that letter, he noted that his efforts to establish a viable scientific and technical directorate had resulted "in a continuous series of frustrations in which, with a few exceptions, the working components have resisted any transfer of their responsibilities." He also observed that although McCone had always supported the basic concept of the Research directorate, other senior agency officials had made it clear they did not, and "no one is willing to face up to the problems of implementing it." One indication of that lack of nerve was that a recent "apparent decision to transfer OSI [to the DDR] was dropped."[72]

Scoville also noted that "during the past year a major part of my activities has also involved joint programs of the Agency and the Department of Defense." However, "I have never been supported and placed in a position where it was possible to direct this program in the manner it deserves. As a consequence, I found myself continuously in the position of being held responsible for matters which I have had neither the authority nor the means to control."[73] The joint programs Scoville was referring to were conducted under the auspices of a secret three-letter organization—the NRO.

The "NRO" was the National Reconnaissance Office—established through a September 6, 1961, letter from Deputy Secretary of Defense Roswell Gilpatric to Allen Dulles and concurred in, on Dulles's behalf, by Deputy DCI Charles P. Cabell. The letter was the initial result of the desire of Killian, Land, and officials in the new administration, particularly McNamara and Gilpatric, to formalize the management of the space reconnaissance program. Under its terms, the Air Force's SAMOS and GAMBIT programs, along with CIA's CORONA, MURAL, ST/POLLY, IDEALIST, and OXCART programs, would become part of a single National Reconnaissance Program (NRP), encompassing space reconnaissance as well as aerial overflight programs. The letter also stipulated joint management of the NRP—via the NRO—by the CIA Deputy Director for Plans (Richard Bissell) and the Under Secretary of the Air Force (Joseph V. Charyk).[74]

Neither the CIA nor the Air Force was forced to transfer its programs to the new organization, whose central headquarters had only a small staff. The CIA's CORONA and other reconnaissance programs were still run by the Deputy Directorate for Plans, while SAMOS and GAMBIT were the responsibility of the Air Force Office of Special Projects, which had been established in August 1960 and reported directly to Charyk. The September 6 agreement allowed each organization to manage its reconnaissance projects as part of a single NRP, with a single security system, and each could be called on to assist the other's programs in areas where it held special capabilities. Thus, in addition to whatever reconnaissance systems it developed or procured, the Air Force would provide launch, tracking, and recovery services. The CIA could be called on to assist with covert contracting and security for individual programs a well as for the NRP as a whole.

Although that arrangement was satisfactory to Dulles and McNamara, the National Security Council's Special Group, which supervised all U.S.

intelligence activities, would not ratify the agreement, believing that the national reconnaissance effort was too important to entrust to divided management. Under those circumstances, and with Bissell's departure from the CIA apparently imminent as a result of the Bay of Pigs, Charyk and his staff moved toward concentrating greater authority in the hands of the NRO and its director. On November 22, the NRO staff completed a draft statement of "NRO Functions and Responsibilities," which suggested the transfer of several, and possibly all, CIA reconnaissance programs to the Air Force. Not long afterward, Charyk went further, advocating the consolidation of all program functions in the NRO "without regard for previous arrangements." The CIA, he now believed, should not be given responsibility for either research and development or technical management of NRP projects.[75]

The radical changes Charyk envisioned became the basis for the serial exchange of memos between the NRO and CIA. In the midst of those exchanges, Scoville assumed the role of DDR in February 1962. He certainly reviewed and approved the CIA's April 19 memo, arguing that covert programs then operated by the CIA should remain the CIA's responsibility and that others assigned to the CIA by the Secretary of Defense and DCI would be the complete responsibility of the CIA.[76]

On the evening of April 19, Scoville and Charyk met, a meeting Charyk recalled as "not all that pleasant." In that meeting and in a subsequent memo, Scoville resisted Charyk's suggestions that Scoville should serve as deputy director of the NRO, arguing that he should be designated the CIA representative to the NRO. The former position implied subservience of the director; the latter did not. The two men also had differences concerning whether the CIA should have a veto on planning of advanced projects.[77]

After some additional wrangling, agreement was reached in the form of the May 2, 1962, "Agreement Between the Secretary of Defense and the Director of Central Intelligence on Responsibilities of the National Reconnaissance Office," signed by McCone and Gilpatric. The agreement, which covered a number of issues, provided for a single Director (the DNRO), a position Gilpatric named Charyk to the next day (which was formally confirmed in a June 14 DOD directive). In addition, the agreement assigned technical management responsibility for all NRP projects to the DNRO, who would be selected by, and be directly responsible to, the Secretary of Defense and the DCI. However, it also specified that, as the CIA had pressed for, the CIA would serve as executive agent for covert projects under its management and any additional projects assigned to it by the Secretary of Defense and DCI. In the view of an NRO historian, the agreement constituted "a relatively strong policy statement on NRO purposes," but in other respects it "conceded to the CIA the key points at issue."[78] Round one had gone to Scoville, but it would be only a temporary victory.

In July, following a late May conference at Greenbrier, West Virginia, attended by key NRO and CIA officials—including Charyk and Scoville—Charyk issued a formal directive on NRO organization and functions. The memo outlined the NRO structure as consisting of a Director, an NRO Staff, and three program elements—A, B, and C. The NRO Staff, consisting largely of Air Force personnel, had an overt identity—the Office of Space Systems in the office of the Secretary of the Air Force. Program A also had an unclassified cover—the Air Force Office of Special Projects. Program B was the designation given to the CIA reconnaissance activities that were the responsibility of the Office of Special Activities. The Navy's satellite reconnaissance effort, consisting of the GRAB ferret satellite, developed and operated by the Naval Research Laboratory, became Program C, with the Director of Naval Intelligence heading the program.[79]

There were some areas where the CIA (Scoville) and NRO (Charyk) were in agreement—among them that responsibility for developing SIGINT satellites belonged to NRO and not NSA. But both the May meeting and the July statement left several important issues unresolved, and the door open for further conflict. In June, Charyk began urging that mission planning, on-orbit target programming, and approval of mission targeting options be centralized at the NRO. Charyk considered such functions to be natural responsibilities of the NRO Staff, but Scoville did not.[80]

In late June, the PFIAB had advised President Kennedy that the NRO charter needed to be strengthened. After Kennedy endorsed the recommendation, McCone and Gilpatric sat down to discuss the matter, with Gilpatric suggesting that the only way to satisfy the PFIAB was to make the Secretary of Defense the executive agent for both DOD and the CIA aspects of the NRP, as had been proposed earlier in the year.[81]

However, while Gilpatric and Charyk were pushing in one direction, Scoville was pushing in the other. In late August and early September, Scoville announced or proposed two de facto alterations of the arrangements made earlier. He told Charyk that the CIA would continue to go directly to the Special Group on matters concerning ongoing projects, which amounted to a rejection of Charyk's May 22 proclamation that he would be the NRO point of contact with the Special Group, a policy he had reiterated in a subsequent memo to Scoville. In addition, Scoville noted his opposition to Charyk's decision to have the CIA award covert contracts for programs not under its exclusive control. He argued that it was inherently undesirable for the CIA to "assume the responsibility for covert procurement" for Air Force programs.[82]

In an August 29 memorandum, Scoville returned to the issue of his role in the NRO, arguing that instead of serving as head of Program B as specified in Charyk's July 23 memo, the DDR should be officially designated as the Senior CIA Representative. Scoville had already transferred the title of Director, Program B, to OSA head Jack Ledford. Scoville also objected to Charyk's claim that the DNRO was responsible for determining the assignment of operational control for reconnaissance systems, arguing that the May 2 agreement gave that authority to the Secretary of Defense and DCI.[83]

Added to disagreements on issues and personality differences was another complicating factor in Scoville's relationship with Charyk and the NRO—DCI John McCone. Part of the problem was that McCone came to the agency without the conviction that the CIA should be involved in space or aerial reconnaissance. John McMahon recalled that one of McCone's first comments was "What are you people doing in the airplane business?" In addition, the new DCI was a good friend of Gilpatric and wanted to avoid a fight with McNamara, at the time the proverbial eight-hundred-pound gorilla of the national security establishment.[84]

Nor did McCone and Scoville mesh personally. McCone was new money, Scoville old money. The DCI was also remote and austere. When Scoville called him "John," McCone flinched. People just didn't call him by his first name, McMahon recalled, observing that "I don't think even his wife did." Further, McCone was a staunch Republican, while Scoville was a liberal Democrat. Scoville was committed to nuclear disarmament and devoted some of his time to chairing an interagency committee on the issue. As a result, McCone felt Scoville was giving less than 100 percent to his job.[85]

Also, although McCone's appearance and demeanor helped generate the appearance of a tough and decisive manager, he often wavered and reversed course. Scoville's deputy Edward Giller recalled that McCone would make instant decisions and then do an about-face, leaving people irritated and requiring deputy DCI Marshall Carter to pick up the pieces.

Albert Wheelon, Scoville's successor as head of OSI and then as chief of the CIA science and technology effort, later wrote that McCone "was regarded as a great manager. . . . In truth, he was no manager at all. . . . He was reluctant to make and implement organizational decisions."[86]

Thus, in a meeting with Charyk on October 1, McCone agreed that the CIA would assume responsibility for all covert contracting—a decision that came less than a month after Scoville had rejected the idea and after McCone had told Scoville of his support.[87] Then, when Scoville proved unhelpful, in Charyk's view, in providing CORONA-experienced personnel for an operational control facility in the Washington, D.C., area, Charyk turned to McCone, who again sided with him despite his initial support for Scoville. Such incidents led Scoville to question Charyk's willingness to deal with him in good faith, whereas Charyk concluded that he was better off dealing with McCone.[88] Those incidents, particularly when added to McCone's failure to deliver OSI and TSD as promised, convinced Scoville that he could not rely on McCone.

McCone's indecisiveness manifested itself in a different way in summer and fall 1962. Charyk and Scoville had reached agreement on several issues, mostly minor, only to have the agreements nullified by McCone's refusal to accept Scoville's judgment. In each case, Scoville had to contact Charyk and announce his withdrawal from the agreement in question. Charyk, apparently unaware of McCone's role, took Scoville's withdrawals as a sign of capriciousness. Charyk believed Scoville to be insincere, and the tone of their exchanges sharpened. The situation was made worse by the shift of U-2 missions to the Air Force during the Cuban missile crisis. By late October, Scoville and Charyk were no longer talking. Written correspondence from one to the other, even of the most formal kind, stopped shortly afterward.[89]

Adding fuel to the fire was McCone's mid-November proposal to McNamara that he sign a letter to the Director of the Budget recommending the direct release to CIA of all funds required for the conduct of covert satellite projects. Charyk responded by writing Gilpatric that "if the NRO is to function it must be responsible for continuous monitoring of financial and technical program status, must control the release of funds to programs and must be able to reallocate between NRP programs." McCone's proposal would have allowed the agency to shift funds among CIA programs and prevented the DNRO from shifting funds between CIA and Air Force programs. Charyk concluded that Scoville had originated the proposal, although it was composed and submitted without his knowledge.[90]

Although personal hostility may have helped embitter the relationship between Charyk and Scoville, as well as between the CIA and NRO, there were also fundamental institutional viewpoints involved that had nothing to do with personality issues or particular acts of the principals and their subordinates. In the view of an NRO historian, "Scoville was the embodiment of CIA esprit de corps in an organization which—with considerable justification—considered itself uniquely more efficient and effective than any other element of the government." That view was fueled not only by the success of programs such as CORONA and the U-2 but also by the Air Force's SAMOS failures and the problems experienced in development of the GAMBIT high-resolution satellite.[91] Although the Air Force element of the NRO eventually would oversee the development of a number of valuable reconnaissance satellites, including GAMBIT, at the time success was elusive.

Scoville and others in the CIA equated the NRO with the Air Force and viewed the NRO as a means by which the Air Force was attempting to hijack a highly successful CIA program to substitute for the Air Force's failed program. As Wheelon would write many years later: "After their initial mistakes in rejecting the U-2 and botching the SAMOS Program, the Air Force knew a good thing when it saw it."[92]

Charyk and his staff had a drastically different viewpoint. It took a year and a half and over thirteen launches before CORONA experienced its first success. The overhauled SAMOS program had been in existence only slightly more than two years, and it had not yet had a chance to prove itself. Charyk and the Air Force were confident that it would succeed.[93]

Of greatest importance, they saw the NRO as "the embodiment of a new spirit in the national defense establishment"—similar to the creation of the National Security Agency a decade earlier and, more recently, a number of centralized defense agencies, such as the Defense Intelligence Agency. Charyk and others in the NRO viewed their organization as a national instrument that only incidentally made use of Air Force resources, and they believed their conception of a national reconnaissance program was much more comprehensive in scope than that of the CIA.[94]

Many in the CIA saw things differently. After all, the CIA was also a national organization—indeed, *the* national intelligence organization. Its components reported to the Director of Central Intelligence, who was charged by the NSC, via National Security Council Intelligence Directive No. 5, with coordinating the collection of intelligence through clandestine means, which included covert reconnaissance.[95] In addition, the DCI was responsible, largely through the CIA, for producing national intelligence for the president and other key decisionmakers—products for which reconnaissance data were essential. If the DCI and CIA agreed to abdicate a major role in directing the national reconnaissance effort, they would be endangering their ability to ensure that the required information was collected.

CIA officials were also not likely to accept the notion of an NRO whose use of Air Force assets was only "incidental"—no matter how strongly Charyk or other NRO officials embraced the idea, and even though there were Air Force officers assigned to the CIA who did not let their military affiliation compromise their work for the CIA. Nor did it matter if the regular Air Force distrusted NRO, or if Air Force officers serving with the NRO were treated as outcasts by the rest of the Air Force. To those in the CIA, blue suits were blue suits.[96]

In December, Charyk received an offer from the COMSAT Corporation, and by January people knew he would be leaving government shortly. But his imminent departure did not stop him from continuing to address the weaknesses he believed existed in NRO's charter and to press for a new one.[97] A new agreement, he argued in a parting analysis of the NRO situation, should state plainly that the NRO was an operating agency and that its director had full management responsibility for all projects. This meant, Charyk contended, that the NRO director should have authority over the reconnaissance activities of both the CIA and DOD. He should have complete authority in funding matters. And in a flashback to the time when he and Bissell worked together without discord, Charyk observed that appointments must be made so as to ensure that the responsible people "will function as an effective working team rather than as representatives of the DoD and CIA."[98]

At the end of February, during his last week in office, he completed a revision of a CIA draft, which had apparently been prepared by McCone's immediate staff rather than by Scoville or his staff. Charyk took the revision to Roswell Gilpatric. It appears that some CIA-suggested changes were incorporated sometime after Charyk left office. On March 13, Gilpatric signed the slightly modified version on behalf of DOD. It was sent to CIA that day and immediately was approved by McCone.[99]

The new agreement, though it did not include all the elements Charyk considered important, did substantially strengthen the authority of the NRO and its director—which did not stop McCone from concluding that it would be more "workable" than its predecessor.[100] The new agreement named the Secretary of Defense as the Executive Agent for the NRP. The program would be "developed, managed, and conducted in accordance with policies and guidance jointly agreed to by the Secretary of Defense and the Director of Central Intelligence."[101]

A "separate operating agency of the Department of Defense," the National Reconnaissance Office, would manage the NRP "under the direction, authority, and control of the Secretary of Defense." The NRO's director would be selected by the Defense Secretary with the concurrence of the DCI and would report to the Defense Secretary. The agreement also settled one issue of repeated contention between Scoville and Charyk, in Charyk's favor—by creating a Deputy Director's position and specifying that its occupant would be selected from CIA personnel. The Deputy Director, the agreement specified, "shall be in the chain of command directly under the Director NRO"—a sharp contrast to Scoville's view that he should be the CIA representative to the NRO. His duties included supervising all NRP tasks assigned to the CIA by the NRO director.[102]

The NRO director was charged with presenting to the Secretary of Defense "all projects" for intelligence collection and mapping and geodetic information via overflights and the associated budgets; scheduling all overflight missions in the NRP; and supervising engineering analysis to correct problems with collection systems. With regard to technical management, the DNRO was to "assign all project tasks such as technical management, contracting, etc., to appropriate elements of the DoD and the CIA, changing such assignments, and taking any such steps he may determine necessary to the efficient management of the NRP."[103]

The charter thus eliminated many of the CIA prerogatives that Charyk and other NRO officials considered impediments to their vision of a truly national reconnaissance program. Absent from the 1963 agreement were earlier provisions that required coordination of missions schedules with the CIA; that gave the CIA supervisory authority for engineering analysis of projects for which it was executive agent; and that gave the CIA responsibility for funding and supporting projects for which it was the executive agent. At the same time, on the other key issues, including technical management and research and development, the NRO director could chose to employ, *or not employ*, CIA resources as he believed best for the NRP.[104]

The breaking point for Scoville arrived in the person of Brockway McMillan, the Assistant Secretary of the Air Force for Research and Development who assumed the DNRO position on March 1 (he became Under Secretary of the Air Force in June). McMillan read the authority given him under the new agreement literally and assumed that he could make impersonal and rational judgments with the unswerving support of both McNamara and McCone.[105]

Thus, McMillan deemed it completely logical to transfer the CORONA project from the CIA to the Air Force Office of Special Projects and to place authority over its elements in the head of Program A. McMillan took a number of minor but unilateral actions to accomplish the transfer and was shocked when Scoville strongly protested each and every one of them. McMillan's response was first to prevent two of the Air Force officers working for the CIA on CORONA from communicating with Langley and then to transfer one officer without coordinating the move with the CIA.[106]

In Los Angeles, the Office of Special Projects was using the Aerospace Corporation to do systems engineering and technical direction for its programs and wished to add CORONA to Aerospace's responsibilities. The CIA considered this to be another takeover maneuver and bitterly opposed it.[107]

McMillan also took a strict stance on his review authority over NRP funds in accordance with an April 5 agreement, signed by McCone and Gilpatric, giving the NRO complete authority over all funds supporting the NRP, regardless of source—a change McCone agreed to so that funding for expensive CIA reconnaissance operations would not officially be part of the CIA's budget. Scoville and others continued to believe that funds marked for CIA-managed projects or studies should come to them automatically. McMillan did not.[108]

The battles with McMillan left Scoville especially bitter. More than twenty years later, he would describe McMillan as an "incompetent whose only talent was empire-building."[109] Those battles, on top of his conflicts with Charyk and difficulties with his own boss, led him to conclude he would be happier elsewhere. It was, deputy Edward Giller later recalled, "an emotional parting."[110]

3

A NEW BEGINNING

Pete Scoville's resignation left the Deputy Directorate for Research without a leader and in disarray. The NRO's new charter threatened to strip the directorate of authority with respect to its most important endeavor. Scoville's organization had never achieved the role originally envisioned, partly because of the refusal of Ray Cline and Richard Helms to turn over the scientific intelligence and technical services portfolios. As one CIA historian observed, the research directorate "never had a fighting chance." It did not help, in the view of some, such as John McMahon, that Scoville was simply "too nice a guy."[1]

But through the efforts of some key individuals, both within and outside the CIA, the directorate would receive a new name and a more extensive mission. It would champion the CIA's role in space reconnaissance—successfully managing the procurement of several new reconnaissance satellites and forcing a revision in the NRO charter. The directorate's ELINT operations would expand in the quest for better intelligence on the Soviet space and missile programs. In addition, technical analysis of foreign space and missile systems would become a major activity for the renovated directorate.

Such achievements did not come without significant intellectual and bureaucratic efforts. Ingenuity and perseverance were required to see some projects through to a successful conclusion. A willingness to engage in bitter and prolonged bureaucratic warfare also proved essential.

A SECOND TRY

Scoville's frustrations with his position had reached the ears of PFIAB chairman James Killian early in 1963. Neither he nor Edwin Land had been fully satisfied with the Deputy Directorate for Research, and they decided to press McCone to strengthen the CIA's technical capabilities. In

March, the rest of the PFIAB approved Killian and Land's "Recommendations to Intelligence Community by PFIAB," which spelled out how this task should be done, and the report was delivered to McCone.[2]

The recommendations included the "creation of an organization for research and development which will couple research (basic science) done outside the intelligence community, both overt and covert, with development and engineering conducted within intelligence agencies, particularly the CIA." It was necessary, they observed, to establish "an administrative arrangement in the CIA whereby the whole spectrum of modern science and technology can be brought into contact with major programs and projects of the Agency." Killian and Land noted that, unfortunately, "the present fragmentation and compartmentation of research and development in CIA severely inhibits this function."[3]

On April 15, McCone informed Killian and Land, through presidential National Security Adviser McGeorge Bundy, of the progress he had made in implementing their recommendations—which was none at all. He had taken no action, acknowledging that he had considered including OSI and TSD in the directorate but had suspended action. He promised to "move ahead with additional changes" that would give the research directorate "expanded responsibilities."[4]

Ten days later, Scoville submitted his resignation. Not long after Scoville departed, McCone decided to offer his position to Albert Wheelon, who had just returned from an overseas trip. Just a year before, Wheelon had replaced Scoville as head of OSI and was now being asked to succeed him a second time.[5]

Wheelon's year at the helm of OSI was his first inside the CIA, although it was not his first contact. The Illinois-born, California-raised, Wheelon had received a bachelor's degree in engineering from Stanford, a school he chose after it became clear to him that West Point was "not interested in those with eyeglasses." Stanford was followed by MIT, where he shared an office with future Nobel laureate Murray Gell-Mann, described in one study of twentieth-century physics as someone "who gave a rich new layer of meaning to the term 'brash.'" The same term would also be applied to Wheelon. After receiving a doctorate in physics in 1952, he worked on guided missiles at the Douglas Aircraft Company and then in 1953 joined the technical staff of Ramo-Woolridge (which would become Thompson-Ramo-Woolridge in 1958 and then TRW). In 1960, he was appointed director of the company's Radio Physics Laboratory, which focused on guidance systems for long-range ballistic missiles and satellites.[6]

As a by-product of his work for TRW, Wheelon published an impressive number of scientific papers, which appeared in prestigious journals such as *The Physical Review* and *Journal of Applied Physics*. One group of papers, bearing titles such as "Spectrum of Turbulent Fluctuations Produced by Convective Mixing of Gradients" and "Radio-Wave Scattering by Tropospheric Irregularities," focused on a phenomenon known as electromagnetic scintillation—the impact of the atmosphere on light, radio, and other electromagnetic signals, a topic of significance to missile guidance. A second group dealt with satellites and missiles and bore equally technical titles, such as "Oblateness Perturbation of Elliptical Satellite Orbits."[7]

His work on U.S. missile systems first brought him to the attention of the CIA. In summer 1957, a U-2 had photographed the Tyuratam ICBM and satellite launching complex. In an attempt to extract more information from those photographs, the CIA and Air Force sought help from individuals involved in U.S. missile programs who might notice things in the photography that others would not. Air Force Ballistic Missile Division chief Bernard Schriever appealed to Simon Ramo, the "R" in TRW, to provide a member of his technical staff. When complications arose with the first two TRW candidates, Wheelon was next in line. He, along with Army missile specialist Carl Duckett, became part of the JAM SESSION program. Many years later, Wheelon would recall that "it was my introduction to intelligence. I found it fascinating."[8]

Between 1960 and 1962, as part of project EARSHOT, Wheelon also helped to decipher the meaning of the telemetry transmitted by Soviet missiles during their test flights and by Soviet satellites that were being orbited at regular intervals. The Army and Air Force had been intercepting the data but needed assistance in making sense of it. The EARSHOT group was soon able to identify the different telemetry channels, calibrate them, and draw some conclusions about the missiles. Through his work on JAM SESSION and EARSHOT, Wheelon came to the attention of Bissell, Scoville, and Robert Amory, the Deputy Director for Intelligence. When Scoville became DD/R, he recruited Wheelon to assume the helm at OSI. With Killian and other key officials urging him to accept, Wheelon packed up and headed to Washington.[9]

At OSI, the brash Wheelon was not inhibited by the fact that he was only thirty-three years old and OSI staffers had to adjust to their new boss. Some, Wheelon felt, had become accustomed to being administrators rather than making technical judgments themselves. He sought to make OSI staffers more self-confident to give them more equal footing in their interactions with technical consultants. He believed some staffers' talents were being wasted. When he discovered that Sayre Stevens (later Deputy Director for Intelligence during the Carter administration) had been assigned to study Soviet windmills, he canceled the assignment and reassigned him to study Soviet air defenses. Some people considered themselves tenured professors, free to spend part of their day playing bridge at the faculty club. Wheelon, who with his wife and children still in California would stay at the office until 10 p.m., "began to press people hard." One division chief soon left for a job at the North American Aerospace Defense Command (NORAD).[10]

At the upper levels of the agency, Wheelon's work received favorable reviews. In late February 1963, deputy director Marshall Carter sent a two-paragraph memo to McCone noting that "I have been singularly impressed over the past months by the calm, unruffled, quietly analytical, and remarkably astute manner in which Bud Wheelon approaches all problems. . . . He is one our finest assets." Carter urged the DCI to "bring him into the family circle at every opportunity and to utilize him as a source of basic judgement . . . in areas which trouble you."[11]

But despite his willingness to take charge at OSI and his awareness of Carter's favorable view, Wheelon was taken aback by McCone's offer of the DD/R job. At the time, he was considering returning to California after just a year at CIA. His California house remained unsold. Also, he was "personally discouraged." He had come to Washington expecting to work for Scoville or Amory, both of whom were gone from the agency, and not Ray Cline. The two did not "hit it off very well," Wheelon later recalled. Cline, Wheelon felt, was more interested in making OSI a "team player" than in improving its performance. Further, he was well aware of the frustrations Scoville had suffered and believed that the position, as constituted, was a no-win situation. He declined the job, telling McCone, "We should not just screw another light bulb into a shorted-out socket."[12]

Wheelon did suggest that he could perform a service for the agency by tracking down Scoville and speaking to him about his reasons for leaving and what needed to be done. Wheelon journeyed to Woods Hole, Massachusetts, where Scoville was attending a conference. After arriving midmorning, Wheelon spent two or three hours with Scoville before returning to Washington that evening.[13]

The theme Wheelon detected in Scoville's comments was that Scoville felt McCone had consistently undermined him. The former deputy director talked about how Killian, Land, and McCone had assured him of his mandate, which was to include TSD, and how its deputy chief, Edward Giller, had become his deputy in anticipation of the transfer—only to have McCone yield when Helms objected. Scoville also noted how McCone similarly backed down in the face of Cline's unwillingness to part with OSI. As a result, Scoville began to question McCone's determination as well as his word.[14]

But those events alone did not cause Scoville's departure. The decisive factor, the former DDR told Wheelon, was McCone's unwillingness to fight the Pentagon over reconnaissance issues. Every time there was a dispute between him and the DNRO (whether Charyk or McMillan), the DCI, Scoville charged, either preemptively surrendered or promised to back him and then folded in negotiations with Gilpatric. Since he didn't know how to work in such an environment, he had to leave.[15]

The next day, Wheelon reported to McCone and deputy DCI Marshall Carter. Diplomatically, he told the two of Scoville's disappointment with regard to TSD and OSI, without stressing the issue of broken promises. The two senior intelligence officials were also apprised of Scoville's belief that the Air Force was moving to phase out the CIA's role in satellite reconnaissance. The question of the CIA's function in that activity was the key issue, Wheelon told McCone and his deputy.[16]

When asked what he thought the CIA should do, Wheelon reminded McCone that when he, McCone, had been head of the Atomic Energy Commission, the Air Force had demanded creation of a second national laboratory to speed development of the H-bomb, and that creation of Lawrence Livermore National Laboratory did produce that result. Wheelon then advanced the thesis that the only thing more important than nuclear weapon design was good intelligence about the Soviet Union, and that the only means of obtaining it was through overhead reconnaissance. The partnership with the Air Force was over, Wheelon continued, and "you must know it." Since there was no place for the CIA in the Air Force's plans, the alternatives were either to withdraw from the field or become the Livermore to the Air Force's Los Alamos.[17]

Wheelon also told McCone that the stage was set for the rapid dissolution of the research directorate. That was one path McCone could have taken. But, having been convinced of the crucial role of reconnaissance, and possibly concerned about the reaction of Killian and Land if, rather than strengthening the CIA's science and technology mandate, he abolished it, McCone decided on another course. In a second meeting with

Wheelon, either that day or the next, McCone again offered Wheelon the job, reminding him of the commitment he had made in 1962 to stay at CIA for at least three years. With McCone pledging complete support, as well as agreeing to rechristen the directorate the Directorate of Science and Technology (to emphasize the concept of the directorate managing all CIA scientific endeavors) and to accept the PFIAB's March 1963 recommendations as the directorate's new charter, Wheelon accepted.[18]*

The change became official on August 5, when a memo from deputy DCI Marshall Carter announced the retitling of the directorate, along with the transfer of two components from the intelligence and support directorates to the science and technology directorate. The following day Wheelon held a meeting with several hundred members of his new directorate. Carter was also present and made an appeal for bureaucratic "peace and harmony."[19]

NO MORE MR. NICE GUY

Jack Ledford, who served under both Scoville and Wheelon, later described Scoville as brilliant. But Wheelon was also brilliant and had "three times the energy level" of his predecessor. He was also very aggressive, fast-moving, and able to "analyze a problem, take it apart, and put it together with a solution better than any man I've ever seen," Ledford recalled. Scoville reminded his OSA chief of a Harvard or Stanford physics professor, whereas Wheelon was a "go-get-'em type" who "understood infighting in Washington very well."[20] Wheelon's skill at waging bureaucratic battles would be one factor in making the Directorate of Science and Technology (DS&T) the organization that Land and Killian had envisioned.

The two components transferred to the new directorate were the Automatic Data Processing Staff from the administration directorate, which became DS&T's Office of Computer Services, and the Office of Scientific Intelligence.[21] Once again the Technical Services Division remained under Richard Helms and the clandestine service. It was not an issue Wheelon wished to contest. He understood that Helms did not want "outsiders" involved in the audio operations, fabrication of identity documents, and secret writing techniques that were an essential part of espionage operations. Nor did he believe that dramatically improving the

---

*As noted earlier, at the time each CIA directorate was known as the "Deputy Directorate for." In July 1965, each became the "Directorate of." That change occurred during Wheelon's tenure, and therefore the new titles are used from this point forward.

quality of TSD would lead to significant improvement in the value of U.S. espionage operations. In addition, TSD was often involved in activities that were somewhat less than scientific—such as commissioning a madam to produce a *Handbook for Courtesans* instructing women on how to excite men (presumably more detailed than a comedian's advice to "show up") or rolling a Russian courier in the expectation of obtaining plans for Soviet subversion (and instead winding up with a briefcase containing $250,000).[22]

OSI was a quite different matter. Wheelon believed Cline to be a political opportunist who did not understand and would not nurture scientific intelligence but would tear it apart. That view was echoed by longtime OSI official Karl Weber—"Cline didn't know diddly-squat" about scientific matters, he stated in 1999. He also recalled telling Wheelon at one point, "Watch out for him [Cline]. He's a street fighter with a Harvard accent."[23]

Weber need not have worried. According to one history of the CIA, Cline "was furious with the shift of OSI" but was "consistently outmaneuvered by Wheelon." One CIA official recalled that "Ray had an uncontrollable ability to make enemies. . . . He and Bud Wheelon were at daggers drawn. When you take on Bud Wheelon, you're taking on a bureaucratic master, and Bud Wheelon ripped Ray to shreds." Wheelon attributed his victory less to bureaucratic skill than to the fact that he and McCone had concluded, prior to the discovery the previous October, that the Soviets had placed offensive missiles in Cuba, whereas Cline's intelligence directorate argued that the Soviets would not take such an action. As a result, Wheelon's stock rose while Cline's fell.[24]

Cline's pique at the transfer of OSI was still evident in his memoirs, published twenty-five years later. He noted that "the one major change in CIA's structure that McCone made was one I disapproved of . . . he took the scientific intelligence analytical staff from the DDI and turned it over to . . . Albert (Bud) Wheelon, who stayed only a short time before going back to industry." As a result, "CIA advocacy of its own scientific collection techniques became mixed up with its objective analysis of all scientific and technical developments." Permitting the same unit to collect and evaluate intelligence "violated a cardinal rule of sound intelligence organization."[25]

THE CHINESE BOMB

During Wheelon's tenure as deputy director for science and technology, OSI focused on a variety of topics—foreign scientific resources; the research, development, and testing of air defense systems; cruise missiles, aircraft, and naval vessels; scientific space activities; unconventional warfare; the physical, engineering, and life sciences; and nuclear energy.[26]

Heading OSI was Donald Chamberlain, a Ph.D. in chemical engineering who had left his professor's position at Washington University in St. Louis to join the agency. Chamberlain was someone Wheelon "had extraordinary confidence" in and would keep "the military guys from going off half-cocked on Russia."[27]

As in the past, a crucial element of the office's work concerned foreign nuclear weapons programs. The division's products included November 1964 studies on the Japanese and Indian nuclear energy programs. The former study covered the number and type of research reactors in Japan, its exploration for and production of uranium, research into the production of heavy water, and a variety of applications—from the study of the use of plutonium for advanced reactors to the application of nuclear energy research, medicine, and industry. A few months earlier, OSI had examined the status of Soviet nuclear research reactors and their contribution to the Soviet atomic energy program.[28]

In 1964 and 1965, OSI helped draft the national intelligence estimates on the Soviet atomic energy program. Topics explored included the Soviet Union's production of fissionable materials, its nuclear-powered submarine program, nuclear weapons developments, and the command and control of nuclear weapons. The 1964 estimate noted that "the Soviets significantly improved their fission and thermonuclear weapon capabilities as a result of the 1961–62 test series."[29]

In addition to Japan's activities, the nuclear programs of two other Asian countries were of concern to OSI. In October 1965, Chamberlain responded to a request from a National Security Council staff member for information on the Indian nuclear weapons capabilities. His memo focused on the possibility of India developing nuclear weapons and on its nuclear facilities, plutonium research, and nuclear power development. Chamberlain noted, "India probably already has on hand enough plutonium for a nuclear device." But he concluded, "We have no firm indication that the Indian Government has decided to develop nuclear weapons."[30]

Of far greater concern was the Chinese program. China was, according to Karl Weber, "a real mystery . . . big, really foreign, hard to get a handle on."[31] Just a year earlier, on October 16, 1964, China had detonated its first atomic bomb at Lop Nur, in northwestern China. The test, in addition to unequivocally demonstrating China's nuclear capability, also highlighted the shortcoming of OSI's analysis of the Chinese program.

Between August 1963 and China's detonation, OSI's work had been conducted against the backdrop of growing concerns by Presidents Kennedy and Johnson and their advisers about the implications of China's joining the nuclear club. They had already considered a number of options—including assisting India in building a bomb (to ensure that the first Asian bomb would not be a Communist one), as well as enlisting the Soviet Union in a joint preventive strike against Chinese nuclear facilities. The first alternative was rejected by Secretary of State Dean Rusk, the second by Nikita Khrushchev.[32]

A Special National Intelligence Estimate (SNIE), published less than two weeks before OSI's transfer to the science and technology directorate and largely the work of OSI, summarized what OSI knew, or believed it knew, about the Chinese program. The estimate, "Communist China's Advanced Weapons Program," reported that since the estimate of the previous year, "we have received a considerable amount of information, mainly from photography"—the results of U-2 and CORONA overflights. But the estimate also noted that "the gaps in our information remain substantial and we are therefore not able to judge the present state or to project the future development of the Chinese program as a whole with any high degree of confidence."[33]

The estimate fully reflected the belief of OSI and Chamberlain that China would seek to join the nuclear club via the same route taken by other emerging nuclear powers—a plutonium bomb. The process of enriching uranium to a level suitable for use in weapons is laborious, and considerably less plutonium than uranium is needed to make a simple atomic weapon. The Chinese might indeed have taken the plutonium route had the Soviets not withdrawn technical assistance in 1960, forcing the Chinese to concentrate their scare resources on the more advanced program—which happened to be uranium enrichment.[34]

The SNIE reported the discovery of what was mistakenly judged to be a plutonium production reactor at Baotou with "elaborate security arrangements." The estimate also said it was unclear whether the reactor had gone critical, and it probably could not have gone critical before early 1962—in which case the earliest a first device could be tested, relying on plutonium from that reactor alone, would be early 1964. If the Chinese ran into a normal number of difficulties, late 1964 or 1965 would be the earliest they could test. If the reactor went critical after early 1962, the detonation would be delayed even further. Although the accumulated overhead photography yielded no signs of the other plutonium reactors that OSI analysts believed China needed, they noted that "the possible existence of another reactor cannot be ignored."[35]

March and June 1963 photographs of the Lanzhou Gaseous Diffusion Plant, which had first been identified in 1959 aerial photography, showed progress being made on a nearby hydroelectric plant believed to have been designed to supply Lanzhou, as well as transmission lines between Lanzhou and a thermal electric plant. The analysts believed Lanzhou was unlikely to produce weapons-grade uranium-235 before 1966, even under the most advantageous conditions, and more likely to do so during 1968 and 1969. What the analysts did not know was that in late 1962, China's Second Ministry of Machine Building, which ran the nuclear program, had directed Lanzhou to produce enough uranium for a bomb by the beginning of 1964.[36]

Based on the faulty identification of Baotou as a plutonium production facility, and the erroneous assumption that plutonium would fuel China's first atomic explosion, the analysts' best guess was late 1964 or 1965. But they added that the possible existence of another, undiscovered plutonium reactor might mean that "the Chinese could achieve a first detonation at any time."[37]

As OSI continued to try to determine the truth about the Chinese program, U.S. policymakers continued to explore their options. In November 1963, Joint Chiefs of Staff (JCS) chairman Maxwell Taylor presented his colleagues with a paper on "how we can prevent or delay the Chinese from succeeding in their nuclear development program." The wording of the title on the agenda—"Unconventional Warfare Program BRAVO"—indicated the paramilitary nature of the contemplated action.[38] A few months later, Walt Rostow, the chief of Policy Planning, asked staff expert Robert Johnson to study the feasibility of disrupting the Chinese nuclear effort by force. Johnson concluded that "preemptive military action is undesirable," in part because the United States had not identified all of the relevant targets.[39]

During the first eight months of 1964, China made steady progress toward building its first atomic bomb. In January, the Lanzhou facility produced its first highly enriched uranium and began regular operations. In April, the Jiuquan complex made the first nuclear components for the bomb. In June, the Ninth Academy conducted a successful full-scale simulation. And on August 19, workers at Jiuquan assembled the first nuclear test explosive, including the nuclear core.[40]

A special national intelligence estimate published on August 26 reflected both the extensive reconnaissance operations directed at China's nuclear facilities and the continued assumption that plutonium would be China's path to its first atomic bomb. Titled "Chances of an Imminent Communist Chinese Nuclear Explosion," the NIE reported that recent CORONA photography of the Lop Nur test facility (first identified as a result of a December 1961 CORONA mission) led analysts to conclude that "the previously suspect facility at Lop Nur . . . is a nuclear test site which could be ready for use in two months."[41]

However, the estimate, reflecting OSI's views, stated "that [the detonation] will not occur until sometime after the end of 1964." That conclusion was driven by the view that China "will not have sufficient fissionable material for a test of a nuclear device in the next few months"—a conclusion based on the continuing belief that China's first bomb would be fueled by plutonium, not uranium, and that the Lanzhou plant, which had already produced sufficient uranium-235 for a bomb, was "behind schedule." Analysts believed that the plutonium reactor assumed to be at Baotou would not produce enough plutonium for a bomb until 1965 at the earliest.[42]

Such conclusions were disputed both within and outside the CIA. Two prominent nuclear advisers, Albert and Richard Latter, told Wheelon that OSI was "screwing up" by assuming that a first bomb would rely on plutonium. Chamberlain had misjudged the Chinese program and "got stubborn about it," Wheelon later recalled. He took the Latters to see McCone.[43]

Allen Whiting of the State Department's Bureau of Intelligence and Research (INR) doubted that the Chinese would have erected the test tower at Lop Nur evident in CORONA imagery unless a test were imminent. That evidence, along with public and private statements by Chinese leaders, led him to recommend to INR director Thomas Hughes that the United States invoke a long-standing contingency plan by announcing the upcoming test before the Chinese did—in an effort to lessen the impact and "reassure neighboring countries that the United States was watching and aware." NPIC director Arthur Lundahl independently recommended a preemptive announcement.[44]

On September 29, after further consideration of more violent options, which may have included another attempt to recruit the Soviet Union to participate in a preemptive strike, a State Department spokesman announced that a Chinese test "might occur in the near future."[45]

On October 15, a memo from Chamberlain to Deputy DCI Carter noted that the most recent information had confirmed that Lop Nur was probably ready to host an atomic test. The memo included descriptions of specific items revealed in overhead photography—including a 340-foot tower surrounded by a double fence, two small towers, and various bunkers and platforms—then stated that the "high priority given to the completion of site construction suggests that a test is scheduled in the fairly near future." It also noted that the high level of flight activity to and from the area halted in September 1963, when the site was essentially complete, but had resumed in September 1964, possibly reflecting final preparations.[46]

According to the OSI chief, a reevaluation of the Baotou reactor site indicated that adequate primary and backup electric power circuits for reactor operation had been installed by March 1963, a finding that reduced confidence in the August 1964 judgment that the reactor did not begin operation until early that year. Analysts also noted that another possible source of fissionable material was a facility in a large complex near Yumen, which might contain a small operational reactor. In addition, they stated that "we no longer believe that evidence on plutonium availability justifies the on-balance judgement reached in August 1964. We believe the Lop Nur evidence indicates that a test could occur at any time." But they hedged their bets by concluding that "we believe a test will occur sometime within the next six to eight months."[47]

The next six to eight months included, of course, the very next day—October 16, when China announced the detonation of its first atomic device. On October 20, the same day a CORONA satellite snapped a picture of ground zero showing clear signs of the detonation, Atomic Energy Commission chairman Glenn Seaborg told a presidential cabinet meeting that analysis of the debris from the radioactive cloud confirmed that the bomb had employed uranium, not plutonium, and that it "had been more sophisticated in design than our own Hiroshima [uranium] weapon."[48]

The misunderstood Baotou facility played no role in the production of China's first nuclear device. Subsequently, it was responsible for the transformation of uranium oxide into uranium tetrafluoride. In 1967, the facility at Yumen was identified as a plutonium reactor, and China detonated its first plutonium device the following year. An article in the CIA's in-house journal, *Studies in Intelligence*, concluded that "there was a preconception of the likely Chinese approach, and a failure to consider seriously alternative options." The OSI, and thus the CIA, had, as Wheelon put it, "missed the boat."[49]

MISSILES AND SPACE

Wheelon's Directorate of Science and Technology began with five components—the three he inherited from the Directorate of Research (OSA, OEL, and ORD) and the two that were transferred from other parts of the agency (OSI and OCS). On November 7, 1963, he created a new component—the Foreign Missile and Space Analysis Center (FMSAC), with a planned staff of 270.[50]

Under its charter, FMSAC was to provide detailed technical intelligence on Soviet, Chinese, and other foreign space and offensive missile systems. OSI and other components of the intelligence community would provide overviews of space and missile programs, monitor deployments, and study strategy. Determining the trajectories, range, number of warheads, and accuracy of ICBMs as well as the precise movements and missions of satellites and space shots would be the job of FMSAC, with the help of OCS's computers.[51]

Part of Wheelon's rationale for establishing the new organization was explained by a *Studies in Intelligence* article he had coauthored in 1961 with OSI analyst Sidney Graybeal. They characterized the space race as having many characteristics of a game, noting that "our stature as a nation, our culture, our way of life and government are tending to be gauged by our skill in playing this game."[52]

In playing the game, it was important for the United States to have as much accurate intelligence as possible about Soviet space plans, capabilities, and operations. Once a space launch occurred, "intelligence must be prepared to move quickly and confidently" into a "tracking, collection, and analysis operation." Such activity would help national leaders make "correct and appropriate comments on each new Soviet space accomplishment." It would also allow the United States to understand when the Soviets failed and give U.S. leaders the option of revealing those failures. If statements by U.S. officials are "as authoritative and complete as possible, Congress and the public will be less likely to give undue weight to the rash of scientific but often ill-informed opinion."[53]

Wheelon also had come to the conclusion that the work of OSI's offensive systems division was not up to his standards and needed an infusion of better-trained personnel—individuals who understood telemetry and other technical issues. Furthermore, missiles and space were not within the expertise of OSI chief Donald Chamberlain. And he also had "too much on his plate" anyway, according to Wheelon. There was also, in Wheelon's view, a need for a forceful leader, someone willing to battle the Air Force over issues such as the capability of a new Soviet missile.[54]

Also needed was an organization that had no institutional conflict of interest in analyzing foreign efforts and had access to the full range of intelligence data. In Wheelon's view, neither the Army's missile intelligence unit nor the Air Force's Foreign Technology Division satisfied both those requirements. FTD, in particular, was to Wheelon a "propaganda mill," and one function of FMSAC would be to "keep FTD honest."[55]

One particular controversy that, to Wheelon, indicated a need for a second voice on missile matters was the continuing debate over the SS-8 missile. In 1961, using data collected from the first tests of the missile earlier that year, scientists working for the Air Force calculated that the SS-8 nose cone weighed around 25,000 pounds—sufficient to carry a warhead in the 100-megaton class. But there were doubters in other corners of the intelligence community, including CIA, and during 1962 the question of the nose cone's size became a matter of intense disagreement and the focus of a major analytical effort. In 1962 and 1963, outside review groups and other members of the intelligence community, including Army intelligence, moved toward the view that the SS-8 warhead was small.[56]

An October 1963 national intelligence estimate stated that the data available indicated that the SS-8, if large, could carry a nose cone weighing about 10,000 pounds, but the best estimate was that it had a payload similar to that of the SS-7—only about 4,500 pounds. The Air Force retreated but did not surrender—insisting that the evidence did not exclude the possibility of the SS-8 carrying a nose cone of up to 18,000 pounds.[57]

Wheelon intended FMSAC to be a center where all incoming information relevant to missile and space activity would arrive and be analyzed, with results distributed to the White House, NASA, and other interested parties. It would also play a role, Wheelon expected, in influencing the development and deployment of collection systems.[58]

Wheelon found a forceful leader for FMSAC in JAM SESSION colleague Carl Duckett, at the time the head of the Directorate of Missile Intelligence of the Army Missile Command at Huntsville, Alabama. Duckett differed from many of those who rose to high levels in the CIA. He grew up in rural North Carolina and never attended an Ivy League university. When he was seventeen, his mother presented him with a new pair of jeans, some money, and instructions to get a job at the mill down the road. Duckett didn't stop for 200 miles, until he got a job at a radio station. He was drafted for service in World War II, and when the results of his IQ tests came in, it was apparent that the military had a genius on its hands. Duckett was then sent to study radio at Johns Hopkins University.[59]

After the war, Duckett was assigned to White Sands Proving Ground and became involved in missile testing and telemetry analysis. From White Sands he moved on to Huntsville to work on range instrumentation. In 1957, he was brought to Washington as part of the JAM SESSION program.[60]

Among those Duckett brought into FMSAC were David Brandwein, a veteran of TRW and EARSHOT, who would succeed Duckett as FMSAC director; M. Corley Wonus, a future head of the directorate's SIGINT operations; and future DS&T chief R. Evans Hineman (commonly referred to as Evan Hineman).[61] In 1956, Hineman, having obtained his degree in mechanical engineering and completed his Reserve Officer Training Course, was headed for two years of Army service. A course in technical intelligence, which he considered preferable to the alternative of learning to repair tanks, was followed by assignment to the Army missile intelligence unit at Huntsville. In his two years there, he had an inside view of Soviet space and missile efforts and was called on to brief notables such as Wernher von Braun and General John Medaris, head of the Army's missile program.[62]

When his two years at Huntsville were up, Hineman joined the Army Ordnance Technical Intelligence Agency at Arlington Hall, Virginia—an organization that would become part of the Army's Foreign Science and Technology Center (FSTC) when it was formed in 1962. Hineman first met Carl Duckett around 1960. When Duckett was subsequently put in charge of the Army's missile intelligence effort, he tried to get Hineman to come back to Huntsville, but both Hineman and his wife felt they had seen enough of the Alabama town. When he became head of FMSAC, Duckett called again, and this time, Hineman signed up.[63]

Not everyone was as enthusiastic about FMSAC as Wheelon, Duckett, and Hineman. Among the least enamored were two powerful Air Force generals, Bernard Schriever, head of the Air Force Systems Command (AFSC) and chief of staff Curtis LeMay. In September 1963, LeMay had been alerted of Wheelon's plans in a letter from Schriever's deputy. In December, after the center's creation and a briefing from Wheelon and Duckett, Schriever wrote to LeMay, urging that "immediate action should be taken to slow down or block CIA action to duplicate DOD missile and space intelligence."[64] By "DOD" Schriever meant "FTD," which reported to his Systems Command.

Schriever complained that "the establishment of this activity within CIA is most certainly the first step in competing with and possibly attempting to usurp the Services' capabilities in this area of scientific and technical intelligence." He also objected that the creation of FMSAC had "resulted in undesirable competition for special talent and special data." Schriever characterized the Air Force capability in the area as representing "a significant investment in manpower and resources and . . . an extremely vital function which must not be lost or permitted to be eroded by another government agency."[65]

He recommended that Joseph Carroll, head of the Defense Intelligence Agency and thus the senior military official on the United States Intelligence Board, be encouraged to protest CIA activities in the area "at least until an agreement on respective responsibilities and mutual support can be reached." But Schriever believed that since "the problem could not be solved through intelligence channels alone . . . I recommend that you and the Secretary act to protest this expensive and unnecessary duplication of DOD space and missile intelligence analysis by CIA."[66]

On January 2, 1964, LeMay asked the head of Air Force intelligence, Brig. Gen. Jack Thomas, and a colleague to prepare a memorandum that would serve as the basis of a JCS request to the Secretary of Defense for OSD action "to oppose the FMSAC program."[67] That was apparently followed by a memo from LeMay to Schriever stating that he shared Schriever's concerns and that the memo he envisioned going to McNamara would request the Defense Secretary to consult with McCone "in an effort to prevent a major CIA effort competing with and largely duplicating activities well under way in Department of Defense agencies."[68]

Ultimately, the Air Force opposition proved futile. But the Defense Department's review of missile and space intelligence activities, which was being conducted during late 1963, did result in a Defense Department competitor, at least in some respects, for FMSAC. Chartered by a Defense Department directive, the Defense Special Missile and Astronautics Center (DEFSMAC), a joint NSA-DIA operation, opened for business on June 1, 1964.[69]

The center was to receive warnings of upcoming foreign missile and space launches, alert all relevant intelligence collectors and officials of the forthcoming launches, and provide initial assessments of the launches. Former DEFSMAC chief Charles Tevis recalled that there was a "great opportunity for these two . . . centers to fight . . . everybody likes to be the first one to get a current report out," and there was a "kind of one-upmanship in reporting." According to Hineman, there was a rivalry with DEFSMAC over "who's going to get to the street first," and the rivalry was probably good for the country. Since the intelligence community was working with incomplete data, it was useful to have organizations that could go down different analytical paths in pursuit of the truth.[70]

There was ample Soviet missile and space activity to keep FMSAC and DEFSMAC busy during Wheelon's tenure. The Soviets began orbiting a variety of military support satellites. Reconnaissance and meteorology spacecraft joined scientific satellites in orbit, usually with the uninformative *Cosmos* designation (which was also used for space probes that never made it out of earth orbit). In 1965, the first Soviet *Molniya* ("Lightning") communications spacecraft was placed in its peculiar orbit—flying at a 63-degree inclination and reaching 24,000 miles above the earth when over the northern Soviet Union and descending to a mere 240 or so miles when it whizzed over the southern portion of the planet.[71]

Manned missions were intended to claim space "firsts" for the Soviets as well as help prepare for a mission to the moon. The cosmonauts stayed close to earth initially; unmanned missions were intended to establish an ability to reach, orbit, and land upon the moon as well as send back photographs. Thus, the October 1964 *Voshkod 1* mission was the first flight without spacesuits and the first with direct in-flight medical observations. The *Voshkod 2* mission of March 1965 included the first space walk, a ten-minute stroll outside the capsule by Alexei Leonov.[72]

Meanwhile, Soviet lunar probes were launched to orbit the moon or achieve a soft landing and in each case also to send back photographs. A string of failures in 1964 and early 1965 was followed by the success of *Zond 3,* which sent back pictures of the lunar surface taken during a flyby. That was followed by several more failed soft landings before *Luna 9* was successful on January 31, 1966.[73]

Probes fired at Mars or Venus included the April 1964 mission of *Zond 1,* which the Soviets apparently lost contact with before it passed by Venus. The *Venera 2* and *Venera 3* missions in November 1965 were partially successful but did not transmit any data because the first flew by and the second crashed into the planet.[74]

One component of FMSAC, the Activities Interpretation Division, served as twenty-four-hour watch center. The time difference between Washington and Soviet launch sites, along with the urgency in determining the mission associated with each launch, required FMSAC to disrupt the sleep of key personnel. Evan Hineman remembers being called in during the middle of the night on several occasions to examine data on trajectories and orbits so that the White House, NASA, and other agencies could be told whether an earth satellite, interplanetary probe, or lunar mission had been launched.[75]

Among the important elements of these inquiries was trajectory analysis. Establishing the launch time to the nearest minute, through tracing the trajectory back to the launch point and incorporating data on velocity, permitted a great deal to be inferred about the objectives of the mission as well as the technology employed. Thus, the launch time of *Luna 1* on January 2, 1959, had enabled U.S. analysts to conclude that the Soviet claim that it was a solar satellite was most likely an attempt to cover up a failed attempt to send the spacecraft crashing into the moon's surface.[76]

Quick assessments were only part of FMSAC's work. Wheelon and Graybeal noted in their 1961 article that although "gross features of a Soviet space shot can usually be . . . established within the first few hours by an experienced technical man," the "variations and nuances of a given flight, however, which can be equally important, may require weeks of concentrated effort by a team of subsystem specialists working together." The results of such analysis would be a clear picture of mission performance and the system's technical features.[77]

Thus, the CIA was able to report to the White House on June 1, 1964, that *Zond 1,* which had been launched two months earlier, would reach the vicinity of Venus on July 20. The report noted that "we cannot yet tell whether it will impact on Venus or fly by, perhaps ejecting an instrumented probe to explore the planet's atmosphere as it goes by." (*Zond 1* came within 62,000 miles of Venus, but the failure of its radio prevented any data from being returned.)[78]

FMSAC personnel also sought to unravel the failure of the unmanned *Cosmos 57* mission, which was placed into orbit on February 12, 1965. Analysts examined the data from radars that tracked the spacecraft's movements in space and scrutinized intercepted telemetry in their attempt to understand the purpose of the mission and why the spacecraft burned up not long after its first orbit.[79]

The space walk of Alexei Leonov a few weeks later pointed FMSAC analysts in the right direction. By comparing the telemetry from *Cosmos 57* and *Voshkod 2*, they were able to determine that *Cosmos 57* was a test for the automated system that operated the airlock Leonov needed to pass through. They also determined, from intercepts of signals to and from *Cosmos 57,* the key channels on which commands were transmitted to the spacecraft from the Soviet control station, as well those from the spacecraft to ground controllers that told how it was responding.[80]

The explanation analysts pried from the intercepted signals was that while the spacecraft was in range of signals from one transmitter, it received a duplicate set from a second transmitter that was intended to pick up communications with the spacecraft when it flew out of range of the first. The double signals were merged into a single signal that instructed the spacecraft to fire its retro-rockets in preparation for descent. Possibly because of the mass of deployed airlock, the spacecraft then began tumbling some seventy-eight times a minute. Only because the airlock operations could be carried out manually was the Leonov space walk able to proceed as planned.[81]

The *Luna 9* mission of early 1966 was also of great interest to FMSAC analysts because a successful soft landing would have returned the Soviet Union to leadership in the lunar race. U.S. collection sites, including the Army's Sinop facility in Turkey and the NSA's STONEHOUSE facility in Ethiopia, enabled U.S. analysts to monitor launch, orbit, and ejection and to determine that *Luna 9*'s trajectory was on target.[82]

From the intercepted telemetry, analysts determined when the spacecraft's engine had been fired to send it cruising toward the moon. On February 3, it was oriented for retromaneuver while STONEHOUSE, Jodrell Bank, and other sites listened in order to provide FMSAC, DEFSMAC, and other interested parties with data to analyze. *Luna 9* landed softly that same day. Its first signals from the moon included telemetry as well as what was soon recognized to be a fax transmission. In the United States and England, fax machines were modified to convert the signal into pictures—with the result that some of the pictures obtained at Jodrell Bank were published before the Soviets officially released them.[83]

Of greater concern than the Soviet space program was the Soviet missile program—particularly the ICBMs and submarine-launched ballistic missiles (SLBMs) that could hit U.S. territory. From 1964 through mid-1966, the Soviets began testing three third-generation ICBMs—the SS-9 Scarp, SS-11 Sego, and SS-13 Savage. They also conducted tests of their SS-7 Saddler and SS-8 Sasin missiles.[84]

Some issues about those programs, such as the numbers produced and deployed, the locations of deployment sites, and targeting policy, were considered outside of FMSAC's charter. The technical intelligence analysts at FMSAC worried about key characteristics of the missiles and their warheads—missile size, yield, accuracy, range, throw weight, vulnerability to defensive systems, whether the warhead could be airburst, and whether the missile was liquid- or solid-fueled.[85]

Such technical details were not merely of academic interest to missile designers, for they could have significant strategic implications. They were a key element in determining whether the Soviet strategic forces could strike certain types of targets, overwhelm missile defenses, or destroy U.S. ICBMs in a preemptive strike.

The information mined by FMSAC analysts, only some types of which were available for any given missile launch, included optical, radar, and telemetry data. To estimate the size and shape of a reentry vehicle, photographs were most helpful but were rarely obtained. Less directly indicative, but still useful, were radar cross-section data.[86] From estimates of size, estimates of yield followed.

Extracting intelligence from telemetry data required not only a facility for technical analysis but also ingenuity. Soviet missile designers knew what aspect of the missile's performance each channel of telemetry measured and how that performance was being measured, but FMSAC analysts did not. In addition, they usually were confronted with an incomplete set of telemetry, since during the 1960s the United States was rarely able to gather telemetry during the earliest launch stage because Tyuratam was over the radio horizon from U.S. eavesdropping antennae.

Despite such handicaps, FMSAC analysts could rely on the fact that certain basic measurements, such as acceleration and fuel pressure, were required during any test, and that the numbers associated with particular aspects of the missile's performance would behave in a certain manner. Thus, when the system feeding propellant to an engine shut off, measured pressure would drop to zero in considerably less than a second, and the turbine would take four to eight seconds to coast to a stop.[87]

An analogy can be drawn to a car: A person riding in a car would expect to have a set of gauges on the dashboard measuring speed, oil pressure, and other aspects of the car's performance. Even if those instruments were placed in unconventional positions in the car and no units of measurement were indicated, it would be possible to correlate specific instruments with the car's behavior to determine both the function of an instrument as well as the units of measurement employed. Thus, "given a fair sample of powered flight telemetry, the analyst can usually say whether the vehicle is liquid or solid-fueled, whether it has a single burning stage or multiple stages, and what ratio of payload to total weight it probably has."[88]

Analysts also examined telemetry to create a record of the liquid level at the bottom of the propellant tank as burnout neared. From that information, they sometimes could determine the shape of the bottom of the tank, a determination that could then be used in estimating missile size—which as the SS-8 debate indicated could be a key issue in assessing the missile's capabilities. Telemetry data could be combined with other data to determine the velocity, acceleration, flight path, and angle of a reentry vehicle's descent—significant data in establishing its vulnerability to missile defense systems.[89]

Turning telemetry and other technical data into estimates of the characteristics of Soviet missiles allowed the national estimates on Soviet strategic forces, such as the October 1964 NIE, to assess the probable range, accuracy, reentry vehicle weight, warhead weight, warhead yield, and type of propellant for each operational Soviet missile.[90] Such data were important not only in assessing the Soviet threat and U.S. strategic requirements but also, a few years down the road, in developing arms control strategies.

EAVESDROPPERS

A significant part of the data that FMSAC and other elements of the intelligence community relied upon in attempting to decipher the Soviet missile and space programs was provided by the directorate's own collection activities—particularly those of the Office of ELINT (OEL).

The CIA-funded Norwegian station at Kirkenes and its subsidiary METRO outpost at Korpfjell continued to intercept communications, telemetry, and other electronic signals. To enhance intercept capability, the CIA budgeted part of $104,000 to replace one of the principal ELINT receivers at the Kirkenes site during the 1966–1967 fiscal year.[91]

The remainder of the money went to "activate an ELINT boat operation in the Barents Sea," which was targeted against Soviet naval operations. In 1965, the *Globe XIV,* a whale catcher, was purchased and converted into the ELINT ship *Marjata I.* The *Marjata I* replaced the *Eger* in 1966. Soon after the *Marjata*'s first operations, it became the subject of intense Soviet interest, and some "incidents" followed, but the Norwegians did not consider them sufficiently serious to halt the operations.[92]

According to John McMahon, the Norwegians were "not intimidated," and the boat operation produced "great intelligence." Included were data on launches out of the White Sea, on air-to-air and air-to-ground missile launches, and on Soviet practice firings from the Barents Sea. The operation also provided "good COMINT coverage."[93]

OEL also sought to improve its ability to monitor missile tests emanating from Tyuratam and antimissile activity at Sary Shagan. In 1965 and 1966, OEL established a second telemetry intercept station in northeastern Iran at Kabkan, forty miles east of Meshed. Code-named TACKSMAN II, the station was only 650 miles southwest of Tyuratam.[94] As with the TACKSMAN I facility at Beshahr, it was a strictly U.S. operation, with no Iranians permitted inside the facilities. It also had, as did the Beshahr site, a communications intercept capability to permit monitoring of test range communications.[95]

TACKSMAN II was located in a remote mountainous area inhabited by nomads, and although the station became home to advanced electronic equipment, living conditions were primitive for those on the site survey team and the initial permanent contingent.[96] Bob Phillips was among the seven people who established the site in 1965, and he returned in 1966 to spend a year as chief engineer. The nine or ten individuals who spent that year at TACKSMAN II had to dig a slit trench to serve as the latrine, carry water up the mountain, and have their supplies flown in from Tehran. It was "like camping out for a year," Phillips recalled, except camping out usually does not involve "sitting on a slit trench [in freezing weather] in the middle of the night." The site was devoid of trees, a factor Phillips believed influenced his later decision to buy a house in an area of northern Virginia that had "trees everywhere."[97]

But the hardships endured by the CIA's personnel on an isolated mountain in Iran paid huge dividends for the FMSAC analysts who were trying to crack the Soviet missile and antimissile programs. At their peak, the Iranian stations provided about 85 percent of the hard intelligence on the Soviet ICBM program. The sites could do what no other U.S. intercept sites could do—monitor the last moments of the firing of the missile's first stage, which meant a greater degree of confidence in determining missile dimensions and throw weight. The material, according to Phillips, came in "pure" and required no exotic processing. To FMSAC chief Duckett, it was "pure gold."[98]

The Norwegian and Iranian stations (along with other stations operated by NSA or its military components) had an assortment of operational and test firings to monitor between 1964 and mid-1966. In 1965, the Soviets began test firing solid-fueled missiles, which the United States designated the SS-13 Savage, from Plesetsk out to the Kamchatka Peninsula, over 3,000 miles away. That same year they also commenced test firings of a solid-propellant missile from Kapustin Yar on journeys of about 1,100 miles. Test firings of the SS-10 from Tyuratam began with a failure in April 1964, but six successful tests followed by the end of September.[99]

Between mid-March and mid-April 1966, four different types of Soviet missiles (SS-7, SS-8, SS-9, SS-11) were test fired from Tyuratam to the Klyuchi impact zone on Kamchatka. One objective of the SS-9 firings may have been to test a major modification of the SS-9 reentry vehicle. Similarly, SS-11 tests appear to have been related to testing of a heavier version of the missile's reentry vehicle.[100]

In 1965 and 1966, while Kirkenes, Beshahr, and Kabkan were listening to Soviet missile tests, another CIA facility was listening for signals from the moon. Out at Stanford University in Palo Alto, California, the CIA was employing a 150-foot dish antenna to monitor the signals of Soviet radars after they had bounced off the earth's only natural satellite.[101]

The "moonbounce" phenomenon had been discovered in 1946, when scientists detected a man-made signal reflected from the moon. Experiments that followed revealed the extraordinary weakness of such signals. A typical signal received via moonbounce was a billion times weaker than if it were intercepted by an airplane ten miles from the transmitter. As a result, only very large antennae could effectively hear such signals and distinguish them from other signals.[102]

By the early 1960s, the possibility of exploiting the moonbounce phenomenon was being investigated by a number of agencies. N. C. Gerson of the National Security Agency used the Arecibo Ionospheric Observatory in Puerto Rico to intercept moonbounce signals from a Soviet radar operating on the Arctic coast. Along with a member of the Army Security Agency, he produced a three-volume study—*Moonbounce Potential from Scooped Antennas*. The Air Force also had a moonbounce project, FLOWER GARDEN, which relied on several antennae, including the 250-foot antenna at Jodrell Bank. Other moonbounce collectors were the antennae at the Grand Bahama tracking station, a Navy intercept site at Sugar Grove, West Virginia, and the Naval Research Laboratory's Chesapeake Bay Annex.[103]

Among the intelligence issues the intercepts helped resolve was the Hen House radar. In January 1964, the NRL's 150-foot antenna at Chesapeake

Bay, programmed with information from other sources about the Hen House's frequency, made the first intercept of the radar's BUEB signal after it ricocheted off the moon—although it was not clear at the time whether the intercept was of a Hen House signal or a Hen Roost signal. Analysts were able to determine that the signal was from a phased-array radar and made considerable progress in determining the radar's signal characteristics. They also determined that the signal came from Sary Shagan.[104]

By 1964, the CIA had received reports that Hen House radars were being deployed at several locations in the Soviet Union, but there was no corresponding evidence of Hen Roost deployment. If the intercepted signal did come from Hen House, the United States had acquired significant intelligence about the radar well before its full deployment. If the signal was from Hen Roost, then the CIA and other members of the intelligence community would have no clue about how Hen House worked. In early 1965, the issue was settled by a CIA contractor, ESL, Inc., founded by future Secretary of Defense Bill Perry. ESL proved with mathematical rigor that the BUEB signal came from Hen House—a radar that would be employed for ABM, early warning, and space tracking purposes.[105]

The CIA's Palo Alto facility, which had been chosen because of its potential with regard to westward-looking Soviet radars, enhanced understanding of the radar system. The facility consisted of "quite sophisticated collection equipment, including two unique receivers," which were built particularly for the moonbounce mission. In August 1965, Palo Alto made its first intercept of a Hen House radar signal, a signal it was able to observe for thirty-eight hours a month.[106]

The data collected at Palo Alto, added to those obtained by the Defense Department's antennae, led to three major conclusions: First, the Hen House signal had a "spread-spectrum" mode—the frequency spread of the signal could be deliberately broadened to increase the radar's range or its accuracy in reading the target's speed. Second, Hen House relied on an advanced scanning system that enabled the radar not only to search for a target but also to dwell on it for a short time. The brief look allowed the identification and measurement of the radar's signal parameters. Finally, the moonbounce data led to estimates that the peak power of the Hen House transmitter was twenty-five megawatts, making it one of the highest-powered radars in the world. These findings led to a fourth conclusion, which proved correct—the Hen House was a new, sophisticated ABM radar. On the basis of that conclusion, the United States could begin developing countermeasures and tactics to reduce its effectiveness.[107]

The Office of ELINT was also pursuing its Quality ELINT program in support of current U-2 and future OXCART operations—flying its Power and Pattern Measurement System (PPMS) on various Air Force planes in order to determine the power and coverage of the Soviet radars designed to detect penetrating aircraft.[108]

Choosing which radars to target involved balancing intelligence priorities, air access, and eavesdropping conditions. Preference was given to targets in isolated areas where signals from other radars would not interfere. Radar signals were identified in advance, using direction finding equipment that was part of the airborne system. Special navigational instruments recorded the aircraft's position and altitude during each collection operation so that analysts would know the exact geometric relationships between the radar and the measurement system. Several projects were completed in six missions or less, whereas others required more than forty flights.[109]

Seventeen Quality ELINT missions were flown between August 1963 and September 1966 (see Table 3.1), with the PPMS being carried on Air Force RB-47H, C-97, and C-135 aircraft. On the September–October 1963 New Breed III mission, an RB-47H flew over the Arctic north of the Soviet Union to monitor Tall King and Spoon Rest radars. In October, an RB-47H mission, designated Iron Lung, monitored signals from a Spoon Rest radar in Cuba. Between May and October 1966, a C-135, as part of Operation Briar Patch, flew over the Barents Sea intercepting signals from a Hen House radar.* During that same period, a C-97 flying over the Gulf of Tonkin intercepted the emanations from a Fan Song radar during Operation See Top.[110]

---

*There was also a land-based component to Briar Patch. Gene Poteat concluded that given the size of the radar and its probable high power, it should be possible to pick up its signal out to several hundred miles, regardless of where the signal was pointed. The signal would be scattered forward and over the horizon via a phenomenon known as tropospheric scatter. Based on intelligence that a Hen House was under construction a couple of hundred miles inland from Riga, Poteat located an island in the Baltic that appeared to be the right distance from the Hen House to install a tropospheric-scatter receiver that could intercept and continuously monitor the radar.

After extensive negotiations to gain access, OEL installed dual antennae, about fifty wavelengths apart, to reduce the expected atmospheric fading, and the receiver was put on automatic pilot. The Briar Patch system finally picked up the transmission from the targeted Hen House and every subsequent transmission. From monitoring the radar, the CIA learned that it traced U.S. satellites from the first orbit. It

TABLE 3.1 Quality ELINT Missions, August 1963–October 1966

Operation	*Dates*	*Platform*	*Targets*	*Location*
Field Day	July–September 1963	C-97	Fan Song	Cuba, EG
New Breed I	July–August 1963	RB-47H	Tall King	Sakhalin
New Breed II	July–August 1963	RB-47H	Spoon Rest Knife Rest	Sea of Japan
Iron Lung	October 1963	RB-47H	Spoon Rest	Cuba
New Breed III	September–October 1963	RB-47H	Tall King Spoon Rest	Arctic above Soviet Union
NewBreed IV	January 1964	RB-47H	Spoon Rest Knife Rest	Arctic above Soviet Union
Winesap I	May–September 1964	RB-47H	Fan Song	East Germany
Iron Lung I	January–September 1964	RB-47H	SCR-270 Tall King	Yellow and East China Sea
Iron Lung II	February–May 1965	RB-47H	Knife Rest Spoon Rest Tall King	Yellow and East China Sea
Winesap II	June–August 1965	C-97	Flat Face	East Germany
Lead Off	August–September 1965	RB-47H	Back Net	Black Sea
High Pitch	January–March 1966	RB-47H	Bar Lock Big Mesh Fan Song	Sea of Japan Yellow and East China Sea
Low Pitch	September 1966	RB-47H	Bar Lock Big Mesh Fan Song	Cuba
Cross Field	May–October 1966	C-97	Fall Song	East Germany
Top Hat	May–October 1966	C-97	Bar Lock Big Mesh Fan Song Side Net	East Germany
Briar Patch	May–October 1966	C-135	Hen House	Barents Sea
See Top	May–October 1966	C-97	Fan Song	Gulf of Tonkin

---

appeared that the Soviets had an "incredibly effective espionage network to tip off the Hen House when a U.S. intelligence satellite was about to be launched." According to Poteat, when there was a lengthy hold of an impending launch from Vandenberg Air Force Base, the Hen House would switch off and come back on the air the instant the satellite lifted off from Vandenberg. (Gene Poteat, "Stealth, Countermeasures, and ELINT, 1960–1975," *Studies in Intelligence* 42, 1 [Spring 1998]: 51–59.)

CHECKROTE

In addition to trying to unravel the secrets of Soviet radars, the Office of Research and Development (ORD) continued to employ over-the-horizon (OTH) radars to help decipher the mysteries of the Soviet and Chinese missile programs. By September 1965, the EARTHLING radar in Pakistan had detected sixty-five missiles launched from Tyuratam; these accounted for 82 percent of the missiles known to have been launched from that site when EARTHLING was operational. A few of the detections had not been noticed by any other collection system, possibly the result of some combination of aborts not picked up by any line-of-sight collection system or false alarms.[111]

In May 1965, as U.S.-Pakistani relations deteriorated and the United States faced loss of all its intelligence facilities in Pakistan, ORD began to install an OTH radar system called CHECKROTE on Taiwan—but only after Wheelon had exerted considerable effort to move a graveyard inconveniently located on the intended site. The radar's primary function was to monitor missile launches from China's Shuangchengzi missile complex. By August 1, 1966, CHECKROTE was up and running. Almost a year earlier, in September 1965, Pakistan had closed the EARTHLING installation.[112]

EMPLACED SENSORS

In 1965 and 1966, the DS&T made at least two attempts to collect intelligence on the Chinese nuclear and missile programs using emplaced sensors—sensors placed at a strategic location and, DS&T hoped, undiscovered by the target.

In 1965, the Indian government gave the CIA permission to plant a device on the summit of Nanda Devi in the Himalayas to monitor telemetry from the Chinese missile center at Shuangchengzi. The device, which was developed by the Office of ELINT in response to FMSAC's requirement, would unfortunately be swept away by an avalanche.[113]

In 1965 or 1966, a U-2 carried a spearlike device on an eleven-hour trip into China and ejected it. At 3,000 feet, its parachute was to open and carry the device to earth, where it was to stick in the ground. The mission was appropriately named Project JAVELIN, and the device was codenamed TOBASCO. ORD and Sandia Labs had developed it for OSI. From its intended location near, but not too near, the Chinese nuclear test site at Lop Nur, the device, equipped with airwave and ground motion sensors, was to provide the CIA with data on the explosive power of Chinese nuclear tests.[114]

TOBASCO had been tested in Nevada and New Mexico during U.S. nuclear tests. But it was never heard from again after being ejected from the U-2. Whether it hit a rock, was discovered by nomads, failed to implant itself because the terrain was harder than expected, or just didn't work, was never discovered. Perhaps it was an omen that upon his return the pilot who handled the aerial javelin toss was forced to crash-land short of his base and came down in a rice paddy.[115]

AERIAL PROJECTS

In addition to javelin tossing, U-2s had continued to fly over China, photographing nuclear and missile facilities. In 1962, Sino-Indian relations deteriorated into war, giving the United States and India a common enemy. The CIA had already provided India with U-2 photographs of the Chinese border.[116] In 1963, the CIA suggested establishment of a temporary U-2 detachment in northern India. From there, the nuclear test site at Lop Nur and other targets in Xinjiang province could be reached on U-2 missions.[117]

The White House approved the idea, which was followed by protracted negotiations with the Indian government. In spring 1964, India agreed to deployment of a U-2 detachment at Charbatia, an old wartime base near Cuttack on the east coast. Two or three missions followed, with the Indian government receiving up-to-the minute intelligence on Chinese military deployments along the border, while the CIA obtained pictures of Lop Nur and other Xinjiang targets.[118]

In 1964, as the United States pondered the status of the Chinese nuclear program, Texas Instruments Corporation developed an infrared scanner, the FDD-4, that could be employed to determine whether nuclear facilities such as Lanzhou were operational. The expectation was that the heat generated by active facilities would show up in infrared photographs.[119]

In 1964 and 1965, the Nationalist Chinese Black Cat squadron made several attempts to fly a U-2 equipped with the FDD-4 scanner over the nuclear facilities at Baotou and Lanzhou to determine if they were active. Previous tests of the scanner on missions over U.S. nuclear facilities indicated that it produced its best results at night.[120]

The first target was the uranium gaseous diffusion plant at Lanzhou. However, the November 1964 mission was aborted due to an electrical failure. The second try, this time targeted on Baotou, was also aborted when a test of the plane's defensive systems failed. The third time appeared to be the charm, at least for a while. The plane got within thirty miles of Lanzhou when its SAM warning device started blinking, indicating a SAM site almost directly ahead and forcing an abort.[121]

Another mission, this time flying out of Korea, also had to be aborted. Finally, on January 8, 1965, a Black Cat pilot took off from Taoyuan on a flight that lasted a little over seven hours, almost six hours of which was spent over the mainland. The pilot made it to Lanzhou without equipment failures or SAM attacks. The infrared camera demonstrated that the facility was operational. Unfortunately, two days later a mission over Baotou resulted in disaster when the plane was shot down.[122]

Indeed, the pilots who participated in Project TACKLE, as the U-2 missions over China were code-named, were in constant danger from China's air defense system. Nationalist Chinese pilots flying from Taiwan as well as U.S. pilots flying from a base at Ban Takhli, Thailand, all faced the prospect of death or incarceration.

During a July 1966 flight, Major "Spike" Chuang Jen Liang ran into a SAM battery when turning over Kunming air base; eight missiles were fired at him in two salvos. Two were photographed as he put his plane into an evasive turn and escaped death. On another overflight targeted on Lanzhou, Major Billy Chang Hsieh spotted two SAMs fly by as he passed over the nuclear facility. As he revisited the site shortly afterward, the camera photographed missile crews scrambling to reload the launchers and fire another salvo.[123]

A device instrumental in saving Chuang's life was the Oscar Sierra warning system, which had been installed in the U-2s in spring 1965. The key to the system was its detection of the change in pulse repetition frequency of the SA-2 radar when the system shifted into firing mode. The change caused a red light labeled "OS" to go on in the U-2 cockpit, giving a pilot flying at 72,000 feet about forty seconds to get out of the way. Pilots soon came to translate the "OS" as Oh Shit![124]

China's nuclear program was not the only target of U-2 overflights. In mid-1963, Deputy DCI Marshall Carter, Jack Ledford, and Kelly Johnson were all at Edwards Air Force Base in California. One day they met at the bachelor officers' quarters. Ledford later recounted that Johnson had a couple of White Horse scotches, the only scotch he would drink, and that the three of them began talking. The question arose of whether it would be possible to operate U-2s from aircraft carriers. Such an ability would alleviate the problem of having to find foreign bases for U-2 operations—since many countries were nervous about a U-2 base on their territory. That conversation was not the first time such a possibility had been raised.[125]

What followed was Project WHALE TALE, the modification of some U-2s to permit carrier operations. The project began in August 1963 with a successful U-2C takeoff from the USS *Kitty Hawk* operating off San Diego. The landing was much less successful: The plane bounced, hit hard on one wing, and barely managed to become airborne again before reaching the end of the deck. To make landings possible, the landing gear was strengthened, an arresting hook was attached to the rear of the fuselage, and "spoilers" were placed on the wings that, with the push of a button by the pilot, would kill the plane's lift.[126]

In May 1964, a U-2G—a U-2C with the necessary modifications—was aboard the USS *Ranger* when it set sail for the mid-Pacific. The plane's target was Mururoa atoll, a twenty-mile-by-ten-mile strip of territory thousands of miles from land. For a U-2 to overfly it would require a carrier as a launch site. Mururoa was part of French Polynesia and was a target because a year earlier France had selected the atoll as its new nuclear test site, to replace the site in what had become independent Algeria. For the next four years, the CIA maintained a contingent of carrier-qualified U-2 pilots as well as three U-2Gs. During that time, France conducted six atmospheric and three underground nuclear tests on Mururoa. But the May 1964 flight was the sole operational mission from a carrier. After the first, senior officials had second thoughts on the propriety (and presumably the public relations risk) of spying on an ally, even a troublesome one.[127]

One proposed modification of the U-2, aimed at a quite different target, never was made. ORD's director, Robert Chapman, advocated building a long-focal-length camera to be put in the nose of a U-2. Rather than looking down, the camera would look up into space and photograph the Soviet satellites that FMSAC was so curious about. Putting the camera in a U-2 would get it up above the atmosphere and avoid the loss of clarity due to atmospheric interference. Chapman hoped the clearer images would allow more precise evaluation of the satellite's mission. However, the proposal was, as Bud Wheelon recalled, "not a very good idea" and was "stomped on" by the NRO.[128]

The NRO also helped terminate the low-altitude overflights of China that began with the ST/POLLY program. In June 1963, a P-3A Orion maritime patrol aircraft arrived at the Naval Aviation Depot at Alameda, California, after having been diverted from Florida-based training flights. The plane was modified by widening the main cabin door and adding a duplicate next to the original door. As a result, both doors swung inward and back out of the way, creating an opening approximately fifty-three inches wide. That Orion was the first of three P-3As that were remodeled as part of ST/SPIN—the follow-on to ST/POLLY.[129]

Assigned to manage the conversion program, which was carried out by the secretive E-Systems of Greenville, Texas, was OEL's Robert Singel. As was the case with its predecessor, the primary function of the aircraft was to fly low into China in order to stir up and monitor China's air defenses, data required by the Strategic Air Command. The modification of its cargo doors reflected the plan to use the planes for the same types of covert-action operations as the P-2V Neptune conducted—dropping equipment, arms, ammunition, and agents on some occasions, and thousands of propaganda leaflets on others.[130]

Along with the ELINT receivers that were carried on the Neptunes, the Orions were equipped with a variety of additional sensors, including side-looking airborne radar for missions flown along the Chinese border, communications intercept equipment, and an infrared detector. Reportedly, an acoustic eavesdropping device was tested, one so sensitive that it could detect engine and machine-manufacturing noises. The planes were also equipped with cameras for slant-range or oblique photography. To help satisfy nuclear intelligence requirements, the planes also carried an air-sampling apparatus that was connected to the ram air scoops to the rear of each side of the cockpit.[131]

The first ST/SPIN aircraft, manned by Nationalist Chinese personnel, began operations in 1964. Some missions involved flying along the southern border of the People's Republic of China (PRC), with occasional penetrations to detect air defense radars and determine the characteristics of their signals. Missions into the interior, in addition to conducting airdrops, also involved locating military installations, intercepting military communications, and air sampling. Missions were eventually conducted over Burma and up into Tibet to collect intelligence on Chinese activities against the civilian population.[132]

The ST/POLLY and ST/SPIN programs were threatened by the behavior of both PRC and Nationalist Chinese officials. The PRC was occasionally able to shoot down an aircraft. P-2Vs were shot down in November 1961, June 1963, and June 1964. Another disappeared in January 1962, possibly as a result of an operational accident. In addition, the PRC's information about the Nationalist Chinese personnel involved was so extensive that the intruding P-3As often received calls from PRC radio operations requesting to speak, by name, to one or more of the Nationalist Chinese on board. Further, the planes carried far more personnel than necessary, often twenty-seven instead of the required fourteen to sixteen. Personnel received bonuses for participating in such missions, and the Nationalist Chinese general who ran the program was willing to assign extra crew members to the missions in exchange for a kickback (which he also required from the first fourteen crewmen). When OSA chief Ledford told Wheelon that the general had been sent to prison for his actions, Wheelon told him that not only should the United States do nothing to get him out, but that the Nationalist Chinese should "throw away the fucking key."[133]

In 1965, before the third P-3A had been modified, Singel received word that the program was being terminated by the NRO, which had provided the funding.[134] It is unclear what combination of PRC and Nationalist Chinese actions, the capabilities exhibited by the NRO's new ferret satellites, and budgetary limitations resulted in the cancellation decision. The last flights in the program occurred in 1966.[135]

In September 1966, the OXCART had still not flown an operational mission. For Wheelon, it proved a "hell of a challenge," a weekly "four-alarm fire" that threatened to destroy the CIA's "reputation for doing things on the cheap [and] quickly." Bureaucratic and technical issues consumed "so god damn much of my time," Wheelon recalled. Along with Ledford, he worked to ensure continued Air Force support, which included allocation of tankers to refuel the planes, for the program.[136]

According to Wheelon, for a while it was unclear if OXCART would ever reach operational status. In contrast to the U-2, it was behind schedule and over budget. The fundamental technical problem was compressor stalls, which induced horrendous shaking and caused pilots to bail out. But more than a plane was lost. One pilot died when his parachute didn't open, and all but one Lockheed test pilot quit. Wheelon threatened to cancel the program unless Kelly Johnson, "who didn't trust electronics," put in an electronic system to correct the problem. Wheelon also put people to work developing a jammer that could limit the threat from hostile radars.[137]

But the reason OXCART was not operational by September 1966 was not problems with the aircraft, which had been corrected. By the end of

1963, there had been 573 flights totaling 765 hours. On July 20, 1963, an OXCART flew at Mach 3 for the first time, and in November it reached Mach 3.2, flying at 78,000 feet. On February 3, 1964, it flew for ten minutes at Mach 3.2 and 83,000 feet. By the end of 1964, there had been 1,160 flights, although the flight time was only 1,616 hours. Eleven aircraft were available, four of which were reserved for testing.[138]

On January 27, 1965, an OXCART took off on its first long-range, high-speed flight. It flew for 1 hour and 40 minutes, with all but 25 minutes of its flight conducted at above Mach 3.1. Its total range was 2,580 nautical miles, at altitudes between 75,600 and 80,000 feet.[139]

OXCART was delayed because higher authorities turned down repeated proposals to employ the plane on operational missions. The first suggestion that OXCART might be ready for operational deployment came in early 1964, when OSA began planning for its use over Cuba under a program designated SKYLARK. On August 5, Deputy DCI Marshall Carter directed that OSA achieve emergency operational readiness by November 5. The plane would operate at Mach 2.8 and 80,000 feet. But SKYLARK was never implemented.[140]

In 1965, Asia became a possible theater for OXCART's first operations. On March 18, McCone, McNamara, and Deputy Secretary of Defense Cyrus Vance met to discuss the growing threat to aerial surveillance of China, a threat manifested in the loss of several Air Force drones. They agreed that the CIA should take all preparatory steps necessary to overfly China with OXCART aircraft, flying out of Kadena Air Base on Okinawa. Deploying the planes to Okinawa, however, would require presidential approval.[141]

Four days after McCone and Vance met, OSA director Ledford briefed Vance on details of the scheme, designated Operation BLACK SHIELD, which had been drawn up for Far East operations. It called for three aircraft to be deployed to Okinawa for sixty-day stints twice a year. About 225 personnel would be involved.[142]

During that period, North Vietnam began to deploy SAMs around Hanoi, threatening U.S. reconnaissance capability. In early June, McNamara inquired about the use of OXCARTs as substitutes for U-2s and was told BLACK SHIELD could operate over Vietnam as soon as the planes could be certified for use.[143]

With deployment expected to take place in the fall, the detachment went about demonstrating the reliability of the aircraft and its systems at Mach 3.05 and 2,300 nautical miles. But longer flights at higher speeds and temperatures resulted in new problems, the most serious being with the electrical wiring system. Such problems prompted CIA program manager John Parangosky to visit Kelly Johnson in early August. Johnson decided to spend full-time at the site in order to get the job finished quickly.[144]

Four primary BLACK SHIELD aircraft were selected, and final validation flights conducted. OXCART achieved a maximum speed of Mach 3.29, an altitude of 90,000 feet, and sustained flight time above Mach 3.2 for 1 hour and 14 minutes. As a result, Johnson wrote Ledford that "my considered opinion is that the aircraft can be successfully deployed for the BLACK SHIELD mission with what I would consider to be at least as low a degree of risk as in the early U-2 deployment days. . . . I think the time has come when the bird should leave its nest."[145]

However, higher authorities did not agree. Their reservations were not technical but political. Two days after Johnson's letter to Ledford, the 303 Committee, the NSC group responsible for reviewing sensitive intelligence operations, received a formal proposal to unleash the OXCART over North Vietnam. It was but one of several proposals for OXCART operations that the 303 Committee vetoed. Vice-Admiral William Raborn, who had replaced McCone as DCI in late April 1965, raised the prospect of deploying OXCART to Okinawa at five 303 meetings during the first half of 1966 but always failed to win sufficient support.[146]

The Joint Chiefs of Staff and the PFIAB supported the CIA proposal, but top officials at State and Defense concluded that the political risks of basing aircraft in Okinawa outweighed any intelligence the OXCART might gather. On August 12, both groups presented their views to President Lyndon Johnson, who sided with the majority of the 303 Committee against deployment.[147]

Even before OXCART was given a go-ahead, the CIA was examining two possible successors. Project ISINGLASS envisioned a plane capable of speeds between Mach 4 and Mach 5 flying at 100,000 feet. A feasibility study by General Dynamics was completed in fall 1964, but OSA took no further action because the proposed aircraft would still be vulnerable to Soviet countermeasures.[148]

An even more radical proposal came in 1965 from McDonnell Aircraft under the designation Project RHEINBERRY (although some of the work apparently also fell initially under the ISINGLASS designation). The RHEINBERRY aircraft would be rocket-powered, launched from a B-52, and ultimately reach speeds as high as Mach 20 and altitudes of up to 200,000 feet.[149]

Favoring the proposal was General Bernard Schriever, who wanted to see ramjet technology developed but who was unsure the NRO would approve such an effort. He suggested to Wheelon that OSA might begin work on it, and the Air Force Systems Command would support the work. Wheelon raised the issue with Raborn, who raised it with McNamara, who told the DCI to forget it. Wheelon was not convinced it was needed, and the plane would be quite inflexible—capable of only one turn around the earth.[150]

Nor would it have produced much in the way of intelligence. After much effort, designers concluded that it was impossible to eliminate the shock wave created when the plane skipped along the atmosphere and impossible to photograph targets through the shock wave. The plane might have provided an exciting ride for the pilot but would have done nothing for intelligence analysts on the ground.[151]

4

SPACE RECONNAISSANCE WARS

Bud Wheelon's greatest and most lasting impact on the revitalized Directorate of Science and Technology (DS&T) and the CIA was in the area of space reconnaissance. During the fourteen months Herbert Scoville served as Deputy Director for Research, the conflict between the CIA and NRO over space reconnaissance had escalated from border skirmishes to war. That war would intensify dramatically between August 1963, when Wheelon assumed the helm at DS&T, and October 1965, when Brockway McMillan would depart the scene.

A variety of factors would fuel the conflict, including the relationship between the men as well as their personalities. There were also disputes relating to CORONA. But the most significant problem was the differing conceptions Wheelon, McMillan, and their organizations had of the roles of the CIA and NRO in the development and operation of space reconnaissance systems. The incompatibility of those views helped to intensify the bitter conflict over the development of new photographic and signals intelligence satellites as well as the authority of the NRO and its director.

The bureaucratic bloodshed would be hard on the psyches and careers of several of those involved—including Wheelon and McMillan. But out of the chaos, order emerged in Washington—in the form of a new, and durable, agreement governing the CIA-NRO relationship. In addition, plans to develop two revolutionary reconnaissance systems would also safely survive the CIA-NRO wars, and the groundwork would be laid for a third revolutionary system. Years after the battles were over, if not forgotten, those systems would be producing valuable intelligence.

THE GREAT DIVIDE

One former CIA official described Wheelon as "the most acerbic . . . son of a bitch" he had ever met.[1] Wheelon recalled being "pretty young . . .

pretty impatient," "brash," and "full of himself." He was "not tactful" with the "committee sitters" at the CIA. As result of his self-imposed time limit at the agency and the "extraordinary pressure" emanating from the Pentagon with respect to the reconnaissance issue, "amenities fell by the wayside."[2]

Nor was McMillan a diplomat—particularly since his reading of the NRO charter convinced him he had been given full authority to manage the National Reconnaissance Program, subject only to the supervision of the Secretary of Defense. To complicate matters, there was already bad blood between the two men. Several years before, McMillan served as referee for a paper Wheelon had submitted to a prestigious technical journal. By the time the process was finished, each questioned the other's intellectual honesty.[3]

The differences between the organizations and their view of their roles that existed during Scoville's tenure carried over to the Wheelon years. That the Air Force element of the NRO was not an intelligence-producing organization and had no direct connection to one, such as DIA, continued to be a problem in the CIA's view. In a meeting with McMillan during the interval between Scoville's resignation and Wheelon's becoming Science and Technology Chief, Deputy DCI Marshall Carter suggested that McMillan authorize a symposium for all his program directors and their deputies "to make abundantly certain that the people running our programs know that their sole purpose is to develop intelligence and not just be shooting another rocket in the air."[4]

According to an NRO history, "NRO people generally lacked the CIA's concern for processed intelligence as an end product. [Their viewpoint] was that film properly exposed and promptly recovered was their 'product.' The photographic content of the film was a secondary matter and one in which few had other than a secondary interest. In that characteristic lay the core of much of CIA's professional antagonism."[5] The differing perspectives also were manifested in disputes over launch schedules.

The CIA's connection to the production of intelligence also influenced its approach to the development of new reconnaissance systems. General Lew Allen Jr. served in a variety of NRO posts beginning in 1965, including director of the NRO Staff and director of Program A, and went on to become director of the National Security Agency and then Air Force Chief of Staff. In Allen's view, the engineers from Program A were "substantially more practical and realistic" than their counterparts at Langley. They placed a much higher value on accomplishing a task on time and within the allotted budget.[6]

But the wizards at Langley had "a different approach to life," according to Allen. They were "less concerned about cost and schedule" and "more concerned about bringing new capabilities into being." They also "looked further ahead" and were substantially better in terms of new ideas and concepts. In his view, a key factor in the different approaches was the CIA's connection with intelligence production.[7]

New issues further exacerbated the relationship. But whereas Scoville found McCone's support in such battles slippery, Wheelon found it far more reliable. He helped instill in McCone a conviction of the importance of a substantial CIA role in reconnaissance, a view McCone evidenced before the end of August 1963. In a meeting with Deputy Secretary of Defense Roswell Gilpatric, Deputy Director of Defense Research and Engineering Eugene Fubini, Carter, and Wheelon, McCone expressed his belief that there had been a departure from the original concept of the NRO as an organization that would combine the reconnaissance operations of the Air Force and CIA under one roof but not assume direct control of them.[8]

CORONA BATTLES

The battle was joined not long after Wheelon's appointment as deputy director. In the view of CIA historians, McMillan "made a frontal attack with a request to McCone that CIA relinquish all responsibility in regard to CORONA."[9] As Wheelon recalled, "The Pentagon observed . . . my appointment with satisfaction. They properly judged me to be quite junior . . . and bureaucratically inexperienced. They did not know of McCone's conversion and so they moved quickly."[10]

At the time, the reconnaissance program was in turmoil. During the first five months of 1963, four of the six satellite reconnaissance missions failed. In one instance, a KH-4 launch on February 28 ended with the destruction of the Thor booster. Twice, the Agena wound up in the Pacific rather than outer space. Another time, during a KH-6/LANYARD mission in May, it failed in orbit. After three successful midair recoveries, a July KH-6 mission produced a limited success, since the camera failed before the scheduled end of the mission. In August, the second recovery capsule on a KH-4A failed to separate from the spacecraft.[11]

The impetus for McMillan's action, in addition to his preferences, included a October 22 memo to him from McNamara, which followed discussions the Secretary had with his NRO director and Fubini. The memo noted the roles of the CIA, the interagency Configuration Control Board, and Air Force in the procurement and operation of the CORONA spacecraft. The Secretary then told McMillan that he "consider[ed] the split of technical responsibilities . . . unsatisfactory, and the CORONA program will benefit in achievement of full operational potential by placing all functions under a single management system." He instructed McMillan to establish "a single authoritative CORONA project director, to whom you can assign personal responsibility for successful and efficient technical management of the CORONA system."[12]

Five days later, a memo from McMillan to McCone noted the NRO director's belief that it was necessary to establish "a single authoritative point of contact between the NRO and contractor." McMillan also informed the DCI of his choice of the director of Program A to fill that role, as well as his expectation that the CIA would continue to supply security and film-courier support.[13]

Rather than settling the issue, McMillan's memo served as the catalyst for more bureaucratic battles. In Wheelon's view, the memo "had the beneficial effect of clarifying their objectives, which had been carefully nuanced by Charyk. With the gauntlet down, we faced an early test of McCone's resolve."[14]

McCone did not disappoint those who most fervently sought to resist any reduction in the CIA's role in CORONA. In late September 1963, McCone wrote to Deputy DCI Carter and Wheelon, noting that he had received "continual complaints that D/NRO is directing NRO activities so that all satellite reconnaissance is an Air Force mission and the CIA capabilities in this field are being ignored." The DCI stated that CIA capabilities in the area should be maintained and "we should consider whether we wish to recapture activities recently pre-empted by the Air Force."[15]

McMillan's October memo was followed by a November 27 meeting between him and McCone and a December 10 memo to McCone noting McMillan's submission of a revised directive. The revision still emphasized the need for a single point of contact and assigned the Program A director "full responsibility for the successful conduct of the CORONA project."[16]

Sometime on December 10, McCone and McMillan met, although whether McCone had yet read the revised directive is not clear. McCone spoke first, charging that McMillan wanted "to take the whole project over," and according to McMillan, warned that "he would not stand for submersion of the project into the bureaucracy of the Air Force and that he would liquidate the NRO if necessary to prevent this." After McMillan presented his views, the DCI agreed to consider the matter further.[17]

That response came three days later, in the form of a memo, and shortly before McCone was due to travel to Saigon. He noted that in several recent discussions with McMillan, he had emphasized that both CIA and Air Force resources related to overhead reconnaissance should be preserved, including the "unique contractor capabilities which have been developed at the insistence of the CIA." He complained that, according to several sources, "major contractors no longer feel free to meet with CIA officials and discuss problems . . . without first securing Air Force permission." Such a limitation, McCone charged, would violate the basic tenet of the NRO agreement providing for full utilization of CIA and Air Force resources. He therefore requested that in the following week, McMillan make it "abundantly clear" to the NRO and Program A staffs that "any remark which carried the above policy implications should be corrected forthwith."[18]

As a means of obtaining the CIA's agreement to transfer responsibility for CORONA to the Air Force, Fubini proposed a deal—in exchange for acquiescing to the transfer, the CIA would be assigned responsibility for development of the next-generation search system. But McMillan disliked the idea, characterizing it as "the trade of a major development responsibility for the job of cleaning up a stinking mess (i.e. CORONA)." McMillan would not agree until "he was satisfied CIA has the development capabilities," and he expressed his fear that "CIA lack of responsiveness to DNRO on such a program is a serious possibility."[19]

In February, McMillan, in responding to the 1963 CORONA problems, which continued with a launch failure in November, tried again. In another memo to McCone, he stated that "the Government's management of this project is a significant factor contributing to the unsatisfactory record of recent performance." He informed the DCI that he had issued a directive requiring "all proposed changes and all significant engineering efforts to be referred to me prior to implementation." The procedures were to be interim ones.[20]

The following month, in a memo to McCone, Wheelon noted two requests from McMillan that the CIA concur in the transfer of the element of the Space Systems Division (of the Air Force Systems Command), which handled CORONA matters, to Program A. Wheelon informed his boss that new information indicated the unit was about to be dissolved and its responsibilities re-created under Program A and that the "program is being transferred to [Program A] without our concurrence."[21]

Five months later, the issue was still an irritant. On August 28, Deputy Secretary of Defense Cyrus Vance assured Deputy DCI Marshall Carter that a portion of a McMillan memo regarding a meeting earlier that month was not taken as concurrence in transferring the contracting responsibility for the CORONA payload from the CIA to the Air Force. "Quite to the contrary," Vance wrote, "it was read to show that there was no agreement on this subject as between Mr. McCone and me."[22]

Less pleasing to some CIA officials was a letter from Vance to McCone on October 15 in which Vance noted their agreement earlier that month that "there will be a single authoritative representative of the Government for technical direction on the entire CORONA system." That representative, Vance noted, would be the head of Program A. Wheelon received a memo characterizing Vance's note as "a real beaut . . . a classic example of de facto negotiation." The key point of contention was, still, which agency was responsible for the CORONA payload and issuing technical directives to the contractors on the subject.[23]

The following month, Jack Ledford, head of the Office of Special Activities, noted: "In two years, the payload responsibility and direction of the CORONA Program has not been resolved. While the NRO and Director, Program A are of the view that they are directing the entire CORONA Program, the Agency still maintains its view that the Agency is responsible for payload management. There have been no formal decisions clarifying this difference of opinion."[24]

On November 17, McCone wrote Vance that at the September 1 NRO Executive Committee meeting (consisting of McCone, Vance, Fubini, and McMillan) "it was agreed that CIA would continue its present responsibility in contracting for all elements of the CORONA payload."[25] That same day a draft of a letter from Carter to McMillan noted areas where the CIA and NRO appeared to be in "complete agreement." Those areas included the need for a "single authoritative program manager for CORONA," who would exercise "over-all technical direction of the program and be responsible to the DNRO for its successful prosecution, who is in turn responsible to Mr. McCone and Mr. Vance." In addition, Carter believed they had agreed that the CIA would continue, under the auspices of the NRO, to handle the Advanced Projects facility at Palo Alto, the camera programming function, and the systems integration contract with Lockheed. Also, the CIA would serve as project manager for the CORONA payload.[26]

The continuing battle was the subject of memos from McCone and McMillan in April and June 1965. On April 21, McCone gave explicit instructions to Wheelon that the CORONA contracts with Lockheed (systems integration), General Electric (reentry vehicle), and Itek (camera) should clearly establish that CIA had the responsibility and authority to provide technical direction for the CORONA payload.[27]

In June, McMillan charged that the CIA had not complied with terms of an agreement reached by McCone and Vance in August concerning the systems engineering and systems integration functions. McMillan's memo alleged that a CIA employee instructed Lockheed personnel not to sign an essential contract due to security issues. Despite resolution of those issues as well as discussions with the DCI, and a written request from McMillan to the Deputy DCI, the CIA injunction against signing this contract had not been lifted.[28]

Launch scheduling also proved an irritant. In the view of CIA officials, the heart of the issue was Program A's detachment from intelligence production. A CIA memo noted that "Personnel from the NRO Staff and Program A who are divorced from the intelligence mission are more interested in launch schedules and recoveries than in the quality of the photography." It mentioned a meeting in February between Col. Frank Buzard of the NRO staff and a CIA representative during which Buzard reportedly stated that sixteen CORONA launches had been scheduled by the DNRO for 1965 and those launches would take place according to the established schedule. The CIA representative responded that "CORONA was an intelligence reconnaissance program and that the missions would be flown in response to intelligence requirements, not in response to preestablished Air Force launch schedules."[29]

Harsh words were also exchanged in 1965 over allegations that the CIA had been withholding data from the Air Force concerning orbiting CORONA payloads. On March 24, McCone placed an urgent call to Vance requesting that he see Carter as soon as possible. At their meeting the next day, Carter told the Deputy Defense Secretary that allegations by McMillan about the CIA withholding information concerning the functioning of the CORONA payload required to conduct launch or recovery operations were baseless. Carter assured Vance that all information on the condition and operation of the payload and the payload section of the vehicle that bore on the decision to de-orbit was provided immediately to Air Force representatives. Carter added that he believed such accusations were "just another attempt to get CIA completely out of the satellite business."[30]

Carter then went to see McMillan, who had put in a call for him, for a much less amicable meeting. He gave McMillan a fact sheet on the allegations. It asserted that the CIA had provided the Air Force with "more, repeat more, operational data on the payload" since August 1964 than at any time prior to that date. According to Carter, McMillan became "visibly disturbed" and confirmed that the allegations were misleading.[31]

Carter told the NRO director that it was apparent to him that "there was a clear-cut effort to run CIA out of the satellite business and make this critical intelligence collection system a complete blue-suit operation." According to Carter, McMillan then attempted to reopen the entire matter, suggesting that the Air Force should receive all the basic telemetry and calibration data. Carter told him that he "would not have it," and had no intention of establishing or allowing to be established a separate diagnostic, analytical function by an agency having no responsibility for the payload."[32]

Matters worsened when McMillan asked Carter to agree that detailed results of the payload telemetry analysis would be provided to the Air Force Satellite Test Center. Carter ignored the exact phrasing, stating that he saw no reason why the results of the analysis should not be made available, but before giving firm agreement, he wished to consult with his staff. McMillan lashed out, saying he had "the impression that McCone and you are captives of your staff and unable to make decisions." Carter fired back, telling McMillan that "he would do well to learn how to use a staff himself as well as exerting some caution in his use of the English language." Carter closed his memo describing the meeting by noting that "while we have clearly won this skirmish, the battle will continue so long as McMillan, [Col. Paul] Worthman, Buzard, . . . are in the act."[33]

EAVESDROPPING FROM SPACE

One day in 1966, Robert Mathams and three other men drove out into the Australian outback, about twelve miles from Alice Springs. They passed through some low hills, took seats on the ground, and opened a case of red wine. A toast followed. At the time, Mathams was head of the Scientific Intelligence Group of Australia's Joint Intelligence Bureau. Joining Mathams in the toast were Bud Wheelon and his deputy, Carl Duckett, and Leslie Dirks, another key DS&T staff member. The celebration concerned the selection of the site for the ground station for a new type of intelligence satellite—a satellite that had its genesis in a newspaper article that appeared in the summer of 1963.[34]

Not long after becoming head of the DS&T, Wheelon was reading a story in the *New York Herald Tribune* about Syncom, a NASA-DOD-

Hughes satellite program. The article discussed what was then a revolutionary means of communications, first suggested by science and science fiction writer Arthur C. Clarke, that allowed communications far beyond the horizon—signals were transmitted from a ground station to a satellite and then back down to another ground station.[35]

The Syncom satellites were not low-earth orbiters whizzing around the earth and thus out of view of one or both ground stations for substantial periods of time. Instead, they flew 22,300 miles above various points on the equator—in geostationary orbit. At that altitude and location, the satellites revolved around the earth at the same speed as the earth turned on its axis. In effect, they hovered over a single point on the equator. In addition, at their high altitude, about one-third of the earth was in view of each satellite. Such satellites thus represented an efficient and always available means of shuttling communications across large portions of the planet. It occurred to Wheelon that it might be possible to employ such an approach to intercept signals from key targets and relay them to a U.S. ground station.[36]

Targets might include telemetry signals from Tyuratam, Plesetsk, the White Sea, and even Sary Shagan, which was located far enough in the Soviet interior to be immune from U.S. land- and air-based eavesdropping efforts. A geosynchronous intercept system would also allow the collection of down-range telemetry from the impact zone on Kamchatka. In addition, such a system promised to provide launch-pad telemetry from all the sites, which would provide better estimates of thrust and warhead capability.[37]

Wheelon assembled some key CIA officials to explore such ideas—including George Miller, chief of the Office of ELINT; Carl Nelson, from the Office of Communications; and Leslie Dirks, who had joined the CIA in 1961 after obtaining a B.S. from MIT in 1958 and a research degree from Oxford University in 1960.[38] Also brought into the discussions was Lloyd K. Lauderdale, a graduate of the U.S. Naval Academy with a Ph.D. from Johns Hopkins. A veteran of OSI's defensive systems division, he had experienced the frustration of trying to understand the Soviet ABM program with its main test center at Sary Shagan.[39]

An initial concern was whether such a program was feasible. Because the telemetry signals were transmitted at very-high and ultra-high frequencies (VHF and UHF), they would not bounce off the atmosphere, as high-frequency communications did, but leak out into space where the satellites would be waiting to scoop them up. But it was feared that the noise from other, and unwanted, transmissions such as television signals would drown the telemetry in an ocean of noise. Spending several hundreds of millions of dollars of the taxpayers' money only to wind up with Soviet television signals would hardly be a wise investment. Before proceeding further, Wheelon asked William Perry, who had just left Sylvania's Electronic Defense Laboratories to form his own company, to study the matter. Six months later, he reported that the idea was workable. Many years later, Perry's work in determining the feasibility of such a satellite would be a key, although unspecified, reason for his winning the CIA's R. V. Jones Award—named after the British physicist who headed the British Secret Intelligence Service's scientific intelligence effort in World War II.[40]

When presented with the idea, both McCone and Carter were supportive, and Lauderdale was tapped as manager of the new program, which was named RHYOLITE—an apparently chance selection of an appropriate designation, as rhyolite is a volcanic rock containing colorful pieces of quartz and glassy feldspar embedded in a mass of tiny crystals. Lauderdale would become the key figure in transforming the idea into a reality—arriving at work one day with a working model of a French umbrella antenna, which would also serve as model for the RHYOLITE antenna.[41]

Not surprisingly, RHYOLITE became another battle in the prolonged conflict between Wheelon and McMillan. Wheelon had no faith that McMillan or the NRO would give RHYOLITE a fair hearing, and the program was started using CIA funds, before McCone went to Vance to ask for NRO funding.[42]

McMillan later recalled that Perry's study convinced him his initial skepticism about the feasibility of RHYOLITE was misguided, but a memo he prepared upon his departure from the NRO questioned whether such a system would be worth the expense. And according to Wheelon and John McMahon, the NRO and Defense Department did what they could to derail the program. Eugene Fubini suggested that the mission could be fulfilled by modifying NASA's Advanced Technology Satellite, then in development. In addition, after RHYOLITE won approval from higher authorities, the NRO tried to slow down funding, while money flowed into a competing Air Force program. That program, code-named CANYON, resulted in placing satellites in geosynchronous orbit to intercept Soviet and other communications.[43]

Meanwhile, the NRO saw the CIA's reluctance to provide details on program specifics or funding as another sign of the agency's unwillingness to accept the authority of the NRO. According to NRO staffer Frank Buzard, comptroller John Holleran "kept trying to get a handle on money for RHYOLITE and never was able to."[44]

In early 1965, while the bureaucratic battle over RHYOLITE was going on back in Washington, the CIA station chief in Canberra, William B. Caldwell, informed Australia's Secretary of Defence, Sir Edwin Hicks, that the CIA wished to establish a ground control station in Australia. Other sites, including Guam, had been considered, but central Australia had a crucial advantage. In May, Hicks was given a more detailed technical description of the program. The following month, Minister of Defence Shane Partridge was briefed on the project, and a senior Defence official was appointed to head a special team to determine the most suitable location for the prospective station.[45]

In late 1965, U.S. and Australian engineers began surveys of the Pine Gap valley in the Australian outback, formerly a grazing area. Official agreement to establish a station was reached in June 1966, when Secretary of State Dean Rusk addressed the Australian cabinet while in Canberra to attend a conference of the Southeast Asia Treaty Organization (SEATO). The station, commonly known as Pine Gap, was built twelve miles southwest of Alice Springs in central Australia—a location that, unlike Guam, ensured immunity from eavesdropping or electronic interference from Soviet spy ships.[46]

PEACE IN THE VALLEY

In the midst of the contention over hardware, McCone, Wheelon, and other DS&T officials were also waging a continuing battle concerning the authority of the NRO and its director. The intensity of the conflict and the importance of the issues had even produced a 1963 summons from President Kennedy for McMillan and Wheelon in an attempt to establish a more amicable relationship. Wheelon's impression was that Kennedy was not very well briefed, and the meeting involved little more than a pep talk in which Kennedy spoke of the importance of their job and how they were both held in high regard.[47] The session had no lasting, or even temporary, effect.

Thus, in 1964, the CIA-NRO rift remained an issue for the Johnson administration to confront. On May 2, the President's Foreign Intelligence Advisory Board, chaired by Clark Clifford, delivered its report on the National Reconnaissance Program. The PFIAB concluded that "the National

Reconnaissance Program despite its achievements, has not yet reached its full potential." The fundamental cause for the NRP's shortcoming was "inadequacies in organizational structure." In addition, there was no clear division of responsibilities and roles among the Defense Department, CIA, and the DCI.[48]

The board's recommendations represented a clear victory for the NRO and its director. The DCI should have a "large and important role" in establishing intelligence collection requirements and in ensuring that the data collected was effectively exploited, according to the board. In addition, his leadership would be a key factor in the work of the United States Intelligence Board relating to the scheduling of space and airborne reconnaissance missions.[49]

But the board also recommended that President Johnson sign a directive that would assign to the Air Force responsibility for management, systems engineering, procurement, and operation of all satellite reconnaissance systems.[50] The CIA might be assigned to do research on concepts for new systems, but the heavy lifting would be left to the Air Force. In a June 2 memorandum to national security adviser McGeorge Bundy, Vance noted his intention to see that several of the board's recommendations, including that one, "be promptly pursued."[51]

Others, including McCone, were less enthusiastic about the report. The DCI objected that he did not believe that if the PFIAB's proposals were adopted, either he or the CIA could perform the missions the report "apparently contemplates" for them. He argued that there needed to be a clear recognition of the DCI's joint responsibility with the Secretary of Defense in developing the reconnaissance program and full participation by the DCI in the development and direction of the program—including decisions concerning the assignment of responsibilities for development of new collection systems and operational activities.[52]

Two NSC staff members also raised questions about the wisdom of the PFIAB's conclusions and recommendations. In a memo to Bundy, Spurgeon Keeny, whose background included a seven-year stint (1948–1955) in Air Force intelligence, argued that the recommendations "would place the Air Force within striking distance of achieving complete control of the [National Reconnaissance Program]" and "would tend to eliminate CIA as a creative force in developing our reconnaissance capabilities"—a move that "seems self-defeating since CIA has been responsible for much of the success in this field." Instead, "there should be formal recognition of the principle that both CIA and DOD should maintain strong, independent organizations in the recon field." Peter Jessup, detailed to the NSC from CIA, attributed the PFIAB's conclusions to a "slick sales job" by "McMillan & Co" combined with a "poor one" by the CIA.[53]

Bundy, sometime in June or July, directed McNamara and McCone to produce a draft directive, with "a clear delineation of . . . roles and responsibilities," that would serve as an agreed charter for the NRP. The memo allowed for the possibility that there would be "significant differences" and invited the two officials to offer alternative provisions to the charter reflecting such differences. Bundy requested the work be finished within two weeks.[54]

It would be far longer than two weeks before the work would be completed. In the meantime, McCone and Wheelon continued having "significant differences" with McMillan and Fubini. In a memorandum concerning an August 1964 meeting of the NRO executive committee, McCone wrote: "I emphasized again and again that there was absolutely no intention of creating in CIA technical assets to conceive, manage, or direct booster operations involved in reconnaissance programs and that the allegations of Dr. Fubini that our purpose was 'to create another NASA' were entirely unfounded and I would like him to withdraw them."[55]

There was, however, an intention by Wheelon to solidify further the status of a unit he created to handle what he had hoped would be reinvigorated and extensive CIA satellite operations. On September 1, McCone approved Wheelon's request to assign the Special Projects Staff (SPS), established in fall 1963, formal responsibility for satellite matters that technically belonged to the Office of Special Activities. Jack Ledford had remained as official head of Program B while Jackson D. Maxey served as head of the new staff, which obtained its personnel from the Systems Analysis Staff and OSA. In addition, the technical personnel working on the CORONA program in California, along with four OSA officers, were assigned to SPS.[56]

In February 1965, Wheelon took another step toward enhancing the CIA's role in space reconnaissance. A memo from Wheelon to Marshall Carter proposed to transform the "small group of Agency employees," operating "under the euphemistic title Special Projects Staff" into the Office of Special Projects. Wheelon noted an earlier reluctance to establish a full-fledged office until the CIA's role in satellite reconnaissance could be clarified.[57]

One rationale for establishing a new office was that the limited personnel available were inadequate to cope with the "lively pace" of space reconnaissance activities. There was also the "cumbersome network of satellite activities . . . spread throughout the Directorate." Included were functions carried out by the SPS but for which OSA and its chief, Jack Ledford, were technically responsible to the NRO. The proposed office would be responsible for the development, operation, and management of the CIA's satellite activities.[58]

Wheelon also informed Carter that his staff was preparing a memo for the Deputy DCI's signature advising McMillan of the transfer of satellite responsibilities within the DS&T, the creation of the new office, the identity of its head, and his designation as "Director, Program E"—which left the aerial reconnaissance functions in Program B, to be managed by OSA.[59] But like the NRO agreement, the creation of a new satellite office within the science and technology directorate took far longer than anticipated. Toward the end of 1964, another round of discussions between McNamara and McCone had commenced toward a new agreement that, it was hoped, would clearly specify CIA responsibilities in the reconnaissance area and "put an end to the continual struggle within NRO over lines of authority."[60]

But in early 1965, McMillan, at a meeting of the National Reconnaissance Program Executive Committee, demonstrated that he was not a prisoner of his staff—disavowing an agreement concerning CORONA management that had been negotiated by them and the CIA and signed by Marshall Carter. McMillan stated that he had agreed only in principle and subsequently refused to address the question, although he made several additional efforts to transfer the CORONA systems engineering responsibility from Lockheed to Aerospace, attempts that were blocked by Carter. On April 21, McCone gave Wheelon instructions to write into CIA contracts with Lockheed, General Electric, and Itek, language that would clearly establish with the contractors the fact that the CIA had the responsibility and the authority to provide technical direction for the CORONA payload.[61]

Meanwhile, both the CIA and NRO continued formulating and advocating their different positions concerning the DS&T's future role in satellite reconnaissance. In an April 2, 1965, presentation to the PFIAB, McMillan made his case for a strengthened NRO—making reference to the continued lack of a clear decision concerning a follow-on to CORONA. His summary of the management status of the NRO began with the remark that "de facto, NRO does not exist." He also complained that the existence of an executive committee had the effect of elevating almost all NRO matters to the Vance-McCone level. Since the principals were busy with other matters, meetings were infrequent, and decisions were delayed. McMillan added that "many of the agreements arrived at in the ExCom have not been implemented."[62]

McMillan contended that the CIA found direct management by an "outsider"—"in particular by one who in their eyes is colored AF blue"—to be "galling and hard to accept." The CIA people he had to work with, he said, "have a history of obstructing or defying my control," which "lends confirmation to charges of bias on my part." Cited as examples were changes within Program B of which he had never been informed and instructions to Lockheed not to communicate with McMillan.[63]

In summing up, the NRO chief stated his belief "in a strong NRO" and maintained that neither "the CIA [n]or the military are capable of accepting effectively autonomous responsibility. Both need the discipline of a central problem-oriented management." He also asserted that "unless the situation that now prevails is changed sharply, the DNRO cannot responsibly spend the taxpayers' money without firm management controls over the way it is spent."[64]

The battle continued throughout April. Possibly in response to McMillan's presentation, McCone proposed that the Satellite Operations Center be removed from the custody of the NRO and given to the CIA. The proposal resulted in a long and despairing letter from McMillan to Vance, which concluded with the comment that "I am convinced that if [the Satellite Operations Center] is removed from the NRO, the NRO will be destroyed and the DOD will experience interminable difficulties in getting its requirements recognized. I am further convinced that this fundamental fact is well understood by others and that the final irrevocable destruction of the NRO is the primary intent behind the proposal to separate the Op Center."[65]

On April 12, McMillan learned that McCone—frustrated by President Johnson's seeming indifference to intelligence reports, except when annoyed at bad news—would be leaving office shortly. On April 22, McMillan formally presented, and recommended quick adoption of, a directive composed by Fubini for the President's signature. The directive, as an NRO history put it, "would have resolved all outstanding issues by enforcing the lines of agreement urged by PFIAB in May 1964—the recommendation from which so much had been expected and from which nothing had come." The proposal would have limited CIA influence to maintenance of a research and development group reporting to the NRO director.[66]

On April 26, McCone, who would leave in a matter of days, fired back, according to an NRO history, with a formal proposal to dissolve the NRO, with the CIA assuming complete responsibility for "research, preliminary design, system development, engineering, and operational employment" in all programs assigned to it. The NRO Satellite Operations Center would become a CIA facility, and Defense Department agencies would conduct support activities—launching, tracking, and recovery. Instead of a DNRO, there would be a Director of National Reconnaissance (DNR), who would be responsible to an executive committee composed of the DCI and Deputy Secretary of Defense. The DNR would have no management authority for CIA programs but could be delegated authority for Defense Department programs. He would be permitted to review but not modify budgets and would report to the operating head of the CIA in all matters of "policy, coordination, and guidance." He would have no staff.[67]

Two days later, McCone departed, taking his deputy out the door with him. At his last staff meeting, he told Wheelon and others, "My only regret is not having done more to straighten out the NRO mess."[68] McCone's and Carter's positions were filled by Vice-Adm. William F. Raborn, who had managed the development of the Polaris missile, and Richard Helms, who had been serving as Deputy Director for Plans since 1962. The departure of McCone and Carter undoubtedly further delayed the conclusion of a new agreement. The main task of negotiating that agreement fell to Raborn, Helms, and longtime agency official John Bross, at the time deputy to the director for National Intelligence Program Evaluation, whose primary function was to coordinate the activities of the intelligence community.[69]

The CIA's basic thesis in support of its continued role was the argument by McCone and Wheelon that

> The acquisition of intelligence by overhead reconnaissance is a responsibility of the Director of Central Intelligence. Satellite photography makes a most important input into the intelligence inventory. The DCI in discharging his statutory responsibilities for producing estimates concerning the security of the United States must direct this intelligence-acquiring facility to meet his needs. To do this the DCI, directly or through subordinates responsible to him, and with the continuing advice of the United States Intelligence Board, should determine the frequency of satellite missions, the targets and priority in which they must be treated, and the control of the

> satellite when in orbit to ensure coverage of the targets and therefore the acquisition of information considered essential by the DCI.[70]

In addition, a paper Wheelon prepared in May, "A Summary of the National Reconnaissance Problem," reviewed various options. He noted that the March 1963 NRO agreement "gave the Air Force virtual control over all CIA programs and established NRO as an operating organization with implied line authority over those elements of CIA involved in reconnaissance."[71] He also observed that an NRO funding agreement signed one month later eliminated direct congressional appropriations to the CIA for its overhead programs "and thereby passed budgetary control of the total effort to DoD."[72]

The "present arrangement," Wheelon wrote, "has been neither a happy nor productive one. External program control has frustrated many CIA activities or forced their development outside the terms of the agreement. Everyone who is aware of the NRO situation is properly concerned about it, and many believe that the present arrangement is basically unworkable."[73]

Wheelon then considered several alternatives for managing the national reconnaissance effort. Responsibility could be assigned to a single agency (NASA, the Air Force, the CIA), which would handle all aspects of the effort—from payload design to launch, operations, and recovery. That alternative was not viable, Wheelon argued, because although the CIA should have significant responsibility in regard to the procurement, tasking, and operation of reconnaissance systems, it needed the Air Force to conduct the launch, tracking, and recovery operations.[74]

Wheelon contended that since launch, tracking, and recovery were clearly DOD functions, and there was agreement at the highest level in DOD that targeting and orbit selection should be handled by the CIA, the only remaining question was who should develop payloads. He noted two alternatives—assigning the CIA the task of developing all payloads, on the grounds that it had to be done secretly and because the design should be responsive to national intelligence needs, or assigning the task to the Air Force. The second alternative was unacceptable because "it would give the Air Force complete control over all satellite reconnaissance," and "its success would depend on continuing, faithful Air Force responsiveness to truly national intelligence needs."[75]

A third possibility was to divide the task. Indeed, Wheelon proposed that there be "an orderly assignment of satellite payload development to the various agencies"—possibly with the Navy handling SIGINT payloads, the Army geodetic and mapping payloads, the Air Force high-resolution photographic systems, and the CIA search systems. Assignments would be made by the DCI and Deputy Secretary of Defense jointly.[76]

A fourth possibility, which Wheelon rejected, would be to assign the basic research role for satellite systems to the CIA, and leave development and procurement to the Air Force. The problem with such an arrangement, he argued, was that the aerospace industry was responsive to procurement agencies that had a large number of dollars at its disposal. It would be unreasonable to expect the aerospace companies to give their best efforts to a group with only a few million dollars to spend, when a half billion dollars would be available from the procurement agencies. In addition, it would be "unreasonable to expect the development and procurement agency to have deep, continuing enthusiasm for another's concepts and become 'a loving foster parent.'"[77]

All-out competition represented a fifth alternative, which Wheelon rejected because it "would be difficult to keep such a competition orderly, especially with a limited technical and industrial base in which to establish such a competition." He concluded by noting that he hoped the CIA proposal would be accepted, but if that were not possible, "the assignment of all reconnaissance payloads to CIA is the only way to preserve dedication of these satellite collection systems to national intelligence needs."[78]

In early summer, before much work was done on the ultimate agreement, the NRO staff learned that McMillan would be leaving in a few months. (He had in fact been fired by Vance.) Vance and John Bross reached agreement on August 6, and the resulting document was signed by Raborn and Vance on August 13, 1965. Vance apparently relied on the advice of Fubini, who may have been its principal author, in accepting the agreement. It incorporated several concepts he had discussed with various members of the NRO staff in the preceding weeks. Final details were worked out by Vance and Raborn.[79]

The agreement assigned responsibilities to the Secretary of Defense, DCI, and NRO and formally established a National Reconnaissance Program Executive Committee (NRPEC). The Secretary was to have "the ultimate responsibility for the management and operation of the NRO and the NRP," choose the Director, concur in the choice of the Deputy Director, and review and have the final power to approve the NRP budget. The Secretary also was empowered to make decisions when the executive committee could not reach agreement.[80] The DCI was to establish collection priorities and requirements for targeting NRP operations, determine frequency of coverage, review the results obtained by the NRP and recommend steps for improving its results if necessary, serve on the executive committee, review and approve the NRP budget, and provide security policy guidance.[81]

The NRP Executive Committee established by the agreement would consist of the DCI, Deputy Secretary of Defense, and Special Assistant to the President for Science and Technology. The DNRO was to sit with the committee but in a nonvoting capacity (a provision from an earlier draft and reinserted by Raborn that eliminated the DOD draft proposal he received that would have made the DNRO a voting member of the NRPEC).[82]

The committee was to recommend to the Secretary of Defense the "appropriate level of effort for the NRP," approve or modify the consolidated NRP and its budget, and approve the allocation of responsibility and the corresponding funds for research and exploratory development for new systems. It was instructed to ensure that funds would be adequate to pursue a vigorous research and development program involving both CIA and DOD.[83]

The executive committee was to assign development of sensors to the agency best equipped to handle the task, while all other engineering development tasks—such as design of the spacecraft, reentry vehicles, and boosters—were assigned to the Air Force, with the proviso that development had to proceed on a coordinated basis to ensure "optimum system development in support of intelligence requirements." At Raborn's suggestion, the agreement also included the provision that "To optimize the primary objective of systems development, design requirement of the sensors will be given priority in their integration within the spacecraft and reentry vehicles."[84]

The Director of the NRO would manage the NRO and execute the NRP "subject to the direction and control of the Secretary of Defense and the guidance of the Executive Committee." His authority to initiate, improve, modify, redirect, or terminate all research and development programs in the NRP would be subject to review by the NRPEC. He could demand that all agencies keep him informed about all programs undertaken as part of the NRP. An annex to the agreement specified assignments of four optical-sensor subsystems to specific agencies. The CIA was assigned responsibility for development of CORONA improvements and development of the new sensor for a new search system once the concept for the full system was selected.[85]

Former CIA and NRO officials concurred on at least one matter—the agreement significantly reduced the independent authority of the NRO director. They disagreed on its wisdom. To McMillan, it was "a victory for the wrong guy." Many at the NRO may have shared that conclusion, but at the CIA there was a different perspective. The DCI didn't "really have a job under the agreement," in Wheelon's view, but the agreement was "a triumph of people who cared about the program," and it "provided adult supervision" for the DNRO. Subordination of the DNRO to the three senior officials who made up the executive committee meant his decisions were subject to review, and he "could not act unilaterally." The intent was "to stop adventurism on the part of the DNRO." Frank Buzard, a member of the NRO staff at the time, later noted that "the creation of the ExCom certainly tied the hands of the DNRO as far as new systems were concerned. In any case there was peace in the valley for a while after it was issued."[86] But that peace would not prevent intense competition between the CIA and Air Force elements of the NRO over the rights to build new generations of imagery and signals intelligence systems.

On September 9, 1965, with the new agreement in place, Wheelon sent a memorandum to Deputy DCI Richard Helms again requesting approval for the creation of an Office of Special Projects. Wheelon argued that in view of the August NRO agreement, which reaffirmed CIA responsibility as a participant and assigned to CIA definite program areas, it was time to implement the planned organization. The office was established on September 15, and John Crowley, who had joined the agency about a year earlier as CORONA program manager, was chosen as the first chief of the new office.[87]

Also on September 15, Raborn designated Huntington D. Sheldon, a graduate of Eton and Yale College and former head of the Office of Current Intelligence, as Director of Reconnaissance, CIA. Sheldon was responsible to Wheelon for the activities of the Office of Special Projects (OSP) and related activities within the science and technology directorate. He was to provide the DNRO with a single point of contact with the CIA for all reconnaissance programs, and as a CIA history of OSP noted, "the assignment of Mr. Sheldon was in the nature of adding a diplomatic negotiator to balance the aggressiveness of the DS&T in handling NRP matters." It was also, Wheelon recalled, a way of "stiff-arming the NRO"—highlighted by Sheldon's title as "Director of Reconnaissance, CIA" rather than "Director, Program B, NRO."[88]

THE NEXT GENERATION

On August 25, 1963, only weeks after Wheelon had assumed command of the Directorate of Science and Technology, the first of the KH-4A CORONA spacecraft blasted off from Vandenberg Air Force Base. The primary difference between the KH-4A and its immediate predecessor was not in terms of resolution—the new camera produced photographs with resolutions in the 9–25 foot range, a trivial improvement on the 10–25 foot resolution of its predecessor. Rather, the new cameras carried a greater film load—enough to fill two reentry vehicles. Missions could be extended to fifteen days in contrast to a maximum of seven for the KH-4, and a greater number of targets could be photographed.[89]

Fifteen KH-4A missions were flown through the end of 1964. In early 1965, Eugene Fubini and John Crowley agreed that studies should be made concerning the weaknesses and limitations of the KH-4A system. On June 29, after completion of the studies, formulation of recommendations, and a CIA–Air Force Office of Special Projects briefing, McMillan approved development of an improved version of CORONA—which would be launched in September 1967 as the KH-4B; it improved CORONA's resolution to approximately six feet.[90]

By that time, Wheelon had completed his stay at the CIA and returned to private industry. In addition to RHYOLITE, his legacy included a technically demanding and ambitious program to develop a next-generation search system. Because the DS&T first began to explore the possibility of a follow-on system in fall 1963 and started early development work in 1964, the questions of what, if any, system to develop and whether the CIA should do the developing became a major issue in the NRO-CIA battles of 1963–1965. It would, in the words of one former NRO staffer, turn into a "real donny-brook."[91]

In July 1964, McMillan had instructed the Itek Corporation to stop work on what was to be a follow-on to CORONA—the M-2—and to concentrate on improving the capability of the existing systems. His instructions followed a report from the Panel for Future Satellite Reconnaissance Operations, whose members included Edward Purcell, the chairman, Richard Garwin, Edwin Land, and NPIC director Arthur Lundahl.[92]

The panel had been briefed by various contractors and military and governmental personnel as to what systems were in design development or under consideration. James Reber, chairman of the interagency Committee on Overhead Reconnaissance (COMOR), which selected targets for the spy satellites, discussed the latest COMOR requirements. Lundahl covered the relationship between the resolution of an image and a photointerpreter's ability to extract intelligence from the photo. There was no difference, the CIA's chief photointerpreter told them, in the intelligence that could be derived from photographs with resolution of ten feet than of five feet. The Purcell group concluded that development of a new search system with resolution between four and six feet was not justified. [93]

McMillan's emphasis on improving CORONA was also based on the findings of the reconnaissance panel. Its report had noted that the KH-4 system operated at its ultimate photographic capability only about 10 percent of the time, partially as a result of recognized factors. The panel observed that "it seems entirely feasible to bring most of these factors under control so that one could count on peak resolution from the . . . system on 90% of the exposed film." The consequence would be "an enormous gain in information acquisition."[94]

But the vision of least one member of the Purcell panel went beyond five-foot resolution. Edwin Land concluded that a system was needed that covered as much territory as CORONA but with the resolution of GAMBIT—the Air Force's new high-resolution satellite whose images had a resolution of eighteen inches. A study by Wheelon's Systems Analysis Staff noted there were no plans for developing such a system.[95]

A high-resolution search system would address one of Wheelon's concerns—that photointerpreters were "drowning in data" and finding it extraordinarily difficult to detect new items of interest with CORONA photography. They were failing to find the needles in the haystack. With too much to look at, they were "getting bleary-eyed."[96]

In October 1963, Wheelon had established the Satellite Photography Working Group "to explore the whole range of engineering and physical limitations for satellite photography." Chaired by Stanford physicist Sidney Drell, with ORD deputy director Robert Chapman serving as their CIA contact, the group was to look at possible ways to improve CORONA and set guidelines for the development of new systems. According to Wheelon, that effort marked the "resurgence of CIA activity in the satellite business."[97]

The project was approved by McCone and Gilpatric during an October 22 meeting, and on November 5, a letter from Wheelon to McMillan provided a detailed outline of the group's agenda and requested NRO funding. McMillan responded on November 18, noting that establishment of the working group "affords an excellent opportunity to achieve a more basic understanding of the reasons for the variations in quality and resolution we have experienced to date with the CORONA system," although he discouraged an analysis of systems still under development. He agreed to provide NRO funds to cover the costs associated with outside consultants.[98]

Wheelon asked Drell's group, which included Rod Scott of Perkin-Elmer and two representatives from Itek, to determine how much CORONA's resolution could be improved and how much intelligence could be extracted from wide-area photos of higher and higher resolution. In an attempt to determine the intelligence value of increasingly sharp images, the group degraded aerial reconnaissance photographs to five different levels of resolution and gave them to photointerpreters at NPIC to see how much intelligence could be extracted at each level.[99]

Drell and his colleagues concluded that CORONA had been pushed about as far as it could be, and that to achieve significantly better resolution would require a new system. Meanwhile, NPIC's photointerpreters demonstrated that a wide-area system with resolution of two feet would dramatically improve their ability to spot new facilities and extract intelligence about them. As a whole, the exercise resulted in the realization that, according to Wheelon, "something a lot better was needed."[100]

But McMillan's willingness to fund a research effort did not mean a willingness to fund a satellite to be developed on the basis of the group's findings and recommendations. Wheelon later recalled that "from the outset McMillan did everything in his power" to stop that program, including refusing to provide funds.[101] But McMillan's decision did not prevent McCone from authorizing the use of CIA funds for the same project. With the Land Reconnaissance Panel and PFIAB suggesting that the expenditure of $10 million would be worthwhile to investigate the feasibility of a new wide-area, high-resolution system, McCone approved the funding.[102]

DS&T representatives talked to both Itek and Perkin-Elmer about the possibility of working on the program. In February 1964, using personnel from various offices and staffs within the science and technology directorate, the systems analysis group began a study in conjunction with Itek, whose ideas were preferred to those of Perkin-Elmer, to determine the feasibility and potential intelligence value of using several individual sensors or combination of sensors in a satellite system. The study led to a camera design believed to be capable of producing high-resolution over a wide swath.[103]

It was not until June that McMillan discovered the CIA effort, code-named FULCRUM, which the agency had concealed not only from the Soviet Union but from the NRO as well. To pursue the project beyond the initial phase would require NRP funding. Wheelon initially proposed a six-month design effort. At the beginning, a project office of five to seven people, reporting directly to Wheelon, would be established within the CIA and be responsible for system engineering and technical direction. The proposal, according to an NRO history, was "precise, carefully detailed, seemingly quite accurate, technologically conservative, and—on the whole—exceptionally well constructed."[104]

But McMillan believed that to approve the proposal would enable the CIA to establish "an independent capability for full-scale development of space systems," even though their feasibility had yet to be determined. To establish such a capability, the CIA would have to recruit a substantial technical establishment. Not surprisingly, the NRO director was thoroughly opposed to the idea.[105]

McMillan also believed that he had Fubini's support. The deputy director of defense research and engineering had observed that over the past two years, no committees had recommended a new search system. Also, Fubini had technical reservations about whether the high-speed film flow envisioned in the FULCRUM system was attainable. He also argued that proceeding toward a new broad-coverage system was unwise while the causes of CORONA's variable performance remained unknown.[106]

McMillan attempted to head off any fait accompli by turning McNamara's attention to the matter. With Fubini's support and Vance's approval, he submitted a McNamara-to-McCone memorandum for the Secretary's signature, but in the end it was revised and signed by Vance. It proposed that the CIA be authorized to do only those tests needed to establish FULCRUM's feasibility while the NRO simultaneously undertook comparative studies. By January 1965, Vance suggested, a determination of development desirability and a selection of a system should be possible. He added, "At that time we can discuss the assignment of responsibilities for development and operational employment."[107]

Wheelon, according to an NRO history, "either did not await DoD action or, more probably, had advance notice of Vance's intentions." On July 9, before Vance's letter could reach McCone, the science and technology chief sent McMillan an outline of "the various tasks for which we require immediate NRO funding." Wheelon's task description went beyond feasibility studies to include funding for spacecraft, booster, and "assembly, integration, and checkout" contracts.[108]

That same month, the United States Intelligence Board formally called for development of a new search system—which still left open the question of the system's characteristics and which agency should manage its development. On August 11, a meeting of Vance, McCone, Fubini, and McMillan addressed the CIA's proposal. McCone accepted in principle a funding level of about $30 million and a set of Vance instructions on FULCRUM issued a week earlier, which was expanded to provide for some system design study work but under the aegis of the NRO.[109]

In a late 1964 presentation to the PFIAB, McMillan noted the Purcell panel's report and apparently referred to its suggestion that the best thing to do was stay with CORONA. In a memo, the DS&T's John McMahon contended that such an argument was misleading. He noted the contents of the briefings given by Reber and Lundahl as well as the panel's being told that the new search system proposed as a follow-on to CORONA was a "10,000 lb. monster" that would require a Titan 3C booster. Thus, "the panel felt that rather than bankrupt the US Treasury . . . we turn to CORONA and make [it] work all the time" at nine-foot resolution. McMahon argued that the Purcell panel members failed to explain the documentation and presentations upon which they based their recommendations, and he suggested that if they were briefed on the current systems under way and the resolutions required, they would reach different conclusions than they did in July 1963.[110]

In any case, McMillan and the NRO were determined that FULCRUM, about which the CIA would tell them little, would not be the only candidate to succeed CORONA. A contract to begin studies for a system designated the S-2 was issued to Eastman-Kodak, whose approach McMillan recalled as "fairly conventional." Some attention was also devoted to a proposal for a smaller system, designated MATCHBOX, that was advertised as being capable of producing equally detailed imagery.[111]

Then, on February 24, 1965, Itek made an announcement that stunned Wheelon and "the NRO Staff found hilariously enjoyable"—that it would undertake no further work on the FULCRUM program.[112] Since Itek began serious work on FULCRUM, it had been faced with a CIA requirement that it felt unnecessary and unreasonable—that the camera be capable of photographing targets up to 60 degrees to the left or right of the satellite's path above the earth—from horizon to horizon. The farther a camera is moved "off axis," the more the atmosphere degrades its resolution, and thus a 35-degree capability in each direction had been the maximum demanded of any CORONA camera. As Walter Levison, a camera designer and senior Itek official at the time, recalled, Itek thought the decline in resolution that would result would be too great to justify attempting to produce a system that could scan 120 degrees.[113]

The difference in viewpoints had apparently led to some hard feelings between Special Projects Staff head Jack Maxey and Itek's FULCRUM program manager John Wolfe. Maxey was, according to Frank Madden, the chief engineer for FULCRUM, "high-handed, demanding." But the event that triggered Itek's withdrawal, according to Levison, occurred at a meeting in Boston of the Land Reconnaissance Panel, attended by, among others, Levison, Itek president Frank Lindsay, Wheelon, and McMillan. The meeting featured a briefing by Leslie Dirks on FULCRUM. Dirks insisted that the requirement for the new satellite to scan 60 degrees in each direction was an Itek recommendation and not made at the CIA's insistence. Levison's reaction, in "the heat of the moment," was "that tears it." Later that afternoon, a meeting among Levison, Lindsay, and other Itek executives resulted in the decision to withdraw from the FULCRUM program.[114]*

After the meeting, Levison called NRO staffer Paul Worthman, who in a memo described Levison's voice "as shaking throughout the conversation." Levison informed Worthman of Itek's decision and requested advice on how to handle the situation. Worthman suggested the first thing to do was inform McCone, which Levison said Itek president Frank Lindsay was trying to do at that moment. When McCone could not be reached, Lindsay called John Bross to give him the bad news.[115] Worthman then called McMillan and told him to call Levison immediately. A meeting among Levison, Wolfe, McMillan, and Land followed, which left the latter two "stunned." Levison told them that Itek felt it could not survive under "the domination of the CIA" and that the CIA had fostered an "immoral environment."[116]

Itek's announcement that it would no longer work on FULCRUM "hit us like a ton," John McMahon recalled. It also led to suspicions on the part of several CIA officials that McMillan or Fubini had offered Itek an inducement to withdraw from the CIA program—such as a guarantee of

---

*Thirty-five years later, Levison wondered "What the hell difference did it make?" and noted that the amount of film a satellite could carry in the case of CORONA, had increased from 20 to 180 pounds. With that much film on board, the sensible reaction to wasting a few frames of film would be "Who cares?" (Telephone interview with Walter Levison, September 17, 1999.)

an NRO contract to build the next search system. McMillan denied any previous arrangement with Itek, and Levison recalled that "nobody made any promises to anybody." McMillan did transfer the S-2 program from Eastman-Kodak to Itek after its withdrawal from FULCRUM. According to Levison, McMillan wanted to keep Itek working in the reconnaissance field, and Eastman-Kodak had plenty of work—including working on the KH-10 optical system for the Air Force's Manned Orbiting Laboratory. Part of McMillan's decision was apparently the result of the technical discussion about a new search system at the February 24 meeting.[117]

Back at Langley, McCone and Wheelon decided they would have to find another contractor, possibly Perkin-Elmer. Meanwhile, McMahon, along with two other CIA officials—Jim MacDonald and Henry Plaster—were sent to Itek, where they seized all records, brassboards, and engineering notebooks related to FULCRUM.[118]

During a visit to Perkin-Elmer, Wheelon asked Rod Scott for any ideas. Scott explained the concept of the "twister," which would allow images to be recorded on film that was see-sawed back and forth—a radical departure from the practice of advancing the film frame by frame past the focal plane. The twister would permit placement of the cameras in the satellite so that they would be parallel to the satellite's motion rather than perpendicular—which in turn meant the satellite could carry cameras of sufficient size to achieve the CIA's resolution and scan objectives. (In other words, placing cameras of sufficient size across the *width* of the spacecraft would require building a spacecraft that would be too large for the nose of the launch vehicle, whereas placing them across the length would not.) The concept also involved rotating the focal plane rather than the camera.[119]

Wheelon next consulted Land, who preferred Perkin-Elmer's design to Itek's. According to McMillan, Land was supportive because he was not a systems engineer but a scientist who "liked nothing more than an innovative, clever device." The twister "just knocked him off his chair." McCone then put up $10 million–$30 million of agency money to keep the project going.[120]

In mid-July, McMillan made one last effort to slow down FULCRUM, sending Vance and Raborn a report in which he asked for a deferred review of progress. McMillan reported to Vance that the original S-2 system still appeared to be the most promising approach, adding that he proposed to select either Itek or Eastman-Kodak to develop an alternate camera configuration.[121]

The reaction from Raborn was similar to the reactions of McCone, Carter, and Wheelon to comparable proposals on similar occasions in the past. First, he politely protested McMillan's apparent intention of unilaterally selecting a specific search system for development. Then he invoked the pending Land panel report as reason for not rushing to judgment. Finally, he made the point that only he and Vance could make the final decision on any specific search system.[122]

Vance had earlier cautioned McMillan to proceed cautiously in making program commitments to Itek, but McMillan, who was convinced that the S-2 system was by far the best prospect, had continued to invest in it. Since the Land panel had proposed no solution, only further study, Raborn suggested that McMillan had exceeded the authority entrusted to him.[123]

According to an NRO history, failure of the Land panel to make a choice was a disappointment for the NRO and McMillan. They had "hoped for selection of some system other than [FULCRUM], a development that would tend to choke off the CIA's involvement in the creation of new satellite systems."[124]

As a result of the August 1965 agreement, the CIA was given responsibility for managing the development of the new search system. But in September, a McMahon memorandum charged that McMillan had indicated that Itek had been selected to build the new search system, despite the fact that the competition was still ongoing.[125]

Perkin-Elmer ultimately won the competition, probably because of the coverage provided. The criteria for evaluation were written by McMillan's successor as NRO director, Al Flax, and the scan angle received high priority. Its optical bar system provided horizon-to-horizon coverage, even though it was not used a majority of the time because the resolution was, as Itek had warned, severely degraded at the extremes. Normally, the camera scanned 30 degrees to either side rather than 60 degrees. The system was intended to yield resolution of three feet at the nadir (when the target was directly underneath) but produced no better than six feet at the extremes.[126]

On April 22, 1966, the USIB gave its blessing to development of a new search system along the lines of FULCRUM rather than its main competitor, the S-2. A new code name, possibly AQUILINE, was assigned to the program that same day, but it was replaced eight days later by the name it was subsequently known by, at least by those with the proper clearances—HEXAGON.[127]

Exactly four months after the USIB gave its approval to HEXAGON, Bud Wheelon wrote to DCI Richard Helms to confirm a conversation they had the previous week. In the letter he noted that "when I accepted

John McCone's invitation to join CIA in early 1962, it was with the understanding that I would serve . . . not more than four years. I believe that I have now accomplished all of the major objectives in creating a technical intelligence component for the Agency." He also noted that "Hughes Aircraft Company has offered me a most attractive position. . . . As we agreed, 23 September 1966 will be my last official day."[128]

A month and a day later, Wheelon put in his last day as Deputy Director for Science and Technology. There would be much more work to be done before HEXAGON or RHYOLITE flew, but they would become two of the three key reasons why, in 1994, he would be named the first winner of the R. V. Jones award. The satellites also provided the foundation for the CIA's continuing role in the development of space reconnaissance systems, which would include a third major system whose origins could be traced to Wheelon's tenure. The same CIA official who recalled Wheelon as "an acerbic son of a bitch" noted that without him, the Air Force "would have run away with the [reconnaissance] program."[129] He might have added that in that case, there would have been no RHYOLITE, HEXAGON, or KH-11.

(Left) Richard Bissell, photographed standing in front of the Brandenburg Gate, joined the CIA in 1954 as a special assistant to DCI Allen Dulles. During his tenure with the CIA (1954–1962), he oversaw the successful development of the U–2 and CORONA reconnaissance systems for the CIA. CREDIT: *Fran Pudlo*

(Below) Edwin Land, second from the left in the second row, with other recipients of the National Medal of Science and President Johnson. Land served as a scientific adviser to the CIA and NRO. He was a key figure in the decision to proceed with the U–2 and KH–11 systems and in the creation of the Directorate of Science and Technology. CREDIT: *LBJ Library*

(top left) Herbert Scoville Jr. joined the CIA as head of the Office of Scientific Intelligence and became Deputy Director for Research in 1962. He resigned a year later, largely because of the problems in his relationship with the National Reconnaissance Office. CREDIT: *CIA*

(bottom left) Albert "Bud" Wheelon replaced Herbert Scoville as OSI chief in 1962. When Scoville resigned from the CIA in 1963, Wheelon was asked to replace him. As Deputy Director for Science and Technology, Wheelon reestablished the CIA's role in space reconnaissance and supervised the initial development of key imagery and signals intelligence systems. CREDIT: *CIA*

(above) Carl Duckett replaced Wheelon as head of the science and technology directorate in 1966 and served in that position until 1976. Under Duckett, two key programs initiated by Wheelon—the RHYOLITE signals intelligence satellite and the HEXAGON imagery satellite—became operational. A third, the KH–11, received presidential approval and was first launched in December 1976. CREDIT: *CIA*

(top left) Leslie Dirks joined the CIA in 1962 and became Deputy Director for Science and Technology in 1976. He played a key role in the KII–11 program from its conception, serving as its program manager prior to replacing Duckett. CREDIT: *CIA*

(bottom left) Lloyd Lauderdale served as Carl Duckett's deputy before leaving government to join E-Systems. He is known as the "father of RHYOLITE," having served as its program manager and guiding its technical development. CREDIT: *Virginia S. Lauderdale*

(above) Ruth David became the first Deputy Director of Science and Technology chosen from outside the CIA's ranks. Her tenure (1995–1998) involved controversy over some of her decisions and a decline in the directorate's status due to changes in the directorate's role in space reconnaissance and imagery interpretation. She also increased the directorate's work in information technology. CREDIT: *CIA*

Central Intelligence Agency, Headquarters, Langley, Virginia. CREDIT: CIA

Headquarters of the National Photographic Interpretation Center at the Washington Navy Yard. NPIC was established in 1961 as "service of common concern" to be managed by the CIA. In 1973, it became part of the DS&T. In 1995, it was merged with a number of other agencies to form the National Imagery and Mapping Agency, which was placed within the Department of Defense. CREDIT: *Federation of American Scientists*

(above) The Matomic Building (second from right) at 1717 H Street N.W. served as headquarters for the U–2 project staff from February 1956 until March 1962, when the staff moved to CIA's new headquarters at Langley, Virginia. CREDIT: *Federation of American Scientists*

(below) The Ames Building in Rosslyn, Virginia, housed a number of CIA offices for several years, including the DS&T's Office of Research and Development. The CIA moved out of the facility in the late 1990s. CREDIT: *Federation of American Scientists*

5

CHANGE OF COMMAND

When Bud Wheelon headed back to California in October 1966 to become vice-president for engineering at Hughes Aircraft, he brought along the Distinguished Intelligence Medal awarded to him shortly before his departure.[1] He left behind a science and technology directorate that had become a key player in scientific and technical intelligence production, signals intelligence collection, and, most important, overhead reconnaissance.

In many ways, the DS&T was an intelligence community in itself—establishing requirements, developing and operating collection systems, and analyzing some of the data collected. What Ray Cline had seen as a problem—collectors and analysts reporting to the same boss—many in the directorate saw as a virtue. The priorities of those developing and operating collection systems flowed, without bureaucratic obstacles, from the priorities of the analysts.

Assuming command of the directorate, as acting deputy director, was former FMSAC chief Carl Duckett, who had become Associate Deputy Director for Science and Technology in mid-May 1966.[2] In some ways, Duckett was no Wheelon; in others, Wheelon was no Duckett.

Although the directorate would relinquish its role in aerial reconnaissance operations to the Air Force on his watch, Duckett's strengths enabled the directorate to flourish and to reach its peak of power and influence. During his decade-long tenure, the objectives of the HEXAGON and RHYOLITE programs would be realized, another battle with the Air Force over development of an advanced satellite system would be fought and won, and collection operations in Iran and Norway would continue to yield vital intelligence on Soviet missile programs. The directorate would also expand its role in the CIA's scientific and technical projects, assuming control over offices previously belonging to the intelligence and operations directorates.

A NEW BOSS

In contrast to Bud Wheelon, who had arrived at the agency with advanced degrees from prestigious institutions and a long list of scientific publications, Carl Duckett brought no impressive scholarly credentials to the job, not even a college degree. The lack of such credentials almost prevented Duckett from becoming Wheelon's successor.

Wheelon himself did not think Duckett should succeed him, despite his having "many fine qualities"—and told Raborn and Helms so. Wheelon believed that the directorate was still in the "creation" stage, that it needed a strong technical person, but that individuals such as Leslie Dirks were too young. Thus, he had lined up his former boss at TRW, Frank Lehan, to replace him. Lehan was familiar with DS&T operations, having served as a key adviser from its birth. But a personal problem, in the form of a wayward daughter, forced Lehan to withdraw his name after Wheelon made it clear he could not stay on for another year.[3]

Wheelon informed Helms and possibly suggested another of the directorate's key advisers—William Perry—for the job. But in April 1967, after more than six months of trying and failing to recruit someone with the appropriate scientific credentials and finding himself satisfied with Duckett, Richard Helms, Director of Central Intelligence since June 1966, removed the "Acting" from Duckett's title.[4]

Duckett lacked an academic background but he had other capabilities that proved of great value to a man in his position. He was, as former Deputy Director for Intelligence Edward Proctor observed, a good briefer, a man who, according to Dino Brugioni, "could turn technical data into laymanese."[5] Such a talent was of great use in marketing, in selling senators and congressmen, many of whom had little or no understanding of technical issues, on the need for a new collection system. Indeed, Duckett was, according to one directorate official, "probably the best marketeer," a man who "could sell Congress anything."[6]

Also crucial to Duckett's ability to sell programs was his personal style. His experience as a disk jockey had made him a "smooth talker" who "had congressmen in the palm of his hand."[7] His smooth talk was aided by his knowledge of the lives and families of key members of the Appropriations and Armed Services committees—who in the 1960s and early 1970s determined which CIA programs would be funded and which would not. His prehearing chats with legislators were often sufficient to ensure that military arguments in opposition to a CIA program fell on deaf ears.[8]

AZORIAN AND NURO

On February 24, 1968, a Soviet Golf-II submarine, one of a class of diesel submarines armed with SS-N-5 Serb nuclear ballistic missiles, left port. Sometime in early March, while on a routine patrol that had taken it about 750 miles northwest of Hawaii, it surfaced to recharge its batteries, air out the crude ventilation system, and communicate with fleet headquarters at Vladivostok. Instead, the submarine imploded and sank in water three miles deep. Taken down with the submarine were its seventy-man crew, three SS-N-5 missiles, each tipped with a four-megaton warhead, and cipher material.[9]

After twenty-four hours of listening in vain to the assigned frequency, the Soviet Pacific Fleet declared an emergency and began to hunt for the missing sub. A dozen ships, including four or five submarines, took part in the search. The first ships to arrive in the search area were greeted by heavy snowfall, gale winds, and waves forty-five feet high. The surface ships and submarines directed their sonar at the ocean below; the subs also dived to look for the missing sub.[10]

Monitoring of the Soviet effort, as well as examination of earlier intercepted communications, led U.S. intelligence analysts to conclude that the sub was lost and that the Soviet navy had no solid idea where it sank. The U.S. Navy, on the other hand, had at least the rough coordinates for the site. That information came from the Navy's Sound Surveillance System (SOSUS), a network of over twenty underwater hydrophone arrays that could pick up the sound generated by a variety of underwater activities—including that of submarines. The acoustic signals gathered by SOSUS could be used not only to distinguish among different submarine classes but also among individual subs in the same class. Analysis of the signals from the SEA SPIDER array, near Hawaii, yielded the conclusion that the sub's most likely resting place was 1,700 miles northwest of Hawaii, at 40 degrees latitude and 180 degrees longitude.[11]

Captain James F. Bradley Jr., who headed the Office of Naval Intelligence's undersea warfare office, brought the news of the missing Soviet submarine to senior Navy officials, who then proposed to Secretary of the Navy Paul Nitze that the USS *Halibut* be assigned to search for the sub. Ultimately, the United States might be able to recover its missiles, codebooks, and technological information.[12]

The *Halibut* had been converted from a guided missile submarine to a "spy sub" under the direction of John P. Craven, the first director of the Navy's Deep Submergence Systems Project. The Brooklyn native, whose credentials included a doctorate in mechanical engineering and service as chief scientist in the Navy's Polaris missile program, had modified the sub so that it could dangle cameras to view the ocean bottom as it hovered below the surface. What he had hoped to find, as part of an operation code-named SAND DOLLAR, were the warheads the Soviets left behind after missile tests in the Pacific.[13]

During summer 1968, the *Halibut* lowered its thick cable toward the ocean floor, the attached lights and cameras searching for the sub. The resulting pictures showed the submarine's sail, the three missile tubes, one of which was intact, and a sailor's skeleton. The photos also showed that the lost submarine had broken into pieces. The rear engineering section had split off from the forward and central sections, which were about 200 feet in length and carried the ship's three missiles.[14]

In early September, the *Halibut* returned with a set of 22,000 photographs of the lost submarine, which were code-named VELVET FIST. Craven later told Congress, in secret testimony, that the "*Halibut* was able to locate, examine, and evaluate the accident and to obtain significant intelligence information concerning the submarine, its mission, and its equipments."[15]

But both the Navy and CIA wanted more than pictures—at the very least, the warheads and cipher material. Examination of the warheads would provide the United States with insight into the state of Soviet nuclear technology—particularly the reliability, accuracy, and detonation mechanisms of the missiles. Equally prized were the cipher machines and code manuals that might be stored in watertight safes.[16]

Other possible items for recovery included the torpedoes, which if recovered would give U.S. analysts their first look at the Soviet devices. Data concerning the homing devices incorporated into the torpedo design would be of aid in developing countermeasures. And there was the submarine itself. Analysts could subject the steel used in the hulls to metallurgical analysis and possibly determine how deep Soviet subs could dive.[17]

The prospect of recovering significant material produced two proposals—one Navy, one CIA. Bradley and Craven suggested sending minisubs to grab a nuclear warhead, the safe containing the crypto codes, and the submarine's burst transmitters and receivers. They considered it unnecessary to recover the missiles, which were primitive, and the submarine hull.[18]

After listening to Bradley and Craven's idea, Duckett and other CIA officials came back with a much more dramatic plan—to recover the forward and central sections of the submarine. According to one account, Bradley and Craven thought they were crazy. And when Duckett proposed mounting a recovery effort to DCI Richard Helms, his first response was "You must be crazy." But, after further consideration, Helms approved Duckett's idea.[19]

With approval from the White House, the CIA contacted eccentric multimillionaire Howard Hughes, whose organization had a passion for secrecy. Hughes, along with its subcontractors, would spend over three years working on the first phase of what was then known as Project AZORIAN. They produced the *Glomar Explorer*—36,000 tons, 618 feet in length, and 115.5 feet in the beam—to serve as a floating, highly stable platform. In the center of the ship, a high derrick passed piping directly through the "moon pool" in the ship's hull—a pool 200 feet long and 65 feet wide. The pool could be opened to allow an object to be lifted into it from the sea. A companion to the ship was a huge submersible barge, the *Hughes Marine Barge-1* (*HMB-1*), roughly the size of a football field, that was covered by an oval roof and lowered below the *Glomar Explorer*. The barge carried gigantic retrieval claws that could embrace the submarine and raise it from its watery grave. The roof prevented Soviet reconnaissance satellites from photographing the cargo.[20]

The loss of the Golf-II submarine, in addition to serving as the catalyst for AZORIAN, also led to the creation of a new reconnaissance office in which Duckett and the DS&T played a key role. The National Underwater Reconnaissance Office (NURO) was established in 1969 to serve as an underwater NRO, coordinating CIA and Navy efforts in underwater reconnaissance operations that included not only AZORIAN but also submarine reconnaissance missions, which often involved covert entry into Soviet ports. The office was headed by the Secretary of the Navy, at the time John Warner, the future senator from Virginia. Bradley served as NURO's first staff director, and Duckett as the senior CIA representative to the new office.[21] At the time NURO was formed, completion of the AZORIAN mission was several years away.

DRAGON LADIES AND NICE GIRLS

Shortly before Bud Wheelon departed, the Office of Special Activities had also undergone a change of command. In August 1966, a month after Jack Ledford returned to regular Air Force duty, Brig. Gen. Paul Bacalis became the new head of the CIA's aerial reconnaissance effort. Bacalis, who had flown fifty combat missions as a B-24 pilot during World War II, had spent the two previous years at SAC headquarters, in the Inspector General's office and the operations directorate.[22]

As with Ledford, the job came as a surprise to Bacalis. In mid-1966, he was on the promotion list for brigadier general when he received a message to report to the Pentagon, where he discovered he had a job interview over at the CIA. Once there, he spent the entire day being interviewed by Wheelon, Duckett, Ledford, and Raborn. After three weeks passed, during which time other candidates were also interviewed, Bacalis was told his new assignment was as chief of OSA. Rather than the desk job he expected, he had his "own little Air Force."[23]

That "little Air Force" included the U-2s as well as the A-12s produced by the OXCART program. At the time Bacalis became OSA chief, the agency's U-2 fleet had dwindled to six. However, on August 1, 1966, McNamara and Helms had decided to order eight upgraded U-2s from Lockheed on behalf of the CIA and Air Force, and in November, they tacked on another four aircraft to their order. Of the total, six eventually went to the CIA.[24]

Of course, while Lockheed worked on producing the new planes, the Nationalist Chinese pilots of Detachment H continued flying the old ones on an assortment of missions. On November 26, 1966, a mission planned to cover twenty-three targets selected by the interagency Committee on Overhead Reconnaissance (COMOR) penetrated the Chinese mainland at 69,000 feet, southeast of Luchiao Airfield. Before the mission was aborted due to an overheated light, the U-2 photographed twenty of the COMOR targets plus another forty of interest to the intelligence community. Coverage was obtained of Chungan Airfield, and a number of KOMAR missile patrol boats were detected at the Santu Naval Base.[25]

On June 5, 1967, twelve days before China's first detonation of a hydrogen bomb, Spike Chuang departed from Ban Takhli, Thailand, and flew a U-2 on a 3,700 mile, 9-hour round-trip flight, taking the plane and its cameras over the Chinese test site at Lop Nur. Captain Tom Hwang Lung Pei's flight, which began at Taoyuan, Taiwan, was considerably shorter, ending when an SA-2 hit his aircraft while it was over Chuhsien.[26] In addition to photographing Lop Nur, U-2s continued dropping sensors in the vicinity of the nuclear test site. A May 7, 1967, mission, also flown by Spike Chuang, involved dropping the fifteen-foot-long TOBASCO pod. Among the functions of an August 31 mission, flown by Bill Chang, was to interrogate the pod, possibly because of problems in relaying the data through a satellite. The mission required Chang to loiter in the vicinity of the pod for about ten minutes.[27]

In mid-1968, OSA deployed the first of the new generation of U-2s, the U-2R, to Taoyuan. The new plane was capable of carrying out long-duration SIGINT missions as well as acquiring valuable imagery through use of a new generation of Long-Range Oblique Photography (LOROP) cameras, which could photograph targets many miles to the side of the aircraft. The main camera, which had been designed with the requirements of technical intelligence analysts in mind, could distinguish objects smaller than four inches.[28]

To permit longer missions, fuel capacity was dramatically increased, with fuel tanks carried within the aircraft as well as on the wings. The plane also carried more sophisticated navigational aids. A typical U-2R mission might involve sensors weighing 3,000 pounds, a fuel load of 12,250 pounds, and flight time of seven and a half hours (most of it spent above 70,000 feet). A U-2R carrying its maximum fuel load of 18,500 pounds could fly a fifteen-hour mission.[29]

The next year, the question arose as to how much longer the agency would be operating U-2s. In March 1969, John McLucas became Under Secretary of the Air Force and Director of the NRO. He concluded early in his tenure that aerial reconnaissance operations could be handled solely by the Air Force and outside of the NRO.[30]

Aside from McLucas's desire to remove the NRO from aerial operations, there was budgetary pressure, and the view that a single manager should be assigned to direct U-2 operations. If only one agency was going to handle the U-2, it would have to be the Air Force. By early December, Deputy Secretary of Defense David Packard had discussed the possibility with Richard Helms. The day before, Packard had instructed McLucas to prepare a plan to consolidate all U-2 operations under the Strategic Air Command. Packard noted that Helms agreed to consider such a plan, but that final agreement as to substance and timing had yet to be obtained.[31]

Those memos marked the beginning of the end for CIA operation of the plane it had brought into being, but the end would not be immediate. On Christmas Day, a memo written by Brig. Gen. Donald H. Ross, who had replaced Paul Bacalis as head of OSA in July 1968, noted that "We have just received word President has reviewed IDEALIST program, including TACKLE arrangements, and has concurred in need for continuation of program." In early August 1970, in anticipation of a breach in the cease-fire in the war of attrition between Israel and Egypt, President Nixon ordered periodic overflights.[32] National security adviser Henry Kissinger asked the Air Force to provide U-2 coverage of the Suez Canal, after discovering that satellite imagery was inadequate to discover gun emplacements and jeeps. But the Air Force said it couldn't move quickly enough—that it would take several weeks to move a U-2 detachment from Del Rio, Texas, to the Middle East.[33]

At a meeting of the NSC, Helms told his audience that the CIA U-2 detachment at Edwards (Detachment G) could deploy aircraft to the region and begin operations over the Suez Canal within a week. The flights began somewhat later than the CIA wished because of problems in acquiring a base from which to launch the missions. Apparently, Italy, Greece, and Spain refused to permit U-2 missions from their territory, while the United States had to "beg" the United Kingdom to permit flights from its base at Akrotiri on Cyprus.[34]

From August 9 through November 10, 1970, after which the Air Force assumed responsibility, CIA U-2s flew twenty-nine missions over the cease-fire zone as part of Project EVEN STEVEN. It also conducted a dozen ELINT missions. The CIA missions did reveal a breach of the cease-fire—Egypt's construction of new missile sites near the Suez Canal, which would place at risk Israeli aircraft flying over Sinai's east bank to defend the Bar-Lev line from an amphibious assault. Talks between Israel and Egypt occurred during and after the CIA's monitoring, although not without interruption. Relations improved after Egyptian strongman Gamal Abdel Nasser died on September 28, 1970, and was replaced by Anwar Sadat, who extended the cease-fire and eased tensions.[35]

The CIA's U-2 effort would extend deep into Carl Duckett's stint as deputy director, but the OXCART project would become the world's most advanced anachronism after fewer than ten operational missions. The CIA was lucky that it reaped even that much benefit from its considerable investment. The Air Force had used the OXCART as the basis for its look-alike SR-71, originally designated the RS-71 (RS for Reconnaissance Strike) until President Johnson inverted the two letters during the 1964 campaign. The existence of an Air Force SR-71 fleet would then be used to justify termination of the OXCART effort.

In November 1965, the Bureau of the Budget had circulated a memo expressing concern about the costs of the OXCART and SR-71 programs. It questioned the total number of planes as well as the necessity for a separate CIA fleet and recommended phasing out the OXCART program by September 1966 as well as halting further SR-71 procurement. OSA director Jack Ledford suggested that the Budget office's proposal would "deny the United States Government a non-military capability to conduct aerial reconnaissance of denied areas . . . in the years ahead."[36]

There was also opposition outside the CIA. Secretary of Defense Robert McNamara rejected the recommendation, presumably because the SR-71 would not be operational by September 1966. In July 1966, at the suggestion of the Budget Bureau, a study group, consisting of the CIA's John Parangosky, C. W. Fischer of the Bureau of the Budget, and Herbert Bennington of the Defense Department, was established to look for ways to reduce the costs associated with the two programs. The group was requested to consider five alternatives, which it transformed into three options—maintain both planes; mothball the A-12s and share the SR-71s between the CIA and Air Force; and mothball the A-12s by January 1968 (assuming SR-71 readiness by September 1967) and turn the mission over to SAC. From the CIA's perspective, the Bureau of the Budget, and in particular one of its staff members, W. R. Thomas, had one specific outcome in mind—termination of the OXCART program.[37]

That belief undoubtedly only increased the urgency OSA felt to give the A-12s a chance to demonstrate their value. During 1966, the CIA proposed to the 303 Committee that OXCART aircraft be deployed to Okinawa and fly reconnaissance missions over North Vietnam or China or both. All such proposals were rejected. The CIA, Joint Chiefs, and the PFIAB favored such operations, but they were opposed by McNamara, Vance, and Under Secretary of State U. Alexis Johnson—who felt that improved intelligence was not so urgently needed as to justify the political risks of basing the planes on Okinawa and the almost certain disclosures that would follow. They also preferred to preserve the nominal cloak of secrecy around the A-12 until events required its use—although the existence of an A-12 type plane, the SR-71, had been acknowledged by President Johnson.[38]

On December 12, 1966, Deputy Defense Secretary Vance, Bureau of the Budget chief Charles Schultze, Helms, and presidential science adviser Donald Hornig met to consider the alternatives. Over Helms's objection, they suggested terminating the OXCART program, leading the DCI to request that the Air Force share the SR-71 fleet. Helms asked Duckett to prepare a letter to the President stating the CIA's reasons for wishing to continue the OXCART effort.[39]

Four days later, Schultze handed Helms a memo for the President requesting a decision either to turn part of the Air Force SR-71 fleet over to the CIA or to terminate the OXCART program entirely. Helms, having just received new information that he believed demonstrated the A-12's superiority, asked for another meeting after January 1 to review the data and requested that the memo to the President be withheld pending the meeting's outcome. Helms believed that the SR-71 could not match the photographic coverage provided by the A-12—since only one of the three SR-71 cameras, its Operational Objective System, was working near specification. It could photograph only a swath twenty-eight miles wide with a maximum resolution of twenty-eight to thirty inches when the target was directly underneath (at nadir).[40]

In contrast, the A-12's Type I camera could photograph a seventy-two-mile swath with a maximum resolution of twelve to eighteen inches at nadir. Oblique images had a resolution of fifty-four inches. Thus, the A-12 camera covered over twice as much territory, with better resolution. In addition, the A-12 could fly 2,000 to 5,000 feet higher and was faster, with a maximum speed of Mach 3.1.[41]

On December 27, a memo from deputy director of central intelligence Vice Adm. Rufus Taylor to national security adviser Walter Rostow noted that the memo that had been received the day before on the SR-71/OXCART issue "did not quite fully reflect Helms' opinion." Taylor noted that the SR-71 could not yet be considered interchangeable with the OXCART, because the OXCART had been fully operational for a year and demonstrated greater performance than the SR-71, "which has not yet achieved operational capability." In spite of Helms's request for delay, the Bureau of the Budget memorandum was submitted to President Johnson. On December 28, he approved the mothballing of the OXCART fleet and its phaseout by January 1968.[42]

The CIA had to develop a schedule for the phaseout of the A-12, an effort it code-named SCOPE COTTON. The agency informed Vance on January 10, 1967, that the A-12s would gradually be placed in storage, with the process to be completed by the end of January 1968. In May, the Deputy Defense Secretary directed that SR-71s would assume responsibility for Cuban overflights by July 1, 1967, and for Southeast Asian overflights by December 1, 1967. Until those capabilities were developed, OXCART was to remain on call, capable of conducting overflights of Southeast Asia (on a fifteen-day notice) and of Cuba (seven-day notice).[43]

In the midst of planning for termination of the program, the CIA continued advocating that an A-12 be employed for a special mission targeted on the Soviet Union. In May 1967, the 303 Committee received a CIA proposal to employ an OXCART, in conjunction with a U-2 carrying ELINT gear, to solve the mystery of the Tallinn system.[44] Although the CIA, Navy, and State Department had concluded that the system was air-defense oriented and had little ABM capability, the Defense Intelligence Agency and Army Intelligence suggested that considerable uncertainty remained, while Air Force Intelligence chief Jack Thomas argued that the Tallinn system "probably was designed for and now possesses an area anti-ballistic missile . . . capability."[45]

Photointerpreters insisted that twelve-to-eighteen-inch-resolution imagery was needed to determine the size of the missile, the antenna pattern, and configuration of the engagement radars associated with the Tallinn system. Unfortunately, attempts to photograph it using the high-resolution GAMBIT satellite had been defeated by cloud cover. In addition, ELINT analysts needed data about the Tallinn radars, but there were no U.S. intercept sites that could monitor emanations when the radars were being tested. The Soviets also never operated the radars in tracking and lock-on modes, preventing analysts from determining the frequency or other performance characteristics of the radars.[46]

To settle the question, the Office of Special Activities suggested a mission that would employ the OXCART's high-resolution camera along with a U-2 flying a peripheral ELINT mission. The highly classified proposal had an unclassified designation—Project SCOPE LOGIC—and a classified code name—Project UPWIND.[47]

OSA proposed flying an OXCART from the United States to the Baltic Sea, where it would rendezvous with a U-2. The A-12 would fly north of Norway and then turn south along the Soviet-Finnish border. Shortly before Leningrad, it would head west-southwest down the Baltic Sea, skirt the coasts of Estonia, Latvia, Lithuania, Poland, and East Germany, and then head west, returning to the United States. The entire flight would cover 11,000 miles, take eight hours and thirty-eight minutes, and require four aerial refuelings.[48]

Although the OXCART would not intrude into Soviet airspace, it would appear to Soviet radar network operators to be headed directly over Leningrad. OSA hoped that the OXCART's journey would provoke Soviet air defense personnel to activate the Tallinn system radars in order to track the aircraft. As the OXCART made its dash down the Baltic, its Type I camera would be filming the entire south coast, including Tallinn. If CIA analysts were correct and the system was designed to counter high-altitude aircraft at long ranges, then OXCART would be in jeopardy during its dash down the Baltic. However, the weapons experts in the Office of Scientific Intelligence believed that the A-12's speed and electronic countermeasures would protect it from standard Soviet SAM installations. The more vulnerable U-2 would be flying farther out to sea, beyond the range of the SAMs. CIA and Defense Department officials supported the proposal, but Secretary of State Dean Rusk strongly opposed it, and the 303 Committee never forwarded the proposal to Johnson.[49]

At the time Project UPWIND was under consideration, the CIA suggested another use for the OXCART—to determine if surface-to-surface missiles had been introduced into North Vietnam. Johnson asked for a proposal on the matter. The CIA briefed the 303 Committee, arguing that OXCART's camera was far superior to the cameras on drones or on the U-2, and the plane was far less vulnerable. While State and Defense were examining the proposed political risks, Helms raised the issue at the President's regular "Tuesday lunch" on May 16 and received approval for the deployment, which was dubbed BLACK SHIELD.[50]

The agency wasted no time, and the airlift of personnel and equipment to Kadena Air Base in Japan began the day after Johnson approved the project. In less than two weeks, three OXCART aircraft arrived. By May 29, the CIA contingent was ready to fly operational missions, and the detachment was alerted to be ready the following day.[51] There was no action that day, but an A-12 got its first taste of action May 31.

A torrential rainstorm blanketed Kadena Air Base that day. Paul Bacalis was there to witness the first launch and later recalled pilot Mel Vojvodich sitting in his plane on the runway awaiting orders. He also recalled aide Col. Slip Slater's question—"What do you say, boss?"—as well as his response—"Launch him!" Bacalis watched "orange balls coming out of the rear of the aircraft" and the plane "disappearing into the overcast."[52]

Vojvodich then headed for Vietnam, flying just off the East China coast, without difficulty, at Mach 3.0. He prepared to enter hostile territory, flying at Mach 3.1 and at 80,000 feet, through the "front door." He first flew over Haiphong and Hanoi, departed North Vietnam near Dien Bien Phu, refueled over Thailand, and penetrated enemy airspace near the demilitarized zone. Clear weather over the target area permitted photography of ten priority target categories as well as 70 of the 190 known SAM sites. In addition to SAM sites, the A-12's cameras photographed Haiphong/Cat Bi Airfield, the port at Haiphong, a military training area, an army barracks, and a segment of the Hanoi/Lao Cai railroad. Three hours and thirty-nine minutes after takeoff, Vojvodich arrived back in Kadena, where it was still pouring—a downpour that forced him to make three instrument approaches before landing.[53]

Over the next six weeks, the detachment was alerted for fifteen missions and flew seven. Four detected radar tracking signals but no hostile action resulted. By mid-July, the imagery obtained from those missions provided enough evidence for analysts to conclude that no surface-to-surface missiles had been deployed in North Vietnam. Those missions also provided imagery of airfields, naval bases, port areas, railroad segments, iron and steel works, and supply depots. Thus, June imagery showed a variety of fighter aircraft at Phuc Yen airfield as well as several different classes of ships. From August 16 to December 31, twenty-six missions were alerted, and fifteen flown. Not until October 28 did a North Vietnamese SAM site fire at an OXCART, an event that was captured on film. The photos showed missile smoke around the SAM site and pictures of the missile and its contrail.[54]

The missile fired that day did not endanger the spy plane, but several missiles fired two days later resulted in the closest call an OXCART would experience. During the plane's first pass over North Vietnam, pilot Denny Sullivan detected that he was being tracked by radar and that two SAM sites were prepared to launch, although neither did. During his second pass, the North Vietnamese tried to bring down the plane with a barrage of at least six missiles. In addition to seeing the vapor trails, Sullivan witnessed three missile detonations near the rear of the A-12, which was traveling at Mach 3.1 at about 84,000 feet. After he returned, an inspection of the aircraft revealed that a piece of metal had penetrated the underside of the right wing, passed through three layers of titanium, and lodged against a wing tank support structure. The fragment was not a warhead pellet but probably debris from one of the detonations.[55]

At least three of the missions conducted between August and December returned not only overhead photographs of North Vietnam but also oblique images of mainland China. The first leg of the September 17 OXCART mission took the plane to the northern reaches of North Vietnam and thus just south of China. During that portion of the flight, the plane's camera captured images of military installations, railroad segments, storage areas, and urban complexes. An October 4 mission produced photography of Chinese air installations, a barracks, electronics/communications sites, and naval and port facilities. Another mission later that month also yielded images of military facilities.[56]

As a result of the capabilities OXCART demonstrated in its missions, high-level presidential advisers and congressional leaders began to question the decision to terminate the program, and the issue was reopened. The CIA continued to argue that the A-12 was a superior aircraft because it flew higher and faster and had better cameras. The Air Force maintained that its two-seat SR-71 had a better collection of sensors, with three different cameras (search, high-resolution, and mapping), infrared detectors, side-looking radar, and ELINT collection gear.[57]

A series of missions, designated NICE GIRL, were conducted in an attempt to settle the issue. The two routes posed no risk to the pilots, since they flew over the continental United States. The first two missions were flown October 20 and October 25, 1967. The final missions were flown November 3, when an A-12 and an SR-71 flew identical flight paths, separated in time by one hour, from north to south, roughly above the Mississippi River. The data collected during the missions were evaluated by representatives of the CIA, DIA, and other Defense Department intelligence organizations.[58]

The results proved inconclusive, with both photographic systems providing imagery of sufficient quality for analysis. The A-12's Type I camera with its seventy-two-mile swath width and 5,000-foot film supply proved superior to the SR-71's Operational Objective camera with its twenty-eight-mile swath and 3,300-foot film supply. On the other hand, the SR-71's infrared, imaging radar, and electronic and communications intelligence equipment provided some unique intelligence not available from the A-12. Air Force planners admitted that some of this equipment would have to be sacrificed to provide the SR-71 with electronic countermeasures gear when it flew over regions of the world more hostile than the central United States.[59]

Although the flyoff did not settle the question of which aircraft was superior, OXCART won a temporary reprieve in late November 1967 when the Johnson administration decided to keep both fleets for the time being. But with war costs rising, a challenge to maintaining competing reconnaissance programs was bound to occur again.[60]

A December 29, 1967, memo from Deputy Defense Secretary Paul Nitze to Gen. Earle G. Wheeler, Chairman of the Joint Chiefs of Staff, and Alexander Flax, director of NRO, announced the decision to maintain an OXCART capability, consisting of five operational aircraft, through June 30, 1968. The memo also called for planning for the introduction of the SR-71 into reconnaissance operations in North Vietnam "as rapidly as

ECM [electronic countermeasures] implementation and other program considerations will permit."[61]

BLACK SHIELD missions continued during the first three months of 1968, with six missions flown of the fifteen alerted—four over Vietnam and two over North Korea. The last OXCART overflight of Vietnam occurred on March 8. On January 26, an A-12 overflew North Korea for the first time, in response to the North Korean seizure three days earlier of the USS *Pueblo*, a signals intelligence ship. The objective was to discover where the *Pueblo* was being held, and whether North Korea was preparing any large-scale hostile move in the wake of the incident.[62] The A-12 pilot, Frank Murray, recounted his flight:

> I left Kadena, topped-off, then entered northern airspace over the Sea of Japan via the Korean Straits. My first pass started off near Vladivostok, then with the camera on I flew down the east coast of North Korea where we thought the boat was. As I approached Wonsan I could see the *Pueblo* through my view sight. The harbour was all iced up except at the very entrance and there she was, sitting off to the right of the main entrance. I continued to the border with South Korea, completed a 180-degree turn and flew back over North Korea. I made four passes, photographing the whole of North Korea from the DMZ to the Yalu border. As far as I knew, I was undetected throughout the flight but when I got back to Kadena some folks told me that the Chinese had detected me and told the North Koreans, but they never reacted.[63]

Murray's mission, which showed no signs of any upcoming action by North Korea, was followed by two further missions on February 19 and May 8. To the extent those missions responded to DIA requirements, they included coverage of seven jet-capable airfields, naval facilities (including the Mayang Do submarine facility), and the North Korean–Chinese border. Dean Rusk had been reluctant to approve a second overflight for fear that the plane might be brought down in hostile territory, but was assured the A-12 would slice through North Korea in seven minutes and was unlikely to land in either China or North Vietnam.[64]

In the midst of the overflights, the question of OXCART's future had remained open, as national security adviser Walter Rostow, members of the PFIAB, key congressmen, and the President's Scientific Advisory Committee questioned whether the program should be terminated. A new study was ordered and completed in spring 1968. Analysts considered four alternatives—transferring the entire OXCART fleet to SAC by October 31, 1968, and turning A-12 test aircraft over to the SR-71 test facility; transferring all OXCART aircraft to SAC and storing eight SR-71s; closing the OXCART home base and collocating the fleet with SR-71s at Beale AFB in California, but with the CIA retaining control and management; continuing OXCART operations at its own base under CIA control and management.[65]

Not surprisingly, Helms preferred the last option, a position he conveyed to Nitze, Hornig, and NRO director Al Flax in an April 18 memo. He questioned the collocation option on the grounds of security and the lower cost figures associated with combining the two fleets. The key point, he argued, was the desirability of retaining a covert reconnaissance capability under civilian management.[66]

On May 16, Clark Clifford, the new Secretary of Defense, reaffirmed the original decision, and President Johnson confirmed it on May 21. Two months earlier, in accord with Vance's orders, SR-71s had begun arriving at Kadena to take over the BLACK SHIELD mission. After the May 8 mission over North Korea, members of the Kadena detachment were advised to pack their bags and prepare to return home. By mid-June, all the OXCARTs were back in the United States, their espionage careers prematurely terminated.[67]

CATS AND BIRDS

While portions of the directorate focused on aerial and underwater reconnaissance, the Office of Research and Development was busy pursuing a variety of projects. By mid-1968, Robert Chapman, a geophysicist, was in his fourth year as head of ORD; he had become acting director in May 1964 and director in March 1965.[68]

ORD continued experimentation on both humans and animals. In 1968, the office established a joint program, Project OFTEN, with the Army Chemical Corps at Edgewood Arsenal Research Laboratories (EARL) in Maryland to study the effects of assorted drugs on human and animal subjects. The Army not only assisted ORD in building a computerized database for drug testing but also supplied military volunteers for some of the experiments.[69]

The research and development office paid EARL $37,000 to perform new tests on a compound that Edgewood had dubbed "EA 3167" and previously tested on volunteers. ORD's Medical and Behavioral Sciences Division suspected that EA 3167, a powerful incapacitant, could be administered through a handshake or other casual contact. In 1971, it contracted with Edgewood for additional tests of EA 3167. The contract ended in 1973 before any tests could be performed, according to the EARL official who oversaw the contract.[70]

Cats and dogs did not have the option of volunteering. Victor Marchetti, who served as executive assistant to the deputy DCI during the late 1960s, recalled an attempt to turn cats into mobile bugging devices—a project commonly referred to as "Acoustic Kitty." The project was "more than just a goofy operation," according to Marchetti. The problem with the microphones of the day was that they picked up all the sound in a room—from voices to tinkling glasses—often producing recordings in which conversation could not be filtered out from other noises. A bug placed in the couch of a Chinese diplomat in France proved ineffective because of the squeaking noises that drowned out conversations, not only when the diplomat was using it for his frequent sexual escapades but when visitors were simply sitting.[71]

The concept behind the Acoustic Kitty project was that unlike a mechanical bugging device, a cat's ear had a cochlea, as did a human ear, that could filter out irrelevant noise. Project staffers attempted to train a cat to listen to conversations and not to the background noise—as an interim step in designing a microphone that could filter out extraneous noise.[72] Then, according to Marchetti,

> they slit the cat open, put batteries in him, wired him up. The tail was used as an antenna. They made a monstrosity. They tested him and tested him. They found he would walk off the job when he got hungry, so they put another wire in to override that. Finally, they're ready. They took it out to a park bench and said "Listen to those two guys. Don't listen to anything else—not the birds, no cat or dog—just those two guys!". . . They put him out of the van, and a taxi comes and runs him over. There they were, sitting in the van with all those dials, and the cat was dead![73]

An undated agency memo that was heavily redacted, possibly largely out of embarrassment, on "[Deleted] Views on Trained Cats [Deleted] for [Deleted] Use," apparently quashed the project. The memo stated that "the program would not lend itself in a practical sense to our highly specialized needs." It also concluded that "the environmental and security factors in using this technique in a real foreign situation force us to conclude that . . . it would not be practical."[74] That would seem to have been an obvious conclusion that staffers could have reached before the first cat was cut open.

In the late 1960s, ORD was also interested in attempting to turn birds—both real and mechanical ones—into spies. One project followed from the refusal, first by the 303 Committee in 1967 and then by President Johnson, to approve an A-12 mission to get better imagery on the Flat Twin engagement radar associated with the Tallinn system.[75]

Over a period of five to six months in California, ORD trained a red-tailed hawk to carry a camera over the site and return with its photographs. The process involved construction of a wooden model of a Flat Twin so that the red-tailed spy would know when to activate the camera—which could take only a single photograph—that would be hung around its neck.* But after training was completed, the CIA discovered that legislation restricted the transport of the bird.[76] Not surprisingly, no one had thought to write a national security exemption into the law.

ORD turned to an unprotected crow, which completed its training in half the time. But the crow would have to be escorted much of the way, carried on a boat up the Baltic and through the canals in Denmark and Sweden. Knowing that the Soviets paid close attention to boat movements through the canals, the CIA decided to cancel the project.[77]

Sometimes the spies were just supposed to look like birds, in one way or another. The objective of another late 1960s ORD project, appropriately code-named ORNITHOPTER (an airplane that flaps its wings), was to produce small mechanical birds, which could perch on windowsills while their little microphone-equipped bodies eavesdropped on conversations within the room.[78]

Project AQUILINE was intended to produce a Remotely Piloted Vehicle (RPV) that would have a radar profile similar to a condor and carry photographic, ELINT, and air-sampling sensors. Its targets were to include the Chinese missile test center and the nuclear test site at Lop Nur and possibly Sary Shagan and the Flat Twin radar that had been the target of Project UPWIND. The vehicle could not be seen or heard at 1,000 feet.

---

*The CIA also tried on at least one occasion to train pigeons to carry a camera and move their heads to activate the device. The initial test run involved releasing a camera-carrying pigeon in the Washington, D.C., area. Almost two days after its release, the pigeon returned to the release site—on foot. The camera around its neck was too heavy to permit sustained flight.

But a key problem emerged during development—directing AQUILINE's movements after it passed over the horizon. Initial experiments employed C-130s, but such aircraft could not communicate with the AQUILINE vehicles if they were more than 250 miles away. U-2s, because of their high altitude, would theoretically permit communication and guidance at far greater distances—except that when flying at 70,000 feet, U-2 pilots would have too many other tasks to permit them to direct the remote spy's movements. Eventually, the program was terminated—although much of the development work was turned over to Israel, which used it in developing its RPVs.[79]

Shortly after the end of AQUILINE, an ORD employee, initially using his own funds, bought a twin-engine model plane set, put a television camera in its belly, and convinced the agency to continue work on the project. Once again a C-130, flying in the same direction, was used to control the aerial spy, which proved capable of producing photographs with resolution of three feet. The CIA turned the technology over to the Army, which used it in its Aquila RPV.[80]

DIFFERENCES OF OPINION

On January 20, 1969, Richard Nixon, having eked out a close victory over Hubert Humphrey in the November elections, became the thirty-seventh president of the United States. On March 21, his Secretary of Defense, Melvin Laird, during prolonged testimony before a skeptical Senate Foreign Relations Committee's subcommittee on disarmament, announced that the Soviet Union had embarked on a buildup of its strategic nuclear forces aimed at wiping out America's ICBM force in a single blow. "There is no question about that," he added.[81]

A week earlier, in accord with a recommendation by the Joint Chiefs of Staff, Nixon had announced that he was scrapping the Johnson administration's plans for the Sentinel ABM defense system. Sentinel's objective had been to protect urban areas from a Chinese attack or a limited Soviet attack, but the proposal had been the focus of protests—particularly from the fifteen metropolitan areas around which the nuclear-armed ABMs were to be installed. The new administration explained that it was changing the system's name and objective. The goal of Safeguard, as it was now called, would be to protect not the U.S. population but the country's land-based missile force—the ICBMs stored in silos in Nebraska, Wyoming, North and South Dakota, Missouri, Kansas, and Arkansas—from a Soviet first strike.[82] The strategic theory was simple. By ensuring that U.S. missiles would survive any Soviet attempt to destroy them in their silos, the United States would preserve its retaliatory capability, and any Soviet incentive to engage in a first strike would be removed.

The feasibility of Safeguard was challenged by both politicians and scientists, including Herbert Scoville, who had left the Arms Control and Disarmament Agency with the advent of the new administration. Opponents suggested that the exposed radars and command and control centers required to operate the system could easily be neutralized, in contrast to ICBMs in hardened silos. The radars could be blinded by the first nuclear detonations. The capability of radars to sort out missiles from debris, decoys, and chaff was questioned, as was the ability of the system's computers to manage a massive missile-against-missile engagement. In addition, it was argued that the Soviets could build additional ICBMs more cheaply than the United States could build the antimissiles to knock them down.[83]

An even more fundamental question revolved around a Soviet missile, designated the SS-9 or Scarp by the U.S. intelligence community. First deployed in 1966, the missile was estimated to weigh 450,000 pounds, stand ten stories high, and be capable of carrying a twenty-five-megaton warhead (weighing between 10,000 and 15,000 pounds) on a 7,000-mile journey. In August and September 1968, the United States monitored an SS-9 test in which three separate warheads, each judged to be capable of carrying enough nuclear material for a five-megaton blast, were dispensed by the missile.[84]

The question facing the intelligence community was whether the new Mod-4 version of the SS-9 was the Soviet Union's first missile with Multiple Independent Reentry Vehicles—MIRVs. A missile with three independently targetable warheads could drop each one on a different target. If they were sufficiently accurate, the warheads would have a high probability of destroying even hardened missile silos—and a Soviet force of 500 SS-9s would have a good chance of destroying a substantial portion of the Strategic Air Command's 1,000 ICBMs. A conclusion that the new version of the SS-9 carried three accurate MIRVed warheads, and would be deployed in sufficient numbers, would provide support to the administration's argument that the United States needed to deploy Safeguard. In contrast, a missile with multiple reentry but not independently targetable warheads—with MRVs—could only dump its warheads within a very narrow area.

The capabilities of the SS-9 Mod-4 had been addressed five months earlier in the annual national intelligence estimate on Soviet strategic forces (NIE 11-8-68). The estimate observed that the three-warhead tests were "not incompatible with tests leading to a multiple independently-targeted reentry vehicle (MIRV) capability." The study observed that "we believe the Soviets could achieve an operational MRV employing three RVs in a modified SS-9 payload by late 1969." However, the reentry vehicle system, as observed, would "degrade the overall accuracy and reliability of the SS-9 system." Thus, an SS-9 with three warheads could still be effective against a single target but not multiple targets. MIRVs that could be employed against Minuteman silos probably could not be deployed until 1972.[85]

The intelligence community's collective judgment was accepted by outgoing Defense Secretary Clark Clifford, whose January 1969 posture statement declared the modified SS-9 triplet to be a MRV missile but not a MIRVed missile.[86] Although the issue did not become public until March, the debate within the administration was already under way within weeks after Nixon assumed the presidency.

Providing some of the intellectual ammunition for the new administration's view was the Air Force's Foreign Technology Division (FTD). FTD argued that the Mod-4 might possess some primitive characteristics of a MIRV. If the Soviets could delay the separation of each reentry vehicle from the launch platform for seconds or even a fraction of a second, they could send the missiles off on different ballistic paths. If the targets were close enough together, the SS-9 would be the functional equivalent of a MIRVed missile.[87]

Among those left unconvinced by such arguments was David Brandwein, Carl Duckett's successor as the director of the Foreign Missile and Space Analysis Center. On February 5, he wrote in his personal notebook that Lloyd Lauderdale had passed him a draft of a memo on the SS-9/triple RV prepared for John Foster, the Defense Department's research and engineering chief. He observed that "it was pretty much the . . . party line, which says it could be made into a MIRV, they might do it without our knowing it, and it looks like this is what the Sovs have in mind. I disagree! My gut feeling is that it is MRV, not MIRV, and that is all it will ever be."[88]

For the next six weeks, Brandwein would attend a variety of meetings on the SS-9 triplet as the CIA and Defense Department battled over the MIRV issue—the outcome of which could support or undermine the new administration's ABM program. Attendance at some meetings was part of a process of debate between rival viewpoints; at others, the objective was to ensure that the views of FMSAC and the CIA were represented along with those of the Defense Department.

On February 7, Brandwein attended a DOD presentation to Secretary of the Air Force Harold Brown, along with Wayne Boring, a CIA analyst. Brandwein recorded in his diary that "as soon as we got into Brown's office he [Boring] proceeded to tell Lloyd [Wilson of DDR&E] why the DDR&E . . . diagnosis of the SS-9/Triple RV = MIRV was much too positive. He had . . . found all the weaknesses which I had found independently! Wayne said I was grinning like a cat & that he felt like standing up and cheering! Afterwards Wilson was thoroughly deflated."[89]

But such efforts had no impact on Laird or the administration's commitment to Safeguard. During his Senate testimony, Laird predicted that unless the United States deployed such an ABM system, the Soviets would have a first-strike capability in five years. At the time, there were only 228 SS-9s deployed, but Laird pointed to intelligence indicating that the Soviets had prepared six new SS-9 silos in December in an entirely new missile field. He suggested that might indicate a new wave of deployment—contradicting the view expressed in NIE 11-8-68 that deployment would soon come to a halt.[90]

Research and engineering director Foster, convinced of the SS-9 MIRV potential by FTD's analysis, provided some specific numbers during congressional testimony that spring. He argued that by the mid-1970s, the Soviet strategic rocket forces could have 420 MIRVed SS-9s with sufficient accuracy and reliability to wipe out 95 percent of the Minuteman force in a single strike. In such briefings, Foster ignored the cost to the Soviets for each missile ($25–30 million) as well as the need to reprogram missiles during flight.[91]

Although Foster was unable to convince Brandwein, Duckett, or others from the CIA with such arguments, he did, at least for as long as it would matter, convince national security adviser Henry Kissinger. The consequence was a meeting in the White House Situation Room on Memorial Day during which Kissinger "beat up on" DCI Richard Helms, Deputy Director for Intelligence R. Jack Smith, Abbot Smith, chairman of the Board of National Estimates, and presumably Duckett, who was also in attendance, for their heretical views on the SS-9—views that were preventing Kissinger from obtaining congressional funding for Safeguard.[92]

Between Laird's March testimony and Kissinger's tantrum, further SS-9 testing seemed to strengthen the Pentagon's position. From April 20 to mid-May, three SS-9 triplets were tested. After analysis of the telemetry, TRW concluded that the triplets were landing in a triangular pattern that resembled the Minuteman deployment pattern. Analysts used such findings to claim that even if the SS-9 triplet was not a true MIRV, it was the "functional equivalent" of one—able to attack three distinct, geographically separated targets.[93]

For a brief period, Laird appeared to believe that new evidence showed the SS-9 Mod-4 to be more than functionally equivalent. On June 6, Duckett asked Brandwein to investigate Laird's claim to Helms that the Defense Intelligence Agency had demonstrated that the last SS-9 MRV test showed a three-in-a-line pattern, and that such evidence proved that a MIRVed missile was involved. Brandwein checked into the story and determined that Laird had been unintentionally misinformed by his research and engineering chief, John Foster, who at the time believed the evidence showed three warheads in a line because the refined, and contrary, data had not been passed on to him by an aide.[94]

By mid-June, the intelligence community was working on a "memorandum to holders" of NIE 11-8-68. Such memos were sometimes prepared to update portions of NIEs concerning issues of immediate importance. On June 12, the United States Intelligence Board had agreed to a memorandum suggesting that the Soviet Union's actions to improve its nuclear forces fell short of an effort to achieve a first-strike capability.[95]

On Saturday June 13, the day after the USIB meeting, Helms, Abbot Smith, Jack Smith, Duckett, and Brandwein were summoned to a meeting with Kissinger and officials from Defense, State, and the NSC Staff. According to Brandwein, "Kissinger made it pretty plain he was unhappy with it! He kept saying he didn't want to influence our judgements—but! It was a difficult 3 hours. Kissinger kept saying 'his most important client' wanted the facts separated from the judgements and identified as such. He also kept claiming he wasn't a technical man, neither was his client—but the 'facts' are the technical details."[96]

Kissinger asked that the memorandum be rewritten to provide more clarification of some points and additional discussion pro and con about the MRV-MIRV issue, including more evidence of the judgment that the SS-9 was not MIRVed. Smith rewrote the draft with assistance from several FMSAC staffers as well as Brandwein, who rewrote the sections on "Is it a MIRV?" and the SS-9 range, but did not change the conclusion.[97]

Then, on June 19, Nixon told a press conference that in proposing Safeguard, he did so "on intelligence information at that time," and since that time, "new intelligence . . . with regard to Soviet success in testing multiple reentry vehicles . . . has convinced me that Safeguard is even more important."[98]

Meanwhile, Duckett had been assigned to help Kissinger understand the technical issues involved. Kissinger referred to Duckett as "Professor" because of his ability to explain technical matters in understandable terms, and Duckett later recalled the relationship:

> What was difficult was, when you have the national security adviser saying, "Look, the president of the United States and secretary of defense have said the following. Now, are you telling me that you are going to argue with them. And the answer was, 'No sir, I'm not going to argue with them, other than to tell you that they're wrong.' But that's when a senior intelligence officer . . . has to be prepared to say, the fact is, we do have enough information . . . And in this case, we felt the technical argument was overwhelming."[99]

On June 23, at a hearing before the Senate Foreign Relations Committee, Richard Helms and Melvin Laird sat side by side. Helms noted that since he had last briefed the committee, the Soviets had conducted two additional long-range tests of the SS-9, and that "the intelligence community is in agreement that vehicles in these tests were not independently guided."[100] Laird, however, pointed to the recent SS-9 tests and argued that although the data were not conclusive, they were consistent with a MIRV capability. In addition, he noted that the level of deployment was not tapering off. He also claimed that there were no differences with regard to the meaning of the intelligence data, only an institutional difference, with the Defense Department planning for the worst case.[101]

But the battle continued behind the scenes. Brandwein addressed the President's Science Advisory Committee on June 25 and gave a two-hour briefing on the SS-9, covering accuracy, range, and whether it was MIRVed. After the FMSAC director presented both sides of the argument, PSAC member Richard Latter, Brandwein wrote, "went on to a blackboard lecture to tell them how *his* calculations showed SS-9 accuracy had improved. I didn't think he convinced the others."[102]

With the issue still before the Senate, and no clear winner, Duckett prepared a July 17 briefing that, he would recall, was "as objective as I know how to do a paper." With only senators allowed on the floor, Henry Jackson of Washington read the paper. Several weeks later, on August 5, Foster addressed a House subcommittee in closed session. He acknowledged that the evidence did not prove without question that the SS-9 was MIRVed but argued that "it very strongly indicates that it is a MIRV."[103]

On August 6, the attempt to stop Safeguard or limit it to a research and development program failed. Vice-President Spiro Agnew broke a fifty-fifty Senate tie in favor of the program. Brandwein later observed that "we lost that battle . . . I mean, I was convinced that the SS-9 was not MIRVed, was not a first-strike weapon, but we just couldn't talk people into it."[104]*

CHECKROTE

One of ORD's most successful projects in the late 1960s that aided U.S. monitoring of launches from the Shuangchengzi missile test complex (SCMC) was the CHECKROTE over-the-horizon radar. Installation of CHECKROTE on Taiwan began in May 1965, and operations started on August 1, 1966.[105]

The United States suspected that the PRC was testing medium- or possibly intermediate-range missiles at the complex, making it necessary to design the radar to detect the missile skin rather than the enhanced image. Thus, the radar had to be three times more sensitive than EARTHLING. CHECKROTE's format was patterned after EARTHLING's, but improved performance was obtained by increasing its power and antenna performance. CHECKROTE's range resolution was also improved, to twenty times better than EARTHLING's—an improvement that was crucial to the acquisition of missile trajectory information.[106]

The first missile detections from Shuangchengzi were made on December 5, 1966. Through September 1968, CHECKROTE identified thirty-eight suspected missile launches—three in 1966, twenty-nine in 1967, and six in 1968. Among the missiles being tested at the time was the CSS-2 intermediate-range missile, with a range of 1,735 miles; it became "the backbone of the Chinese missile force." Analysts studied the detected signatures to determine if they were consistent with characteristics of missiles expected to be launched from SCMC and with expected radar performance. The conclusion was that the great majority of the signatures collected were bona fide detections. By spring 1969, a major upgrade of the target-identification capabilities of CHECKROTE was in progress.[107]

---

*The CIA's view proved correct. The SS-9 Mod-4 was never deployed, apparently because it could not be made sufficiently accurate. The first genuine MIRV was tested on the SS-18 Mod-2 in August 1973. A later SS-18 Mod was deployed with MIRVs. The first operational missile to be deployed with MIRVs was the SS-19 Mod-1 in December 1974. (Kirsten Lundberg, "The SS-19 Controversy: Intelligence as Political Football," Kennedy School of Government, Harvard University, 1989, p. 20.)

NEW BIRDS IN SPACE

In October 1966, Richard Lee Stallings, a senior official of the Office of ELINT, arrived in Australia to oversee the construction of the RHYOLITE ground station at Pine Gap, near Alice Springs in central Australia. Earlier, Stallings had been stationed in West Germany, where he was responsible for management of OEL's efforts in that country and the coordination of the CIA's SIGINT activities with those of the West German Federal Intelligence Service (BND). Stallings remained in Canberra until final arrangements for establishment of the station had been made, then moved to Alice Springs toward the end of January 1967.[108]

OEL's Ground Systems Division operated the station on behalf of RHYOLITE's "owner"—the Office of Special Projects. Back in Washington, John McMahon, who had become deputy director of OSP, directed the construction effort. As he put it, simply and emphatically, many years later, "I built Pine Gap."[109]

Before the end of 1968, the first two radomes (radar domes), made of Perspex and mounted on concrete structures, had been built. The radomes, about 110 feet and 70 feet, respectively, protected the enclosed antenna against dust, wind, and the prying cameras of Soviet spy satellites. Construction of the third and fourth radomes apparently began in November 1968; they were completed in mid-1969. In early December 1968, with initial construction of the facility completed, Stallings was succeeded by Harry E. Fitzwater, who would remain at the station until 1972.[110]

By the time Stallings departed, the Air Force's "alternative" to RHYOLITE had already made it into space. Indeed, the first CANYON launch attracted the attention of the *New York Times*'s John Noble Wilford. His August 7, 1968, article, "A Secret Payload Is Orbited by U.S.," noted that the satellite, launched from Cape Kennedy on an Atlas-Agena rocket, carried a "super-secret payload." In that pre-Watergate era, launch officials told inquisitive reporters, "You wouldn't want to know what's on that bird. It's that secret." The secrecy resulted in the first closed launch from the Cape since 1963. The erroneous belief persisted for two decades afterward that the CANYON launches were part of Program 949, a program to detect missile launches via the heat emitted by the missiles.[111]

Ultimately, seven CANYON spacecraft, bearing the numerical designations 7501 through 7507, were orbited, the second on April 12, 1969. Six were successful. Each CANYON spacecraft transmitted its intercepted material to a ground station at Bad Aibling, Germany.* Approximately two months after the launch of 7502, another Atlas-Agena D blasted off from Cape Kennedy. This time, rather than placing a spacecraft in an approximately 20,000- by 24,000-mile orbit with a 9.9-degree inclination, the rocket sent the first RHYOLITE, 7601, into geostationary orbit above the equator just south of Borneo. From that location, it could intercept the telemetry signals from solid-fueled missiles fired from Plesetsk, as well as monitor SLBMs fired from the White Sea. Once RHYOLITE was in orbit, its antenna, about sixty to seventy feet in diameter, was unfurled, and after a period of testing, it began operations. Because of the similarities between the CANYON and RHYOLITE launches, which employed Atlas-Agena Ds and were launched from Cape Kennedy into high-altitude orbits, outside observers also believed 7601 to be a Program 949 satellite.[112]

The primary mission of "Bird 1," as Pine Gap personnel called 7601, was to intercept the telemetry from Soviet missile tests. But it was soon discovered that 7601 also had a significant capability against communications in the VHF and UHF bands, and it was used to monitor both the Indo-Pakistani War in 1971 and the Vietnam theater.[113]

For part of 1969, it seemed that RHYOLITE might be the only one of Wheelon's satellite programs that would make it off the drawing board and onto the launchpad. The HEXAGON/KH-9 program was abruptly canceled. The budget crunch, created by the Vietnam War and Lyndon Johnson's Great Society, threatened to end the HEXAGON program before it reached the launch stage.[114]

As a substitute, plans code-named HIGHER BOY were developed to put some KH-8/GAMBIT spacecraft into an area surveillance orbit. Such ad hoc substitutions were not acceptable to those running the reconnaissance program. In an attempt to restart the flow of funds, Roland Inlow, chairman of the Committee on Imagery Requirements and Exploitation (which had replaced the Committee on Overhead Reconnaissance in 1967), was sent to talk to James Schlesinger, who was responsible for na-

---

*A number of CANYON spacecraft often had problems communicating with the Bad Aibling ground station. However, over the life of the program, CANYON satellites produced a massive volume of intercepted material—covering North Vietnam, the Soviet Union, China, and the Middle East. The volume was so great that the United States arranged with Canada and Britain to have their SIGINT services provide analysts in exchange for access to the CANYON product. Unfortunately, one of the British personnel assigned to translate CANYON's Soviet intercepts was Geoffrey Prime—who provided the Soviet Union with details of the program.

tional security programs at the Bureau of the Budget. Inlow explained that the KH-9 was essential to arms control verification, and the money began to flow again.[115]

One last delay occurred in late 1970 as the spacecraft was being prepared for a January launch. A minor change, involving a single resistor, was ordered on paper but never actually made. The result was catastrophic damage to the film supply during thermal tests. Preparations then were begun to make the second HEXAGON vehicle the first to fly.[116]

The spacecraft lifted off from a Vandenberg AFB launchpad on June 15, 1971, propelled into space by a Titan 3D with 3 million pounds of thrust. The newest addition to the U.S. reconnaissance arsenal was a 30,000-pound cylinder, forty feet long and ten feet in diameter. Its size enabled it to host a variety of other projects. Thus, the new-generation surveillance satellites often carried antennae for SIGINT collection and relaying messages from U.S. covert agents in the Soviet Union and elsewhere. The additional missions often led NRO to keep the spacecraft in orbit even after all the film had been returned to earth. HEXAGON launches also often carried a second payload, a ferret spacecraft designated 989 and designed to detect and record the signals from Soviet and other radar systems.[117]

The camera system, designated the KH-9, consisted of two cameras with 60-inch lenses. The cameras could operate individually or be employed to obtain overlapping photos of a target—which could then be used with a stereoscope to extract additional information about a target's dimensions. In addition, the cameras could produce images covering a much wider area than the KH-4B but with a resolution of two feet, almost as good as the eighteen-inch resolution of the KH-7. Whereas the KH-4B camera system had a swath width of 40-by-180 miles, the KH-9 system was twice that—80-by-360 miles; the result was a fourfold increase in the territory that could be covered by a single photo. And whereas the KH-4B returned two film capsules, the KH-9 returned four.[118]

The KH-9 represented a major advance in U.S. reconnaissance capabilities. The greater film capacity meant longer lifetimes, and in normal circumstances, film could be returned as frequently as with the KH-4B. Thus, in the early days of the program, the KH-9 returned film capsules every three or four days. In emergencies, an incomplete reel could be returned without drastic damage to the overall mission. But most important, the tremendous swath width of the KH-9 meant an ability to conduct true wide-area searches to find new missile fields, test ranges, and nuclear facilities. It also meant that a greater number of requests for photography could be accommodated because of the ability to incorporate a wider area in a single scene. Thus, lower-priority targets had a better chance of being photographed.[119]

The ability of the KH-9 to photograph huge chunks of territory was a delight to the mappers of the newly created Defense Mapping Agency. The fewer photos needed to cover a part of the world, the easier it was to construct an accurate map. When the KH-9 program was terminated, the mappers at DMA "wept blood," according to one intelligence official.[120]

The first KH-9, designated 1901, operated in an elliptical 114-by-186-mile orbit, with a 96.4-degree inclination. The inclination ensured that 1901 not only covered the entire earth from pole to pole in the course of its operations but also that its orbit was sun-synchronous—meaning that each daylight pass over an area could be made at an identical sun-angle and thus avoid differences in pictures of the same area that might result when photos were taken from different angles. Each ground track repeated every three and a half days. On days when a particular area was overflown, it was overflown twice, once in daylight and once in darkness.[121]

Between its launch on June 15 and its destructive reentry on July 6, fifty-two days later, 1901's operators checked out its imaging, communications, and propulsion systems. It was also extensively calibrated to determine how well the new camera system held up to its theoretical promise. As with all new satellites, photographs were taken of a variety of locations in the United States and where the dimensions of the target and energy emissions could be precisely determined.[122] Once checkout was completed, 1901 could begin snapping pictures of the usual targets of interest—including a variety of Soviet and Chinese nuclear and missile installations.

PROJECT IMPACT

Reconnaissance was not the only directorate activity conducted to support U.S. efforts in Vietnam. OSI's Project IMPACT, whose objective was to diagnose the nature of epidemics, predict their spread, and estimate their impact on military and civilian activities, was employed in an attempt to guide U.S. military actions.[123]

IMPACT's earliest success was in December 1966, when OSI identified an outbreak of meningitis in China based on reports portraying the disease as viral encephalitis but stating that officials were using antibiotics to fight the epidemic, an ineffective medical strategy against encephalitis. IMPACT analysts proceeded to predict the spread of the disease from one province to the next and to note how it hampered the movements and activities of the Red Guard.[124]

In summer 1968, a new strain of influenza rolled out of China and into a substantial portion of the world, including Vietnam. Project IMPACT was assigned to forecast and quantify the effects upon the Vietcong (VC) and North Vietnamese Army (NVA). The effort involved establishing a chronology of the times and locations of outbreaks, using reports over the 1968–1970 period—including any quantifiable figures on the rates of sickness and the frequency of VC-NVA requests for drugs and other medical supplies.[125]

A pattern evolved in which occurrence of the flu was a function of traffic density and personnel moving south from North Vietnam, and the trend coincided with the dry season—when the bulk of all military supplies moved down the Ho Chi Minh Trail. Incapacitation rates ranged from about 40 to 70 percent, and analysts had very good evidence that except for isolation and quarantine of patients, the enemy had no capability to protect VC-NVA personnel by mass vaccinations.[126]

In December 1970, reports of outbreaks among VC-NVA forces in the North Vietnam–Laos border area increased, indicating the stage was set for the beginning of the 1971 influenza epidemic there. Members of the CIA's Office of the Special Assistant for Vietnamese Affairs (SAVA) were consulted, and analysts used their data on traffic routes, troop concentration, and location of way stations to construct a model of the movement of the flu epidemic. Tchepone was a key junction on the Communist road network that extended into the south. If Tchepone became infected, the disease would move from way station to way station north and south in Laos and back to North Vietnam.[127]

In late December, there were indications that the NVA 4th and 16th AAA Battalions at Tchepone had become infected. It was estimated that in the primary infected area of Quang Binh province, the epidemic would peak about January 30, and in the secondary infected areas south of Tchepone, the peak would occur about mid-February. An overall 50 percent infection rate was calculated for VC-NVA personnel in those areas, and estimates were that half of those infected would be incapable of performing normal duties for about one week.[128]

Indigenous intelligence teams operating in Laos and Cambodia were warned to take special precautions during the peak influenza periods. South Vietnamese Army units entered Laos and conducted extensive operations near Tchepone and other areas around the primary infectious zone during February, hoping to take advantage of a weakened enemy. However, these operations weren't mounted until just after the time analysts predicted the enemy would be most affected. As a result, the combat effectiveness of the VC-NVA forces was probably degraded to a lesser degree than if the operations had been launched earlier.[129]

6

EMPIRE

By 1972, Duckett's leadership had helped solidify the position of the Directorate of Science and Technology, which had become a worldwide enterprise—with CORONA, HEXAGON/KH-9, and RHYOLITE spacecraft orbiting the earth, U-2s patrolling the skies, and ELINT stations in Iran and Norway intercepting Soviet missile telemetry. In Washington, the Foreign Missile and Space Analysis Center and OSI were analyzing foreign nuclear and missile programs. ORD, meanwhile, was looking toward the future.

The directorate had also exhibited unusual organizational stability. The six offices Duckett had inherited—Computer Services, Special Projects, Special Activities, Research and Development, ELINT, and Scientific Intelligence—along with FMSAC, were still on the directorate's organizational chart. Nor had there been any additions. That would change, with the reorganization of the responsibilities of FMSAC and OSI, the renaming and expansion of the mandate of Special Projects, and the acquisition of units that had been part of the intelligence and operations directorates.

Meanwhile, the CIA role in the U-2 effort it had forged would end in 1974. The directorate would also enter into new areas—some of which, such as covert communications, would become permanent missions. Others such as parapsychology would, fortunately, not survive much longer than Duckett's tenure.

NEW ACQUISITIONS

Three organizational changes occurred within the science and technology directorate in 1973. In September, responsibility for the analysis of the characteristics and capabilities of defensive missile and other weapons systems was transferred from OSI to FMSAC, which then became the Office of Weapons Intelligence (OWI).[1]

Because the analysis of weapons systems had significant common elements—such as the dependence on telemetry and data processing techniques—all weapons research was consolidated in a single office. OSI remained responsible for producing finished intelligence on foreign nuclear capabilities, biological and chemical warfare, advanced technologies, and the physical and life sciences.[2]

The transfer of the National Photographic Interpretation Center from the intelligence directorate to DS&T had been in the works for several years. By 1973, NPIC was no longer operating over a car dealership on K Street. In 1962, Defense Secretary Robert McNamara and members of the President's Foreign Intelligence Advisory Board visited and were shocked by the conditions at 5th and K and advised the President that NPIC needed a new building.[3]

Kennedy promptly told DCI John McCone "to get them out of that structure" and wanted to know how soon a move could be accomplished. McCone responded that the Naval Gun Factory appeared to be a reasonable choice but that it would require a year to refurbish it. Kennedy's reply was "All right, you do it."[4]

On January 1, 1963, NPIC moved into its new home—Building 213 in the Washington Navy Yard, often referred to as the "Lundahl Hilton." It was, according to McCone, a "rags-to-riches" situation. The 200,000 square feet of floor space meant that hundreds of more workers could be added. The building had large elevators, air conditioning, and good security. Most of all, it was the national center that Lundahl had envisioned almost ten years earlier. Most people in the building worked for the CIA—the people who typed the letters, drove courier trucks, ran the computers and library searches, and produced the graphics.[5] But the photointerpreters came from the CIA, DIA, Army, Navy, Air Force, and other organizations. An Air Force interpreter who studied photos of Soviet silos might ride the elevator with a CIA interpreter who pored over photos of Chinese nuclear facilities and a Navy representative whose safe was filled with the latest photography of Soviet submarines.

Of course, the environment at the Washington Navy Yard, itself located in a rundown area of Washington, was far from luxurious. And working in a building whose windows, for security reasons, were bricked up certainly could be claustrophobic. But at least NPIC personnel were located in a larger facility with some amenities.

Even before the first KH-9 mission, NPIC officials, including director Arthur Lundahl and senior manager Dino Brugioni, realized that upgraded equipment would be needed to exploit the imagery fully. Using lasers rather than crosshairs for measurement would increase precision. Lundahl helped sell Richard Helms on the idea by arguing that better equipment would enable photointerpreters to extract more data from KH-9 images and thus reduce the chances of successful Soviet deception, a particular fear of Helms.[6]

Also required was other new equipment that would make the photointerpreters' work easier and more productive, such as new light tables, microstereoscopes, and adjustable chairs. The new light tables would employ cold light to eliminate the unpleasant effects of hot lights, such as dry skin. Adjustable chairs would allow both short and tall interpreters to work in comfort.[7]

But the funding required was difficult to obtain while NPIC was in the intelligence directorate, where spending large amounts of money on equipment was not a common practice. Further, according to Brugioni, contractors were not interested in working with NPIC because it had relatively little money to spend. A million-dollar contract was not worth the trouble, and the intelligence directorate had no leverage with such contractors. However, the science and technology directorate did hundreds of millions of dollars of business with such contractors, giving it considerable influence. Accepting work from NPIC, even if it was for relatively little money, would be a smart business move if it was done for a valued customer. Helms was sufficiently convinced to authorize NPIC's transfer to the DS&T, a move not without opposition.[8]

On February 2, 1973, Richard Helms's tenure as DCI ended, a consequence of his refusal to permit President Nixon to use the agency to help cover up the Watergate break-in. Helms was shipped off to Iran as the new ambassador, and James R. Schlesinger, the former Bureau of the Budget official who almost terminated the HEXAGON program, became the nation's new intelligence chief. Serving at that time as the agency's executive director, its number-three official, was William Colby, a veteran of the OSS and the CIA's Plans directorate. Colby quickly convinced Schlesinger that the executive director position was of little value, and that Colby would be more useful as the head of Plans.[9]

In his memoirs, Colby recalled that as the new head of Plans, he changed its designation to Operations and, on Schlesinger's orders, transferred the Technical Services Division—which Helms had insisted remain in the Plans directorate when he headed it—to the DS&T. The change was, he wrote, "a start in breaking down the walls of compartmentation between the Operations Directorate and the Agency's other directorates." In return, Schlesinger agreed to shift to Operations the unit of the intelligence directorate that operated overtly within the United States to gather information from U.S. citizens with knowledge of foreign developments or personalities.[10] As a result of the transfer, TSD became OTS—Office of Technical Service.

Colby's boss had more in mind for TSD than a change in name and a transfer from one part of the agency to another. One day in April 1973, Schlesinger summoned John McMahon to appear at his office at nine o'clock the next morning. At the time, McMahon was in his second year as director of the ELINT office, after having served as deputy director of both the Office of Special Projects (1965–1970) and the Office of ELINT (1970–1971). Having no idea why Schlesinger wanted to see him, McMahon called Duckett, who joined him in the director's seventh-floor office the next morning.[11]

Schlesinger told a surprised McMahon that he wanted him to assume command of OTS, replacing Sidney Gottlieb. The CIA veteran noted that his last real contact with the office and its activities was in the 1950s. Schlesinger's response—"close enough"—settled the issue. With the issue of "whether" settled, the only question left was "when?" Duckett suggested the first of the month, but Schlesinger looked at his watch and said, "How about ten o'clock?" McMahon never returned to his office at OEL.[12]

McMahon's immediate transfer reflected the DCI's belief that it was necessary to clean house at OTS and do so without delay. According to McMahon, the key issue was that the drug research OTS was conducting with the Army had "got out of hand."[13] Schlesinger was also probably aware that in July 1971, TSD had provided former CIA officer and then White House employee Howard Hunt with an assortment of its products—a wig, a speech-altering device that would give him a lisp, a gait-altering device that would make him limp, a pair of thick glasses that provided clear vision, and false identification papers. Hunt's projects included trying to dig up derogatory information on the Kennedys, in particular potential Democratic presidential nominee Edward Kennedy, as well as trying to obtain information that could be used to discredit Daniel Ellsberg, who had leaked a copy of the Defense Department's top-secret *Pentagon Papers* study of U.S. involvement in Vietnam to the *New York Times*.[14] In May, Schlesinger issued a directive requiring all elements of the agency to report any activities that were conducted outside the agency's charter.

Aside from cleaning house, McMahon had two other missions. One was to build up office morale, which had been damaged as a result of the negative publicity the CIA had received as fallout from Watergate and other matters. The other was to push improved technologies through the R&D phase and into operations.[15]

OTS, McMahon later recalled, "made any kind of James Bond device you could think of."[16] Those devices, in addition to the kind provided to Howard Hunt, included personal weapons such as the "cigarette pistol" (a .22-caliber weapon disguised as a European king-sized cigarette); a "pen" that could fire a .38-caliber tear gas cartridge; and a specially modified version of the Walter PPK—James Bond's gun. Among the photographic and agent communications equipment developed and produced by OTS were cameras disguised as cigarette lighters and wristwatches and a complete radio station in an attaché case.[17]

Audio surveillance gadgets included briefcases and attaché cases equipped with recording equipment; clandestine listening devices disguised as batteries, appliance plugs, and other innocuous items; and hot-miked telephones—telephones wired to permit the mouthpiece to be activated even with the handset in the hung-up position. To help with surreptitious entry were such OTS products as assorted lock-picking devices, a kit to make key impressions, and an electronic stethoscope to aid in safecracking. There were also means for destroying equipment or cryptographic material (a combustible notebook), for producing explosions (explosive flour), or for incapacitating an adversary's automobile (the gas tank pill, battery destroyer, or tire spike).[18]

OTS also produced a variety of means to open envelopes, including a flaps and seals kit, and a flaps and seals hot plate, which provided a portable heat source to aid in steaming open envelopes. In addition, there was the dead-drop device—an aluminum spike that could be unscrewed to insert microfilm or other material, rescrewed, and then driven into the ground—as well as a hollow coin that could be opened only by applying pressure to a specific point on one side of the coin.[19]

DEVELOPMENT AND ENGINEERING

Schlesinger's brief tenure in early 1973 as director was also marked by the April transformation of the Office of Special Projects into the Office of Development and Engineering (OD&E). The change in title reflected a change in mandate. Whereas OSP's sole responsibility had been the development of satellite systems, OD&E was to provide engineering and system development support for the entire agency, with the Office of Research and Development focusing on "exploratory development."[20]

Along with the new name came a new director for the office. Leslie Dirks, who had become OSP's deputy director in September 1970 when John McMahon was assigned to head the ELINT office, became the first head of the office.[21] Despite its more extensive responsibilities, OD&E's primary business remained the same—development of satellite reconnaissance systems.

By the time Dirks assumed office, both the HEXAGON/KH-9 and RHYOLITE programs were well established. All three HEXAGON missions in 1972 had been successful, with the last staying in orbit for ninety days. The first of those missions was part of stepped-up U.S. reconnaissance activities designed to provide an updated survey of Soviet strategic forces in preparation for final negotiations on the Strategic Arms Limitation Treaty. On April 23, the first 1973 mission was in its forty-fifth day.[22]

The first RHYOLITE continued to monitor telemetry from Soviet ICBM and SLBM tests. In June 1969, testing of a new SLBM, the SS-N-X-8, began and continued for several years. In October 1970, SS-9 Mod-4 tests resumed after a six-month hiatus, and by November 5, there had been four more. An October 1972 national intelligence estimate noted that the Soviets were continuing to test the Mod-3 version of the SS-11, which then constituted 60 percent of the Soviet ICBM force. The Soviets also began testing the Mod-2 version of the SS-N-6 Sawfly in 1972.[23]

The second RHYOLITE was launched March 6, 1973, and once its checkout was complete, a two-satellite constellation was established. The second RHYOLITE apparently was placed south of the Horn of Africa to receive telemetry from liquid-fueled ICBMs launched from Tyuratam toward the Kamchatka Peninsula impact zone.[24] Both were kept busy by Soviet ballistic missile tests for years to come.

But OD&E was doing more than living off its past accomplishments. It was working on a follow-on to RHYOLITE, code-named ARGUS, which became the subject of an internal intelligence community battle and ultimately was killed by Congress.[25] Most important, OD&E was proceeding with the KENNAN program, which promised to provide imagery in "near real-time"—as the satellite passed over its target—via a television-like electro-optical system. That program represented another victory for the directorate and Program B over their rivals in the Air Force Office of Special Projects (Program A)—but one obtained only through the intercession of some prominent scientists. KENNAN was also part of Bud

Wheelon's legacy and a personal triumph for Dirks, whose work on developing a real-time capability went back to the earliest days of the directorate.

In 1963, Dirks and several colleagues began pondering whether the United States could launch a truly secret reconnaissance satellite, one that could be kept secret not only from the American public but from the Soviet Union as well. An April 1963 memo from OSA deputy director James Cunningham to John Parangosky, his deputy for technology, argued that if, in the future, the United States relied solely on the heavy reconnaissance satellites under development, "an intense Soviet effort will seriously reduce our coverage and may deprive us of coverage completely."[26]

Cunningham believed that specter justified development of "a backup covert system which would rely, above all, on concealment" and "be kept on the shelf until needed." Requirements of a covert system would include a clandestine and preferably mobile launch system, silent launch and operations, and radar cross-sections that did not show up on Soviet radar screens. Although the resolution of the photographs would be inferior to that of the more conventional systems, it was believed that "useful coverage can be obtained."[27]

But Dirks and his colleagues quickly concluded that a secret satellite in low-earth orbit was not feasible. The Soviet space detection and tracking network would easily pick up the launch and orbit of the satellite. An alternative was to place the spacecraft in a much higher parking orbit, bringing it down only when needed. Possibly the Soviets would miss or be confused by this unusual maneuver. But this strategy also had a fatal flaw. As the film sat in space, unused, it would begin to degrade. By the time the secret satellite received NRO's call, the entire film supply might be worthless.[28]

The alternative to film brought Dirks and his colleagues full circle to the concept of a television-type imagery return system, which had been suggested in the 1950s by Merton Davies and Amrom Katz of the RAND Corporation.[29] The desirability of such a system had not been forgotten, despite the success of CORONA and the failure of SAMOS. Whether or not such a satellite could be kept secret from Soviet space watchers, it could send back timely data. The Cuban missile crisis was one dramatic example of the potential value of "real-time"—an example appreciated by both Bud Wheelon and a young Leslie Dirks. One day they visited AT&T's Bell Labs in New Jersey to take a peek at something the company was working on, a special dispensation from Bell Labs president and PFIAB member William Baker, whose organization didn't ordinarily allow outsiders to see work in progress. The two CIA officials saw work being done on charge-coupled devices (CCDs), which AT&T hoped would serve as key technology in videophones.[30]

Such technology was not mature in 1963, but Dirks realized that it might be in 1973. Over the rest of the decade and into the next, he and other OSP staffers, including Robert Kohler and Julian Caballero, kept the project alive, looking for advances in technology that would permit such a system and seeking support for research into areas relevant to its development.[31]

By the end of the 1960s, several crises had demonstrated the limitations of film-recovery systems for warning of imminent attacks and the monitoring of the wars that followed. There was an appreciation that existing satellite imagery sensors were "rigid and unresponsive on timely basis."[32]

On June 5, 1967, Israel launched a series of devastating air strikes on Egyptian air bases. The attacks followed the mid-May withdrawal of U.N. troops from the Sinai and Gaza, the closure of the Suez Canal to Israeli shipping, the blockade of the Straits of Tiran, and the U.S. government's assessment that a serious international effort to open the canal was unlikely.[33]

Over the next six days, Israeli forces racked up devastating victories against Egyptian, Syrian, and Jordanian air and ground forces on three fronts. By noon on June 5, Egypt had lost 309 of its 340 serviceable aircraft, including all thirty of its TU-16 bombers that could be used against cities. Three Israeli Defense Force armored corps broke into Egyptian territory, took the Gaza Strip, and penetrated to the heart of the Sinai.[34]

In response to the Jordanian strafing of a small Israeli airfield, the Israeli air force struck back, catching thirty Jordanian planes on the ground. Israeli ground forces rolled through to the West Bank in a matter of days. Syria had also struck against Israel on the opening day of the war, bombing an oil refinery, Israeli positions at the Sea of Galilee, and an air base. An Israeli air strike followed, all but eliminating the Syrian air force. On June 9, Minister of Defense Moshe Dayan instructed the Israeli Defense Forces (IDF) to seize the Golan Heights, from which Syria had been conducting artillery attacks in peacetime. By noon the next day, the Syrian town of Kuneitra had fallen into IDF hands, and the road to Damascus was open.[35]

From the beginning of the war, the United States was monitoring events as closely as possible. But neither CORONA nor KH-7/GAMBIT satellites made a contribution. A KH-7 had been launched the day before the war. In addition, a CORONA mission that began May 9 continued for sixty-four days, including the entire period of the war. In an attempt to get better coverage, technicians altered the orbit of one of the satellites, but the returned film was apparently of poor quality. Not surprisingly, former Defense Secretary Robert McNamara later did not recall that satellite reconnaissance played any role in U.S. intelligence gathering during the war.[36]

Former JCS chairman Maxwell Taylor, then a member of the PFIAB, was among those whose interest in the possible value of real-time photography was stimulated by the war. After a July briefing by Helms, he sent the CIA a series of questions concerning intelligence collection capabilities in the context of the Six-Day War, leading Dirks, then head of OSP's Design and Analysis Division, to explain CORONA capabilities during crisis situations. In a memo, Dirks noted that "I particularly emphasized the problems associated with using recovery film type systems in a crisis situation."[37] During a joint CIA-NSA-DIA briefing on August 31, Taylor indicated his continuing interest in the question of satellite reconnaissance in crisis situations. In particular, he inquired about the relationship between technological developments and the prospect of obtaining imagery in near real-time to support decisionmakers during a crisis.[38]

Less than a year after that briefing, on August 20, 1968, Soviet and other Warsaw Pact forces stormed into Czechoslovakia to put an end to Alexander Dubcek's "socialism with a human face." In the months leading up to the invasion, attention in the West had turned to the question of whether the Soviets would use brute force, as they did in Hungary in 1956. A memorandum by the CIA's Office of Strategic Research on August 2 noted, "It appears the Soviet high command has in about two weeks time completed military preparations sufficient for intervening in Czechoslovakia if that is deemed necessary by the political leadership."[39] Although a minority of analysts in each of the major analytical agencies (CIA, DIA, the State Department's Bureau of Intelligence and Research) believed that the Soviets would invade, a majority in each of those agencies expected the Soviets to exercise restraint.[40]

In an attempt to accumulate hard data on Soviet plans, the intelligence community relied on monitoring the Soviet press, diplomatic reporting, clandestine agents, and signals intelligence. KEYHOLE satellites also could provide important data. Signs of impending invasion that might show up in satellite photography included increased activities at airfields, troop departures, extensive logistics activities, and, most dramatic, the massing of troops near the Czech border.

A KH-8/GAMBIT launched on August 6 performed poorly and was deorbited after nine days. As a result, the CIA was forced to rely solely on the KH-4B launched on August 7. A film package returned prior to August 21 proved reassuring. It showed no indications of Soviet preparations for an invasion.[41] But on August 20, Warsaw Pact troops, led by those from the Soviet Union, entered Czechoslovakia and brought an end to the Prague Spring.

When, subsequent to the invasion, the second and last of the CORONA film buckets was recovered and analyzed, the imagery showed "unmistakable Soviet preparations for invasion," according to Roland Inlow, former chairman of the Committee on Imagery Requirements and Exploitation. Photointerpreters could see that the Soviets had placed crosses on their mobile equipment to distinguish it from similar equipment they had given to the Czech army. The film also showed the presence of large numbers of transport aircraft "lined up wing-tip to wing-tip at an airfield near the western border." The transports had moved to the airfield under radio silence and would be used to transport the airborne forces that secured Prague.[42]

The experience was not forgotten by many of those involved in the photo reconnaissance program. One former CIA official recalled that people were "still talking about it years later." Furthermore, "a lot of good work was done in retrospect"—the photo intelligence did prove valuable in developing warning indicators.[43]

The Sino-Soviet border hostilities of 1969 marked the fourth significant conflict between the countries since 1962. Notable about 1969 was not only that recent events seemed to highlight the limitations of film recovery systems and the potential value of a real-time system, but that technologies that might permit development of such a system had matured. Thus, in 1969, Leslie Dirks traveled up the Washington-Baltimore Parkway to visit Westinghouse, which was producing light-sensing diodes. Dirks felt that until CCDs were available, those diodes could be used in a real-time electro-optical system, recording the light levels of small segments of a scene; this information could be converted into electronic signals, transmitted to a relay satellite, and then converted on the ground to a photograph of the scene viewed by the satellite seconds earlier.[44]

Dirks's investigation of technological developments that could make real-time imagery possible was complemented by two 1969 studies concerning its utility and impact. A June 1969 study, "The Implications of Near-Real Time Imagery on Intelligence Production and Processes," examined the impact on the CIA of the acquisition of a real-time capability, including the disruption to staffing and schedules. A slightly later study, focused on fifty different crises (including Suez, Cuba, the Six-Day War, and Czechoslovakia) and categorized the crises by their rise, duration, location, and decline; the warning available; and the demands for information. It also addressed what information could have been obtained in each situation, how it might have changed perceptions of the crisis, and the potential utility of such information. It attempted to determine how different degrees of timeliness could have aided decisionmakers.[45]

The study's conclusions were sufficiently positive to encourage the DS&T to begin a full-scale effort to develop a real-time system along the lines envisioned by Dirks. Not surprisingly, the CIA and Air Force were soon in competition. As had been the case for many years, the Air Force sought incremental improvements to currently operating systems rather than quantum leaps. Thus, Program A proposed development of FROG—Film-Readout GAMBIT. As its name indicated, FROG would take the film-return KH-8/GAMBIT satellite and add a film-scanning capability, in the manner of SAMOS.[46]

FROG had been under development since at least the mid-1960s. In an August 1966 memo, Bruce C. Clarke, then the special assistant for special projects to the Deputy Director of Intelligence, noted the system's projected capabilities. It would have a thirty-to-ninety-day lifetime, the ability to transmit imagery three to four times a day, several ground stations in the United States, and a resolution of three to five feet. For targets at certain latitudes, there might be no more than a twenty-minute gap between photographs being taken and the image being received on the ground. For other targets, there might be a five-day gap resulting from the locations of the target and closest ground station along with the movement of the earth and the satellite. FROG was, according to Bud Wheelon, "a really dumb idea," whose only purpose was to block the CIA program.[47]

Secretary of Defense Melvin Laird apparently disagreed, selecting FROG as the next-generation KEYHOLE system. FROG had the advantage of being a modification of an existing system and thus could be brought into operation more quickly than a more revolutionary approach.

But Laird's decision, if not reversed, would probably mean that it would be a long time before any revolutionary change was made. That prospect did not sit well with Carl Duckett and some of the eminent scientists who served as advisers to the CIA and NRO.[48]

Duckett journeyed to Capitol Hill to talk to Senator Allen Ellender, the powerful Louisiana Democrat and chairman of the Appropriations Committee. Duckett persuasively explained the need for a more revolutionary system than the Air Force was proposing.[49]

When a panel headed by former deputy chief of defense research and engineering Eugene Fubini concluded that the CIA's advanced concept was not feasible, a member of that panel who strongly disagreed, Richard Garwin of IBM, convened a meeting of the advisory Reconnaissance Panel, of which he was vice-chairman and Edwin Land was chairman. The panel concluded that the CIA's concept was quite feasible. Garwin, along with Stanford physicist Sidney Drell, visited the White House to talk with Henry Kissinger. And Edwin Land talked to the President, advising him that there was nothing simpler than a tube with a mirror in front of it, which was the essence of the CIA approach.[50]

Further consideration took place at a 1971 meeting of the PFIAB, whose members included Edwin Land, William Baker of Bell Labs, Nelson Rockefeller, Gordon Gray, John Connally, and Maxwell Taylor. Usually Henry Kissinger and his deputy attended, representing the President. But this meeting also drew Nixon himself, along with James Schlesinger—then of the Office of Management and Budget and a supporter of the FROG concept. At that meeting Land said that FROG would be "the cautious choice," whereas the "adventurous choice, and one which would be a quantum technological advance, is to push the development of an electronic imaging system which can be read out through a relay satellite while the sensor is over the target." Nixon promised to take a "hard look."[51]

Nixon's ultimate decision to approve the CIA approach was, according to an individual present, "a direct consequence" of the meeting. The decision pleased Duckett, Helms, and especially Leslie Dirks—but not Ralph Jacobson of the Air Force Office of Special Projects, who saw FROG, a potential $2 billion program, vanish into thin air.[52]

THE DRAGON LADY FLIES AWAY

Proposals to turn the CIA's U-2Rs over to the Air Force had been considered almost yearly, since NRO director John McLucas first suggested the action in 1969. In December of that year, President Nixon decided to maintain a CIA program through 1971 and requested that the issue be reviewed by the 40 Committee, which had succeeded the 303 Committee in reviewing sensitive intelligence operations for the NSC. In August 1970, the committee recommended that the CIA continue flying the spy planes through 1972. On August 12, 1972, the committee made the same recommendation.[53]

Overseeing those operations was Brig. Gen. Wendell L. Bevan Jr. A 1943 West Point graduate, Bevan had flown thirty World War II missions, and gone on to serve at Air Force headquarters, as assistant air attaché for Central America, and as a reconnaissance wing commander. He flew 111 combat sorties, including twenty over Vietnam, on both fighter and reconnaissance missions. In June 1971, Bevan was snatched from his position on the Joint Staff to become OSA's fifth director. He would also be its next to last.[54]

Pressure to place the entire U-2 fleet under single management continued. A memo from the Secretary of Defense to the DCI, undated but apparently sent in spring 1973, noted that "the Air Force's U-2R fleet has been under considerable operational and resource pressure to satisfy current mission needs," including overflights of Cuba. It also asserted that a consolidation would eliminate duplicative functions and could save over $40 million. Thus, Schlesinger proposed that the four U-2Rs assigned to the CIA be transferred to the Air Force. In June 1973, he informed the 40 Committee that the CIA role in U-2 operations could be terminated without difficulty. On August 30, the committee approved the CIA plan to terminate its U-2 activities on August 1, 1974.[55]

Operations in the final year included those over the Middle East, a result of the October 1973 Arab-Israeli war. Two U-2s from Detachment G (based at Edwards Air Force Base in California) deployed to Britain's Akrotiri base on Cyprus on October 7 and 8 in anticipation of being ordered to monitor the conflict, but no tasking ever arrived.[56] Eventually, the war did lead to CIA U-2 flights over the region when the participants in the conflict agreed to U.S. monitoring of the Israeli-Egyptian and Israeli-Syrian disengagement areas. On April 21, a U-2 from Detachment G arrived at Akrotiri and conducted six overflights between May 12 and July 28, with each side being provided the photographs as well as reports specifying the deployment of the other's forces.[57]

During those Middle East overflights, Detachment H on Taiwan ceased its operations against China, partially as result of the U.S.-PRC rapprochement. In June, the Republic of China officially agreed to termination of the TACKLE program. On August 1, 1974, the Air Force assumed responsibility for monitoring the Arab-Israeli cease-fire, ending the CIA's U-2 program. The 1130th Air Technical Training Group (Detachment G) at Edwards was disestablished, and the CIA's Office of Special Activities, with the OXCART in mothballs and the U-2 in the hands of the Air Force, was phased out.[58]

HOBBY SHOP

In July 1972, Sayre Stevens replaced Robert Chapman as director of ORD. It was a change that, according to an Inspector General's report completed that July and issued in October, was overdue. The report was critical of Chapman's management style, noting that "the arrangements for overseeing the work of ORD seemed to us to be very loose and unstructured . . . many of the tasks that occupy [staff members] are self-generated as a consequence of a personal interest in a particular subject." As a result, "many [technical officers] have been allowed to drift into fields of activity . . . which offer little or no prospect of benefiting the Agency." As Stevens recalled many years later, ORD had become too much of a "hobby shop."[59]

The report also noted that ORD's project officers "are very much isolated from the rest of the Agency and have little familiarity with the work of the offices whose missions they are trying to support." That isolation resulted in very different views of the value of ORD's work—"many of ORD's completed R&D projects are evaluated as successes by ORD's definition but as failures by [their] customers . . . some of them achieved the technological objectives that were sought, but there was no requirement for the product at the time it became available."[60]

Stevens's mission was to rejuvenate the 105-person office (which was located not at CIA headquarters but on several floors of the CIA facility in Rosslyn—the Ames Center Building). Over the three years and two months that Stevens and then James Hirsch, who came from OEL and returned there in 1976, ran ORD, they sought to move away from the "sterile" system under which ORD's scientists would come up with their "sandbox projects" and then seek to generate interest somewhere in the directorate or rest of the agency. Instead, they wanted ORD to identify the specific needs of both analysts and operators and seek to develop means of fulfilling those needs.[61]

One program, the Large-Area Crop Inventory Experiment (LACIE), also known as Project UPSTREET, was intended to help analysts produce more precise predictions of Soviet agricultural production. The project was conceived and developed under Stevens and implemented under Hirsch. The impetus for it was the Soviet Union's disastrous 1972 grain harvest. Soviet purchase of far greater quantities of grain on the international market led to an increase in the cost of bread and other grain-based products in the United States.[62]

Prior to 1974, the standard means of estimating a Soviet harvest was applying statistical analysis, specifically a technique known as regression analysis, to the data collected by U.S. agricultural attachés. However, when a particular area experienced a bad harvest, the attachés were prohibited from traveling there. And in the absence of the required data, the reliability of the estimates suffered.[63]

Stevens, at the suggestion of the group in ORD that focused on improving analytical methodologies, sought to make use of a resource that had first become available in 1972—the Earth Resources Technology Satellite (ERTS), which would become better known as LANDSAT. In contrast to the high-resolution imagery satellites developed by the CIA and Air Force, the first LANDSAT satellite, which operated in a 570-mile orbits, produced imagery with a resolution of about 100 feet.[64] However, the satellite was able to cover wide areas in a single photo and carried a multispectral scanner that could produce images using four different channels. The data could then be used to produce "false-color" images in which cloudy water would appear blue, while living vegetation would show up as bright red.[65]

From 1964 to 1968, ORD had developed an airborne multispectral system that was used for predicting and assessing crop yields, which provided an impetus for LANDSAT. Aerial reconnaissance of the Soviet Union was not possible, but LANDSAT imagery was—and if full use was made of its multispectral capabilities, LANDSAT could aid analysts trying to determine how well or poorly the Soviet Union's socialist farming system had done in a given year. That imagery would be combined with meteorological data and other information in a computer simulation model that "grew" the Soviet grain crop up through its harvest. The model started with a maximum estimate for grain production and then adjusted the estimate in reaction to data obtained from LANDSAT and other sources.[66]

The experiment, carried out between 1974 and 1977, proved useful in determining wheat acreage, data that could then be used in producing estimates before harvesting began. Because of budget limitations,

LANDSAT images were replaced by weather satellite images, but the basic methodology remained in use.[67]

During Stevens's tenure, ORD also pioneered soft-copy imagery exploitation—extracting data from imagery on computer screens rather than through the traditional method, an analyst examining film on a light-table. ORD sought to implement an idea that had been discussed in the scientific literature—to scan photographs (such as those sent back on film from the KH-8 and KH-9 satellites) into a computer, then enhance and manipulate them. At the time, computers were not capable of performing such functions without long delays—but by the early 1980s, computer technology would advance sufficiently.[68]

Under Hirsch, ORD pioneered computer networking for the agency. Initially, twenty users were hooked into CIA mainframes. Three and half years later, there were only forty participants. But the idea took off after that, with more new employees being familiar with computers, and the number tied into CIA mainframes would grow exponentially.[69]

Of course, various hardware programs continued—particularly unmanned aerial vehicles programs like AQUILINE. Stevens later recalled that when he joined ORD, it had about eight ongoing airplane programs—something the Inspector General's report considered a sign of poor management. There were also microprocessed electronics "which didn't weight anything" and were "small as hell."[70]

One area in which ORD had difficulty in making an impact was support of clandestine operations. The office was, in Stevens's words, "kind of a Johnny-come-lately research organization" in supporting such operations. It was in severe competition with the "very spooky" technical services unit. Attempts by the research and development office to simply hand off a product to the Operations directorate usually didn't work, and TSD/OTS would wind up reengineering ORD's invention.[71]

THE CIA'S PSYCHIC FRIENDS

In June 1973, OTS chief John McMahon and Carl Duckett were briefed by Harold Puthoff and Russell Targ from the Stanford Research Institute (SRI). Puthoff had obtained a doctorate from Stanford University, was the holder of a patent for a tunable infrared laser, and had coauthored an influential textbook on quantum electronics. Targ, a physicist whose father was a devotee of the paranormal, had spent the previous decade conducting laser research.[72] But the SRI scientists did not come to Langley to brief Duckett and McMahon on the use of lasers for intelligence purposes. Rather, the two senior CIA officials heard about a very different, and unconventional, area of research—psychic spying.

Four years earlier, Puthoff had experienced a number of personal and professional changes. Separation from his wife, a visit to the Esalen Institute, and boredom with teaching in Stanford's electrical engineering department had been followed by his moving over to SRI, which had close ties to Stanford University but was funded largely by government contracts. Puthoff joined SRI to assist with a laser-related project, but when funding dwindled, he sought permission from his boss and obtained $10,000 from the part-owner of a fried-chicken franchise to test for the existence of psychic abilities.[73] Puthoff's turn toward fringe science was not exactly a radical departure. For several years, he had been an active member of the Church of Scientology, and he provided the church with a letter referring to Scientology as a "highly sophisticated and highly technological system more characteristic of the best of modern corporate planning and applied technology." In addition, he wrote that he found Scientology "to be an uplifting and workable system of concepts which blend the best of Eastern and Western traditions."[74]

In April 1972, Targ met with personnel from the Office of Scientific Intelligence to discuss the subject of paranormal abilities, and stated that he knew individuals who claimed they witnessed Soviet research into psychokinesis—the alleged movement of objects using only a mind-generated force—and made films of such activities available to the CIA representatives. In turn, OSI contacted both the research and development and technical service offices, whose past research (including in the case of TSD, research into ESP) made them candidates to fund further investigation.[75]

The first test subject was Ingo Swann, a New York artist who had been involved in psychic experiments at the City College of New York. In June 1972, Puthoff invited him to SRI to demonstrate his alleged abilities. For the first test, Swann was taken to a superconducting shielded magnetometer at Stanford University that was being used in quark experiments. According to accounts that accept the existence of psychic abilities, when Swann directed his attention to the interior of the magnetometer, there was a disturbance in its output signal, indicating a change in the internal magnetic field. In addition, other signal variations were observed in response to his mental efforts, variations never witnessed before or after his visit. A description of the events was transmitted in a letter to OSI and in discussions with OTS and ORD representatives.[76]

TSD followed up by arranging for an experiment, costing less than $1,000, in which Swann was asked to describe objects hidden by TSD personnel—specifically, a live brown moth placed in a sealed box. Reportedly, Swann stated that "I see something small, brown, and irregular, sort of like a leaf, or something that resembles it, except that it seems very much alive, like it's even moving!" The results led then TSD head Sidney Gottlieb to approve another $2,500 in funding and suggest development of a more detailed research agenda.[77]

Just as was the case with the MKULTRA experiments, part of the interest was in determining what results the Soviets might be achieving in their work and how those results might be used in operations against the CIA and the United States. In July 1972, the Defense Intelligence Agency published one of what would be several studies dealing with Soviet bloc research in the parapsychology field. The study examined purported Soviet efforts with respect to ESP, pyschokinesis, astral projection, clairvoyance, and other reputed paranormal phenomena.[78]

By October 1972, TSD authorized a $50,000 Biofield Measurements Program and appointed Kenneth Kress to monitor the activity. Over the next eight months, experiments progressed from attempts to "remote view" objects hidden in boxes to viewing sites in the San Francisco Bay area to which SRI employees had been sent as "beacons." In February 1973, halfway through the contract, a review of the results led several ORD officers to favor contributing personnel and funding from their office. At about the same time, a third remote viewer, Pat Price, joined the project. Price was a small-building contractor, who had served as a local councilman in Burbank in the 1950s and briefly had been the town's police commissioner. He had met Puthoff at a lecture in Los Angeles a few years earlier, and had run into Puthoff and Swann in late 1972 while he was selling Christmas trees.[79]

In late April 1973, a management review involving OTS, ORD, and Executive Director William Colby allowed the project to continue, although Kress was told not to increase the scope of the project or anticipate any follow-on funding. There was a potential for significant embarrassment, and OTS already had enough problems—it was being investigated for possible involvement in Watergate.[80] But this guidance did not prevent a somewhat different approach. Swann had suggested that instead of relying on a "beacon" individual at sites to be viewed (which certainly would not be feasible with regard to the sensitive Soviet and Chinese sites), the viewer be given geographic coordinates and asked to view the facility or activity at those coordinates. Such a procedure was dubbed Scanate—*Scan*ning by coord*inate*.[81]

That approach was a step in the direction McMahon wanted the effort to go—away from experimentation and toward application. He considered parapsychology an "extremely attractive" approach to intelligence collection and argued that standard intelligence sensors operated "in narrow bands." Thus, there was reason to expect, in his view, that information in other bands could be obtained if "the right receiver" could be developed. OTS, however, was not in business to conduct pure research but rather to support the CIA's clandestine operators.[82]

In summer 1973, Puthoff asked an OSI official to give him "coordinates of a place I don't know anything about" for him to pass on to the remote viewers. The official responded, "I'll do you one better. I'll get you the coordinates of some place even *I* don't know about." A colleague in the CIA provided the OSI official with a set of coordinates, without further explanation.[83]

In late May, Ingo Swann sat at one end of a table in the SRI conference room, wrote down the coordinates read by Puthoff, and began his 3,000-mile psychic journey. After six minutes, he had produced an account that included rolling hills, a city to the north, lawns similar to the ones found at a military base, and a flagpole. He also spent an hour at home the following morning viewing the target, although the effort didn't add much to his description.[84]

On June 1, two days after Swann's at-home viewing, Price was given the same coordinates as Swann. On June 4, Price's report, dated June 2, of his viewing was received in the mail. The result was a more detailed account of the site, although one that was consistent with Swann's report. Beyond descriptions of the terrain and the assertion that it was a former missile base, Price claimed that he saw an underground area used for record storage as well as to house computers, communication equipment, and large maps. He also saw personnel from the Army 5th Corps of Engineers and the Army Signal Corps.[85]

Subsequently, he was asked to revisit the site and report on any information concerning code words stamped on documents at the site. According to Price, there was a file cabinet on one wall. The first two words on its label were "Operation Pool . . ." with the final word unclear. Files inside the cabinet were labeled CUEBALL, 14 BALL, 4 BALL, 8 BALL, and RACKUP. On the top of one desk were papers labeled FLYTRAP and MINERVA, and the code name associated with the site seemed to be

HAYFORK or HAYSTACK. Price also came up with the names of personnel—a Colonel R. J. Hamilton, Major General George Nash, and possibly a Major John C. Calhoun.[86]

The OSI officer took the information to the colleague who had provided him with the coordinates, who said that Swann and Price were not even close, that their reports were "bullshit"—the coordinates corresponded to his summer cabin in the Blue Ridge Mountains. However, the OSI officer remained intrigued with the similarity of the descriptions and decided to find out if there was an installation near his friend's retreat similar to that described by the two remote viewers.[87]

Indeed, the OSI staffer discovered a huge facility at Sugar Grove, West Virginia. Nominally a U.S. Navy communications facility, it actually was a National Security Agency intercept site, with a variety of eavesdropping antennae, including a sixty-foot receiving dish for pulling in the traffic from INTELSAT and other satellites. Operations were directed from a two-story underground building.[88] The intelligence mission was secret, but the facility, given its ostensible function, was not.

The results of Swann's and Price's psychic journeys to the West Virginia mountains were the subject of an October 1 report to the CIA. The following month, a "Top-Secret/Codeword Eyes Only" memo evaluated selected results of the experiments. A map drawn by Swann was "correct," while the terrain was "exactly as drawn" by Price, and was "not otherwise accessible to non-base personnel." Elevations given by Price were correct to within 100 feet, and there was "an astonishing similarity between [Price's] description of the facility, some dissimilarities, but most of the important ones do match."[89]

The code words elicited by Price were "current or past active COMINT descriptives." An initial survey showed all the code words to be inactive by 1966, but subsequent investigation turned up two that were relevant to the site but unfamiliar to current personnel. In addition, the site reference (code name) was also among the words reported by Price. One individual named by Price was an NSA security officer, although the memo noted that it was not known whether "he was present during [Price's] alleged 'visit.'" The other individuals named were also DOD personnel but were not familiar to personnel at the site who were asked.[90]

The same memo also evaluated summer remote-viewing sessions that involved a Soviet installation in the Urals and a joint French-Soviet meteorological station on Kerguelen Island in the southern Indian Ocean. Price had "discovered" the Urals site at Mount Narodnaya on his own, without the apparent provision of coordinates. He described an underground facility, helipads, a railway, and a radar installation 30 miles to the north of the site with a 165-foot dish and two small dishes.[91]

The CIA memo referred to Price's description as generally correct with regard to "topography and location of radar dishes." There was a discrepancy between the number of dishes "viewed" by Price and those shown in KH-4 satellite imagery from 1972. There was only one radar dome visible, and that was 60–100 miles from the facility as opposed to 30 miles. There was no evidence on the satellite imagery of a railway or helipads. Despite the discrepancies, Price's descriptions of the site, the Abez space tracking facility, ranged from "similar to identical." The memo also commented that the odds were "over one million to one" that Price could have provided the description based on coincidence or guess, even with the inaccuracies—although there was no explanation as to the basis upon which those odds were calculated.[92]

The description of the Indian Ocean facility was produced by Swann after Puthoff had been given the coordinates by his OSI contact. In addition to its acknowledged function, the site was rumored to double, at least for the Soviets, as an intercept or missile tracking station.[93] The CIA assessment noted that the "descriptions are rather precise, and correct to the limits of KH-4 photography" and that "description of installation functions correct." Other descriptions were not verifiable on the basis of information available to the CIA.[94]

The memo's author noted that he had no "explanation in fact or in principle" for the results and verified that [Price] "is a highly gifted subject capable of obtaining accurate 'visual' information at a distance by non-ordinary means." He went on to state that "whether this information is obtained by paranormal ability or not remains open to speculation."[95]

An attached memo from Puthoff's OSI contact noted that he was informed that Puthoff's laboratory would likely be terminated "unless at least a modest level of support can be obtained . . . from a reputable Governmental agency such as CIA." The OSI official also noted that the SRI vice-president for research informed him that SRI could find no evidence of fraud. Nor could the CIA official, although he refused to offer an ironclad statement with regard to experiments in which he had not participated.[96]

The memo, however, did not discuss a number of issues that would be expected to arise in evaluating the extraordinary claims arising from the remote-viewing experiments—in particular with regard to the Sugar Grove site. Neither Swann nor Price conducted his remote viewing under circumstances in which his lack of access to outside information could be verified. In addition, there was no concern expressed, at least in the memo, about Puthoff's having worked at NSA in the early 1960s—which might have given him access to information about Sugar Grove, including about code words and personnel. Suspicion might have been heightened by Price's reporting of a number of obsolete code words—the type of error that could be explained by his having been provided the information by someone who had access at an earlier time but not any longer. Nor did there appear to be any examination of public information, such as media coverage about the targets, information that certainly was available about the existence of a facility at Sugar Grove.[97]

In any case, the summer 1973 experiments were reviewed by Colby, who had replaced Schlesinger as DCI in September; McMahon; and Sayre Stevens, who had become director of ORD in July 1972 and was far less enthusiastic than McMahon about such activities. He even told Duckett he "was out of his mind" to approve such research.* Nevertheless, a jointly funded ORD-OTS program commenced in February 1974. The premise behind the program was that paranormal phenomena such as remote viewing existed; the objective was to develop and exploit them for intelligence purposes. ORD funds were used for research into measurable physiological or psychological characteristics of individuals believed to have psychic capabilities and the establishment of protocols for verifying such abilities. OTS funding was used to assess the operational utility of paranormal capabilities.[98]

It was not long before a number of problems developed with the program, including the objection of ORD scientists that the tests being conducted by SRI were not sufficiently rigorous.[99] Such objections were also raised by the broader scientific community. Later in 1974, Puthoff and Targ published some of their remote-viewing experiments in the prestigious science journal *Nature*. However, an accompanying editorial comment noted that "there was agreement that the paper was weak in design and presentation, to the extent that details given as to the precise way in which the experiment was carried out were disconcertingly vague." Further, all the referees felt that the details of the various safeguards taken to rule out fraud were "uncomfortably vague."[100]

---

*In a 1999 interview, Stevens said he would not assert that such phenomena were impossible, but that as a means of intelligence, they were "useless" and "absolute bullshit." (Interview with Sayre Stevens, Springfield, Virginia, March 18, 1999.)

By the time the paper was published in fall 1974, there were new directors of both OTS and ORD. In August, John McMahon took another step in his rise through the agency, becoming Associate Deputy Director for Administration. He was replaced by former FMSAC head David Brandwein, who was skeptical about the value of the program. Meanwhile, Stevens became Duckett's deputy in June. He was replaced as head of ORD by James V. Hirsch, who had graduated from MIT with a master's degree in electrical engineering in 1959 and had been lured away from General Electric by the directorate's ELINT office in 1968. Hirsch told Kress that he could not accept that paranormal capabilities existed, but, realizing his bias, would accept the advice of his staff.[101] That willingness would give the project further life.

But an experiment conducted in summer 1974 and evaluated in the fall confirmed Brandwein's and Hirsch's skepticism. That experiment, the result of the push by Duckett and McMahon for viewing of sensitive targets, began on July 9 at SRI, four days after the United States had obtained satellite imagery of a target of special interest—located at 50 degrees, 9 minutes, 59 seconds north, and 78 degrees, 22 minutes, 22 seconds east. Targ and Puthoff informed Pat Price of the coordinates.[102]

Of interest to the CIA at those coordinates was an installation the agency had designated URDF-3 for Unidentified Research and Development Facility-3. The Air Force designated the same site, which was sixty miles southwest of the Semipalatinsk nuclear test site in Kazakhstan, as a PNUTS—possible nuclear underground test site. The chief of Air Force intelligence, Maj. Gen. George Keegan, and key aides believed the site could well be a center for particle-beam research. Concern that such activity might be taking place was first aroused in the late 1960s, when satellite images showed workers assembling four steel spheres nearly sixty feet in diameter. The spheres were then lowered into underground chambers that had been dug out of rock. In the particle-beam scenario, they would serve to contain nuclear low-yield explosions that would create the energy required for producing the particle beam's "lightning bolt."[103]

Price was shown maps of the area and told only that the target was a scientific military research and test facility and was 25–30 miles southwest of the Irtysh River. He was instructed to start with a view of the general area as it would be seen from 50,000 feet and get the layout of any complexes or buildings.[104]

The July 9 session, the first of four over four days, lasted about two hours. From the beginning, Price made the assumption, which was incorrect, that the facility was related to ongoing Soviet space launch and recovery activities. He gave what the experiment's evaluator, a Los Alamos scientist, judged to be "an almost perfect description of someone's first look at the Operations Area of URDF-3"—as low one-story buildings partially dug into the ground.[105]

Price also reported seeing nine other items that the evaluator noted "simply don't appear at or near URDF-3." The imagined objects included a road from the river to the target area, a 500-foot-tall antenna, an array of outdoor telephone poles, an outdoor pool, an airstrip twelve miles from URDF-3, a small village to the northeast, a city sixty miles southwest of the facility, and a three-story building (which Price claimed was the dominant building in the complex).[106]

On the night of July 9, Price completed and turned over, presumably to Puthoff, drawings of part of a perimeter fence and a rail-mounted gantry crane; the drawings were then passed to the CIA monitors the next day. The fence, Price stated, was electrified, but he did not mention its unique shape or the existence of four perimeter fences at URDF-3. His drawing of the gantry crane was evaluated as "remarkably close in detail to the actual gantry crane at URDF-3." Then, on the afternoon of July 10, Price described a complicated relationship involving three gantry cranes at the facility, which the evaluator wrote "does not exist at URDF-3."[107]

Price also reported by phone to Targ that he saw a 55-foot-tall dome-shaped building as well as a 65- to 75-foot-tall cement silo-like building south of the dome-shaped building. However, there were no buildings at URDF-3 that resembled either of the buildings Price described. In the general area where Price claimed the buildings were located were a partially earth-covered tank and a tall cylindrical tank or tower.[108]

For the evaluator, it seemed impossible to imagine how Price came up with a likeness to the actual crane unless he either saw it through remote viewing or was "informed of what to draw by someone knowledgeable of URDF-3." The evaluator also noted that "the experiment was not controlled to discount the possibility that [Price] could talk to other people—such as the Disinformation Section of the KGB." (Price did speak to Targ, with only the SRI experimenter's side of the conversation audible to the CIA monitors.) But the evaluator also found Price's repeated reporting of objects that did not exist at URDF-3 as "difficult to understand." He suggested one rather obvious explanation—if Price "mentions enough specific objects (such as three different types of gantry cranes when there is really only one), he will surely hit on one object that is actually present."

He went on to ask, "if the user of Price's remote viewing talents had no way of checking, how could he differentiate fact from fiction?"[109]

The third day produced "the most negative evidence yet and tends to discredit Price's ability to remotely view URDF-3." That evidence was Price's response to a request that he investigate whether four buildings that he described as separate were really the surface elements of a single underground building. He "looked" underground as requested and reported, "No, that's a concrete apron, and there's nothing subterranean right in that particular area." In fact, the four separate buildings were four sections of a 50-foot-deep underground building.[110]

The overall judgment of the evaluator was that "the validity of Price's remote viewing of URDF-3 appears to be a failure . . . the only positive evidence of the rail-mounted gantry crane was far outweighed by the large amount of negative evidence noted in the body of this analysis." The evaluator also said it was unfortunate that much of the experiment was conducted over the phone with only the SRI experimenter's voice being recorded. He suggested that "future experiments be more tightly controlled to discount the possibility of the subject discussing the material with people not involved in the experiment."[111]

(Only years later, after the fall of the Soviet Union, would American scientists tour the facility and discover what the Soviet scientists were working on there. They were not trying to avoid nuclear testing restrictions or build a particle-beam weapon. Rather, research at URDF-3 was geared to developing a nuclear-powered rocket for space flight.)[112]

In 1974 and in succeeding years, Puthoff and Targ claimed the experiment a success, pointing to the description of the large crane.* ORD officers did not agree, feeling that in the absence of control experiments, Price's successes could be described as lucky guessing. Such skepticism led OTS to issue a challenge to SRI—do something of genuine operational value. A number of ideas were elicited from personnel in OTS and the Operations directorate. The idea selected was to seek to aid Division D in its job of installing audio collection systems.[113]

The targets chosen were the code rooms of two Chinese embassies, one of which was in Africa, whose interiors were known to the audio teams

*In a 1996 article, Targ stated that "the psychic description that we and our viewer provided to our sponsor was so outstanding that it alone assured our funding for the next several years." (Russell Targ, "Remote Viewing at Stanford Research Institute in the 1970s: A Memoir," *Journal of Scientific Exploration* 10, 1 [Spring 1996]: 77–88 at 77.)

because they had made surreptitious entries several years earlier. Price was instructed to view the embassies remotely, locate the code rooms, and extract information that could enable a member of the audio team to determine whether Price was likely to be of operational value in future undertakings.[114]

According to project officer Ken Kress, Price "correctly located code-rooms, produced copious data, such as the location of interior doors and colors of marble stairs and fireplaces that were accurate and specific." At the same time, "much was also vague and incorrect." One operations officer did conclude, according to Kress, that remote viewing "offers definite operational possibilities."[115]

Not everyone was as enthusiastic. The experiments were followed by a review by the Operations directorate, OTS, and ORD. ORD project officers felt that the results "were not productive or even competent" and therefore decided to terminate funding to SRI. James Hirsch, then ORD director, later recalled that the experiments were conducted without proper scientific protocols—that CIA officers present during the experiments knew where the code rooms were and thus were subject to the "unconscious elicitation of information." OTS also ceased funding SRI's experiments—but it did sign Price to a personal services contract, and Price was assigned to work with an OTS psychologist.[116]

Several OTS staffers who had volunteered to attempt remote viewing were chosen and given the geographic coordinates of a site in Libya. They described new construction that "could be an SA-5 missile training site." According to Kress, the "Libyan desk officer was immediately impressed" and told him that an agent had reported essentially the same story.[117]

The OTS psychologist passed a second set of Libyan coordinates to Pat Price, who quickly responded with a report describing a guerrilla training site along with a maplike drawing of the installation. He also described an alleged related underwater sabotage training facility several hundred kilometers away on the coast. The data were passed to the Libyan Desk, which evaluated part of the report immediately and part after obtaining special reconnaissance coverage. According to Kress, some of Price's information was verified by reconnaissance, and his description of the underwater facility was similar to an agent's report. A follow-up request to Price to provide information on activities inside the facilities as well as on plans and intentions went unanswered when Price, whose paranormal abilities apparently didn't extend to precognition, died of a heart attack a few days later.[118]

Price had been the last vestige of the CIA's remote-viewing effort, and his death soon ended the CIA's efforts to employ parapsychology for intelligence purposes—although not the efforts of other agencies or the CIA's study of Soviet efforts. In August 1977, Adm. Stansfield Turner, Jimmy Carter's DCI, was asked about CIA support of parapsychology research after the *Washington Post* ran an article about the government's support of psychic research. Turner noted that the CIA had a man gifted with "visio-perception" of places he had never seen but, he added with a smile, the man had died two years earlier, "and we haven't heard from him since." According to Gene Poteat, the CIA's support of psychic research was a "dumb exercise" that produced "lots of laughing," but it was born out of a knowledge that the Soviets were conducting such experiments and an attitude of "let's not leave anything uncovered."[119]*

PYRAMIDER

Before its transformation into OTS, the technical services division also was largely responsible for electronic agent communication systems—which for many decades had meant radio. During World War II and many years after, counterespionage agencies around the world monitored illicit radio signals that might reveal the identity, location, and activities of foreign agents. During the war, U.S. intelligence officers behind enemy lines sometimes transmitted data via a system designated JOAN-ELEANOR—receivers and tape recorders carried on an aircraft flying overhead.[120]

The space age brought new possibilities. Communications could be sent to a satellite. Depending on the satellite's orbit, the message could either be stored onboard and then "dumped" when the satellite flew over the appropriate ground station or simply relayed immediately to a ground station. By the late 1970s, the Soviet Union was operating a network of

* ORD's efforts were terminated in 1977 by its new director, Philip Eckman, although he did allow Ken Kress to attend committee meetings dealing with the military-run psychic research program. The support of some influential congressmen for the program made it impossible, Eckman recalled, to just "put a thumb in their eye." He commissioned a reputable experimental psychologist to do a year-and-a-half study reviewing experiments going back to J. B. Rhine. The psychologist concluded that whenever there were adequate controls, there were no positive results. Eckman also recalled that ORD personnel reviewed the remote-viewer notes and concluded they were gibberish—that a description one person could interpret as being of a house, another might believe to describe a bowling alley. (Interview with Philip K. Eckman, Alexandria, Virginia, May 17, 2000.)

low-earth satellites, code-named STRELA, to communicate with illegals in the United States and elsewhere.

The first U.S. effort in the field dated back to 1965–1966. The system, designated BIRDBOOK, was, by subsequent standards, primitive. The intelligence officer or agent would carry the briefcase antenna system into a suitable building, encode the message, load it, go to a windowsill on an upper floor of a building directly under the path of the satellite, open the antenna, and point it in the direction of the satellite. The satellite would send an unlocking signal, and the transmission would begin. To verify that the signal had been properly received, the opening and closing portions were transmitted back by the satellite. The whole process had to be completed in less than five minutes, so that the Committee for State Security (KGB) would be unlikely to locate the site.[121]

That effort was, according to John McMahon, "not all that successful."[122] Two years later, plans for a new system involved only one satellite in low-earth orbit. In addition to collecting transmissions from agents, the CIA gave some consideration to using the satellite to transmit misleading data that would be intercepted by the Soviets. According to Victor Marchetti, "the Russians would go bananas trying to figure out what it meant, when actually it meant nothing." But there was some concern that Soviet fears might lead the Soviet Union to take drastic action, including an attack on the satellite. In addition, there were doubts that the technology existed to develop the system properly.[123]

By late 1972, the concept for an agent communications satellite system had changed dramatically. In addition, the science and technology directorate, and particularly the Office of Special Projects, had taken the lead in managing the design of the planned system. Les Dirks, then the deputy director of OSP (and soon to become director of OD&E), was charged with supervising the project. A possible system was described in a December 14, 1972, TRW submission, "Proposal for Covert Communications Satellite Study." That study, along with related studies, had been designated Project PYRAMIDER. So secret were the studies that the CIA specified that only individuals holding BYEMAN clearances—those cleared to know of NRO projects—were eligible to work on PYRAMIDER.[124]

Dirks's office envisioned three basic types of signals that the satellite should be able to receive. The most important were those from human assets, whether officers or agents, in the field. The system would also be used to receive signals from emplaced sensors, which might detect seismic waves from a nuclear blast or telemetry from a missile test. In addition, the satellite system should be able to serve as a backup communications system to installations and facilities in the event that regular communications were knocked out or otherwise impaired.[125]

The CIA had a number of other requirements: The system should "provide maximum protection of the user against signal detection and direction finding leading to determination of user location." Without the necessary security, the covert satellites would simply be mute witnesses as CIA intelligence assets were hauled away to a grim fate. The system also must minimize dependence on overseas ground stations. A third characteristic required was "multiple simultaneous access capability to users employing different types of traffic, data rates, modulation techniques, and radiated power levels." And in contrast to BIRDBOOK, PYRAMIDER had to enable senders to transmit data at the time and place of their choosing. The system should also "provide protection against traffic analysis, which could imply numbers, types, purpose and location of users."[126]

In attempting to satisfy such concerns, agency-contractor TRW considered a variety of approaches, both with respect to the satellite and the means of communicating with them. Transmission techniques examined included "spread spectrum," burst, or concealed transmissions, as well as frequency-hopping. In the first case, the power level of the signal was reduced and thus harder to detect. In the second, the signal would be compressed and transmitted very rapidly—the expectation being that the extremely short transmission time would minimize the probability of detection. The contractor also examined the possibility of hiding the signal in existing radio or television signals. The apparently innocent signal when received in the United States would be stripped of its cover to reveal the secret signal. Encryption was also considered. Finally, TRW looked at frequency-hopping techniques, in which the frequency on which the signal was transmitted would repeatedly change over the course of the transmission. In its report, TRW noted that use of a frequency-hopping strategy would "reduce aircraft intercept radius in remote areas to twenty nautical miles."[127]

It is not clear exactly what communications strategy TRW recommended. What is clear is that the proposed space segment would consist of three satellites in geosynchronous orbit—at 60, 180, and 300 degrees from CIA headquarters. The locations above which the satellites would "hover" would apparently be the Atlantic Ocean (about 10 degrees east), the Indian Ocean (about 70 degrees east), and the Pacific Ocean (about 135 degrees west). Signals sent to the Atlantic and Pacific satellites would be relayed straight to the CIA; those from the Indian Ocean satellite would be relayed through another satellite or from a ground station, which for the purposes of the study was assumed to be on Guam.[128]

The spacecraft itself would be launched from Cape Canaveral and have a 100-foot-wide concave antenna. The PYRAMIDER study was completed in July 1973. That fall, the CIA realized Congress would not provide the funding required to transform PYRAMIDER from a study to a functioning system and shelved the project.[129] But that would not be the end of DS&T's work on covert communications satellites.

JENNIFER*

On November 4, 1972, the *Glomar Explorer* was launched, ostensibly to mine the ocean floor for metals, especially manganese, which is important for producing steel. Of its CIA-selected 170-man crew, 40 formed the mining staff and knew of the ship's secret mission to retrieve parts of the Soviet Gulf submarine that had imploded in 1968. After its test run, the ship returned to Los Angeles, rendezvoused with the *HMB-1,* and on June 20, 1974, headed out to sea on the recovery mission. At that point, Project AZORIAN became Project JENNIFER.[130]

New York Times investigative reporter Seymour Hersh had learned of the *Glomar Explorer*'s true mission but had agreed to withhold exposing it at the request of DCI William Colby, and the cover story had held. To those interested at all, the ship would be mining manganese nodules from the Pacific depths in a purely commercial enterprise. Although several foreign ships came near to watch the *Glomar* at work, they didn't stay long and floated off, their captains apparently convinced that nothing more than the advertised mission was under way.[131]

By the middle of July, the *Glomar Explorer* reached the submarine site, and the crew set to work with the guidance of a computer and bottom-placed transducer so that the barge would stray no more than fifty feet from the mother ship. Pipe from the ship was attached to giant grappling

---

*A review of one of the books on the *Glomar Explorer,* written by an official knowledgeable about technical intelligence projects, referred to "the JENNIFER (sic) project"—indicating that the term as employed in public accounts is misspelled. Logical alternatives include JENIFER and GENNIFER. (John Milligan, Review of "The Jennifer Project," *Studies in Intelligence* 23, 1 [Spring 1979]: 45.)

claws, which resembled a series of six interconnected ice tongs hanging from a long platform. The ship's crew then began to feed length after length of pipe through the hole. By the time the claw reached the target portion of submarine (the bow and center structure) 16,000 feet below, the pipe itself weighed more than 40,000 pounds. Claw operators used television cameras equipped with strobe lights to see what they were doing.[132]

After fourteen-plus hours, the almost 200-foot-long target was about 5,000 feet off the ocean floor, with another 11,000 to go. But, according to accounts given by U.S. officials, two or three prongs of the claw had become entangled in the seabed. The claws were pulled through the seabed to encircle the submarine, but in the process some of the prongs were bent out of shape and thus were unable to fully support the submarine segment. Most of it fell back into the ocean, including the conning tower, three missiles, and the vessel's code room (with the codebooks, decoding machines, and burst transmitters), and sank to the seabed. Only about a 38-foot section was retrieved. Among the items reportedly recovered were two nuclear torpedoes and the bodies of six Soviet seamen, including the submarine's nuclear weapons officer. The journal he had kept of his training and assignments was also recovered, and it provided detailed information on Soviet naval nuclear systems operation and procedures. The *Glomar* returned on August 12, 1974.[133]

It was also discovered that the Soviets used wooden two-by-fours in the building of some of the sub's compartments—an extremely crude method—and the exterior welding of the hull was uneven and pitted, with the hull itself an uneven thickness. Hatch covers and valves also were crudely constructed, compared with those on U.S. submarines. Two torpedoes recovered were determined to be powered by electric motors, and another two were steam-powered, which indicated that the submarine's firing tubes were not interchangeable. Several books and journals were recovered, and some of the pages could be deciphered after chemical treatment. Apparently included was a partial description of Soviet ciphers in effect in 1968.[134]

The six Soviet seamen were buried at sea in a nighttime ceremony on September 4, 1974. Before the vault carrying their bodies was lowered into the ocean, the U.S. and Soviet national anthems were played, and a short address followed. The speaker noted that "the fact that our nations have had disagreements doesn't lessen in any way our respect for [the seamen]," and that "as long as nations are suspicious of each other . . . brave men will die as these men have died in the service of their country."

(The fifteen-minute ceremony was filmed by the CIA, and in 1992, DCI Robert Gates gave a tape of the ceremony to Russian President Boris Yeltsin.)[135]

The *Glomar Explorer* never got a second chance at the rest of the submarine, although the CIA wanted one. On February 7, 1975, a *Los Angeles Times* story, "U.S. Reported After Russian Submarine/Sunken Ship Deal by CIA, Hughes Told," revealed the project, although the story was pushed onto page eighteen at Colby's request. Similarly, the *New York Times* buried the story on page thirty. But the CIA had to believe that even if KGB officials didn't read newspapers beyond page one, they would not have missed Jack Anderson's discussion of the project on national television. As a result, Colby later wrote, "There was not a chance that we could send the *Glomar* out again on an intelligence project without risking the lives of our crew and inciting a major international incident."[136]

DEPARTURE

In early November 1975, just after getting off a plane at Washington's National Airport, Colby was summoned to a Sunday morning meeting with President Gerald Ford. Ford told the DCI he was "going to do some reorganizing of the national-security structure." Henry Kissinger would have to adjust to being merely Secretary of State; the position of national security adviser would be filled by his deputy, Brent Scowcroft. Colby's predecessor as DCI, Secretary of Defense James Schlesinger, was also being fired—due to a lack of rapport with Ford and Kissinger. Colby was "offered" a new job—ambassador to NATO, which he would decline. Colby's mistake was that he had been too willing to provide Frank Church's select Senate committee, in the midst of its high-profile, public investigation of the CIA, with information that the White House and Kissinger would have preferred remain secret.[137]

Colby stayed on at the CIA for a few months until his replacement, George Bush, returned from Beijing, where he had headed the U.S. liaison office. For Bush, the directorship would be another in a series of national security jobs on his way to the presidency. But by the end of his one year in office, the ten-year tenure of Carl Duckett as head of DS&T would be over. When Bush took over the agency, he was told that he had two alcoholics to deal with, including Duckett. Bush, according to Duckett's deputy, Sayre Stevens, "treated Carl delicately, with genuine concern," and "gave Carl every chance in the world."[138]

But Duckett found it impossible to stop drinking. His alcoholism may have been fueled by family problems as well as his disappointment in not having been made either director or deputy director. He had expected that promotion when Richard Helms departed in 1973. Since Schlesinger's appointment was clearly a short-term one, he held out hope that he would be next in line—only to find Colby grabbing the brass ring.[139] Subsequently, he acknowledged that the reports of his drinking led to a discussion with Bush. He would claim that Bush's unwillingness to promote him to deputy director was the true cause of his departure in June 1976.[140]

But the combination of his drinking and his tendency to be indiscreet proved to be a lethal combination for his career. On March 11, 1976, Duckett participated in an informal seminar in front of local members of the American Institute of Aeronautics and Astronautics. The briefing was part of a campaign of increased CIA openness to offset the unfavorable publicity from press and congressional disclosures. One hundred and fifty individuals paid $6.50 for cocktails, a light buffet, and close to two hours of discussion with high-ranking CIA officials. Although the briefing was unclassified, they were asked not to take notes or quote the officials to the press.[141]

Among the topics of discussion was the state of the Soviet space program, which was, according to the CIA representatives, in a "shambles" following a series of launch failures. When asked about Israel's nuclear capability, Duckett didn't hesitate but responded that the CIA estimated Israel had ten to twenty nuclear weapons available for use. If the disclosure of such secret information had stayed with members of the group, perhaps there would have been no repercussions.[142]

But in attendance were several reporters, including Arthur Kranish, editor of *Science Trends*, a Washington newsletter. On March 15, the *Washington Post* published an article by Kranish titled "CIA: Israel Has 10–20 A-Weapons." He did not name Duckett as the source, but there were plenty of witnesses.[143]

Bush issued a public statement accepting "full responsibility" for the disclosure of the highly classified information. It didn't help the situation that Duckett was rumored to have been drinking at the time of his indiscretion. Not long afterward, his request for retirement, for reasons of health, was received and accepted by the DCI.[144]

7

CRACKS IN THE EMPIRE

Carl Duckett's departure would be a key event in the history of the Directorate of Science and Technology. Just as Bud Wheelon's arrival allowed an empire to be established, Duckett's departure marked the beginning of the empire's decline—although it would not be a steep one. Within months, the directorate's scientific and technical intelligence units would be transferred to the intelligence directorate. Several years later, the TACKSMAN sites would be gone. In addition, the CIA's near-autonomy in signals intelligence operations would yield to congressional insistence that NSA manage all the government's SIGINT activities.

Had Duckett remained, the transfer of the DS&T's intelligence analysis components may have never been proposed, and if it had, he might have been able to block it. He might have convinced Congress to leave the CIA's SIGINT operations alone. But his skill as a smooth talker would have been of no help in preventing the fall of the Shah of Iran and the loss of the TACKSMAN sites. Ayatollahs and fanatical Iranian students would, undoubtedly, have been impervious to his charms.

When Duckett departed on June 1, 1976, Leslie Dirks moved up from director of the development and engineering office to take Duckett's place. Duckett's deputy, Sayre Stevens, had left a few weeks earlier to become deputy director for intelligence. Replacing Stevens as the directorate's number-two man was Ernest J. Zellmer, a former submariner, who had served in the Office of Scientific Intelligence under Wheelon and who would play a major role as the directorate's voice in the National Underwater Reconnaissance Program.[1]

Dirks was different from Duckett both in looks and personality. One account described Dirks, halfway through his tenure as DS&T head, as "a tall, gaunt, balding physicist with the sterile aura of a pathology lab."[2] Robert Phillips, who had helped establish the TACKSMAN II site and served in the directorate for three decades, recalled that of all the deputy directors he served under, Dirks was the one for whom he had the least appreciation—considering him aloof, which was perhaps exacerbated by his preoccupation in 1976 with an ill wife. Phillips also found him too heavily focused on the satellite programs he had been managing before his promotion.* He recalled an incident in which he escorted the senior leadership of a foreign intelligence service, one Phillips had helped develop a facet of its technical collection capability, in to see Dirks, only to have him tell the visitors that he "didn't know you had that capability."[3]

Philip Eckman, who headed the Office of Research and Development during most of Dirks's term as deputy director, characterized his boss as a perfectionist who could be "tough to work for, pretty demanding"—a description some would probably have used to describe Bud Wheelon. At the same time, Dirks had "an excellent eye for identifying the right person for the right job."[4]

Although some aspects of Dirks's personality may have irritated some, and although the directorate did not remain quite the empire that Wheelon and Duckett created, it did experience a number of triumphs during Dirks's tenure—the most important being the success of the satellite program he had nurtured for more than a decade. It resulted in his receiving a medal from President Carter and in a nation with dramatically enhanced intelligence capabilities.

LOSS, GAIN, AND REFORM

Shortly after becoming deputy director for intelligence, Sayre Stevens proposed that the Office of Scientific Intelligence and the Office of Weapons Intelligence be transferred to the intelligence directorate. Stevens felt that the separation of the two offices from the rest of the intelligence-production effort was artificial. Furthermore, he was concerned about the lack of interdisciplinary analysis on foreign military forces—particularly with regard to nuclear proliferation. Analysts from OSI and OWI did not communicate with those from the intelligence directorate. When OSI's nuclear energy division suggested China might follow a certain path with regard to its nuclear weapons program, it did so

---

*Indeed, Dirks's continued intense focus on such programs was exceedingly annoying to Robert Kohler, one of his successors as director of development and engineering. At one point, Kohler told Dirks that "if you want to run the fucking program, we can trade jobs." (Telephone interview with Robert Kohler, July 6, 1999.)

without any discussion with the political and economic analysts from the intelligence directorate. Bringing the technical people into his organization, Stevens felt at the time, was a solution.[5]

One source of opposition was Dirks, who pointed to the close relationship that existed among the analysts, collectors, and collection system developers in his directorate. In addition, Dirks warned Stevens that "you'll leave or get thrown out, and they'll put some political scientist in there" who would ruin everything. Stevens himself was concerned that the funding for OSI and OWI contracts with outside consultants would be jeopardized. Not only was the money involved many times the entire budget for the intelligence directorate, but the DI did not favor contracting.[6]

But Stevens was able to convince DCI George Bush, and the offices were transferred. The wisdom of that transfer is, even today, a subject of disagreement. Evan Hineman, who served as OWI deputy director from 1974 to 1976 and as its director from 1976 to 1979, believes the transfer was "the right thing to do" because all analytical efforts should have been brought together. According to Hineman, the result was an improved product, with some of the softer sciences rubbing off on the engineering types and some of the harder sciences rubbing off on the social scientists. When he became science and technology chief in 1982, it never entered his mind to attempt to reclaim OWI.[7]

That view was shared by Rae Huffstutler, who served as director of the Office of Strategic Research (1979–1982) and then as head of the Office of Soviet Analysis (1982–1984). In his view, if one was going to do Soviet analysis, it was necessary to have all the analytical threads; political and military analysts had to work together to capture the threat. In 1996, Stevens, however, characterized the transfer as a "foolish move on my part," and said that "to some extent" Dirks's warning about the consequences of his departure proved accurate.[8]

Dirks's directorate did receive something in return—the Foreign Broadcast Information Service (FBIS), whose open source collection activities provided a significant portion of the information used by agency analysts. The loss "caused a good deal of heartburn in the DI," according to Stevens. But it was felt that FBIS was more of a collection activity than an analytical unit and thus belonged in the science and technology directorate.* More important, FBIS was badly in need of modernization, par-

*That did not stop FBIS analysts in 1979 from anticipating the Chinese invasion of Vietnam by demonstrating, with rare exceptions, that the wording of authoritative

ticularly automation, and the DS&T was much better at such tasks than the intelligence directorate. The "DI culture had them just struggling along," according to Huffstutler, because the intelligence directorate "didn't know how to run programs" or justify modernization budgets to Congress.[9]

The transfer would eventually pave the way for a 1982 modernization program, designated MIDAS, to update FBIS—to move it out of the "green-eyeshade" era and allow it to catch up with industry. CIA representatives visited the *New York Times* as well as the *Philadelphia Inquirer* to learn how a modern news organization worked.[10]

In addition to losses and gains, Dirks's tenure was also marked by continued efforts to "reform" the Office of Research and Development, which still had a reputation as a "rogue" group, according to Dirks's choice to lead the reform effort, Philip Eckman. In October 1976, Eckman, who held a doctorate from Carnegie Tech in electrical engineering, was working at Cal Tech's Jet Propulsion Laboratory in Pasadena. That month he received a call from Dirks, who told him he was coming to Los Angeles and would like to have dinner. Eckman, who was recommended to Dirks by Bud Wheelon's intended successor, Frank Lehan, almost didn't go, but finally agreed to meet the CIA's science and technology chief.[11]

At dinner, Dirks briefed Eckman, who knew little about the agency, on the CIA's science and technology effort and offered him the ORD directorship. According to a brief memoir written by Eckman, Dirks "pitched the wonders of ORD [but] gave absolutely no hint that he had recently proposed to the CIA's executive council that ORD be abolished!" In late February 1977, Eckman arrived for his first day at work. He expected to stay a few years but remained through March 1989.[12]

When he arrived, Eckman found an office "which carried considerable baggage, with some questioning its relevance to the rest of the Agency." In addition, two acting directors followed the tenures of Stevens and Hirsch, giving the office four directors in less than five years. Eckman's charter from Dirks was to make the office relevant, "make it grow . . . and make it central." Before attempting to carry out that mandate, ORD's se-

---

Chinese warnings to Vietnam had been used only in instances in which Beijing used military force. (Remarks by William O. Studeman, Deputy Director of Central Intelligence, Symposium on "National Security and National Competitiveness: Open Source Solutions," December 1, 1992, McLean, Va., p. 9.)

nior officials spent time identifying the roles of the CIA and ORD and settled on technology development in support of collection and analysis as ORD's mission. A reorganization followed that involved creation of a Collection Technology Group and a Processing and Analysis Group. And "for the free spirits who shunned structure, regular management, and orthodoxy, we formed an Advanced Concepts Staff that was intended to be counter-cultural and light on its feet."[13]

In addition to organizational changes and streamlining the project approval process, ORD soon sought to change its relationship with its customers. Eckman credited his first deputy, Ed Cates, with getting ORD to reach out to its customers through annual briefings to customer office directors and promoting awareness of the office's work through an annual accomplishments book.[14]

REAL TIME

On the morning of December 19, 1976, a Titan 3D rocket blasted off from Vandenberg Air Force Base. Its mission was to propel yet another KEYHOLE satellite into orbit. Through December 18, there had been 296 days of satellite coverage that year. Although there had been no crises equivalent to the Middle East wars, the Soviet invasion of Czechoslovakia, or the Cuban missile crisis to monitor, U.S. spy satellites certainly had not lacked targets.

The launch went smoothly, with the Titan 3D sending its payload into a polar orbit. Seemingly, yet another KH-9/HEXAGON had been lofted into space. But close observers noted at least one difference. The new satellite had a markedly higher perigee and apogee than previous KH-9 satellites, coming no closer than 165 miles to the earth's surface—as compared with the normal KH-9 perigee of a little over 100 miles. In an article published in early 1978, space expert Anthony Kenden noted: "A Big Bird was launched on 19 December 1976 into an unusually high orbit, from [153 to 330 miles]. . . . This new type of orbit may indicate that it was the first test of a Program 1010 vehicle."[15]

Indeed, the payload that was placed in orbit on December 19 was the first launch of the KENNAN program (designated 1010 by Lockheed, the primary contractor), which had successfully produced a spacecraft with an electro-optical system—known as the KH-11. The specific spacecraft bore the designation 5501 to specify the particular satellite and mission number.[16]

The KH-11 was launched within two months of the target date, and despite reports to the contrary, it came in substantially under budget. Before Dirks's tenure would end, another three KH-11s would be successfully launched—on June 14, 1978, February 7, 1980, and September 3, 1981. In addition, the code name for the program would be changed from KENNAN to CRYSTAL in 1982.[17]

In general, no two versions of any imaging satellite are necessarily identical, because modifications are often made to sensors and other equipment. The basic dimensions of the KH-11 remained the same from the initial launch—the cylindrical spacecraft measured about 64 feet long and 10 feet in diameter and weighed about 30,000 pounds.[18]

The optical system, however, underwent a major change between the first and subsequent satellites. The first satellite relied on light-sensing diodes to collect the light reflected from the target. By the time the second spacecraft was constructed, Lockheed was able to turn to charge-coupled devices, or CCDs. The CCD originated at Bell Telephone Laboratories in the late 1960s when two researchers, William S. Boyle and George E. Smith, invented a new type of memory circuit—a development that had been in the works for most of the decade. The researchers quickly realized that the tiny chip of semiconducting silicon they first demonstrated in 1970 had a variety of other applications, including signal processing and imaging (the latter because silicon responds to visible light). By 1975, scientists from the California Institute of Technology's Jet Propulsion Laboratory and the University of Arizona were using a CCD in conjunction with a 61-inch telescope to produce a picture of Uranus, about 1.7 billion miles from earth.[19]

The optical system of the KH-11 (and its successors) scanned its target in long, narrow strips and focused the light onto an array of CCDs with several thousand elements. The light falling on each CCD during a short, fixed period of time was then transformed into a proportional amount of electrical charge. In turn, the electrical charge was read and fed into an amplifier, which converted the current into a whole number, between 0 and 256, representing a shade of color ranging from pure black to pure white. Thus each picture was transmitted as a string of numbers—one from each element.[20]

More specifically, the CCD captured particles of energy, visible light, in an array of picture elements known as pixels. The pixels automatically measured the intensity of the particles and then would "send them on their way in orderly rows until they are electronically stacked up to form a kind of mosaic." The standard CCD used in the Hubble Space Telescope has a total of 640,000 pixels arranged in an 800-by-800 format and occupies less than half a square inch.[21]

The KH-11's charge-coupled devices could not, however, do the job alone. Without a good mirror in front of them, even the best CCDs produce photographs with poor resolution. But the mirror for the first KH-11 was quite good and quite large—seven feet, eight inches wide. (Subsequently, mirror size increased). The secondary mirror, greater than one foot in diameter, narrowed the image coming off the primary mirror and sharply focused it.[22]

Another key to the KH-11's ability to produce high-quality photographs was its computer. About the size of a sleek VCR, the computer was fundamental to maintaining the KH-11 in a stable position, pointing the mirror and obtaining photographs of the desired targets.[23]

Once the visible light was collected and transformed into an electrical charge, the signals were then transmitted to one of two Satellite Data System (SDS) spacecraft as the relay spacecraft passed slowly over the northern Soviet Union. The SDS orbit was identical to that first employed by Soviet *Molniya* satellites. Orbiting with a 63-degree inclination, the satellite approached to within 250 miles of earth when passing over the Southern hemisphere, and it moved as far away as 24,000 miles as it drifted over the Northern Hemisphere. A spacecraft in such an orbit took eight to nine hours to pass over Soviet territory, leaving it available to receive and transmit imagery for long stretches of time.[24]

The SDS spacecraft, the first two of which were launched in June and August of 1976, performed a variety of functions. In addition to transmitting the KH-11 digital signals, they relayed communications to any B-52s flying on a polar route, served as communications links between the various parts of the Air Force Satellite Control Facility, and carried nuclear detonation detection sensors. Those other functions, Bud Wheelon noted, were "strictly a sideshow," a nice bonus if they worked but a minor loss if they did not.[25]

The SDS satellite then transmitted the KH-11 signals for initial processing to a ground station at Fort Belvoir, Virginia, about twenty miles south of Washington. The Mission Ground Site—a large, windowless, two-story concrete building—was given the cover title of Defense Communications Electronics Evaluation and Testing Activity and also was designated as Area 58.[26]

Its method of transmitting data permitted the first KH-11 to remain in orbit for over two years—770 days. The next three lasted 1,166, 973, and

1,175 days, respectively.[27] The KH-11 was not limited, as were the KH-8 and KH-9, by the amount of film that could be carried on board. In addition, it had a higher orbit, approximately 150 by 250 miles, that reduced atmospheric drag on the spacecraft.

The new system had one serious initial limitation. Although it could transmit its data instantaneously, it could do so only for two hours per day. So much power was required to transmit the data to the relay satellite (via the KH-11's traveling wave tube amplifier) that the system drained power far faster than it could be replaced by the satellite's solar panels. Thus, the new model of the spy satellite fleet could be used only sparingly at first.[28]

The KH-11 operated along with KH-8 and KH-9 satellites for several years before becoming America's sole type of photographic reconnaissance satellite. Only a few, very select government officials were permitted to know of the KH-11's existence or even see its product. The KH-11 was treated with even greater secrecy than usual in the black world of reconnaissance satellites—the photographs and data derived from them were not incorporated with data from the KH-8 and KH-9 systems. The decision to restrict the data to a very small group of individuals was taken at the urging of senior CIA officials, including COMIREX chairman Roland Inlow, but it was opposed by military officers who wanted the information to be more widely distributed throughout the armed forces.[29]

Among the officials who did know about KENNAN in early 1977 were president-elect Jimmy Carter and his national security adviser, Zbigniew Brzezinski. The latter had been briefed extensively on the new system after Carter's election in November. On December 30, 1976, Enno Henry "Hank" Knoche, the Deputy Director of Central Intelligence, along with John McMahon and other CIA representatives, met with Brzezinski. As part of the briefing, which covered human and technical collection operations, McMahon described the KENNAN system "at some length." Knoche suggested to Brzezinski that he think of the new real-time capability in the context of new approaches to crisis management. He noted that a KH-11 could be tasked by crisis managers, "made responsive to live needs," and be the "basis for re-thinking the organization of current crisis management."[30]

In the month between its launch and Carter's inauguration, the KH-11 underwent checkout and testing and that day finally transmitted its first photos. By this time, Knoche was the CIA's acting director, pending confirmation of the new President's choice for DCI. George Bush had wanted to remain as DCI, but Carter would not extend the stalwart Republican's tenure, not even until his own choice could be confirmed. Until that happened—and confirmation took longer than usual because Carter's first nominee, former Kennedy White House aide Theodore Sorensen, withdrew when it became clear he could not win approval—Knoche was head of the world's most technically accomplished intelligence establishment. Among Knoche's first roles was to show Carter the capabilities of America's newest spy satellite—one way of demonstrating the CIA's value to the new President.[31]

The most dramatic demonstration would have been for Carter to see the photos within moments of their arrival. But he was busy on Inauguration Day—taking the oath of office, strolling down Pennsylvania Avenue in subfreezing weather, and attending the various traditional celebrations. In addition, to have the most dramatic effect would have required either that Carter make the trip to Ft. Belvoir or that Ft. Belvoir come to Carter, neither of which was feasible. As a result, Knoche decided to wait a day before visiting the new President.[32]

So it was 3:15 in the afternoon of January 21 when Knoche and Admiral Daniel J. Murphy, the DCI's deputy for intelligence community affairs, began a fifteen-minute meeting with Carter and Brzezinski in the White House's second-floor Map Room. Knoche had a handful of six-inch square black-and-white photos with him.[33] McMahon had told Carter what the KH-11 could do; now Knoche would show him. Carter examined the photographs that Knoche spread on the map table. The photographs did not reveal some secret, nefarious activity on the other side of the world, but provided an overhead perspective of something much closer to home—Carter's inauguration. After peering at the photos for a few moments, Carter looked up at Knoche, grinned, and then laughed appreciatively. He congratulated Knoche and Murphy on the apparent quality of their latest reconnaissance system and requested Knoche to send over some more samples for the next day's National Security Council meeting, his first as President. "Of course," Carter said as he turned to Brzezinski, "this will also be of value in our arms control work."[34]

Carter and Brzezinski knew they had something of immense value. Indeed, it was more obvious to them than to some in the CIA, for it was the president and his advisers who might be pressed in a crisis to make crucial decisions that could dramatically affect the fate of the United States. Now they would be able to make those decisions with timely information.[35]

PROSECUTION WITNESS

By 1977, Leslie Dirks had been with the CIA for sixteen years. He had participated in countless meetings to discuss U.S. satellite reconnaissance activities—meetings that were conducted under strict security guidelines, often in vault areas. But in April 1977 and November 1978, Dirks would appear in a quite different setting—U.S. District Court. In each case, he would be the key prosecution witness in a trial that resulted from the sale of secrets about one of the CIA's greatest technical accomplishments. The buyer was the Soviet Union. The secrets concerned RHYOLITE and the KH-11.

The sequence of events that led to Dirks's first court appearance began on July 29, 1974, when twenty-one-year-old Christopher John Boyce began work at TRW as a general clerk at a salary of $140 a week. On November 15, he was briefed on RHYOLITE, described by the briefer as "a multipurpose covert electronic surveillance system."[36] He was also told about the PYRAMIDER and ARGUS programs.

The revelations were necessary because Boyce had been assigned to work in TRW's "black vault"—a bank-style vault with a three-number combination and an inside door with a key lock. Within the vault, he monitored secret communications traffic relating to various CIA-TRW satellite projects. Less than six months after joining TRW, Boyce was using a boyhood friend, Andrew Daulton Lee, to sell the vault's secrets to the KGB. In April 1975, Lee, who was more familiar with peddling marijuana than crypto cards, walked through the front door of the Soviet embassy in Mexico City and handed a typewritten note to the first official he encountered. It read, "Enclosed is a computer card from the National Security Agency, crypto system. . . . If you want to do business, please advise the courier."[37]

The KGB, naturally, was interested. And Boyce had a wealth of material to choose from, with fifty to sixty messages a day passing through his hands, messages kept on file for a year. Altogether, Lee would make seven trips to meet with KGB officers. On March 15, 1976, he arrived in Vienna and delivered ten rolls of film containing a month of ciphers; RHYOLITE communications traffic among TRW, the CIA, and Pine Gap; and a thick technical report on the proposed ARGUS system.[38]

In early October 1976, Boyce joined Lee, for the first time, in Mexico City. Once there, it became apparent that as much as KGB officials valued the intelligence Boyce was providing on U.S. satellites, they thought he could be more useful elsewhere. The KGB would be willing, Boyce was told, to provide $40,000 to pay for college and graduate school. They envisioned that Boyce would become a Soviet or Chinese specialist and find a job with the State Department or CIA. Before the month was out, Boyce had applied for admission to the University of California at Riverside.[39]

But the KGB's plan to turn Boyce into a mole was torpedoed by Lee's impulsive behavior. On one occasion, such behavior had led his KGB contact, Boris, to pack Lee in a car and toss him out onto the road. But the lesson did not stick. On January 6, 1977, eager to get money to purchase drugs from a Mexican supplier, Lee tried to get Boris's attention by throwing a Spanish-American dictionary, on which he had marked "KGB," onto the embassy grounds. Fearing that Lee was a terrorist and the dictionary a bomb, the Mexican police immediately arrested him and discovered a sealed envelope with microfilm strips inside the dictionary. The strips contained 450 frames concerning PYRAMIDER.[40]

Within a few months, Boyce and Lee were standing trial, though separately. On April 20, 1977, Leslie Dirks began his testimony in a Los Angeles courtroom, which would conclude the prosecution's case. After eliciting a detailed description of his background, the prosecution went on to establish Dirks's authority to classify projects, including PYRAMIDER. Dirks described the origins and some of the details of the PYRAMIDER studies and his decision that they should be classified as top secret.[41]

He also testified that even though no operational system ever emerged from the studies, U.S. intelligence would sustain significant damage if the Soviet Union had access to information about PYRAMIDER. It would, the science and technology chief argued, provide the KGB with valuable information about the state of covert communications technology as well as the options and strategies that had been considered.[42]

Such information could be used to compromise the communications of both agents and emplaced sensors. Such communications were vital, for the "plans and intents [of foreign governments], in the hands of an agent, does no good. Those plans and intents must be communicated and frequently it's important to do so rapidly to ourselves, the CIA, and ultimately to the President of the United States so that he may be forewarned of a plan or an intent to initiate . . . hostilities in some part of the world." Without a link between U.S. agents and the President, "the national security would indeed be exposed to great damage."[43]

Dirks's testimony for the prosecution concluded with his observation that among the reasons the PYRAMIDER studies needed to be classified was that "they reveal the requirements for covert communications which are still . . . valid requirements." Then, according to author Robert Lindsey, "in more than four hours of cross-examination, [defense attorney] George Chelius did not knock any significant holes in Dirks's testimony. He had left a solid impression with the jury that Chris's actions involved grave harm to the United States."[44]

That impression undoubtedly carried great weight with the jury, which returned a guilty verdict. On July 18, Lee, who had also been convicted, received life imprisonment. Boyce, who had been granted the clearances and had the responsibility for protecting the information, received forty years. Throughout the trials, convictions, and sentencing, there was not a word uttered about RHYOLITE or ARGUS, or the fact that based on Boyce's revelations the Soviet Union began encrypting the telemetry that RHYOLITE had been intercepting, topics the CIA and NRO considered too sensitive for discussion in open court. Further, Boyce's and Lee's disclosure of the PYRAMIDER material was enough to seal their fate. At the time, the very existence of the SIGINT satellite program was highly classified. Out of public view, at least one change was made—the code name RHYOLITE was replaced by AQUACADE.[45]

In November 1978, Dirks was back in court, again as the result of the compromise of a key satellite system. But rather than being in Los Angeles in early spring, Dirks was in Indianapolis in early winter. This time the defendant was a CIA rather than a contractor employee. And the trial revolved around the key secrets that had been divulged. Finally, the recipient was not the KGB but the GRU—the Chief Intelligence Directorate of the Soviet General Staff.

On trial was William Kampiles, who in March 1977 had begun his brief and undistinguished CIA career as a watch analyst in the Operations Center. Watch analysts, although junior officers, received information from the full range of intelligence community sources—CIA agent reports, KEYHOLE imagery, NSA communication intercepts, as well as Defense attaché and Foreign Service reports. They monitored the incoming intelligence reports from around the world and routed them inside the agency.[46]

Among the documents provided to help them understand the significance of the incoming data was Copy 155 of the *KH-11 System Technical*

Manual. Once someone was within the vaulted confines of the watch office, there was no further restriction on access to the manual, and it was not locked up. Its normal resting spot was on a shelf alongside a copy of an almanac in an unlocked cabinet, known as the CONSERVA file, beneath an ordinary copying machine.[47]

Despite access to such documents, Kampiles found the work tedious. He had envisioned using his fluent Greek in clandestine work overseas. But his undistinguished early record in the agency did not stimulate interest in him within the operations directorate. As his performance deteriorated, all hopes of a transfer disappeared. An operations center supervisor recommended that Kampiles be fired before his probationary period was up. He pawed the women in the office, bragged of his sexual exploits, and "stood out markedly from the rest of the people; he was a bullshitter." In November 1977, after only eight months in the CIA and receipt of a formal letter indicating dissatisfaction with his work, he resigned.[48]

Before departing for good, Kampiles pilfered the KH-11 manual, which was not regularly inventoried. One day, he stuffed a copy of the manual into his sports jacket and carried it out of the building. Doing so was not particularly difficult. Removal of classified documents from the agency by employees who wanted to do some work at home had reached such proportions that DCI Stansfield Turner had sent a memo to agency employees ordering a halt to the practice.[49]

On February 19, 1978, Kampiles left for Greece. Three or four days later, he went to the Soviet embassy and offered to deliver documents. He provided a GRU officer with two to three pages of the KH-11 manual—its table of contents, summary, and an artist's conception of the satellite. At a second meeting, Kampiles demonstrated his lack of skill as a covert operator—turning over the rest of the manual for a mere $3,000.[50]

Back in the United States, having received guidance from the GRU about topics of interest and instructions concerning further meetings, Kampiles was anything but discreet. On April 29, 1978, Kampiles sat on a bench outside CIA headquarters telling George Joannides, a friend and employee of the General Counsel's office, how he had conned the Soviets out of $3,000—apparently believing that would make him more attractive to the operations directorate he still longed to join.[51]

That talk was followed by a letter Kampiles wrote to Joannides at the latter's suggestion, which he then passed on to an officer in the Soviet division, Vivian Psachos. She suggested that Kampiles, who was in Indiana, return to Washington to discuss the matter. Attending the discussions on August 14, along with Kampiles, were Psachos, the FBI's Donald Stukey and John Denton, and Bruce Solie of the CIA's Office of Security. Those officials were aware of the CIA's conclusion that the KH-11 had been compromised and also knew, from a GRU officer, of the sale of the satellite manual to the Soviets in Greece and when it was sold—as well as when Kampiles had been in Greece. They were also aware that the Soviets never paid money for promises, only for hard information or documents. Thus, they were more than skeptical about Kampiles's claim of having swindled the GRU.[52]

The next day, in an interview at the Washington field office, James Murphy told Kampiles he didn't believe him, and that if he didn't believe it, "nobody in the whole world would believe it." Kampiles, who had failed two polygraphs, slumped down in his chair and buried his head in his hands. After several seconds, Kampiles looked up at Murphy. "You're right," he said. "I didn't get the $3,000 for nothing. I sold them the document."[53]

Less than three months later, Kampiles was facing a jury, charged with espionage. The trial was the product of a Carter administration decision to prosecute espionage cases, even at the risk of further disclosures.[54] In addition to the testimony of Murphy and Stukey, who recounted their interrogation of Kampiles and his ultimate confession, the prosecution relied heavily on the testimony of Leslie Dirks.

Dirks told the jury that U.S. national defense could be "seriously harmed" if the Soviet Union had access to the KH-11 manual. He said knowledge of the manual would suggest ways that the Soviet Union could hide its nuclear and military capabilities from the satellite.[55] He explained that the "KH-11 system is a photographic satellite with associated ground facilities for controlling [the] satellite and distributing its products" and "one of the principal intelligence collection sources used to verify that the Soviet Union is indeed living up to the terms of their [SALT] agreement with the United States."[56]

Disclosure of the top-secret manual to a hostile foreign power, Dirks testified, would do serious harm to national defense. The manual described "the characteristics, capabilities and limitations of the satellite" and described the "process of photography employed by the KH-11 system and illustrates the quality of the photos and the process used in passing the product along to the users of the system." Further, the manual detailed the "responsiveness and timeliness in the delivery of the 'product.'" Page eight of the sixty-four-page manual described the satellite's "limitations in geographic coverage."[57]

In addition, possession of the manual would "put the Soviet Union in a position to avoid coverage from this system. For example, by rolling . . . new aircraft [under development] into hangars when the system passes overhead, thereby preventing photographs of the new airplanes." Knowledge of the quality of the photographs could enable the Soviets to devise "effective camouflage."[58] Compromise of the KH-11 system would, according to Dirks, cost the United States the advantage of being able to produce "accurate and current information" on Soviet capability for the U.S. president "in a time of crisis."[59]

The jury deliberated for just ten hours before returning their verdict—guilty on all counts. Two counts dealt with espionage and the defendant's intent to injure the United States and carried the possibility of a life sentence. Other counts, carrying lesser penalties, concerned passing U.S. documents to unauthorized persons and the sale of U.S. documents valued at more than $100.[60]

At his December 22 sentencing, Kampiles said, "First of all, Your Honor, I'm sorry for everything that has happened. Not at any time did I want to injure my country in any way. I only wanted to serve my country." Prosecuting attorney David T. Ready suggested a "substantial sentence." Kampiles "chose to casually disregard the safety and well-being of 200 million Americans."[61]

Judge McNagny sentenced Kampiles to forty years in prison stating that "This case is a complete tragedy for a young man who has never been in trouble before" but that "the United States has suffered a severe setback because of the sale to the Russians."[62]

MERGERS

At the beginning of 1976, the Office of ELINT was not the only CIA component with a signals intelligence mission. In the operations directorate, Division D continued its mission of collecting COMINT from outposts in various U.S. embassies and consulates as well as from vans loaded with eavesdropping equipment. The primary mission of those outposts was "close support" of CIA operations—including monitoring the communications of the local security service.[63]

But in February 1977, Division D and OEL were merged into the Office of SIGINT Operations (OSO), which would be part of the science and technology directorate. The consolidation may have been a means of eliminating the "constant battles" that former OEL chief Robert Singel recalled being fought by the two organizations. But according to Roy Burks, who became head of the OSO operations group when it was formed and then its director in September 1981, the merger was a friendly one, with no opposition from the operations directorate.[64]

Heading up the new office during its first fifteen months was Edward Ryan, a veteran of the operations directorate whose previous assignments had included chief of station in Stockholm, chief of base in Berlin, and, until the merger, head of Division D. In May 1978, he was succeeded by another operations officer, David Barry Kelly, whose CIA service had included stints in Nepal, Vietnam, and Moscow.[65]

Kelly would play a key role in the creation of a new and still classified secret signals intelligence organization, which merged the embassy eavesdropping operations of the DS&T and NSA. In 1976, Charlie Snodgrass, staff director for the House Armed Services Committee, conducted a study on U.S. SIGINT activities—and didn't like what he found: too much duplication, not enough coordination, and lack of clear lines of authority in key areas. It had been the practice under Duckett for the CIA to conduct SIGINT activities as it wished, ignoring whatever edicts came from NSA.[66] As a result of Snodgrass's study, and the pressure from Congress that followed, the CIA was forced to acknowledge the NSA as the national SIGINT authority. NSA was quite willing to take over responsibility for all SIGINT. A memorandum of agreement between the two agencies followed, covering liaison, overhead collection, and a number of other subjects.[67] In addition, agreement was reached for the CIA and NSA to merge embassy intercept operations. The CIA really had no choice, as the congressional oversight committees' perception of too much overlap and competition between CIA and NSA embassy operations led Congress to cut off funding for the CIA operation.[68]

The issue was somewhat more complex than that, according to Roy Burks. The CIA viewed the primary purpose of its embassy sites, not surprisingly given Division D's origin, as to assist CIA stations and their officers in the field. For NSA, the mandate was different. It had no operatives in the field to support, so the focus of its intelligence activity was to support national and military policymakers.[69]

The embassy operations, both CIA and NSA, had produced some valuable intelligence. In the late 1960s and early 1970s, the Moscow operation, code-named BROADSIDE, intercepted the radiotelephone conversations of Soviet Politburo members—including General Secretary Leonid Brezhnev, President Nikolai Podgorny, and Premier Alexei Kosygin—as they drove around Moscow. Traffic from the interception operation was transmitted to a special CIA facility a few miles from the agency's Langley headquarters.[70]

Originally, the conversations simply needed to be translated, since no attempt had been made to scramble or encipher the conversations. After columnist Jack Anderson disclosed the operation in 1971, the Soviets began enciphering their limousine telephone calls to plug leaks. Despite that effort, the United States was able to intercept and decode a conversation between Brezhnev and Minister of Defense A. A. Grechko that took place shortly before the signing of the SALT I Treaty. Grechko assured Brezhnev that the heavy Soviet SS-19 missiles under construction would fit inside the launch tubes of lighter SS-11 missiles, making the missiles permissible under the SALT treaty.[71]

In general, however, the intelligence obtained, code-named GAMMA GUPY, was less than earthshaking. According to a former intelligence official involved in the operation, the CIA "didn't find out about, say, the invasion of Czechoslovakia. It was very gossipy—Brezhnev's health and maybe Podgorny's sex life." At the same time, the official said that the operation "gave us extremely valuable information on the personalities of top Soviet leaders."[72]

When the United States opened a liaison office in Beijing in late May 1973, CIA station chief James Lilley set up limousine watches to monitor high-level meetings at the Great Hall and Zhongnanhai, the walled compound that has served as the seat of government in the Communist era. Subsequently, advanced eavesdropping equipment was brought in by diplomatic pouch and placed on the office's roof. The equipment was used to monitor Chinese aircraft movements and intercept both military and civilian communications. It was not long before the liaison office, by monitoring the arrival of flights from the provinces, was able to determine when a Central Committee meeting was imminent.[73]

Details of the merger of embassy intercept operations were worked out between Vice-Adm. Bobby Inman, who became NSA director in July 1977, and OSO chief Barry Kelly. It was agreed that the joint enterprise, to be called the Special Collection Service (SCS), would be initially headed by a CIA official who would serve a two-year term. The deputy director of the SCS would be selected from NSA, and an NSA official would become director after the CIA official completed his term. The director's job would continue to alternate between CIA and NSA officials, with the director's deputy succeeding him.[74]

Things did not get off to a smooth start. Many in OSO were not happy with the formation of the SCS and didn't want to be part of a group that would be managed by an NSA official half the time. Appointed to be the first head of the new service was Roy Burks. From NSA, Bill Black, a senior operations official, was selected to serve as deputy. Neither man, Burks later recalled, was involved in the bitter fighting that preceded the merger, a factor that gave them a better chance to make the new arrangement work.[75]

According to Burks, there were people on both sides who seemed to want to make things difficult. Among the obstacles SCS faced was getting the CIA to courier documents to its College Park headquarters, forcing Burks to send a cleared secretary. The CIA did not want to send material to College Park because NSA people, at that time, were not polygraphed. Only when NSA began routinely giving polygraphs to its employees did the CIA feel comfortable in sending classified documents to SCS headquarters.[76]

But by the end of 1983, joint CIA-NSA Special Collection Elements would be present in about a third of U.S. embassies abroad. The teams, which might consist of only two or three people, produced excellent intelligence, particularly if the embassy was located on high ground or near the foreign or defense ministries or other key offices in the capital. The sites were particularly effective in East European capitals.[77]

ROCKET SCIENTISTS

The early years of the operational KH-11 program also brought a further infusion of talented people into the development and engineering office, many of whom would go on to serve as senior office or NRO officials. Replacing Dirks as director of the development and engineering office was Donald L. Haas, an OD&E veteran who had been serving as director of ORD. He left in August 1978 to become deputy director of the NRO. Five months later, Haas's position was filled by Bernard Lubarsky.[78]

Lubarsky, who knew relatively little about the world of spies before joining it, was recruited from outside the intelligence community because the logical candidates to succeed Haas had left the CIA for jobs in industry and those remaining were not considered ready to assume the directorship. In 1947, after receiving his doctorate in mathematics (his bachelor's and master's degrees were in electrical engineering) from Case Institute of Technology, Lubarsky went to work at the National Advisory

Council on Aeronautics (NACA) and became an employee of the National Aeronautics and Space Administration (NASA) when that agency was created in 1958 and absorbed NACA. While at NASA, he got to know Hans Mark, the director of the space agency's Ames Research Center. In 1977, Mark became Under Secretary of the Air Force and director of the NRO, and in 1978 he recommended Lubarsky as a possible replacement for Haas. In January 1979, Lubarsky assumed command of the 500-person office.[79]

His impression of the people who worked for him was that they were "just outstanding . . . no humpty-dumpties." His deputy, Bert Aschenbrenner, who had served as acting director during part of the period between Haas's departure and Lubarsky's arrival, was a "very dedicated guy." Heading up the office's two satellite reconnaissance programs were Bob Kohler, who "was very aggressive [and] played hardball," and managed the KENNAN program, and Julian Caballero Jr., who managed the AQUACADE (née RHYOLITE) program. Ed Nowinski served as Kohler's systems engineering chief. All three eventually became directors of OD&E.[80]

Many people who worked for Kohler and Caballero would go on to senior positions in the world of reconnaissance. In 1978, Jeffrey K. Harris, a twenty-five-year-old graduate of the Rochester Institute of Technology, transferred from NPIC to OD&E, eventually becoming manager of the KH-11 program and subsequently director of the NRO (1995–1997).[81] Dennis Fitzgerald received a master's from Johns Hopkins University in applied physics, mathematics, electrical engineering, and space technology. He joined the science and technology directorate in 1974 as a member of the OD&E Systems Analysis Group, working on developing new concepts for intelligence collection. In 1980, he became involved in collection systems procurement. Fitzgerald went on to hold senior positions in NPIC and the development and engineering and the research and development offices. In November 1997, he became the head of NRO's signals intelligence directorate.[82]

In 1981, David Kier left NASA, where he was responsible for "aeronautic interfaces" with the Defense Department and intelligence community, to join OD&E, where he would work on a highly secret aerial reconnaissance program (discussed in Chapter 8). In 1997, he became the NRO's deputy director.[83]

Modifications and improvements to the KH-11 and AQUACADE systems were part of the work of the rocket scientists. One proposal, made sometime early in the Carter administration, to modify the KH-11 system reflected the continuing competition between the Air Force and CIA. In response to a 1979 Air Force proposal to develop a dedicated radar imagery satellite to allow the collection of imagery at night and in the presence of cloud cover, OD&E proposed adding a radar imagery payload to the KH-11. The CIA suggested attaching a radar imagery payload developed by the Air Force, code-named QUILL, and orbited only once—in December 1964. The 1964 version returned its images in a recoverable capsule; the version proposed in 1979 would relay its data back to earth as the KH-11 did. The plan was opposed by Secretary of Defense Harold Brown, who objected to placing so many reconnaissance eggs in a single basket. The issue, with Brown and DCI Stansfield Turner on opposite sides, went to President Carter, who sided with Brown.[84]

But the development wizards did create other improvements and modifications. When problems in the performance of an orbiting KH-11 were discovered, the models still on the ground were modified to avoid a recurrence. Before leaving the CIA, Jeffrey Harris led the successful effort to design an advanced version of the KH-11, which had higher resolution and greater swath width than the original model and thus could perform both high-resolution and area surveillance missions. Harris also oversaw the addition of an infrared imagery capability, code-named DRAGON, to the advanced spy satellite.[85]

NEW ENEMIES, NEW ALLIES

By the beginning of 1979, the TACKSMAN I facility consisted of four major units—a command center built into a hilltop, a radar antenna inside a thirty-foot-high dome, a radio monitoring device atop a steel tower, and a relay station pointed upward for communication with U.S. satellites. The radio monitoring device, built by Scientific Atlanta Inc., was a Pedestal Model 310—a device with four eight-foot-long arms studded with quill-like protrusions. The arms were almost joined at the front and pointed toward the Caspian Sea. Nearby was Scientific Atlanta's "power with Pedestal Model 300-L," a dish-shaped device fifteen feet high that pointed upward. There were 100 U.S. technicians who operated the equipment.[86]

The TACKSMAN II facility at Kabkan, Iran, forty miles east of Meshed, was described by a CIA staff member as a twenty-first-century facility with advanced electronic equipment. The facility itself was in stark contrast to the surrounding area—a remote mountainous locale inhabited by nomads. However, it was not the local environment that interested the CIA but rather the fact that Kabkan was only 650 miles south of the Tyuratam space center and ICBM test facility and was capable of eavesdropping on the ABM test center at Sary Shagan.[87]

President Carter considered the sites sufficiently important that he told his ambassador to Iran, William Sullivan, that intelligence cooperation between the CIA and Iran should continue despite the Shah's poor human rights record.[88] But in January 1979, the Shah of Iran, in the wake of increasing protests and riots, fled the country he had ruled so autocratically for twenty-five years.

The Shah's end took the U.S. intelligence community by surprise. A sixty-page CIA study completed in August 1977, *Iran in the 1980s*, had asserted that "there will be no radical change in Iranian political behavior in the near future" and that "the Shah will be an active participant in Iranian life well into the 1980s." A year later, a twenty-three-page CIA Intelligence Assessment, "Iran After the Shah," proclaimed that "Iran is not in a revolutionary or even a 'prerevolutionary' situation." A month later, the DIA issued an Intelligence Appraisal stating that the Shah "is expected to remain actively in power over the next ten years."[89]

From the time the Shah left, Iran became a priority U.S. intelligence target. Among the resources used to gather information were the KEYHOLE satellites. Targets included all of Tehran, Iranian military facilities, and the TACKSMAN sites.[90] Photography of the intelligence facilities could tell the United States whether they had been discovered by the new regime.

The CIA apparently had a plan for airlifting equipment and personnel out of the TACKSMAN II site using C-130 aircraft but never got the chance to implement it. Soon the CIA's prize telemetry intercept sites were in the hands of the ayatollahs. Kabkan was besieged by militiamen, and twenty-two U.S. technicians were captured. Subsequently, they were returned to the United States.[91] (The facility's chief, Richard A. Krueger, later in the year became chief of another CIA SIGINT facility also located in a remote area. However, although Pine Gap's location in the Australian outback was physically remote, his new assignment was in a considerably less hazardous and friendlier political environment.)[92]

On January 31, the U.S. technicians at Beshahr abandoned the facility, leaving the equipment running—perhaps because its intercepts were being remotely transmitted to a satellite. Ambassador William Sullivan engaged in negotiations with the authorities in Tehran, which apparently included payment of ransom, to get the CIA employees out of the country safely.[93]

Although losing the stations was a serious blow, U.S. officials hoped to avoid compounding the disaster by loss of the equipment to hostile powers. One reason the Iranians did not shut off the electricity when they took over was fear of damaging the equipment and therefore their ability to sell it. An Iranian logistics supervisor at the facility stated, "We don't know who will get the equipment. Maybe Iran will sell it to someone. Maybe we will use it. It might hurt the machinery if we turned off the electricity." Thus, the U.S. ambassador to Iran was informed on February 12 that "preventing sensitive military and intelligence equipment from falling into unfriendly hands" was one of two immediate U.S. concerns. In May, a visit by two newspaper correspondents found the Beshahr post "intact and whirring." The bungalows that had housed U.S. personnel had been sealed, but station employees still mowed the lawns occasionally.[94]

The loss of the stations was damaging in both an intelligence and a political sense. The Iranian sites had unique capabilities. In 1979, a worst-case view was given by one official:

> Kabkan is not replaceable. No tricks are going to overcome that in the short run, and the short run could be three or four years. It is going to affect our capability on verification. I don't think people realize how important that base was, not just for SALT, but generally for keeping up with the Soviet missile program. It provided basic information on Soviet missile testing and development. You're talking about a pretty big loss. It's serious.[95]

In addition, coming as it did on the heels of public exposure of Boyce's sale of RHYOLITE data, the loss further exacerbated concern over U.S. ability to verify the new SALT II Treaty. Cyrus Vance, Secretary of State at the time, noted: "The loss of the collection stations in Iran . . . was a serious setback, both in the sense of temporarily impairing our ability to check Soviet compliance with certain SALT limitations and in its impact on key senators, such as John Glenn, who had become the Senate's leading expert on verification."[96]

Also left behind in Kabkan was a system designated LAZY CAT, which had been only recently installed in reaction to concern expressed by intelligence directorate analysts that the Soviets might be testing an antisatellite laser weapon at Sary Shagan. But neither signals intelligence nor imagery was conclusive. In an attempt to provide answers, the Office of SIGINT Operations installed a system similar to the TEAL AMBER space surveillance telescope at Malabar, Florida.[97] The expectation was that if the Soviets were conducting such tests, the laser signal would "scatter stuff our way" after hitting the target, according to one CIA officer knowledgeable about the project.[98]

That same official, William "Al" Nance, was dubious about whether the project would have provided any intelligence of value—even assuming the Soviets were conducting such tests and not simply using the laser for tracking. Potential problems included the need for the LAZY CAT system to be looking in the right direction as well as the need for clear air and an absence of cloud cover. Nance assessed the probability of success as "near zero."[99]

By the time the Shah was heading off into exile, a replacement for the TACKSMAN sites was in sight. During his secret trip to Beijing in July 1971, national security adviser Henry Kissinger offered Zhou Enlai communications intelligence and high-resolution satellite imagery concerning Soviet forces on China's border. Zhou accepted. Additional offers were made in October 1971 during another Kissinger trip, in December 1971 at a CIA safehouse in Manhattan, and again in Beijing in November 1973.[100]

Originally, the visits to China in the early 1970s by Kissinger, and then Nixon, struck the CIA not so much as an opportunity to share intelligence as to collect it. During that time, the Office of ELINT received a query from Richard Helms's office about what opportunities the trips afforded for SIGINT collection. The office's Clandestine ELINT Team examined the possibility of placing concealed eavesdropping equipment on the aircraft as well as in luggage, but ultimately Kissinger decided he wanted no part of such covert collection schemes, and the entire idea was dropped.[101]

A substitute plan was the concept of working jointly with the Chinese to spy on the mutual enemy—the Soviet Union. According to William Nance, the CIA had been looking for an intercept site in the Far East that would be a counterpart to the sites in Turkey and Iran. He examined possible sites in China, their field of view, how far the horizon extended, and what part of a missile test could be monitored. Of particular interest were possible sites in Xinjiang province where intercept antennae could eavesdrop through the gaps in the mountains. Nance took the work to Jim Hirsch, at the time deputy director of OEL.[102]

Not until September 1975 was the possibility raised with the Chinese government. As Henry Kissinger and Qiao Guanhua, the Chinese Foreign

Minister, rode in from the Beijing airport, Kissinger told Qiao that he had a particularly sensitive intelligence-sharing proposal he wanted to propose to Deng Xiaoping. Kissinger explained that in light of U.S. concern over activities at Semipalatinsk, the home of URDF-3, the United States would be interested in establishing a joint seismic and electronic intelligence base in the western mountains of China. Undoubtedly, activities at Tyuratam and Sary Shagan also motivated Kissinger. But Deng's first order of business when they met the following day was to reject the idea.[103]

In January 1979, with the Shah's regime in ruins, Deng Xiaoping arrived in Washington to begin his U.S. tour. Before he departed to see the rest of the country, he held a final private meeting with the President and national security adviser Zbigniew Brzezinski. Brzezinski noted that the United States had been cooperating with the Shah to monitor Soviet missile tests and other developments. A joint U.S.-Chinese intelligence facility, Brzezinski argued, would be a valuable act of cooperation in opposing the Soviet menace.[104]

In an April 1979 meeting with a visiting U.S. Senate delegation, Deng indicated that China was willing to use U.S. equipment to "monitor Soviet compliance with a proposed new arms limitation treaty"—although Deng was certainly more concerned with intelligence about Soviet actions that might directly affect China. Deng also indicated that the monitoring stations would have to be run by the Chinese and the data would have to be shared with the PRC.[105]

There is some disagreement as to when a final agreement was concluded and when operations began. According to one account, when Vice-President Walter Mondale visited China during August 1979, Deng told him that China accepted the proposal and that "we would have given you an answer earlier, but we had some problems on our side. Now they are resolved." According to this same account, from August 1979 to December 1979, C-141 Starlifters ferried equipment to China.[106]

But according to a CIA official, China agreed to the project in November 1979, leading to the project's initial designation—"7911."[107] However, in his memoirs, former DCI Robert Gates recalled that "negotiations culminated at the very end of December 1980–early January 1981" with a secret trip to China by DCI Stansfield Turner and Gates. They left Andrews Air Force Base on December 27 and returned on January 7, with Turner having grown a mustache to help disguise his identity.[108]

Whatever the exact timing, by the fall of 1981, if not before, the two stations at Qitai and Korla in Xinjiang province were in operation. To teach the Chinese technicians how to operate the equipment and change the rolls of magnetic tape that recorded the intercepted signals, the CIA set up a school in Beijing.[109]

The stations, which were code-named CHESTNUT, could monitor military communications from central Asia to the Far East, air traffic, radar signals from Soviet air defenses, KGB communications, and the alert status of Soviet nuclear forces. Of particular interest to the CIA was CHESTNUT's ability to monitor the telemetry from the beginning of missile tests and space shots from Tyuratam, and to follow missiles through their flight over Siberia and the dispersion of warheads. Also in view of the eavesdropping equipment was the Sary Shagan ABM test site.[110]

ESCAPE

The CIA's loss of its TACKSMAN sites did not halt its effort to use Iran as a base for monitoring Soviet missile testing. But without the cooperation of the new government, the project had to be covert. The CIA's Tehran station assigned an agent to purchase a hunting lodge in the Elburz Mountains, with the expectation that an antenna and other ELINT equipment placed in the attic and around the premises would enable the agency to continue intercepting Soviet missile telemetry. But on November 4, 1979, only days after the agent was given approximately $250,000 to make the purchase, Iranian militants seized the U.S. embassy, taking its occupants hostage.[111]

The embassy takeover ended the ELINT project and shifted the CIA's focus to gathering information on the status of the U.S. hostages and supporting the Carter administration's efforts to obtain their release. Those efforts, both military and diplomatic, would prove futile.

In addition to supporting efforts to gain the release of the hostages, the CIA also sought to prevent another six Americans from becoming captives. In the midst of the takeover, aided by a rainstorm, five Americans who were working in the consular section building at the rear of the embassy compound were able to escape. Included were the consul general and his wife, the consul and his wife, and a second vice-consul. The agricultural attaché, who had been working in a nearby office, also avoided capture.[112]

Refuge for the consul and his wife was provided by the Canadian ambassador, Kenneth Taylor, at his official residence in the suburbs—a white two-story masonry building set well back from the eight-foot wall that surrounded it. The other four Americans were hidden in a nearby villa where the Canadian chief immigration officer, John Sheardown, and his wife lived. The six were kept out of view of prowling Revolutionary Guards and Iranian security forces. But if the Iranians realized that six potential hostages were missing, they would start searching for them, possibly without restraint. In any case, the sooner the Americans could escape the country, the better off for them and their hosts—particularly since the *New York Times* had already learned of the Canadians' houseguests. At the request of Secretary of State Cyrus Vance, the editors of the *Times* agreed not to publish that information, but it was only a matter of time before the wrong people would discover the truth.[113]

In mid-December 1979, Antonio J. Mendez was chief of Authentication Branch, Graphics and Authentication Division, Office of Technical Service—responsible for disguise, false documentation, and the forensic examination of questioned (and possibly forged) documents and materials in support of counterterrorism and counterintelligence operations. Mendez had been with the agency, and its technical services unit, since 1965. His career had taken him to Southeast Asia and Moscow as well as Langley and ultimately resulted in his being named one of the CIA's fifty trailblazers.[114]

The assignment his division chief presented him that day in December would be among his most challenging—arrange for a cover story and documentation that would enable the six Americans to be rescued from Iran. Since any cover that relied on U.S. passports would draw unwanted attention, the first option that was consistent with the fact that they all spoke North American English was to make them Canadians.[115]

To do so, to give them Canadian passports, would first require Canada to approve and provide valid blank passports. On January 2, 1980, Mendez and an OTS document specialist flew to Canada, hoping to demonstrate to Canadian officials how OTS could turn the blank passports into convincing cover. They were confronted with a decision that had already been made during a rump session of Parliament—to make an exception to Canadian passport law and provide the six passports. But the Canadians were not willing to deliver another two blank passports for CIA escorts.[116]

Providing unimpeachable passports was only one element required for a successful rescue. If the Americans were to leave via Tehran's Mehrabad Airport, the CIA would also need to know about the departure process—including whether the forms that travelers received on arrival and were collected upon departure (to verify that they left before their visa expired) were actually collected and checked. Since the agency had recently moved one agent out of Iran through the airport, it had a body of information on airport controls and personnel.[117]

Also needed was a cover story that would be the basis for any documentation. OTS and other agency elements began an all-source search for information on the types of groups traveling in and out of Iran's major airport, while the operations directorate's Near East Division collected data on covert, overland exfiltration options.[118]

None of the groups traveling legally to Iran fit the CIA's requirements, and the agency came up with three purely fictional possibilities. The first option for a cover story was that the six were an advance party scouting overseas locations for a motion picture. Such a team would include a production manager, a cameraman, an art director, a script consultant, a transportation manager, a business manger, and a director. There were two other options—a group of Canadian nutritionists conducting a survey of the Third World, or a group of unemployed teachers seeking jobs at international schools in the region.[119]

While Mendez traveled between Ottawa and Washington to work on the logistical details associated with the options, an OTS team in Ottawa worked on the documentation and disguise items, which the Canadians had agreed to send via courier to Tehran. Back at Langley, Mendez's team collected and analyzed the most recent information available on Iranian border controls.[120]

Mendez also traveled to Hollywood to consult with John Chambers, a Hollywood makeup artist best known for his work on *Planet of the Apes*, who was one of several film-industry specialists Mendez had consulted when he headed the technical service's disguise section. While there, Mendez created a name for the movie, *Argo*, designed a logo, and ordered ads in *Variety* and the *Hollywood Reporter* describing the notional film as a "cosmic conflagration." He also brought back Hollywood "pocket litter," such as matchbooks from the Brown Derby, to provide the Americans.[121]

On January 21, one of the CIA officers who would escort the Americans out of Iran left Frankfurt for Geneva to apply for an Iranian visa. Mendez left Dulles Airport the same day for Frankfurt. He traveled on his official U.S. passport, but when he arrived at the Iranian embassy on January 22, he had altered his appearance and carried OTS-produced documentation showing him to be Kevin Costa Harkins, a film producer associated with Studio Six Productions in Los Angeles.[122]

In the meantime, the OTS-prepared exfiltration material had arrived in Tehran, including material to be used if Mendez and his associate failed to arrive, for whatever reason. An urgent message soon arrived for Mendez, after Taylor and one of his aides discovered that one of the passports showed a date of issue of the Iranian visa as sometime in the future.[123]

But Mendez and his colleague arrived in Iran on January 25, carrying the *Argo* script, one completed before the rescue mission was planned and based on a science fiction novel. Later that day, they briefed the Americans on the three possible cover stories, who decided to leave as a group using the Studio Six cover. Mendez then provided the exfiltrators with *Argo* supporting documents and résumés from the portfolio. Three days before their departure, the Americans also received disguise materials and clothing props from Mendez so they could transform their appearances to match what might be expected of a film crew.[124]

In the early morning hours of January 28, the six American diplomats—Joseph and Kathleen Stafford, Mark and Cora Lijek, Bob Anders, and Lee Schatz—escorted by Mendez and his colleague, headed for Mehrabad Airport carrying their OTS-prepared Canadian passports along with the OTS-produced material that padded their wallets. A delay in departure of the scheduled 5:30 a.m. flight, along with the close questioning of one of the diplomats about his passport photo, increased the tension. But both the documentation and disguises proved sufficient. On January 28, 1980, the six Americans flew out of Iran—almost a year before their less fortunate colleagues at the U.S. embassy.[125]

Several weeks after the rescue, Studio Six folded, having already received twenty-six scripts, including one from Steven Spielberg. In 1997, Mendez, who had retired in late 1990, found a Federal Express envelope inside his studio's screen door. It contained a letter from Director of Central Intelligence George J. Tennet informing Mendez that although his trickery may have gone undetected by Iran and other targets, it had not gone unnoticed by the CIA. The letter informed him that he had been named one of the CIA's fifty trailblazers—people "who by their actions, example or initiative helped shape the history of the first half century of this agency."[126]

8

BREAKING DOWN BARRIERS

Leslie Dirks resigned as head of the Directorate of Science and Technology in 1982. Perhaps he was already beginning to experience the effects of what would turn out to be the early onset of Alzheimer's disease.* By 1999, he could no longer even remember the people he worked with at CIA, or what they had accomplished together.

The directorate Dirks left behind on July 3, 1982, if not quite the empire that Wheelon and Duckett had created, was still a key component of the CIA and intelligence community. The damage from the loss of the Iranian stations had been partially alleviated by the establishment of the CHESTNUT sites in China. The KH-11/CRYSTAL program had progressed to the point where it would soon become America's sole satellite imagery system. A follow-on to RHYOLITE was in the works and would make its debut in 1985.

Rather than replace Dirks with his deputy James Taylor, William Casey, who became Ronald Reagan's first DCI, brought Evan Hineman back from the intelligence directorate, where he was serving as associate deputy director. Taylor stayed on as associate deputy director for science and technology until late September and subsequently become the agency's executive director.[1]

Recruiting a successor for Taylor proved difficult, and the job remained vacant for over six months, when James Hirsch returned to the CIA. After a stint on the Intelligence Community Staff, Hirsch had left the agency in late 1978 to do national security analysis for the BETAC Corporation. When Hineman called him in 1983, he had been doing private consulting for over a year and had grown tired of the life. One condition he placed on

*After leaving the CIA, Dirks went to work for Raytheon but did not stay long. Bud Wheelon helped bring him to Hughes, but it soon became apparent that he was ill. (Telephone conversation with Bud Wheelon, November 15, 1999.)

accepting the job was that in addition to his overt position as Hineman's deputy in the directorate, he also become his Program B deputy. With that issue settled, Hirsch resumed his career at the CIA in early May 1983.[2]

TEARING DOWN THE WALLS

In 1997, Hineman addressed a gathering at CIA headquarters, which celebrated the thirty-fifth anniversary of the science and technology directorate. He recalled that when he had taken charge of the directorate fifteen years earlier, all of its six offices had "built walls around themselves."[3]

At staff meetings, each office director would warily share a bit of information about his office's activities. After the meeting, they would visit Hineman individually for far more detailed discussions of their projects. The new deputy director, who felt that he didn't have "depth in technical smarts," wanted a more team-oriented approach. Given the considerable talent spread across the directorate, each office could benefit from the insights and suggestions of people in other offices.[4]

To try to correct the problem, Hineman, along with the directors and deputy directors of each office, met away from CIA headquarters for a few days in September 1982. Officials from each office disclosed about 90 percent of what they doing, far more than they had in any previous staff meeting. One result was to "put the problems of the directorate on the table," to be addressed across the DS&T. The meeting also resulted in shifting some people and funds from one part of the directorate to another.[5]

Second, Hineman sought to break down the barriers between offices in different directorates, particularly between NPIC, the technical service, and development and engineering offices and their consumers in the operations directorate. By 1982, OTS had been outside of the operations directorate for almost a decade and had lost some of its feel for that culture. Both NPIC and OD&E provided support to clandestine operations through the acquisition and analysis of imagery to aid covert action and espionage operations. Hineman arranged for an interchange of staffers from the relevant offices to help improve understanding across the directorate. During his early years in office, Hineman recruited Thomas Twetten, a veteran of the operations directorate and subsequently its chief, to serve as a chief of operations of the Office of Technical Service.[6]

According to Twetten, he was able to serve as a bridge between the operations directorate and OTS. In some cases, the operations people would get a "silly notion" about some equipment they thought would be useful, and Twetten would go "have a chat" with them and talk them out of it. On other occasions, he would talk OTS out of canceling work on some project that was likely to be of great use to the operations side of the agency within a decade—a use that "there was no way for them to see." The apparent value of such interaction led to the creation of communications mechanisms between OTS and the Directorate of Operations at a number of levels. In addition, Jack Downing subsequently succeeded Twetten as the operations directorate's senior representative in OTS, serving as its deputy director. (Downing would also eventually succeed Twetten as the CIA's Deputy Director for Operations.)[7]*

UAVS

Among the projects that ORD director Philip Eckman might have briefed his fellow office chiefs on in September 1982 was one being undertaken by AeroEnvironment, a small California firm with a reputation for innovation, whose involvement was part of a series of studies to find the lightest practical aircraft. AeroEnvironment's assignment was to build an unmanned, solar-powered, propeller-driven aerial vehicle (UAV). The UAV, designated HALSOL (high-altitude solar energy), was expected to fly at 65,000 feet for weeks at a time.[8] Such an aircraft would allow prolonged observation of a target by a single platform (and at relatively low cost)—something that neither aircraft nor satellites could accomplish. Such a "stationary" eye in the sky could enable the CIA to monitor developments at a nuclear test site, the massing of troops near a neighbor's borders, or a battle in progress.

---

*Twetten also noted that there were "two distinct cultures" within the OTS—the engineers who built things and those who went into the field to conduct operations. The former did not necessarily have a good understanding of the operational or weather environment in some areas of the world—for example, Burma. In addition, OTS projects often involved far less money than the DS&T's large projects—which meant they might receive far less attention from some DS&T managers than the directorate's larger programs. At the time he served in OTS, Twetten believed it was important to keep the office in the DS&T—as long as there were people in the office who could bridge the gap between engineers and operators. Subsequently, he was not so sure, after becoming aware of increasing frustration from people in OTS about getting funding for their projects. However, he did not attempt, after becoming Deputy Director for Operations in 1991, to have OTS transferred back to the Operations directorate, because it was not worth the "angst" and the "wounds it would cause." He did establish a small rival group in Operations to help drive OTS to produce the "right equipment." (Telephone interview with Thomas Twetten, March 12, 2001.)

The HALSOL prototype, completed in 1983, was constructed of state-of-the art composites, plastics, and foam. It made nine flights that year at the top-secret Area 51 at Groom Lake, Nevada. The plane, with a 100-foot wingspan, eventually flew at 2,000 feet for thirty to sixty minutes, powered by rechargeable zinc batteries. The flights demonstrated that if the plane had been equipped with the solar arrays and power-control equipment available at the time, it would have become too heavy when any useful sensor payload was added. The plane was parked in long-term storage, in the event that lighter materials became available in the future.[9]

HALSOL never became a CIA asset, but it was one of a number of projects that eventually found their way to other parts of the government or the civilian sector. HALSOL was first resurrected as a Department of Defense project and then as a NASA program. In 1994, the Defense Department, under the code name RAPTOR TALON, took the aircraft, then designated PATHFINDER, out of storage and began testing its capability as a platform that could be used to detect missile launches. When that program was also canceled, NASA was next in line, and PATHFINDER became part of NASA's Environmental Research Aircraft and Sensor Technology program.[10]

In 1983, the CIA became involved in another, much more expensive and more secretive aerial program—which was expected to satisfy requirements for a number of potential users, particularly the Strategic Air Command. Among those working on it was OD&E's David Kier. The "Q Program," with the Q standing for QUARTZ, became the planned successor to the SR-71 after plans for a Mach 5 reconnaissance plane were scrapped sometime in the 1980s. The projected development of QUARTZ pushed aside a Navy program, AXILLIARY, to produce an aircraft that would hover off the Soviet coast. The aircraft was to detect the launch of the Backfire bombers that would attack the U.S. fleet in the advent of war.[11]

The planned QUARTZ vehicle was a Lockheed design, which bested Boeing's blueprint in a highly secret competition—although Boeing did win a subsequent competition to design the wings and flight controls (with Lockheed handling the sensors and fuselage). It would look like a B-2, fly at subsonic speeds at high altitudes, and have a 250-foot wingspan. In addition, it was to have alternative pods—one that permitted it to be flown by a pilot for ferry flights and testing, the other that allowed unmanned flight for dangerous reconnaissance missions. "It was going to do everything and cook breakfast too," said one official.[12]

But the cost per vehicle would be enormous—somewhere between $500 million to $1 billion. "It was so goddamn expensive nobody could even envision how to pay for it," the same official noted. In addition, there was concern about loss of the plane's secrets if it was brought down over enemy territory. "We would have to bomb the country to keep them from getting their hands on it," according to another official. As a result, QUARTZ was canceled during a late 1991 meeting whose participants included NRO director Martin Faga and DCI Robert Gates.[13]

QUARTZ did spawn plans for two successively less expensive versions—the Tier 3 and Tier 3- (subsequently designated Dark Star) UAVs. But both programs were canceled before any aircraft were built. Eventually the United States would have to settle for a more modest UAV program—the Air Force's Global Hawk.[14]

SECRET WARS

When Hineman took office, the Reagan administration, including DCI William Casey, was already committed to a secret war to undermine the Sandinista regime in Nicaragua, a war that the Office of Technical Service would be called upon to assist. In March 1981, President Reagan transmitted his first "Presidential Finding on Central America" to Congress. It authorized CIA funding of selected Sandinista opponents and an "arms interdiction program" whose stated aim was to halt the flow of weapons from Nicaragua to guerrillas in El Salvador, Honduras, and Guatemala.[15]

The main guerrilla force took shape in August 1981 when the 15th of September Legion and the Nicaragua Democratic Union joined with other anti-Sandinista forces to form the Nicaraguan Democratic Force, with 4,000 to 5,000 soldiers. A November 16, 1981, National Security Council meeting resulted in the CIA's being assigned responsibility for creating a paramilitary squad of exiles, working with the governments of Honduras and Argentina as "appropriate." A 500-man force would supplement the 1,000-man force being trained by Argentina. On December 1, Casey presented a second presidential finding to Congress and depicted the program as being limited to attacks against the Cuban presence and the Cuban/Sandinista support infrastructure in Nicaragua.[16]

On January 4, 1982, Reagan signed National Security Decision Directive 17, which noted that it was U.S. policy "to assist in defeating the insurgency in El Salvador, and to oppose actions by Cuba, Nicaragua, or others to introduce into Central America heavy weapons, troops from outside the region, trained subversives, or arms and military supplies for insurgents."[17]

Shortly after Casey's appearance before Congress, the CIA station in Tegucigalpa doubled in size. The initial phase of CIA training in weapon uses, tactics, and communications, conducted in Honduras, was followed by Contra raids in January and February 1982 on small village outposts in northern Nicaragua. On March 14, 1982, CIA-equipped saboteurs blew up two major bridges in Chinandega and Nueva Segovia provinces. According to the DIA's July 16, 1982, *Weekly Intelligence Summary*, between March 14 and June 21, the Contras sabotaged highway bridges, attempted to destroy fuel tanks, and attacked small military patrols and individual Sandinista soldiers. Targets included a customs warehouse, buildings belonging to the Ministry of Construction, crops, and civilian personnel involved in Nicaraguan social service programs.[18]

In July 1983, the CIA began aiding another anti-Sandinista group, Eden Pastora's Democratic Revolutionary Alliance (ARDE). The agency supplied ARDE with 500 Soviet AK-47 assault rifles, transporting them from Israel to Venezuela and finally to Tortuguero, a Costa Rican fishing lodge near the Nicaraguan border.[19]

In addition to supporting the Contras, the CIA initiated its own campaign against the Sandinistas. It recruited a group of specially trained "unilaterally controlled Latino assets" (UCLAs)—Spanish-speaking operatives recruited from El Salvador, Honduras, Chile, Argentina, Ecuador, and Bolivia. The operations were authorized by a presidential finding submitted to Congress in September 1983. Between then and April 1984, the agency carried out twenty-two or more attacks against vital Nicaraguan installations, in particular industrial and transportation targets, apparently in an effort to deliver quicker and more effective strikes against the Sandinistas than had been provided by previous efforts.[20]

The first attack by U.S.-supported Contras occurred on September 8, 1983. Speedboats manned by the UCLAs, and launched from a mother ship anchored twelve miles offshore, hit an oil pipeline at Puerto Sandino, temporarily halting the unloading of oil. On October 2, two 380,000-gallon fuel tanks were blown up at Puerto Benjamin Zeledon on Nicaragua's east coast. Eight days later, the port of Corinto, Nicaragua's largest commercial port, was hit. The CIA's Latino commandos positioned their speedboats behind a South Korean ship and then fired mortars and grenades at five large oil and gasoline storage tanks, igniting 3.4 million gallons of fuel. The Nicaraguan government claimed that more than 100 people were injured in the attack and 25,000 inhabitants of the city had to be evacuated while a fire raged out of control for two days.[21]

In 1984, the Office of Technical Service began to play a significant role in the anti-Sandinista effort. Starting in January, the CIA's UCLAs and Contra guerrillas, operating from a mother ship, used speedboats to begin depositing mines in the shipping channels of Nicaragua's major Atlantic and Pacific coast ports—Corinto, Puerto Sandino, and El Bluff. The mines were large metal cylinders, about 10 feet long and 21 inches in diameter, stuffed with 300 pounds of C-4 plastic explosive and another 300 pounds of inert material to enhance their stability on the seabed. They were placed 2 to 3 feet below the surface of the water, anchored into the bottom, in all channels of the 3 ports. The mines were generally magnetic, but some may have been acoustic. A total of 39 mines were planted between January 7 and March 30, 20 in Corinto, 15 in Puerto Sandino, and 4 in El Bluff.[22]

The first victim was a Japanese ship that struck a mine outside Corinto on January 3 and had to be towed back into port. On the night of February 29, the CIA's Latino assets placed four magnetic mines in Corinto's harbor. ARDE's "Barracuda Commandos" took credit for the operation. As NSC staffer Oliver North wrote to national security adviser Robert McFarlane, "our intention is to severely disrupt the flow of shipping essential to Nicaraguan trade during the peak export period." There was also the desire to "further impair the already critical fuel capacity in Nicaragua." North noted that in one particular case, "while we could probably find a way to overtly stop the tanker from loading/departing, it is our judgement that destroying the vessel and its cargo will be far more effective in accomplishing our overall goal of applying stringent economic pressure. It is entirely likely that once a ship has been sunk no insurers will cover ships calling in Nicaraguan ports."[23]

By early April 1984, ten commercial ships had been hit by CIA mines—four Nicaraguan and six non-Nicaraguan (registered to Japan, the Netherlands, Liberia, Panama, and the Soviet Union). At least eight merchant marine vessels turned back from Nicaraguan ports to find safer waters, including a Mexican oil tanker carrying 75,000 barrels of much-needed fuel. The mining operation cost the Nicaraguans more than $10 million—cotton and coffee piled up on the docks, and imports and exports had to be trucked to and from ports in neighboring Central American countries.[24]

OTS had been responsible for establishing the technical requirements for the demolitions. Its Weapons Group produced the mine casings from sewer pipes, and the fuses were apparently provided by the Naval Surface Weapons Center in Silver Spring, Maryland. The mines were designed not to sink ships but to damage and disable them.[25]

HAZARDOUS DUTY

Among those attending Hineman's off-site meeting in September 1982 was Gen. Rutledge Parker Hazard, also known as "Hap" Hazard. A 1946 West Point graduate, Hazard spent the next twenty-seven years in the U.S. Army, including tours of duty as missile intelligence officer, an artillery group commander in Vietnam, and the manager of three different guided missile systems. When he retired from the Army in late 1973, he immediately joined the CIA. In 1978, he became the director of NPIC.[26]

Hazard's tenure as NPIC director ended in February 1984, shortly after Robert M. "Rae" Huffstutler received a call from Hineman. At the time, Huffstutler was a twenty-five-year veteran of the agency and head of the intelligence directorate's Office of Soviet Analysis. From 1967 to 1982, he had served in the Office of Strategic Research.[27]

Hineman believed that it was necessary to upgrade NPIC. Just as the advent of the KH-9 had required changes, so had the arrival of the KH-11—only more so. Part of that transition had been the creation of a Priority Exploitation Group (PEG) at Ft. Belvoir that could scan incoming imagery. Meanwhile, at NPIC headquarters, Building 213 in the Washington Navy Yard, the Imagery Exploitation Group (IEG), except in crises situations, waited, as in the past, for the product to arrive. But the transition had not been fully made, which was not surprising. There had always been more emphasis on funding expensive collection systems and less on assuring that resources had been earmarked for the processing and exploitation of the data collected. But in 1984, with the end of the KH-8 and KH-9 film-return programs in sight, the need to adjust to the digital world was even more pressing.[28]

Early in his tenure, Hineman went to NPIC for a briefing on the center's ability to exploit "soft-copy" data—KH-11 digital imagery that resided in an interpreter's computer rather than in "hard-copy" form on a light table. He discovered that NPIC was unable to transfer the digital signals into a computer so that imagery analysts could fully exploit the data using a variety of algorithms. It was still necessary to use the digital signals to produce a hard-copy image, and then scan the image into the computer—a time-consuming, expensive process that also limited the extent to which the images could be enhanced.[29]

At the time Hineman called Huffstutler, NPIC was about eighteen months into the major modernization program required but clearly was not going to meet its 1986 target date. The deputy director told Hufstutler that NPIC was having some problems and he would like him to move into the director's chair. Huffstutler had served as deputy to Hineman in the weapons intelligence office, they had gotten along, and they thought alike in approaching problems. And after working on Soviet issues for fifteen years, Huffstutler was ready for a change. He was also quite familiar with NPIC's product, since the strategic affairs and Soviet analysis offices had been among the interpretation center's biggest customers.[30]

In addition to getting the modernization plan back on track, NPIC's new director had two other concerns—ensuring that NPIC's products could be used effectively by its customers and straightening out internal procedures. One of Huffstutler's first acts was to review all of NPIC's reporting. He concluded that imagery analysts did not really understand their role in the analytic process, that they didn't quite have the proper feel for how their products were used by analysts in the intelligence directorate. Their reporting did not "separate in consistent and clear ways" what imagery analysts actually saw from their inferences. They might see a group of tanks but state without further explanation that the picture "showed" a military exercise taking place. A reader could not separate what the interpreter actually saw (the tanks) and what he inferred (the exercise) from the picture. Only three days after Huffstutler informed NPIC analysts of his views, their reporting began to change.[31]

He also addressed two other problems. One was the standard usage of "NPIC believes" in imagery interpretation reports, which he noted "made everyone mad" because it appeared to allow no room for dissent. He told his analysts they could say anything they wanted that met the standards of professionalism and reporting, but they could not turn their conclusions into NPIC's conclusions. Huffstutler assured them that others would take their advice more often than not. There were no further complaints about NPIC reporting after that time, according to Huffstutler.[32]

He also moved to alleviate a feeling by his imagery interpreters that they were second-class citizens in the intelligence community, an effort that took most of his first year in office. The interpreters were referred to, both by analysts in the intelligence directorate and themselves, as "one-source" analysts. On the analytical totem pole, this seemed to place them under the "all-source" analysts in the intelligence directorate who worked with imagery, SIGINT, human intelligence, and open source data. Huffstutler argued that it was really a question of different jobs. The imagery analysts had access to data from all sources and used that data in moving from what they saw to what they inferred. They were not simply describing what was in a picture but analyzing the significance of the picture.[33]

It took far longer than a year to complete the modernization process—indeed it extended into the terms of Hineman's and Huffstutler's successors. Two major aspects to the modernization program were causing the delays. One factor was changes in requirements coming out of the program office. The second was software problems.[34]

The program itself involved new work stations, new data bases, new connectivity to facilities (such as DIA and field activities), and new measurement equipment. Other steps needed were to put the Priority Exploitation Group at Ft. Belvoir on a twenty-four-hour-a-day basis, to ensure that all data came down in a usable form, and to update the requirements process.[35]

In addition to pursuing the modernization program, Huffstutler launched what he dubbed the National Exploitation Initiative, which involved the creation of a National Exploitation Laboratory (NEL). The concept was to create a "users program office" to speak with a unified voice with the procurement program office—the NRO. An early part of the initiative was to invite the directors of the military service's imagery interpretation units to NPIC, update them on the modernization program, and try to establish a dialogue. The NEL, in addition to serving as a single voice for users in evaluating proposals from the Air Force and CIA elements of the NRO, served as a center for the development of equipment to be used in the exploitation process—helping create the best monitors, software, and other components of modernization.[36]

Huffstutler also initiated a database audit to determine the adequacy of the national imagery files, which had never been graded. The NPIC director arranged with the other imagery centers—those in DIA and the military services—to go back and sample past imagery and evaluate the accuracy of the reporting in the written cables. The Strategic Air Command assumed responsibility for the process with respect to air defense imagery, and NPIC took the leadership role for the remainder of the imagery. The audit revealed 96 percent accuracy. Plugging some of the holes discovered in reporting raised accuracy another 1 percent two years later, according to NPIC's customers.[37]

Beyond the problems of modernization, Huffstutler's NPIC had one major world crisis to deal with—one that required around-the-clock operations.[38] On Saturday, April 26, 1986, a nuclear accident occurred eighty miles from Kiev, at the Chernobyl nuclear power plant's reactor No. 4. As the result of a series of safety violations—including running the reactor without the emergency cooling system and removing too many control rods—a small part of the reactor went "prompt critical." The effect was the equivalent of a half ton of TNT exploding on the core. Four seconds later, a second explosion blasted the 1,000-ton lid off the reactor, destroyed part of the building, and brought the 200-ton refueling crane crashing down on the core. A "fireworks" display of glowing particles and fragments escaping from the units followed, setting off thirty fires in the building. In addition, the huge blocks of granite in the reactor core also caught fire, spewing out plumes of highly radioactive fission products.[39]

The first solid indication that the United States received concerning the accident was from an official Soviet statement on Monday, April 28. There had been signs of unusual activity around Kiev on Sunday, probably from communications intelligence, but what was happening was unclear. Only the following day was the situation clarified.[40]

Once alerted to the disaster, the intelligence community responded by turning its full set of resources on the Kiev area. A VORTEX signals intelligence satellite sucked up all military and relevant civilian communications within several hundred miles of Chernobyl. Due to launch failures in August 1985 and earlier in April, the U.S. space imagery capability consisted of a lone KH-11, 5506. It was reprogrammed to obtain photography of the nuclear reactor at the first opportunity. Its last visit had been almost two weeks before, and the first chance for 5506 to provide imagery came on Monday afternoon. However, given its orbital path, the image had to be obtained from a considerable distance and even with computer enhancement didn't show much. Even had 5506 been closer to its target, the smoke hovering over the reactor area probably would have obscured the site. The following morning, the distance was still too great to produce a good photo, but by evening the KH-11 had approached close enough to return the first good imagery of the accident site. The picture was reported to be "good and overhead." Huffstutler recalled the imagery as being "right down the core," showing the concrete cap blasted right out and helicopters and firemen trying to deal with the consequences of the accident.[41]

With the photos in hand, analysts at NPIC began assessing the situation. The photos revealed that the roof of the reactor had been blown off and the walls were pushed out, "like a barn collapsing in a high wind," said one source. Inside what was left of the building, there was an incandescent mass of graphite. Some tendrils of smoke and the blackened roof of the adjoining building indicated that at some point the fire had been more active. The graphite settled down into a glowing mass, while radioactive material from a pile that had contained 100 tons of uranium was still being vented through the open roof and into the atmosphere.[42]

The photos revealed activity in the surrounding areas, activity that was quite remarkable given the perilous situation at Chernobyl: A barge was sailing peacefully down the Pripyat River, and men were playing soccer inside the plant fence less than a mile from the burned-out reactor. The photos of the town of Pripyat showed that there had been no evacuation.[43]

Among those briefed by NPIC with the satellite photos was the House Permanent Select Committee on Intelligence. "We were shown satellite pictures of the reactor building from before and immediately after the explosion," committee member George D. Brown Jr. (D.–Calif.) said after a closed-door hearing on Thursday, May 1. "They were dramatic, with the roof beams collapsed and debris scattered around the plant. No bodies were visible," he added.[44]

KH-11 photos taken on Thursday morning May 2 showed no smoke at all, leading an interagency panel to believe that it was possible the fire had been put out. Only the day before, despite Soviet claims that the fire had been extinguished, the panel had predicted that it might burn for weeks. Some analysts believed they detected shimmering over the reactor, suggesting that the graphite was still burning. It appeared that the Soviets were dumping dirt or sand on the fire from helicopters. One KH-11 photo showed a helicopter hovering directly in the plume of the radiation.[45]

The satellite photos provided data that enabled NPIC's analysts to determine the validity of reports that Unit 3, adjacent to the damaged Unit 4, was affected by a meltdown or fire. From further satellite photos, a federal task force concluded on May 3 that the other Chernobyl reactors were not at risk. Lee M. Thomas, head of the task force, announced that on the basis of the photos, "we see no problems with the other units."[46]

NPIC undoubtedly continued to monitor the cleanup, examining KH-11 images of the Mi-8 helicopters (with lead shields on their floors). The helicopters flew hundreds of missions day after day, dropping sacks of sand through the broken roof of the reactor from heights of more than 650 feet. Workers then sealed the roof shut with tons of lead pellets, which rolled into whatever cracks remained between the sandbags.[47]

A VERSUS B

On January 24, 1985, about fifteen months before the Chernobyl accident, the space shuttle orbiter *Discovery* was launched on the first secret mission in fifteen shuttle flights, carrying another product of OD&E's efforts. Earlier that week, Brig. Gen. Richard F. Abel, the Air Force director of public affairs, warned reporters not to speculate about the payload and threatened that the Department of Defense was ready to launch an investigation in the event of any unwelcome stories.[48]

But times had changed dramatically since Air Force representatives could get away with telling reporters (as they did for the first CANYON launch) that they wouldn't want to know the nature of the payload. They certainly did, and the warning did not stop the *Washington Post* from revealing that the secret payload was a new SIGINT spacecraft. The spacecraft had been developed under the code name MAGNUM, but that name had been changed to ORION by the time of launch. Most important to the U.S. intelligence community was that the shuttle's military astronauts were able to release the satellite safely into space, so that the rocket attached to it could place it in its proper geosynchronous orbit.[49]

The spacecraft, which weighed about 6,000 pounds, was apparently placed in orbit over Borneo. It was reported to have two huge parabolic antennae, one for intercepting communications and telemetry signals and the other for relaying the signals to the ground station at Pine Gap, Australia. ORION was the successor to the RHYOLITE/AQUACADE program, and an improvement both on RHYOLITE and ARGUS, its intended successor. Compared with RHYOLITE, it could pick up lower-powered signals, such as "turned-down" telemetry signals, intercept a wider range of frequencies, and due to its bigger transmitting antenna focus its signal more sharply to its ground station. In addition to intercepting signals never intended for U.S. intelligence analysts, it apparently also received data from emplaced sensors in the Soviet Union and elsewhere.[50]

In 1985, not long after celebrating the successful launch of ORION, Robert Kohler, the former KENNAN program head who in March 1982 succeeded Bernie Lubarsky as chief of the Office of Development and Engineering (i.e., NRO Program B), found himself in a battle with the Air Force and the NRO over the plans for the next SIGINT satellite program.

A native of Rochester, New York, Kohler had considered the snowiest city in the United States no place to live. He graduated from the Rochester Institute of Technology, married, and left town in about a week, refusing to interview at the Rochester-based Xerox and Kodak corporations. His first exposure to space reconnaissance was as head of the photo science technology department at Itek in Boston, where he worked on the CORONA program. In 1967, he joined the CIA for what he expected would be a few years of government service before returning to Itek.

When time came to return, he decided to stay at the agency because he was "having too much fun."[51]

Kohler was certainly not one to avoid a battle when he believed someone else was headed down the wrong path. The Air Force Office of Special Projects (NRO Program A) and its director, Ralph Jacobson, was proposing that the follow-on to ORION be a far bigger system, which they believed was necessary to cope with a new type of Soviet microwave signal.[52]

Kohler thought it was feasible to take the system then in operation and modify each successive satellite, never spending too much money at any one time. He also believed that NRO director Pete Aldridge felt that with a budget squeeze on the horizon, it might be his last chance to get approval for a major new initiative. In addition, according to Kohler, the CIA's Program B had continually bested the Air Force's Program A during Aldridge's tenure, and Aldridge wanted to give Program A a victory.[53]

Kohler's position as head of development and engineering was somewhat different from those of his predecessors in earlier eras. When Kohler took the job, John McMahon, then deputy director of central intelligence, told him he should act as if he worked for the director of the NRO—unless he believed that DCI William Casey was not being adequately served by the NRO director. In 1985, Kohler felt that caveat applied—particularly when Aldridge did not present Kohler's alternative to Casey.[54]

Made aware of the differences, Casey asked to hear from both Air Force and CIA elements of the NRO. Two critical meetings followed involving Casey and Secretary of Defense Caspar Weinberger. McMahon asked to see the briefing Aldridge was planning to give and told the NRO director that it should not contain a recommendation. But at the first meeting, Weinberger asked Aldridge for his recommendation and got it. Casey demurred making a decision then, telling Weinberger that he had not had an opportunity to study the options. When Casey was briefed by the NRO Staff, he found they omitted the Program B option. Again he refused to make a decision.[55]

The following Monday morning, Kohler drafted and sent a four-page memo to Casey through Hineman. According to Kohler, he faced opposition not only from Aldridge but also from the CIA's Executive Director, former DS&T associate deputy director James Taylor, who wanted Casey to accept Aldridge's option. The memo laid out the NRO briefing as well as what was omitted and invited a decision. Instead of a decision, Kohler got a call that night from Casey, telling him he wanted to see him the next day.[56]

Casey, according to Kohler, "had ignored the DS&T for the first four and a half years of his tenure." The next day, he asked the development and engineering chief to tell him how signal recognition worked. After ten minutes, Casey walked over and opened the door to McMahon's adjacent office and asked his deputy to join them. They talked for several hours, with Kohler addressing the issue of the intelligence value per dollar from each of the proposed SIGINT systems, using different scenarios constructed by the intelligence directorate.[57]

The presentation convinced Casey to consider the Program B proposal. He transmitted a sanitized version of Kohler's memo to Aldridge, PFIAB chairman Anne Armstrong, and two technical people on the board—John Foster and Bud Wheelon. Kohler then heard from McMahon, who told him to expect a call from NRO deputy director Jimmie Hill, who would arrange for him to brief Anne Armstrong. When twenty-four hours went by without the call, Kohler called McMahon, who then sent him to La Jolla, California, to see the PFIAB chairman.[58]

Wheelon later recalled first speaking to Casey on his way from Denver to Aspen to attend an Aspen Institute summer study meeting, apparently sometime after Kohler left the agency in August 1985. He considered it "an unwelcome assignment," which couldn't do the Hughes company any good, but he agreed to meet with Aldridge and some of his staff at a motel near the Aspen airport. Wheelon examined the issue, relying on Hughes official Harold Rosen as technical backup.[59]

Wheelon concluded that extensive improvements suggested by Program A were not necessary—that its staff had missed two key technical points—and that the CIA proposal to stay with the same basic system and same contractor (TRW) made the most sense. He spoke to Jacobson about the matter, and the Program A head accepted his analysis.[60]

Two years later, it seemed Kohler's effort had been wasted. Casey had approved the Program B alternative, but he died in 1987. Robert Gates became the acting DCI, and although he had supported the program as chairman of the Intelligence Producers Council, he decided to sacrifice the program to budgetary requirements. But the program's death would be only temporary.[61]

KODIAK

In 1985, Kohler was succeeded by Julian Caballero, who would remain as office director until fall 1993.[62] A system on the drawing board when he assumed command was one dedicated to controlling and relaying data for the entire reconnaissance fleet. The proposed system, originally codenamed IRIDIUM and then KODIAK, would have consisted of four geosynchronous satellites, with one satellite in view of the Washington-area downlinks at Ft. Belvoir and Ft. Meade. That satellite would have been capable of downlinking the information in such a narrow beam as to make it virtually immune to interception. The other three satellites, in addition to their control functions, would be able to receive data from reconnaissance satellites and then transmit the data to the downlink satellite or, via a laser crosslink, to another satellite that would then transmit the information to the downlink satellite. Because of funding limitations, the proposal was killed in 1987. Funding for KODIAK would have required cuts in the Strategic Defense Initiative budget that the administration was unwilling to make.[63]

Beginning in 1984, in an attempt to get part of the job accomplished at no cost to the intelligence community, Aldridge pushed for development of a laser crosslink, rather than a radio crosslink, for the Defense Support Program infrared launch detection satellites operated by the Air Force. As part of a modernization program, the Air Force planned to deploy satellites with crosslinks, eliminating the need for ground stations. Former OD&E chief Bernard Lubarsky, who worked for TRW after leaving the CIA in 1982, later recalled that the DSP contractor recommended the use of radio crosslinks to the Air Force for DSP. According to several individuals who worked on the DSP program for another contractor, radio crosslinks would have accomplished the mission for DSP. But Aldridge pushed for the laser crosslinks, figuring that once developed they could then be used on a system such as KODIAK.[64] But although the Air Force contracted with McDonnell-Douglas to develop such a crosslink, the program had one problem after another until it was finally canceled in the early 1990s.[65] However, as with OD&E's proposed SIGINT satellite system, KODIAK's death would be only temporary.

A TRAITOR IN FBIS

On November 22, 1985, the FBI ended the espionage career of Larry Wu-Tai Chin. Chin began his employment with the U.S. government in 1943 with the U.S. Army Liaison Mission in China. In 1948, he worked as an interpreter in the U.S. consulate in Shanghai and two years later took a job as a secretary-interpreter at the U.S. embassy in Hong Kong. During the Korean War, Chin interviewed Chinese prisoners captured by U.S. and Korean troops.[66]

He began monitoring Chinese radio broadcasts in 1952 for the Foreign Broadcast Information Service's Okinawa unit. In 1961, he moved to Santa Rosa, California, where he continued to work for FBIS. From

1970 until his retirement in 1981, Chin worked as an analyst in the FBIS office in northern Virginia and also served as the FBIS document control officer.[67]

Chin's career as a spy may have begun in the early 1940s, when he apparently received espionage training while still a student in college. In 1952, Chinese intelligence agents paid him $2,000 for having located Chinese POWs in Korea. He also provided Chinese agents with information on the intelligence being sought from Chinese prisoners by U.S. and Korean intelligence officers. Regular meetings in Hong Kong between Chin and his PRC controllers began in 1967. Between 1976 and 1982, Chin met four times with a courier for Chinese intelligence, "Mr. Lee," at a shopping mall near Toronto International Airport. Speaking in Cantonese, Chin handed over undeveloped film of classified documents from FBIS.[68]

The information Chin provided led the PRC to pay him several hundred thousand dollars over a thirty-year career. Although the FBIS is best known for its translation of the public broadcasts of foreign nations (and less known for its translations of the broadcasts of clandestine and black radios), the service's analysts also used classified intelligence reports to help assess the significance of foreign broadcasts. Further, Chin's skill as an interpreter and his long tenure gave him access to a great deal of highly classified data. Thus, Chin "was more than a guy . . . listening to People's Republic of China broadcasts and translating People's Daily." According to testimony given at his indictment, Chin "reviewed, translated and analyzed classified documents from covert and overt human and technical collection sources which went into the West's assessment of Chinese strategic, military, economic, scientific and technical capabilities and intentions," and in 1979 he passed on that assessment to "Mr. Lee."[69]

Chin continued his intelligence activities on behalf of China into the 1980s. In 1981, he met with the vice-minister of the Chinese Ministry of Public Security in Hong Kong and Macao. In February 1982, he traveled to Beijing, where high government officials honored him with a banquet, told him he had been promoted to Deputy Bureau Chief in the MPS, and awarded him $50,000. As late as February 1985 he met Chinese officials in Hong Kong.[70]

Chin's life as a double agent, indeed his life, was undone by Yu Shensan, the son of two prominent Chinese revolutionaries. Before his defection in 1986, Yu headed the Foreign Affairs Bureau of the Ministry of State Security, which had been established in 1983 to improve coordination of China's foreign intelligence operations and reduce leaks of internal government discussions. The new ministry took over the intelligence, counterintelligence, and security functions of the Ministry of Public Security, as well as the intelligence functions of the Investigation Department.[71]

Yu was able to provide the United States with extensive information about Chinese intelligence operations abroad, including the names of Chinese agents. He may have provided information concerning Chin's activities, possibly as early as 1982, the year the FBI first placed a wiretap on Chin's phone.[72]

Chin's jury returned a guilty verdict on February 6, 1986. Sometime during the early morning of February 21, he tied a garbage bag over his head. Discovered by a guard at 8:45, he was pronounced dead forty-five minutes later.[73]

Chin's treason did far more harm to the CIA's sensitive collection operations than to those of FBIS, which continued to monitor and analyze the foreign media. A change in policy leading to the February 1989 Soviet military withdrawal from Afghanistan was identified in FBIS media analysis. During May 1989, FBIS monitoring of Chinese radio broadcasts provided important information on the support for the student protesters in Beijing. The reports indicated that 40,000 students, teachers, and writers in Chengdu marched in support of democracy in mid-May. Altogether, radio reports indicated that there had been demonstrations of more than 10,000 people in at least nine other provinces.[74]

SPECIAL PROJECTS: THE SEQUEL

During the mid-1960s, the DS&T had deployed a number of emplaced sensor systems—such as those targeted on the Chinese missile program or those that Leslie Dirks referred to in his testimony in the trial of Christopher Boyce. In *VEIL*, Bob Woodward described a system designated CERVICAL RUB—"a sophisticated electronic device disguised and constructed to look like a tree limb, complete with bark covering." It was to be "planted" in a tree outside a Soviet air base in Eastern Europe to collect data on advanced Soviet MiG radars. There was also a round device camouflaged as a tree stump and discovered near a military facility that could transmit the data collected to a satellite.[75]

There was also TAW. In 1979, the CIA had discovered that the Soviets were building a highly secret communications center near Troitsk, a town twenty-five miles southwest of Moscow. Underground tunnels connected the center to the headquarters of the KGB's foreign directorate at Yasenovo as well as main headquarters in Moscow. Running through the tunnels were cables for telephone, fax machines, and teletype—all of which the KGB believed to be secure. However, the CIA had managed to bribe a member of the construction crew, who provided the agency with the blueprint for the tunnels. In 1980, a CIA technician, possibly from OTS or OSO, left the U.S. embassy in Moscow hidden in a van. After determining the van was not under surveillance, its driver took him to a remote area, where the technician jumped from the van and hid in the woods. After locating the tunnel, he climbed inside and installed a monitoring and recording device. The coup gave the CIA an ability to record the KGB's most sensitive communications traffic in the Soviet Union.[76]

ABSORB was the result of the directorate's desire to determine the number of warheads carried by Soviet missiles. Those numbers could be estimated from missile telemetry but depended on some assumptions. The United States had never actually seen inside a Soviet missile nose cone to verify the number of warheads being carried. ABSORB did not let the CIA look inside but rather provided an indirect means of assessing warhead numbers. It was known that each warhead emitted a tiny amount of radiation. By measuring the amount of radiation being emitted from each missile, the system could help analysts determine just how many warheads sat on top of the missile. The problem was how to get an accurate radiation reading.[77]

Someone realized that most Soviet nuclear warheads were manufactured in the western USSR and shipped over the Ural Mountains to the Far East, where they were installed on missiles. The only way the Soviets could move those warheads was on the Trans-Siberian Railroad, which starts in Moscow and travels about 5,750 miles east until it arrives at Vladivostok. Branch lines connect Moscow with the rest of Europe. A train from Vladivostok to Moscow had a good chance, at some point in its journey, of passing an eastbound train carrying a nuclear cargo. Even though the trains might pass for only a few seconds, an advanced Geiger counter on the westbound train might be able to get a reading.[78]

By 1983, the CIA had spent about $50 million on the project but had not yet perfected its Radiation Detection Device (RDD)—although it had made some interesting test runs. One test involved hiding a number of sophisticated cameras inside a false wall built in the side of a cargo container. A friendly Japanese company agreed to ship the container across the Soviet Union, from Vladivostok to Eastern Europe. The cameras would snap photographs whenever a train crossed the connecting track. Many of the tracks connected the railway to military manufacturing plants, so each time a train went by a weapons plant, the cameras snapped a photograph for the CIA. Thus, the CIA knew that ABSORB was possible. While the RDD was still being developed, the CIA sent another rigged container, with electronic sensors, to Japan. In February 1986, it learned that the KGB had stopped a cargo container filled with electronic sensors. ABSORB was over before it began. TAW and ABSORB had been betrayed to the KGB by Aldrich Ames in 1985, although that was not known at the time.[79]

The CIA had also deployed seismic sensors in East Germany. In one operation, nuclear detection equipment was installed in a series of road posts on an East German road. The equipment transmitted back to an antenna on a pile of rubble in West Berlin. In another instance, seismic monitoring devices were placed underground, near a road. The data they transmitted (to a satellite) allowed intelligence analysts to differentiate among seven different weight classes, including those for jeeps, passenger cars, trucks, and tanks.[80]

The design of such systems was handled by various offices in the directorate—usually either research and development, development and engineering, or SIGINT operations offices. Many of the projects, such as the seismic systems, fell in the category of MASINT (Measurement and Signature Intelligence). Intelligence was derived from the data collected by such systems through the analysis of acoustic or seismic signals (which did not fall within the electronic signals covered by the SIGINT designation), of debris from an explosion, or of the heat emitted by an object.

The DS&T had achieved some successes by 1987, but Hineman believed they were not enough.[81] There were also some notable failures. In the early 1980s, the counterintelligence services of several East European countries, including Bulgaria, discovered a number of emplaced sensor systems near air bases, ammunition depots, and other strategic sites. The systems were camouflaged as tree limbs, rocks, and other natural objects. In 1983, the CIA gave an individual it believed was an asset, but who was actually a double agent, three of the devices. He quickly turned them over to the East German Ministry of State Security, which then consulted the KGB. The East Germans' Soviet colleagues informed them that similar gadgets had been found in the Soviet Union. Eventually it became clear that the devices recorded traffic around the strategic sites or registered the emissions from nuclear weapons.[82]

Hineman later recalled that as the world evolved and more was discovered about intelligence, countries took countermeasures. The United States needed to develop new capabilities and new technologies, to get closer and closer access.[83]

One problem that Hineman believed was plaguing the program was a lack of proper coordination among the different groups that set requirements, developed the system, deployed the system, and exfiltrated the data. Those in the operations directorate designated to deploy a device in a tree might discover only months or years into development that the device weighed a hundred pounds. To get everybody on the same page from the beginning, it made sense, in Hineman's view, to put everybody in the same organization—so that they could understand problems and difficulties and influence the design.[84]

Just as Bud Wheelon had removed the responsibility for satellites from OSA and created the Special Projects Staff in 1963, Hineman removed the responsibility for emplaced sensors from the other directorate offices and placed it in a new Special Projects Staff in summer 1987. At the beginning of the 1988 fiscal year, it became the Office of Special Projects. The office's director was "responsible for the development and operational support of [emplaced sensor] systems to collect Measurement and Signature Intelligence, Nuclear and Signals Intelligence." In order to carry out that mission, the office was to analyze potential targets, plan the operation, develop collective devices appropriate for the specific targets, and provide operational support during deployment. It was headed by a DS&T official, Gary Goodrich. Its chief of operations came from the operations directorate, its Systems Development Group came from the SIGINT and development and engineering units, and its Collection Group came from the Office of SIGINT Operations.[85]

In Hineman's view, the creation of the separate office improved the emplaced sensor program. As with all such changes, there were some who were less than enthusiastic. Robert Phillips, who worked on a clandestine program that wound up in OSP, acknowledged the importance and sensitivity of the programs. But he wondered if the growing size of OSO helped create a bureaucratic requirement to establish OSP as a way to authorize more Senior Intelligence Service positions, equivalent to Senior Executive Service positions.[86]

According to Phillips, Hineman told him that he wanted more management attention devoted to the emplaced sensor programs. The political fallout from being caught in unacknowledged operations using invasive techniques even in friendly countries could be enormous. But after four years the program had less management than before. OSP was just another bureaucracy and "provided no added value," and it "didn't help solve problems." The people from OSO who formed the core of OSP, Phillips believed, "should have stayed in OSO."[87] In a few years, both OSP and OSO would disappear and be reunited under a new name.

The CIA has funded a number of SIGINT facilities operated by U.S. allies. The functions of this Norwegian facility, code-named METRO, which began operations in 1958, included the interception of Soviet missile telemetry. CREDIT: *Norwegian Intelligence Service*

MARJATA

(top left) The Marjata II was among the Norwegian vessels that carried eavesdropping equipment to spy on Soviet naval activities, equipment provided by the CIA. CREDIT: *Norwegian Intelligence Service*

(bottom left) A U-2 reconnaissance aircraft, developed by the Lockheed Corporation for the CIA. CIA U-2 flights began in 1956 and continued until 1974 when the Air Force assumed full control of U-2 operations. The first CIA U-2 flights helped end fears of a "bomber gap." CREDIT: *Lockheed*

(above) U-2 photograph of Almaza airbase, Cairo, after British-French airstrike, November 1, 1956. CREDIT: *CIA.*

(above) The A-12/OXCART aircraft was developed by Lockheed for the CIA as a successor to the U-2. The plane could fly at over 2,100 miles per hour and at an altitude of over 90,000 feet. The A-12 had a brief operational life, beginning in May 1967 and ending in June 1968, when it was retired in favor of the Air Force's A-12 derivative—the SR-71. CREDIT: *Lockheed*

(top right) The U.S. Navy was the primary purchaser of the P-2V Neptune, which it used in maritime surveillance operations. However, in 1954, the CIA procured several of the aircraft to use in both covert action and intelligence collection operations—including operations over the Chinese mainland. CREDIT: *Lockheed*

(bottom right) The CIA Directorate of Science and Technology has been heavily involved in the development of unmanned aerial vehicle programs. In 1982, the Office of Research and Development funded work by a small California firm to develop a solar-powered UAV for surveillance. Today the plane's successor is used by NASA for environmental research. CREDIT: *AeroVironment*

NAVY

(above) The SS-9 missile was the source of a major dispute in the intelligence community in the late 1960s. President Nixon justified the decision to build the Safeguard ABM on the conclusion, disputed by the DS&T's Foreign Missile and Space Analysis Center, that the SS-9 was a MIRVed ICBM, and therefore gave the Soviets a capability for a preemptive strike on the U.S. ICBM force. The CIA was eventually proved correct. CREDIT: *U.S. Air Force*

(top right) The Sary Ozek IRBM complex as it appeared in September 1971 CORONA/KH-4B imagery. The KH-4B images has a resolution of about six feet. The first launch of the successor system, the KH-9/HEXAGON, had taken place in June. KH-9 images had a resolution of about two feet. The final CORONA launch occurred in May 1972. CREDIT: *National Reconnaissance Office*

(bottom right) Somewhat degraded 1998 advanced KH-11 images of the Baghdad Barracks Brigade and Depot, Abu Ghurayb, Iraq, before and after U.S. air strikes. CREDIT: *Department of Defense*

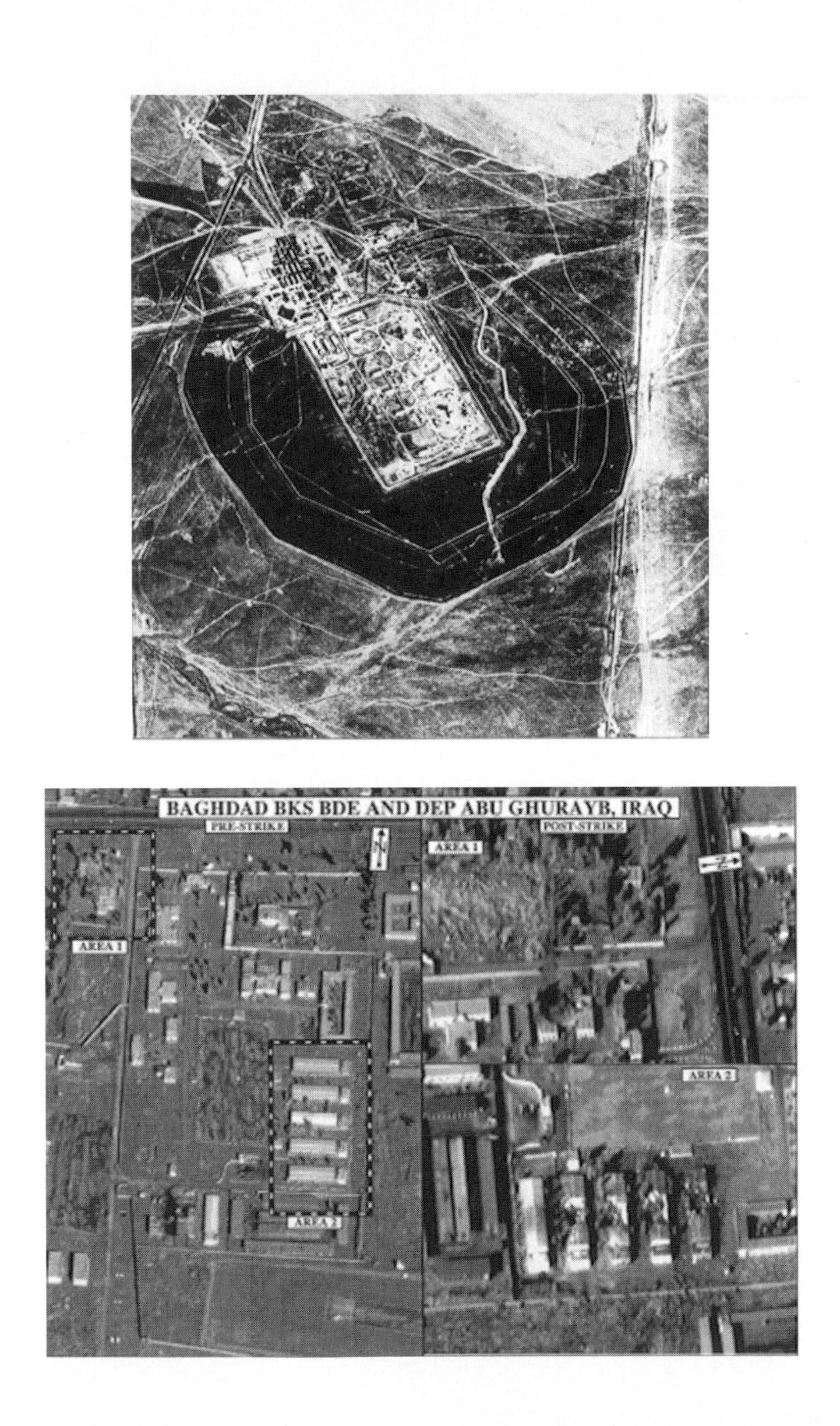
BAGHDAD BKS BDE AND DEP ABU GHURAYB, IRAQ
PRE-STRIKE
POST-STRIKE
AREA 1
AREA 2
AREA 1
AREA 2

(above) The main ground station for receipt of advanced KH-11 imagery, located at Fort Belvoir, Virginia. Given the public cover designation Defense Communications Electronics Evaluation and Testing Activity (DCEETA), within the intelligence community it is designated Area 58. CREDIT: *Robert Windrem*

(below) The Joint Defense Space Research Facility at Alice Springs, Australia. The facility has served as the ground control station for CIA-TRW–developed geostationary signals intelligence satellites, including RHYOLITE/AQUACADE and MAGNUM/ORION. CREDIT: *Desmond Ball*

9

A NEW WORLD

Evan Hineman's tenure as Deputy Director for Science and Technology ended on September 5, 1989, his seven years on the job second in length only to Duckett's among all CIA directorate heads. Stepping into Hineman's shoes was deputy James Hirsch—the first science and technology deputy since Duckett to move up to the top job.

The world had changed dramatically during Hineman's time in office. During his first years as deputy director, the United States and the Soviet Union clashed over the deployment of intermediate-range missiles in Europe, the Strategic Defense Initiative, Afghanistan, the shootdown of KAL flight 007, and a number of other issues. President Ronald Reagan denounced the Soviet Union as an evil empire and "the focus of evil in the modern world." But a combination of Reagan administration policies and Mikhail Gorbachev's rise to the top of the Soviet hierarchy in 1985 had a dramatic impact on world events. At the beginning of 1990, Gorbachev would declare that the Cold War had ended.[1]

CIA historian Benjamin Fischer labeled 1989 as "the year that changed the world."[2] The Communist regimes of Eastern Europe fell that year, along with the Berlin Wall. Before another two years were up, the Soviet Union disintegrated—a collapse that removed the restraints on various Soviet client states, including Iraq.

There were also changes in the offing for the intelligence community. There was pressure to do more with less—as many expected to take part of the expected peace dividend out of the intelligence community's budget. CIA personnel cutbacks reduced its workforce by about 20 percent before the end of the decade. There was also pressure for more openness. In addition, the disappearance of the Soviet enemy brought to the forefront questions of intelligence community structure and targets.

Between 1989 and 1995, those changes affected the DS&T in a variety of ways. The new international environment created new challenges, including a war that stressed NPIC's resources. A restructuring of the NRO would have a significant impact on the nature of the directorate's role in the development of reconnaissance satellites. And since the DS&T's budget was far greater than that of the other directorates, it was the most vulnerable to cuts.

CHALLENGES

When James Hirsch assumed command of the science and technology directorate, the Soviet Union was a "fast fading" nation. But the prolonged focus on the Soviet target "skewed the way we did things." The DS&T had invested heavily in a "frontal technical attack against the Soviet Union." As a result, the CIA "knew more about [Soviet] telemetry systems than [the Soviets] did."[3]

The heavy focus on the Soviet target meant that the directorate wasn't entirely prepared to deal with a radically different world. Thus, a study of "imagery collection requirements for the new world order" concluded that the United States would need to obtain images of five times as many point (individual) targets, and photograph ten times the area it did in earlier years. Such conclusions, Hirsch observed, were based on applying the "Soviet model" to the new era, and would not work.[4]

The Soviet model involved taking on new missions, regardless of the cost. But money had already been taken out of infrastructure and modernization, and the best the DS&T could hope for in coming years was a flat budget. Stricter priorities would have to be set, particularly given the need to modernize further in several areas, including NPIC.[5]

Improving NPIC was only one component of a broader challenge—coping with the digital and information revolutions. The volume of data collected was exploding, the result of more capable collection systems that used digital technology, such as the KH-11, and, in the SIGINT area, the increased volume of signals. There was a need to align processing techniques and capabilities with collection activities. Included was the need to "fuse" data—to combine various types of imagery and other technical data and produce enhanced products.[6]

There were also changes in the workforce, and these required that "careers . . . be managed differently." Career training could no longer be a one-time event that concluded early in the employee's career. The DS&T required long-term career training to keep personnel conversant with changing targets and technologies.[7]

THE GULF WAR

On July 16, 1990, Walter P. "Pat" Lang, the Defense Intelligence Officer for the Middle East and South Asia, carefully studied satellite imagery obtained that morning. A day earlier, nothing was to be seen in southeastern Iraq except empty desert, but on the sixteenth, the story was different. Lang could see part of an Iraqi brigade equipped with Soviet-made T-72 tanks.[8]

The next day's photos were even more disturbing. They showed the entire Hammurabi Division of the Republican Guard—300 tanks and over 10,000 men—positioned near the Kuwaiti border, along with another Republican Guard division. One day later, a third division also showed up in photographs of the border area.[9]

The movement of those three divisions to the border was not what the U.S. intelligence community expected. A national intelligence estimate in fall 1989, *Iraq: Foreign Policy of a Major Regional Power*, had concluded that despite Saddam Hussein's desire to dominate the Gulf region, the eight-year war with Iran had so drained Iraq's resources that the murderous dictator was unlikely to resort to military action.[10]

On July 24, DCI William Webster and Richard Stoltz, the CIA's deputy director for operations, presented President George Bush with hard evidence of Iraqi movements during an emergency meeting at the White House. The evidence was based substantially on the imagery interpretation efforts of the NPIC analysts who had worked overtime extracting intelligence from the satellite images of southern Iraq.[11]

Toward the end of the month, NPIC's interpreters examined imagery showing that three Iraqi Republican Guard divisions had moved into southern Iraq, and the division normally stationed in the south had moved closer to the Kuwaiti border. In addition, the interpreters were able to identify pontoon-bridging equipment, along with hundreds of heavy tank carriers that would enable Saddam's heavy armored divisions to move south swiftly before depositing the tanks in the sand to conclude the conquest of Kuwait.[12]

A reassuring explanation, accepted by many intelligence analysts, was that the Iraqi dictator was simply using the troop movements to pressure Kuwait in the two countries' ongoing negotiations over oil. Another was that although Saddam would take some action against Kuwait, it was unlikely that he would try to seize most of the country. That was the prevailing opinion in the CIA until August 2.[13]

But such explanations became less believable to Lang as the end of the month approached. The National Intelligence Officer for Warning,

Charles Allen, also believed a major attack was coming. On July 30, Lang prepared a memo for Lt. Gen. Harry Soyster, the DIA's director, in which he reported that Iraqi movements did not make sense if the only objective was to intimidate Kuwait. Lang wrote, "I do not believe that he is bluffing. I have looked at his personality profile. He doesn't know how to bluff. It is not in his past pattern of behavior." The photographs Lang examined on the morning of August 1 led him to issue a warning message predicting an attack by that night or the next morning.[14]

On the morning of August 2, 1990, the mechanized infantry, armor, and tank units of the Iraqi Republican Guard invaded Kuwait and seized control of the country. The invasion triggered a U.S. response, Operation Desert Shield, to deter any invasion of Kuwait's oil-rich neighbor, Saudi Arabia. On August 7, deployment of U.S. forces began. U.N. resolutions condemned Iraq's invasion and annexation and called for the immediate and unconditional withdrawal of Iraqi forces. On August 20, President Bush signed a national security directive outlining U.S. objectives—which included the "immediate, complete, and unconditional withdrawal of all Iraqi forces from Kuwait" and the "restoration of Kuwait's legitimate government to replace the puppet regime installed by Iraq."[15]

Implementing that policy would require an intense diplomatic, military, and intelligence effort in the months ahead. A multinational force had to be assembled, operations plan drawn up, and information collected about Iraqi defense systems, conventional offensive capabilities, command and control links, and nuclear, biological, and chemical weapons programs. In the interim, forces would be deployed to Saudi Arabia, as part of Operation Desert Shield, to deter any further hostile action.

A November 29 U.N. ultimatum stipulated that if Saddam did not remove his troops from Kuwait by January 15, a U.S.-led coalition was authorized to drive them out. On January 15, 1991, President Bush signed National Security Directive 54. In the directive's first paragraph, he observed: "Economic sanctions . . . have had a measurable impact upon Iraq's economy but have not accomplished the intended objective of ending Iraq's occupation of Kuwait. There is no persuasive evidence that they will do so in a timely manner." Later in the directive, he stated that "I hereby authorize military actions designed to bring about Iraq's withdrawal from Kuwait."[16]

The first step of the campaign began on January 17 with predawn bombing raids on targets in Baghdad and other key locations in Iraq. The targets included command and control facilities, airfields, communication centers, early warning radars, chemical and biological weapons bunkers, and Baath Party headquarters. Also on the target list were Scud storage and launch sites.[17] The devastating air campaign that began that day was followed on February 22 by the "Hail Mary" ground campaign that would force Iraqi troops out of Kuwait.

U.S. space reconnaissance systems were the primary means of collecting intelligence on Iraq and Kuwait, particularly in the period before military action began. Of particular importance were the imagery satellites the United States had in operation. Three KH-11s were in orbit, although the oldest, launched in 1984, had limited capability.

In addition, there was a satellite, known by the numerical designation 3101 and the code name ONYX, that had been launched in December 1988. Earlier, it (or the program to produce it) had been known as LACROSSE, and before that INDIGO. It was the program that nine years earlier the OD&E had tried to kill by offering to put a radar imagery capability on future versions of the KH-11. Rather than passively depending on reflected visible light or heat to produce imagery, ONYX, as QUILL had three decades earlier, relied on the active radio pulses it generated and then received back from its target. Unlike QUILL, its imagery was not stored in a capsule but transmitted to a relay satellite and then back to the United States. Although the resulting imagery was not in the same class as that of the KH-11, with a resolution of three to five feet, ONYX did have two major advantages. The KH-11 could not produce imagery in the presence of significant cloud cover, which prevented light or heat from reaching the spacecraft sensors, but ONYX could. And whereas the KH-11's visible light sensors were of little value during darkness, radar imagery systems worked well at night.[18]

ONYX had been developed and built by Martin Marietta under the supervision of the Air Force Office of Special Projects, but there was another imagery satellite in orbit—and that was an OD&E product. When first launched from the space shuttle *Atlantis* on March 1, 1990, it was believed to be the first advanced KH-11 spacecraft (the first of which would be launched in 1992). Within weeks, both U.S. and Soviet sources reported it had malfunctioned and would make a "fiery reentry . . . in the next 30 days."[19]

Both assessments were wrong. The payload was a stealth imaging satellite code-named MISTY, which had been developed under the supervision of the DS&T's development and engineering office.[20]

MISTY was one of at least two satellites developed in exceptional secrecy subsequent to the 1983 Reagan administration decision to establish a stealth satellite program.* The idea for MISTY came from OD&E engineers, some of whom had been enamored of the idea of a stealth satellite since the 1970s—having rediscovered the concept first suggested in the 1960s. The objective was to reduce the threat to U.S. satellites from the Soviet Union—whose antisatellite program was of significant concern during the early 1980s.[21]

To help define that threat, OD&E turned to the Directorate of Intelligence's Office of Scientific and Weapons Research (OSWR)—the office formed in 1980 by the merger of the scientific and weapons intelligence offices that had been transferred to the intelligence directorate in 1976. A Threat Assessment Branch (later Center) in the OSWR Space Systems Division was established and produced an analysis that supported the idea that MISTY could be successful—it argued that Soviet radars and cameras were not very capable and were unlikely to track the satellite. But because the program was so highly compartmented, OD&E did not consult several agencies that had experience in satellite tracking—including the Naval Research Laboratory (NRL), whose engineers might have provided a different assessment about MISTY's vulnerability to detection.[22]

A clue to possible U.S. government interest in stealth satellites was supplied just weeks after MISTY's launch. To the anger of many in the NRO, a patent application was filed, apparently by the SDIO, for a "Satellite Signature Suppression Shield." The application described an inflatable shield that could protect satellites from detection by radar, laser, infrared, and optical systems.[23]

But despite MISTY's intended stealthiness, when the shuttle placed it into orbit, four civilian space observers—Russell Eberst, Daniel Karcher, and Pierre Neirinck in Europe and Ted Molczan in Canada—were able to determine that the satellite was in a 494-by-503-mile, 65-degree orbit, an orbit that did not match any other U.S. military spacecraft. In addition, the civilian observers were able to monitor a series of maneuvers performed by the satellite—including the "explosion" that may have been a tactic to deceive those monitoring the satellite or may have been the result of the jettisoning of operational debris.[24]

---

*The program was so secret that there was a special compartment, designated ZIRCONIC, established within the already highly secret BYEMAN Control System to designate information relating to stealth satellites. Within ZIRCONIC, yet another term, NEBULA, designated stealth satellite technology.

The satellite did finally disappear around November 1990. In 2000, one space observer, examining orbital data from the North American Defense Command, came to the conclusion that in May 1995, the satellite was in a 451-by-461-mile orbit. Where the satellite is today is unclear, as is how much additional intelligence MISTY has yielded.[25]

In addition to satellites, the United States relied on several other intelligence assets, which were either deployed to Saudi Arabia or were traditionally operated from territory close to Iraq. U-2s flew imagery and SIGINT missions lasting up to ten hours. RC-135 RIVET JOINT aircraft deployed to Riyadh monitored Iraqi communications. RF-4C Phantoms, F-14s with tactical reconnaissance pods, P-3 Orion ocean surveillance aircraft (flown over land), and unmanned aerial vehicles also gathered imagery. Further, U.S. and British ground-based SIGINT collection sites in the vicinity—on Cyprus and in Turkey, Italy, and Oman—were undoubtedly targeted on Iran and Kuwait.[26]

The United States used these and allied assets, along with human intelligence, to update its database on the Iraqi military, economic, and political systems as a prelude to target selection for an air war and planning for a possible ground offensive. Imagery played a key part in intelligence support to the air war. It provided information about the deployment of Iraqi forces in Iraq and Kuwait, enabled identification of facilities to be attacked, and was vital in assessing the damage caused by the attacks. Imagery revealing the location of Iraqi troops also let the Central Command's war planners devise the "Hail Mary" strategy by which allied forces entered Iraq with minimal resistance. The task of interpreting the imagery was divided between theater organizations such as the Central Command's Joint Intelligence Center, the DIA and military service imagery interpretation units in the United States, and, of course, the National Photographic Interpretation Center. Within a month of the Iraqi invasion, some interpreters working at NPIC's Washington Navy Yard headquarters were working eighteen-hour days to provide a steady flow of intelligence to the President and other senior officials as well as U.S. forces in Saudi Arabia. When a reporter surveyed the NPIC parking lot one midnight in late August, he found more than 100 cars.[27]

Meanwhile, the NPIC's Priority Exploitation Group at Ft. Belvoir was also working at a more intense pace. Normally, the work of examining incoming imagery was handled in two or three shifts, with analysts working ten-and-a-half-hour shifts, four days a week. For those working the day shift, a typical day began at 7 a.m. and ended at 5:30 p.m. After a half-hour "shift change" meeting, the day interpreters went to their Dilbert-style cubicles and, using either a light table or a computer (the Imagery Data Exploitation Station), extracted intelligence from the overhead imagery.[28]

Once Iraqi troops began moving, six to seven ground forces analysts were selected to cover Iraq. Their shifts increased to fourteen to sixteen hours a day. Not surprisingly, people grew tired and made mistakes, including incorrectly entering the coordinates of SA-6 antiaircraft missile sites into the database.[29] Meanwhile, back at Building 213, the interpreters were being overwhelmed by the flood of incoming imagery. Further complicating matters was the lack of sufficient broad-band transmission capability to send much of the imagery to Central Command (CENTCOM) headquarters in Riyadh electronically. Thus, a message based on KH-11 imagery would normally take over an hour to get to the field, and an actual image would take between four and fourteen hours to arrive. Messages based on radar imagery would take two to three hours, whereas images would take between six and twenty-four hours. Those images that took the longest to arrive might arrive via aircraft rather than the airwaves. An Air Force jet was dispatched each evening carrying overhead images.[30]

The war also revealed differences in the interpretation cultures at NPIC and the theater with respect to bomb-damage assessment. NPIC judged aircraft or tanks to be destroyed if destruction was clearly shown by satellite or aerial photography, whereas CENTCOM analysts factored in pilot reports in assessing the impact of bombing raids. In addition, many of the small holes on the outside of a target, which meant serious internal damage, were not detectable—even by high-resolution U.S. imagery satellites. As a result, CENTCOM concluded that 1,400 of the 4,280 Iraqi tanks believed to be deployed in Kuwait were destroyed, but NPIC could confirm only 358 as destroyed.[31]

THE END OF PROGRAM B

The late 1980s ushered in the beginning of what eventually would be a wide-ranging restructuring of the NRO, a restructuring that would have significant implications for the CIA's Directorate of Science and Technology. In a November 1988 letter to Senator David Boren, chairman of the Senate Select Committee on Intelligence, NRO director Pete Aldridge observed:

> As you are aware, over the last year and a half we have conducted an extensive study of the organizational structure of the NRO. While I am convinced that the NRO is extremely effective and responsive to the many needs of the national intelligence community, the dramatically expanding collection requirements, the increasing technical complexity of the targets, the constrained budgets, and the growing diversity of the operational users demand that the NRO become even more effective and efficient.[32]

Aldridge reported that he had discussed the study's recommendations with Secretary of Defense Richard Cheney and Director of Central Intelligence William Webster and he was directing the development of plans to implement the recommendations. Specific changes would include the creation of a centralized systems analysis function "to conduct cross-system trades and simulations within the NRO"; creation of a "User Support" function to improve NRO support to intelligence community users as well as to the growing number of operational military users; and the dispersal of the NRO staff to the new units, with the staff being replaced by a group of policy advisers. In addition, Aldridge foresaw the establishment of an interim facility "to house the buildup of the new functions and senior management." The ultimate goal, projected for the 1991–1992 period, would be the "collocation of all NRO elements . . . in the Washington, D.C., area."[33]

Not planned, and Aldridge pointed this out in his letter, was any change in the nature of Programs A, B, and C as "distinct elements" of the NRO. A study of the NRO conducted by former OSO director Barry Kelly and Rear Admiral Robert K. Geiger, former head of the NRO's Program C, and completed in July 1989 had not recommended any change in that twenty-year-old arrangement.[34]

But they did recommend collocation as a means of increasing the DNRO's authority—as well as installing the Director of OD&E as the head of Program B. They noted that "because the DDS&T reports directly to the DCI, there are real and perceptual problems regarding his willingness to support a DNRO decision that is unfavorable to the CIA, or to appeal it with the DNRO. Instead, the DDS&T can . . . take the issue directly to the DNRO's boss, the DCI." In addition, they noted that "the proximity of the DDS&T to the DCI also tends to cause the DCI to look first to the DDS&T for support regarding NRO issues." Finally, they observed that "the DDS&T is limited by other responsibilities and can spend only about 20 percent of his time on NRO and Program B matters," but that "the effective management of . . . Program B requires . . . someone who spends the majority of his time working Program B and NRO issues."[35]

In July 1989, Webster and Cheney wrote Boren a joint letter reporting on further plans for restructuring NRO's internal operations. The proposed changes, which were largely based on the Geiger-Kelly study, would include establishing a planning, analysis, and evaluation capability within the NRO to support program decisions; creating a deputy director for military support; and formally designating the CIA's Director of the Office of Development and Engineering as Director of Program B in order "to provide a full-time manager for Program B."[36]

Cheney and Webster also informed Boren that the Program A, B, C structure would remain in place:

> [W]e reaffirm our previous conviction, supported by the DNRO's current reassessment, that a business-line structure, that would attempt to give each Program Office the responsibility for a unique mission area, is neither a viable or effective restructure alternative. We want to preserve a beneficial degree of competition between the Program Offices, as appropriate to a problem. Competition is also vital to sustaining the motivation of the Program Offices and our ability to develop creative solutions to intelligence requirements.[37]

However, the policy of maintaining the traditional structure would not last through the Bush administration. In the late 1980s, Congress, particularly the Senate Select Committee on Intelligence and chairman David Boren, had suggested the need for NRO to reorganize and consolidate. The feeling, as described in 1994 by DCI James Woolsey, was that the "NRO . . . was a somewhat decentralized organization, and the various parts of it, from time to time, fell into competition with one another. And that involved, sometimes, competing . . . satellite programs."[38]

Thus, in October 1991, Senator Boren and committee Vice-Chairman Frank Murkowski, in correspondence with the DCI and Secretary of Defense, noted that their committee "recommends reorganization into several directorates and collocation of major NRO elements as expeditiously as possible." The proposal was approved by Robert Gates, who had replaced Webster as DCI in 1992, Cheney, and Bush.[39] The President formally ordered the restructuring in National Security Directive 67, "Intelligence Capabilities, 1992–2005," which he signed in late March.[40]

By the time Bush signed the directive, he had been apprised of the suggestions of a task force chaired by former Lockheed CEO Robert Fuhrman. Its members included four former senior intelligence community officials—Lt. Gen. Lincoln Faurer (NSA), Lt. Gen. Edward J. Heinz (Intelligence Community Staff director), Maj. Gen. Ralph Jacobson (Program A), and Evan Hineman—and two serving intelligence officials, John P. Devine, the NSA's Deputy Director for Research and Engineering, and NPIC director Leo Hazelwood.[41]

Among the panel's recommendations was the termination of the Program A, B, C structure. The panel observed that the traditional organizational arrangement did not "enhance mission effectiveness." Rather, it had led to "counterproductive competition," which "makes it more difficult to foster loyalty and to maintain the focus on the NRO mission." They recommended, "in order to foster an improved NRO corporate spirit, and to better serve the intelligence needs of the nation," that the NRO be organized around the imagery and SIGINT disciplines. The panel noted that "such a restructure will lessen competition between NRO program offices as a driving force for creativity," but believed that the NRO director would be able to find "other and more effective ways of eliciting the most creative and effective ideas for meeting the nation's intelligence needs."[42]

Gates publicly announced the restructuring before a joint public hearing of the Senate and House intelligence oversight committees in April 1992, at a time when the NRO's existence was still officially secret. Gates told his audience that there would be a "far-reaching internal restructuring of the Intelligence Community organization responsible for designing, building, and operating our overhead reconnaissance assets."[43]

The restructuring that Gates referred to took effect the following month. Initially, imagery activities were assigned to the CIA's Office of Development and Engineering, and SIGINT became the responsibility of the Air Force Office of Special Projects. Two tasks that remained were the transfer of all 700 Program A personnel from Los Angeles to Washington—a prospect that perturbed some southern California congressmen and no doubt many of Program A's staff—and the creation of NRO imagery and SIGINT directorates that were purely NRO entities (and that fully integrated Air Force and CIA personnel, along with personnel from the Navy, NSA, DIA, and other organizations).[44]

A major question not yet resolved in late 1992 concerned the impact of the restructuring on the Office of Development and Engineering. It was clear that it would continue to be the source of personnel to work on NRO programs. And in accord with McMahon's instructions to Kohler, it had often functioned more as a component of the NRO than of the CIA. The distinction was emphasized by its having its own building, as well as its own career service—distinct not just from the agency's but from that of the rest of the science and technology directorate. But the restructuring meant that eventually there would be no more CIA/Program B satellite programs, only NRO programs that CIA personnel participated in—which had been Charyk's and McMillan's vision three decades earlier.

BACK TO THE FUTURE

In August 1993, James Hirsch, faced with budgetary and personnel downsizing, effectively reversed one of his and Evan Hineman's changes, when he established the Office of Technical Collection (OTC). OTC absorbed, in their entirety, the Office of SIGINT Operations and the Office of Special Projects. It also took charge of some of the projects that were assigned to the Office of Technical Service, including some of its clandestine imaging activities.[45] Since the OSP-managed activities had largely been the responsibility of OSO until the special projects office was established in 1987, in one sense the clock had been turned back.

The merger returned responsibility to a single office for the CHESTNUT sites, the Special Collection Service operations, and emplaced sensors—and once again assigned one office responsibility for both SIGINT and MASINT collection. But as its name implied, OTC gave the two activities more equal standing. Indeed, the first head of OTC was Peter Daniher, who had headed OSP and was chosen over OSO head Joseph B. Castillo Jr. to run the new office.[46]

Daniher had served in the intelligence directorate's Office of Scientific and Weapons Research (established in 1980 by merging OSI and OWI) and had ambitions to be the Deputy Director for Intelligence. When it became clear to him that he was unlikely to achieve that position, he shifted his focus to the DS&T and became director of the special projects office in October 1989 when Gary W. Goodrich moved up to become Hirsch's deputy.[47]

Hirsch had a number of reasons for establishing OTC in addition to resource pressures. The seemingly disparate activities had some significant common aspects. The data they produced could all be processed using digital techniques, and Hirsch believed it was important that any advances be shared. Developing access to sites to place sensor equipment, whether clandestine SIGINT, clandestine imaging, or clandestine MASINT, involved common problems and challenges. There was also commonality in development and testing. In Hirsch's view, there was no good, logical way to divide the activities perfectly, and that what was important was proper development and testing, irrespective of whether the system was electronic, optical, or chemical.[48]

THE WALKING STICK

In late 1992, President Bush authorized Operation Restore Hope—the deployment of 25,000 U.S. troops to Somalia to ensure that U.N. food, medicine, and other supplies were delivered to those in the war-torn country in need of such assistance. By May 1993, the supplies were reaching their targets, famine was receding, and the nation was relatively peaceful. Most U.S. troops were withdrawn, and Somalia was turned over to a U.N. peacekeeping force.[49]

Then, in a move supported by the Clinton administration, the U.N. mandate was expanded to include the rehabilitation of Somali political institutions as well as the nation's economy. The action infuriated Gen. Mohammed Farah Aideed, a warlord whose Somali National Alliance (SNA) had become the primary power in Mogadishu, the Somali capital. In early June, Pakistani peacekeepers were ambushed and killed after inspecting Aideed's radio transmission center. Not long after, the U.N. senior representative in Somalia, Adm. Jonathan Howe, issued an arrest warrant for Aideed and offered a $25,000 reward for his capture.[50]

The next month, the situation took a turn for the worse, when a U.S. component of the peacekeeping force, the Army's 10th Mountain Division, killed between twenty and fifty Aideed aides and operatives in an attack on the SNA's command center. The attack not only failed to achieve its objective of eliminating Aideed and the SNA as an obstacle to the U.N. mission but also led the warlord to declare war on the U.N. forces.[51]

Finding and capturing Aideed became a top priority for the CIA in Somalia. Trying to locate the warlord through intercepted radio traffic proved impossible in Mogadishu's "pre-electronic state."[52] In early October 1993, an article in the *Washington Post* recounted how intelligence problems, including a lack of intelligence exchange between the nations involved in the peacekeeping effort, hampered the search for the elusive warlord.[53]

One problem not mentioned was the fatal flaw of a CIA asset, which possibly prevented his case officer from using him to plant a homing beacon on Aideed. OTS had implanted such a beacon in an ivory-handled walking stick. The asset, a minor warlord, was to give the stick to Aideed as a symbol of friendship. As long as Aideed carried the stick with him, the CIA would be able to find him.[54]

But in late August, before the CIA's man could deliver the stick to Aideed, he played Russian roulette once too often. By late September, with pressure building to produce a success for the Clinton administration, the deceased warlord's case officer was told that another troublemaker might be captured. The potential target was Osman Ato, a wealthy businessman, arms importer, and Aideed financial supporter. Another CIA contact was willing to deliver Ato for the right amount of money.[55]

Cane in hand, the contact was soon climbing into a car that would take him to Ato. Helicopters tracked the car, using the stick's beacon, on its winding ride through north Mogadishu. When the car stopped for gas, an operative on the ground reported that Ato was in the car. Commandos from the Delta Force, which had arrived in late August expecting to capture Aideed, were launched in pursuit of their new target.[56]

Minutes later, a helicopter descended, and a sniper leaned out and placed three shots into the car's engine block. As the car came to a stop, the commandos slid down ropes dangling from Blackhawk helicopters, surrounded the car, and put Ato in handcuffs. An hour later, Delta's commander, Maj. Gen. Walter F. Garrison, had a big grin on his face and was telling CIA officer Garrett Jones that "I like this cane."[57]

SPYING ON CANCER

On October 11, 1994, James Woolsey, the Clinton administration's first DCI, appeared at a Capitol Hill briefing. He was not there to discuss terrorism, arms proliferation, drug trafficking, or the threat from rogue states. At the request of Susan Blumenthal, the deputy assistant secretary for women's health at the Department of Health and Human Services, he was attending a briefing on breast cancer. He was not there as an observer but as the most senior representative of a CIA effort to make some of its technologies available to fight the disease. Woolsey told the audience that "what we are trying to do is to use the tools developed to protect the lives of 250,000,000 Americans [to] help save the lives of a substantial share of the 46,000 women who die annually of breast cancer."[58]

Earlier in the year, Blumenthal had written to other government agencies inquiring whether they had technologies that might contribute to President Clinton's initiative to fight breast cancer. In July, ORD invited the National Information Display Laboratory (NIDL), an organization sponsored by the intelligence community to help bring advanced commercial and consumer technologies into the government, to prepare a background paper for Blumenthal. The paper described some of the advanced image-processing techniques that might be applied to the field of mammography.[59]

The Defense Intelligence Agency digitized some sample mammography for NIDL experimentation, which proved sufficiently interesting that Blumenthal and a committee of medical experts visited the laboratory in September 1994. The image-processing technique demonstrated to the group led Blumenthal to invite the laboratory to participate in the Capitol Hill symposium. For that meeting, NIDL, with the assistance of the Community Management Staff and ORD, set up several demonstrations of advanced, but unclassified, image-processing techniques that were applicable to medical procedures.[60]

The techniques included using experimental high-definition television and head-mounted displays to examine digital images, pattern recognition tools, and a three-dimensional system for detecting lesions in magnetic resonance breast scans. The briefing also included a demonstration of serial change detection—the subtraction of the images in one photo from a later photo to identify new objects—applied to serial mammograms.[61] Such a system had been developed to enable NPIC to identify new missile sites or other new military developments at a target area.

The following spring, Adm. William O. Studeman, who had become acting director upon Woolsey's resignation, announced that the CIA, NRO, and Community Management Staff would contribute $375,000 to continue research into application of such techniques to breast cancer detection.*

DANGEROUS MISSIONS

In spring 1995, U.S. officials met the flag-draped coffin of Gary C. Durrell at Maryland's Andrews Air Force Base. Durrell, a forty-four-year-old

*It was not the first time CIA research had benefited medical science. In the 1970s, CIA research into lithium iodine batteries, conducted to ensure the prolonged operation of reconnaissance satellites, was made available to the medical community. It subsequently became the dominant technology used in heart pacemakers. (Interview with senior DS&T official, 1996.)

father of two, had died shortly before in Pakistan, the victim of terrorist gunfire. His death was another reminder that, for some, working for the Directorate of Science and Technology could be just as dangerous as working for the Directorate of Operations; Durrell had been in Pakistan as part of the Special Collection Service's Karachi element.[62]

The SCS had continued to pay significant intelligence dividends during the Hineman and Hirsch years. SCS elements could be found in embassies in Moscow, Beijing, Buenos Aires, Santiago, Tel Aviv, Tegucigalpa, and another forty capitals. In Tegucigalpa, the SCS element monitored the police and military as well as the terrorist activities of some of the forces opposing the government. The Tel Aviv outpost intercepted Israeli military and national police communications—allowing the State Department to be informed about, among other things, police activities directed at the Palestinians.[63] Undoubtedly, during the abortive attempt to oust Mikhail Gorbachev in August 1991, the Moscow embassy listening post intercepted whatever communications of the coup plotters, including the KGB chairman and Minister of Defense, could be snatched from the airwaves.[64]

Other SCS missions involved a closer approach to the target. An SCS operation might involve eavesdropping from a van outside the window of a foreign ministry official—which might make it possible for an analyst to read every message being written in the official's office at the time it was being written. Another project allegedly involved capturing pigeons that roosted outside the Soviet embassy in Washington and attaching small microphones to them. After returning to their perch outside an open office window, they produced "incredibly good results," according to a former Canadian intelligence officer.[65]

One operation involved bugging the Chinese ambassador to Washington, who frequently talked about sensitive matters while sitting on a bench in the embassy compound. SCS technicians developed a fiberglass "twig," which contained a listening device. It was tossed into the compound near the bench. SCS bugging operations also involved crystal objects, mugs, porcelain roses, dried floral arrangements, a small totem pole, as well as an icon of the Virgin Mary holding the baby Jesus painted on a one-inch-thick piece of wood. All were planted in offices or offered to diplomats as gifts.[66]

One SCS officer arrived in Kabul toward the end of 1984 and spent several hours a day pretending to be a diplomat, meeting with Afghanis who wanted to travel to the United States, visiting the Foreign Ministry, and attending receptions. But he spent most of his time, usually in twelve-hour stretches, in a windowless suite of three small rooms protected by an electronic lock. One room was a lounge; another served as a storage area for the eavesdropping equipment. In the third room, electronic devices were piled up to the ceiling—creating a wall of knobs, buttons, tape recorders, and glowing oscilloscopes. Relying on a massive guide labeled TEXTA (for Technical Extracts from Traffic Analysis), the eavesdroppers could find what frequencies their targets employed.[67]

The SCS officer monitored Afghan troops as well as the military airport tower, noting on three-by-five index cards aircraft types, arrival and departure times, and destinations. A copy of each teletype message sent by an Afghan government official appeared on a printer in the room. The SCS element in Kabul was able to provide coverage across the country. Included was a grisly intercept reporting that the Afghan resistance had peeled off the skin of a captured Soviet soldier while he was still alive. According to a former Reagan administration Middle East expert, "They were plugged in on Afghanistan. . . . We were soaking up everything."[68]

In Pakistan, Gary Durrell and his SCS colleagues were undoubtedly soaking up as much information as they could. Durrell was a native of Alliance, Ohio. As a member of the Air Force Security Service, the Air Force component of NSA, he worked at eavesdropping sites in Texas and Italy. In 1977, he joined NSA, and spent the next eight years in England at the RAF Chicksands eavesdropping site—which intercepted both Soviet and West European communications. In 1987, he "resigned" from NSA, ostensibly to join the State Department. In fact, he joined the SCS, which by then had moved into its new headquarters in Beltsville, Maryland. The sign outside those headquarters indicated the site housed the State Department's "Communications Systems Support Group."[69]

Before heading overseas, Durrell trained at a site in Maryland that had the appearance of a high-tech company. At the "Maryland field site," as it is referred to in unclassified documents, Durrell and his fellow trainees were instructed on the use of sophisticated listening equipment, some of the equipment no bigger than a briefcase and some stacked like the stereo equipment one might find in a living room. They were trained to do their eavesdropping from locked rooms inside embassies and consulates.[70]

When he left the Maryland field site, Durrell had a cover story, foreign currency, and business cards, with the phone number of a notional boss who would vouch for him. Durrell had also studied photographic albums showing the landmarks and intersections in what was to be his new neighborhood, so as to eliminate the need to ask directions or otherwise call attention to himself. To further enhance his State Department cover, he memorized his purported travel route to the department's Foggy Bottom headquarters, including the bus route and closest Metro stop. He probably, as was usually the case, had also been formally appointed to the United States Foreign Service, with a certificate signed by President Reagan and his Secretary of State as proof.[71]

In the first five years after joining the SCS, Durrell worked under State Department cover in Bangkok, Bombay, and Djibouti. His reports were sent via satellite to a complex of antennae adjacent to the Maryland field site. Inside the consulate in Karachi, Durrell spent four months intercepting communications concerning narcotics trafficking, terrorism, and nuclear proliferation.[72]

That mission came to an end on March 8, 1995. As he was riding in a consulate van on his way to work, terrorists leaped from a stolen taxi and fired their AK-47 assault rifles at the van. Sixteen bullets ripped into the van, killing Durrell and a consulate secretary and wounding another employee. The attack may have been a response to the arrest in Pakistan of Ramzi Ahmed Yousef, who would be convicted in the 1993 bombing of the World Trade Center in New York.[73]

CLOSING DOWN THE X-FILES

When the CIA ended its support for remote viewing and other parapsychology research in 1976, other agencies were willing to take its place. Until 1995, either Army Intelligence or the Defense Intelligence Agency supported such activities as part of projects with exotic names such as GRILL FLAME and STARGATE. In 1979, the DIA asked alleged psychics to provide information on a Soviet submarine program as well as the functions of key buildings in foreign countries. Psychics were also asked to help locate some missing Americans in Iran during the 1979–1980 hostage crisis. The Army's Special Operations Division asked a psychic to help them locate Brig. Gen. James Dozier, who was kidnapped in Italy in December 1981.[74]

In 1986, the military's psychic friends were asked to locate Muammar Gadhafi before the U.S. bombing raid on Libya. The next year, the DIA requested some of the purported psychics to divine the purpose of a Soviet facility at Dushanbe, and in 1989 the Joint Staff asked for help in determining the exact function of a suspected terrorist training facility in Libya. In 1993, the DIA asked the psychics to locate tunnels that the agency suspected the North Koreans were digging under the demilitarized zone separating their country from South Korea. In 1994, some of the alleged psychics were tasked to find plutonium in North Korea.[75]

In 1995, despite its claim that the program produced some successes—including the 1979 prediction that a new Soviet submarine would be launched within 100 days and the identification of a building where Lt. Col. William Higgins was being held in Lebanon—DIA was planning on terminating its STARGATE program.[76]

By that time, CIA supporters such as Carl Duckett and John McMahon were gone, and James Hirsch had not grown any less skeptical than when he headed the research and development office. There was, however, pressure on the CIA from influential members of Congress and staffers—including Senators Daniel Inouye (D.–Hawaii), Robert Byrd (D.–West Virginia), and Claiborne Pell (D.–Rhode Island). For Pell, sometimes referred to as "The Senator from Outer Space," STARGATE was not the first New Age program he had supported.[77]

Several staffers from the intelligence oversight committees who believed, according to Hirsch, that the program had "tremendous potential" pressed the CIA to resume funding. In the late 1980s, the CIA had asked the National Research Council for an assessment of the intelligence value of paranormal spying, and was told there was no reason to support such activities. With Congress mandating that the CIA review the possible utility of remote viewing for intelligence collection, Hirsch, who believed there was "absolutely zero intelligence payoff," decided to obtain an updated, outside assessment of the military's use of psychic spies.[78]

In June 1995, ORD contracted with the nonprofit American Institutes for Research (AIR) for a review of the STARGATE program.[79] An assessment was to be made of two of the three components of STARGATE—the operations program, which relied on remote viewers to provide intelligence on foreign targets, and the research and development program, which used laboratory studies in an attempt to find improved methods of remote viewing for intelligence purposes. (The third component of STARGATE was "foreign assessment," which focused on foreign activities to develop or exploit purported paranormal phenomena in ways that might affect U.S. national security.)[80]

The CIA asked AIR to produce a comprehensive evaluation of the research and development in this area, with a focus on the scientific validity of the technical approaches. In addition, AIR was to evaluate the overall utility of the program to the government and consider whether any changes in the operational or research and development activities of the program might produce better results. Finally, AIR was to provide the CIA with recommendations "as to appropriate strategies for program activity in the future."[81]

Focusing on the laboratory component of the program were two outside experts—Dr. Jessica Utts, a professor of statistics at the Davis campus of the University of California, and Dr. Ray Hyman, of the University of Oregon's psychology department. Utts had written articles that supported the existence of paranormal phenomena, whereas Hyman was a well-known skeptic. In 1986, he had published a lengthy review article on parapsychological research that questioned whether any of the claims of positive results from paranormal experimentation could stand up to scientific scrutiny. In 1989, he had written a highly skeptical report for the NRC on DIA's remote-viewing activities, noting that experiments conducted by DIA had been graded solely by DIA officials and the results had not proven replicable by independent experts. Meanwhile, two senior AIR scientists examined the operational aspect of the STARGATE program.[82]

Utts and Hyman prepared written reviews of the laboratory studies, which echoed their previous work and formed the basis of the AIR report's observation that although the laboratory results were statistically significant, in that hits occurred significantly more often than by chance, it was "unclear whether the observed effects can unambiguously be attributed to the paranormal ability of the remote viewers." Other possible explanations included the characteristics of the judges or the targets. The report noted that "use of the same remote viewers, the same judge, and the same target photographs makes it impossible to identify their independent effects." The report further noted that the laboratory experiments had not identified the origins or nature of the remote-viewing phenomenon, "if, indeed, it exists at all."[83]

In an attempt to assess the operational component of STARGATE, the two AIR representatives interviewed users of the information produced, the remote viewers, and the program manager. The report noted that although the end users found some accuracy with regard to broad background characteristics, the "remote viewing reports failed to produce the concrete, specific information valued in intelligence reporting." The study also observed that the information provided by the remote viewers was "inconsistent, inaccurate with regard to specifics, and required substantial subjective interpretation." Finally, it reported that "in no case had the information provided ever been used to guide intelligence operations," and that "remote viewing failed to produce actionable intelligence."[84]

The report concluded that such observations "provide a compelling argument against continuation of the program within the intelligence community."[85] Not surprisingly, Hirsch agreed. He went to Nora Slatkin, the agency's Executive Director, who accepted his recommendation that the CIA should remain out of the paranormal field. If DIA officials wanted to reorient the program to give it some scientific validity, they could continue it, but DIA was not interested, and the government's psychic friends network was shut down.[86]

10

AGILE INTELLIGENCE

During his years as associate deputy director and then deputy director for science and technology, Jim Hirsch had witnessed turmoil not only throughout the world but at the CIA. From Bill Casey's death in 1987 through 1995, there had been a parade of DCIs. Casey's replacement, William Webster, was succeeded by Robert Gates. When Bill Clinton took office, he replaced Gates with James Woolsey—who after two years of finding it hard to get an appointment with his boss, decided to call it quits. Woolsey's proposed successor, national security adviser Anthony Lake, withdrew in the midst of a very hostile reception from the Republicans on the Senate Select Committee on Intelligence. Then, after having to withdraw the nomination of his next candidate, a former Air Force general, Clinton turned to Deputy Secretary of Defense John Deutch, whose longer-term goal was to become Secretary of Defense.

Not long after Deutch arrived, Hirsch was planning his departure. His replacement was an outsider. Unlike previous deputy directors for science and technology, Ruth David had no previous experience within, or even contact with, the agency. Her tenure at the head of the directorate was the shortest since Bud Wheelon's and was marked by turmoil and change.

Several new offices were created, and one of the original three established in 1962 was abolished. There was internal strife due to David's plan for funding the new offices. The directorate also lost responsibility for national photographic interpretation as a result of a major reorganization orchestrated by Deutch. To some, David's tenure marked a decline in the importance and status of the directorate—in part, due to her own decisions.

BLUE-RIBBON PANELS

Before Hirsch departed, he appointed two blue-ribbon panels to take a look at the directorate. One was headed by Ed McMahon, the executive vice-president of MRJ, a high-technology company whose president was Donald Haas—the former head of the research and development and development and engineering offices who had also served as NRO deputy director. McMahon's group focused on the organization and management of the directorate.[1]

Gordon J. MacDonald, a geophysicist at the University of California, San Diego, who had been one of the first scientists recruited by the CIA to help it employ the intelligence community's technical systems in support of environmental research, chaired the second panel. Joining MacDonald in trying to identify technologies the directorate should pursue was longtime adviser Richard Garwin; William Dally, a professor of computer science at MIT; William Press, a professor of astronomy at Harvard; and Steven Koonin, a theoretical physicist at the California Institute of Technology. Press, Dally, and Koonin were all members of the JASON group of scientists who advised the Defense Department.[2]

According to Koonin, who had become a full professor at Cal Tech in 1981 at the age of thirty, his group received briefings during summer 1995 at secure facilities in northern Virginia, where they held a couple of all-day meetings. It was "a whirlwind look at all pieces of the DS&T." The impression he took away from the briefings was that although there was "isolated . . . technical excellence," the directorate was "somewhat fragmented and in disarray." There were several specific problems—technologies that had evolved in the Cold War were less useful with respect to post–Cold War targets and threats; there was poor interaction between the directorate and the agency's intelligence and operations components (including between the Office of Technical Service and the Directorate of Operations); there was a lack of new talent; and analysts were disappointed with respect to the information support available to them.[3]

Ultimately, the two separate panels came together to give a joint briefing on their findings. With respect to organization and management, the scientists recommended flattening the organizational structure of the directorate, which could involve establishing new offices directly under the deputy director. They also suggested an increased reliance on use of outside consultants to help deal with vastly different issues such as diseases, chemical and biological warfare, and the environment. Perhaps most significant, they suggested placing greater emphasis on information technologies.[4]

In September, as Hirsch was preparing to leave, he discussed the two panels' findings with his successor—findings that probably reinforced some of her basic notions about what needed to be done.

THE NEW NUMBER ONE

In his search for a successor to Hirsch, Deutch looked in a number of places and asked the national labs, which included Sandia, Los Alamos, and Livermore, for nominations. Sandia's nominee, and Deutch's choice, was Ruth David, who at the time was director of Sandia's Strategic Thrust in Advanced Information Technologies.[5]

David was truly an outsider, although one with an impressive résumé. She held a doctorate from Stanford in electrical engineering and had taught at the University of New Mexico. Her academic credentials included a number of technical papers and coauthorship of two reference works on digital signal processing. At Sandia she had managed the development of data acquisition systems to monitor underground nuclear testing at the Energy Department's Nevada test site, as well as the development of various engineering test facilities for Sandia programs. But she had never had any contact with the CIA, either as an employee or consultant.[6]

David's selection was announced on the last day of July; on September 15, ten days after Jim Hirsch's last day as deputy director, she started work as his successor.[7] Her deputy at the time was Gary W. Goodrich, who had become associate deputy director in October 1989. But he would not be around for long—December 31 would be his last day at the agency. On January 1, Pete Daniher, chief of the Office of Technical Collection, who had long coveted David's job and whose chance to get it may have left the building with Jim Woolsey, became her deputy.[8]

NEW OFFICES

While still at Sandia, David had participated in the "Agile Enterprise Manufacturing Forum" at Lehigh University. The meeting focused on how corporations could deal with a rapidly changing business environment—forming teams quickly to solve problems and then moving on to the next problem.[9] David brought the concept with her to her new job. When she arrived in Washington, she noted that the distinct organizations that made up the intelligence community faced rapidly changing priorities, tight budgets, and consumers who wanted intelligence tailored to their needs. Part of the answer, she believed, was to form new alliances within the community and with consumers as well as with individuals and groups from academia and think tanks. She was soon giving briefings on the notion of "Agile Intelligence."[10]

A key to being able to operate an agile intelligence community was to increase the directorate's focus on information technology, as the blue-ribbon panel had suggested. She believed that it had not received sufficient attention but "touch[ed] every aspect of what we do."[11] Even as resources were becoming tighter, the volume of information was continuing to expand dramatically—due to the Internet, the loosening of political constraints in the former Soviet Union and elsewhere, and increased volumes of radio, television, and other telecommunications and of scientific and technical data. In addition, demand grew for the intelligence community to provide its product with greater speed. Further, there was the growing U.S. involvement in military and humanitarian missions in areas of the world not traditionally of great concern—which meant rapidly shifting priorities.[12]

Traditionally, analysts received data only after the information had gone through one or more stages of human processing. Open source data, for example, were "once carefully selected, translated, edited, and organized by people who brought . . . a great deal of knowledge" to the task.[13] David later noted in a 1998 speech that on one occasion the CIA received a collection of 100 diskettes containing information of potential interest. Examining their content required two to three dozen analysts and technical experts.[14]

In today's world, she observed in the same speech, an analyst might need to sort through a vast volume of data, possibly data whose content was completely unknown, looking for relevant information. Even if the general content was familiar to the analyst, the volume of data could make any search tedious and time-consuming. Or the analyst might need to identify a pattern in a huge data set. Such jobs might use so much of an analyst's time that they simply could not be done. Automated processing, using keywords, was one solution.[15]

Such concerns and her belief that improved information technology capabilities held the solution led David in 1996 to establish three new offices in the directorate—the Office of Advanced Analytical Tools (OAAT), the Office of Advanced Projects (OAP), and the Clandestine Information Technology Office (CITO).[16]

The advanced analytical tools office was established as a joint effort with the Directorate of Intelligence—combining technology push with user pull. The CIA described the office as having been chartered "to investigate, develop, and deploy innovative information systems to enhance . . . capabilities to collect, process, and disseminate intelligence." Solutions would "reduce information overload, increase analyst collaboration, improve the intelligence knowledge base, and automate foreign text translation."[17] Appointed to head the office was Susan Gordon, an intelligence analyst who had specialized in foreign weapons and space systems. By the time David departed the agency in fall 1998, the office had a staff of 100 and was focusing on five areas: information extraction, data mining, data visualization, machine translation, and security.[18]

The office's work on information extraction sought to give analysts a means of picking out data they would want to enter in a database from a collection of intelligence reports. As Gordon expressed the problem, "spotting trends in the data is an area where we really need extractors." Data-mining efforts are geared to developing tools to employ keywords to build a database or bases from a number of large databases designed for uses different from those required by the analyst. Software that could prowl through a body of data and respond by isolating specific information for an analyst to review could ease the analyst's task.[19]

Developing machine translation capabilities had become more pressing, due to the multitude of languages that have become important in recent years. The CIA is short of human translators, particularly in languages such as Farsi. At the same time, there is no significant commercial market for such a translation capability in many of the required languages, which requires the analytical tools office to oversee development of such a capability.[20]

The advanced projects office was established to overcome problems in inserting technology into the intelligence process, transferring technology from the research and development stage to operational use. It was to provide a bridge between development and use by "taking things out of R&D and deploy[ing them] quickly," David recalled.[21] Doing that job required the office to look ahead to what technologies would be needed for the collection and analysis of information, identify relevant commercially developed technologies, and seek to develop required technologies when none were commercially available.[22]

The Clandestine Information Technology Office was established as a joint office with the Directorate of Operations. According to a CIA press release, the office would "address collection capabilities within emerging information technologies"—including fiber optics and the Internet.[23]

ALIENATION

Robert Phillips, who served in the directorate for over thirty years, "liked Ruth a lot," but felt that as the deputy director for science and technology she was "way in over her head" and had "no feel for the politics of the agency." There were "things going on in the CIA that none of her experiences ever prepared her for" and "things [that she did] that turned out awkward."[24]

One of those things was her creation of "new offices without [any] idea as to how to staff them" and pay for them. Phillips's views were echoed by former ORD director Philip Eckman, who noted that David's creation of the new offices was done "without any real understanding of or caring about the culture of the organization," and without taking the necessary steps to ensure funding. Ultimately, the new deputy director found a directorate component that she felt could be cut back in order to help fund the new offices—the Foreign Broadcast Information Service. Her plans apparently called for a 20 percent cut in personnel and a 38 percent cut in the nonpersonnel budget. Approximately one-third of FBIS's fourteen foreign bureaus would be closed as part of a plan to save $20 million.[25]

FBIS was older than the agency itself—the "purveyors of fine open source intelligence since 1941"—according to an FBIS briefing slide. It had been nearly exempt from cuts, because its cost was minimal and it made an enormous contribution, according to Phillips and others. David believed the FBIS mission was important but not as important as the new offices she was establishing.[26]

Naturally, many in FBIS were annoyed with their new directorate head. One of David's early actions had been to establish a Lotus Notes system that enabled personnel to send her anonymous e-mail, which she promised she would read and answer. Her unpopular decision, at least with FBIS personnel, to slash funding for the unit, led to "some very cruel messages" calling her an amateur and an interloper.[27]

David felt that if she could explain her views and how important the new offices were, the animosity could be neutralized. To get those views across, she began holding a series of town meetings. Fifty to sixty FBIS members were in attendance at one, and after her opening speech they launched a verbal assault, objecting that she had just arrived at the agency and didn't know what she was doing. David, Phillips recalled, was "almost in tears." In his view, the situation could have been alleviated if her deputy, Pete Daniher, who had been in the agency for over twenty years and had credibility with the dissidents, had spoken up in her defense. But Daniher, who was sitting with her, "never said a word."[28]

And it was not only agency insiders who objected to the planned cutbacks. Academics, who made great use of the unclassified digests of the foreign press, were not pleased.[29] Congressional oversight committees were also supporters of FBIS, noting in 1997 that "comprehensive open source collection, translation, and analytic effort is crucial to the [intelligence community's] ability to maintain global coverage," and that "careful scrutiny of 'closed society' media . . . can also reveal valuable information on trends, new developments, and leadership plans."[30]

Earlier in the year, David backed off on plans to cut the broadcast service, and a CIA spokeswoman announced that FBIS would be spared from proposed funding cuts. She also noted that FBIS would continue to monitor, translate, and publish accounts from about 3,500 foreign broadcast and press outlets in fifty-five languages and newspapers—which represented "virtually 100 percent" of current coverage.[31]

Congressional concern and interest were expressed in the House intelligence committee's report on the 1998 *Intelligence Authorization Act*, published in summer 1997. The committee noted that FBIS's "re-engineering strategy" called for "using more modern and commercially available technologies as FBIS's operational linchpin and to transition from traditional large-scale, static collection and processing centers toward a more agile and less expensive architecture." The committee applauded the effort to "adapt FBIS's infrastructure and operating practices to incorporate new technologies and to meet intelligence requirements more efficiently."[32]

The committee did express concern about resource-allocation decisions that were being made "without fully taking into consideration 'customer' requirements." In short, it was unclear to many FBIS customers what regions of the world would be "affected by significant decreases in collection, translation, and analytical activities." It was necessary, the committee believed, that "open source collection . . . be driven by the direct input of major customers, particularly the all-source analysts who best understood where their information gaps lie."[33]

THE BEST SCIENTIST

In a brief statement in April 1996, the CIA announced that ORD's John Craven, then fifty-seven, had been named the agency's best scientist. The statement said his "breakthroughs in areas of computer logic, digital signal processing and laser technology are truly remarkable." The following year he was named one of the fifty CIA trailblazers.[34]

That Craven was able to contribute even a fraction of what he has is astonishing. In 1968, he received a doctorate in solid-state physics from the University of Chicago; his dissertation topic was "The Fermi Surface and

Band Structure of White Tin as Derived from de Haas–van Alphen Data." After Chicago, he joined the CIA and was placed in a special career-development track for the agency's top prospects. The six-month program took him from Cape Cod to a U-2 base to Strategic Air Command headquarters and onto a nuclear submarine. Then in 1971, a swimming accident left him paralyzed from the neck down.[35]

Today, Craven lives in a modest apartment in a Maryland suburb of Washington, where he has an around-the-clock caregiver. Once or twice a week, he travels to the CIA for briefings. Mostly, he works at home, relying on a computer, a voice-activated phone, and a fax machine. He holds a pointer in his mouth to tap out letters, never more than fifteen a minute, on his computer keyboard. His phone has special encoding devices that allow him to conduct secure conversations with colleagues.[36]

Those circumstances did not prevent Craven from doing award-winning work on three projects, one of which is classified. One project involved the use of microwave technology to create a 100-fold increase in the speed at which computers could operate. The speed of computers is limited by the power they consume and the heat they generate while operating. Microwave technology could operate at much lower power levels, conserving energy and reducing heat.[37]

The focus of the second project was laser cross-links. One problem with using laser beams as communication devices over long distances was that they had to be perfectly aimed and were easy to interrupt, with even a slight misalignment resulting in the loss of the signal. Craven led a team of scientists who figured out a way to reduce those problems.[38]

Craven told an interviewer, "Our charter is to push the state of the art," whereas his "goal is not to nudge the state of the art but to try to make a quantum leap."[39]

NIMA

On October 1, 1996, the National Imagery and Mapping Agency (NIMA) opened its doors with a staff of 9,000—more than any intelligence agency other than CIA and NSA. That day marked the conclusion of over five years of studies and debates over the organization of the U.S. imagery intelligence effort.

In his April 1992 testimony before the House and Senate intelligence committees, then DCI Robert Gates noted that the Imagery Task Force he had established upon becoming DCI had recommended the creation of a National Imagery Agency (NIA), which would absorb the CIA's National

Photographic Interpretation Center as well as the Defense Mapping Agency (DMA).[40]

The task force's vision for an NIA was not as broad as what had been recommended by some people in congressional hearings and written into proposed legislation by both the House and Senate intelligence committees. The broader vision would have created an agency that would control the entire range of imagery intelligence—research and development of future collection systems, operation of current systems, tasking (the selection of targets), and analysis of the images collected.[41]

During his testimony, Gates rejected the recommendations of both his task force and the congressional committees, noting he had no desire to establish a new, large agency. Gates was not alone in his reluctance to merge NPIC with DMA. Joint Chiefs chairman Colin Powell did not want to relinquish authority over DMA, which was vital to providing support to military operations.[42]

Gates and Powell did agree to the creation of a small Central Imagery Office (CIO), which was established within the Department of Defense in early May. The new office was to address the problems perceived to exist within the imagery intelligence effort, particularly by many in Congress and the military. Those problems included a lack of coherent imagery management, imagery collection and dissemination difficulties, budgetary constraints, and changing requirements for the support of military operations.[43]

The CIO was officially a joint CIA-DOD enterprise, chartered by both DCI and Defense Department directives.[44] In contrast to the alternative national imagery agencies that had been proposed, the CIO was not designed to absorb existing agencies or take on their collection and analysis functions.

Rather, the mission of the CIO included tasking of national imagery systems (assuming that role in place of the DCI Committee on Imagery Requirements and Exploitation, or COMIREX) to ensure more effective imagery support to the Department of Defense, combat commanders, the CIA, and other agencies; advising the Secretary of Defense and the DCI regarding future imagery requirements; and evaluating the performance of imagery organizations. The most important role assigned to the new office was ensuring that imagery dissemination systems were "interoperable"—that an image transmitted on one system (an Army system) could be received on another system (a Navy system). During the Gulf War, there had been fourteen different imagery transmission systems in the Middle East theater, only a few of which were interoperable.[45]

Creation of the CIO delayed, but did not prevent, creation of NIMA. In April 1995, then DCI-designate John Deutch told the Senate Select Committee on Intelligence that, if confirmed, he would "move immediately to consolidate the management of all imagery collection, analysis, and distribution." He argued that "both effectiveness and economy can be improved by managing imagery in a manner similar to the National Security Agency's organization for signals intelligence."[46]

After his confirmation, Deutch established a National Imagery Agency (NIA) steering group, which in turn chartered an NIA task force. The terms of reference for the task force included among its key assumptions that "at a minimum, the NIA will be formed from the Central Imagery Office, Defense Mapping Agency, National Photographic Interpretation Center, and portions of the Defense Intelligence Agency and the Services."[47]

In late November 1995, Deutch and Secretary of Defense William Perry sent a joint letter to congressional leaders and relevant committees on their plan to establish NIMA as a combat support agency within the Department of Defense on October 1, 1996—thus ensuring that the Secretary and JCS chairman would not lose control of the mapping function. Their letter noted that the proposed agency would be formed by consolidating the DMA, CIO, NPIC, the imagery exploitation element of the Defense Intelligence Agency, and portions of the Defense Airborne Reconnaissance Office and NRO that were involved in imagery exploitation and dissemination.[48] The planned agency would thus leave the acquisition and operation of space systems and their ground stations to the NRO, and would also leave untouched the imagery exploitation activities of the service intelligence organizations and unified combat commands.

According to the letter, the task force recommended the consolidation for three basic reasons. It argued that a "single, streamlined and focused agency" could best serve the imagery and mapping needs of the growing and diverse customers throughout the government. The task force also contended that the dispersion of imagery and mapping responsibilities that then existed did not "allow one agency to exploit the tremendous potential of enhanced collection systems, digital processing technology and the prospective expansion in commercial imagery." Finally, the panel felt that developments in information technology made it possible to conduct imagery intelligence and mapping as joint enterprises, which could be best realized through more centralized management.[49]

The wisdom of the plan was questioned by both former intelligence (particularly CIA) officials and many within Congress. Former deputy

DCI John McMahon was "dead set against it" and argued with Deutch, telling him he was taking DCI prerogatives and placing them where they didn't belong—in the Defense Department. Such a move would represent an "erosion of DCI independent responsibility for national intelligence." Of course, McMahon and others believed Deutch wanted to ensure that NPIC would be reporting to him when he moved on (he hoped) to become Secretary of Defense.[50]

When Deutch asked Jim Hirsch for his view, the deputy director for science and technology told him it would be a good idea to consolidate development and operation of imagery satellites with interpretation, as suggested in 1992. He was concerned, however, that the quality of each of the three pillars of imagery interpretation—mapping and geodesy, military support, and intelligence analysis—not be compromised as a result of a merger, and that each be preserved as a distinct function. Mapping and geodesy is geared to the measurement and depiction of terrain as well as the atmosphere. Military support functions largely involve describing what is in a picture and counting, for targeting, order-of-battle or battle-damage assessment purposes. The questions are how many objects (aircraft, missiles, tanks) there are, where they are, and how many have been destroyed. Intelligence analysis is a multidisciplinary approach in which the analysts use other data, along with the imagery, to determine the function of a facility, to describe a nation's nuclear weapons program, or to estimate the likelihood that a country will attack its neighbor or conduct a nuclear test.[51]

Although Hirsch saw some potential gains in the creation of a unified agency—including being able to achieve the military's coveted goal of information superiority and "dominant battlefield awareness"—he was also concerned that the intelligence analysis function might be shortchanged in a unified military agency. He believed that rather than such a unified agency, a unified program with three elements, NPIC being one, would be a reasonable alternative.[52]

When the Defense Department insisted that the military services retain their imagery interpretation capabilities, Hirsch unsuccessfully suggested that the CIA should maintain the intelligence directorate's Office of Imagery Analysis (OIA), which supported the intelligence and operations directorates—albeit with equipment and analysts on loan from NPIC.[53]

Evan Hineman, who had been asked by Deutch to chair a task force on national imagery, believed the proposal had merit, but he also had reservations. He hoped that NPIC's relation to the new agency would be similar to OD&E's relationship to NRO—still officially part of the CIA, even though it reported to another boss. He also recommended that the head of the new agency be someone from the CIA, selected by the DCI with the Secretary of Defense's concurrence.[54]

At the analyst level, there were also concerns. Patrick Eddington joined the CIA in 1987 after graduating from Southwest Missouri State. After attending the agency's National Imagery Analysis Course, he reported to NPIC in February 1988. Over the next seven years, he served in both the Priority Exploitation Group at Ft. Belvoir and the Imagery Exploitation Group at the Washington Navy Yard, as well as with the intelligence directorate's Office of Scientific and Weapons Research. Over those years, his interpretation efforts had been focused on imagery of the Soviet Union and Iraq.[55]

He later wrote that NIMA was "derisively referred to as 'the Enema' by NPIC analysts" and "was seen as little more than a power grab by the Pentagon, orchestrated by Deutch to gain a monopoly over the national imagery system." "No self-respecting imagery analyst," Eddington wrote, "wanted to become a 'human photomat' producing a mountain of meaningless briefing boards for the Joint Chiefs of Staff or any other Pentagon 'customer.'"[56]

Objections also came from the vice-chairman of the Senate Select Committee on Intelligence, Robert Kerrey (D.–Nebr.), and the House Permanent Select Committee on Intelligence. The primary concern was that as a result of the transfer of NPIC personnel from the CIA to DOD, imagery support to national policymakers would suffer in order to support the requirements of military commanders. Although the opposition was unable to block the creation of the new agency, the Senate Select Committee on Intelligence did persuade the Senate Armed Services Committee to amend the legislation creating NIMA. Thus, the final legislation stipulated that the DCI retained tasking authority over national imagery systems, and that the Secretary of Defense must obtain the DCI's concurrence before appointing the NIMA director or note the DCI's lack of concurrence before recommending a candidate to the president. In addition, the Armed Services committee agreed to modification of the National Security Act to explicitly state NIMA's responsibility to provide intelligence for national policymakers.[57]

When NIMA came into being on October 1, 1996, it incorporated all the elements mentioned in the late November statement as well as the Air Force's Defense Dissemination Program Office, which disseminated satellite imagery, and the CIA's Office of Imagery Analysis—effectively removing from the CIA any responsibility for imagery interpretation. Heading the agency was Rear Admiral Joseph Dantone, with former NPIC director Leo Hazelwood as deputy director.[58]

LEGACY

At approximately 10 a.m. on December 20, 1996, a Titan 4 rocket, with about 3 million pounds of thrust, blasted off from its launchpad at Vandenberg AFB in California. To some extent, there was no mystery as to what was sitting atop the rocket as it headed for outer space. NRO spokeswoman Katherine Schneider acknowledged that the payload was a reconnaissance satellite, the first time NRO acknowledged such activity within two decades of its taking place. Other details, such as orbit and mission, remained classified.[59]

However, it was soon clear to observers that the payload was the third and final piece of the advanced KH-11 constellation, satellites whose numerical designations were 2104, 2105, and 2106. It was operating in an orbit of 155-by-620 miles and at an inclination of 98 degrees. Its two predecessors had been launched on November 28, 1992, and December 5, 1995, also using Titan 4 boosters, and were operating in similar orbits.[60]

Although in late 1997 they were "owned" by the NRO, they were the legacy of the Office of Development and Engineering and the work of Robert Kohler, Julian Caballero, Ed Nowinski, and Jeffrey Harris. Each satellite, often referred to as an Improved CRYSTAL, was enhanced in four ways: It had greater resolution than the KH-11 models (better than six inches); it was better able to perform area surveillance missions; it carried an infrared imagery capability, code-named DRAGON, which allowed it to image targets at night; and it carried the Improved CRYSTAL Metric System that allowed "fiduciary marks" to be incorporated in imagery—marks that enhanced the ability to use the imagery for precision mapping.[61]

By the time the third advanced KH-11 was launched, its two predecessors had provided the intelligence community and its customers with high-resolution imagery of an array of global targets—a massacre site in Bosnia, Chinese military deployments, Indian preparations for a nuclear test in 1995, Iraqi military facilities, a Libyan chemical weapons plant, and North Korean missile test preparations.[62]

DEMISE

In the mid-1990s, the vision statement of the Office of Research and Development promised that "when the future arrives ORD will have been there." Few people expected in 1995 that the office had a very limited future. But in addition to creating three new offices in 1996, in 1998 Ruth David abolished ORD—the only surviving original office.

Part of ORD's mission had been to "fail"—to separate ideas that would work from those that wouldn't before millions of dollars were wasted. But it had a number of outright successes and made contributions to the technical collection, clandestine collection, and analytical activities of the CIA and intelligence community—as well as to other parts of the government and private sector.

In 1984 and 1985, ORD sponsored the development of a "problem structuring aid" that was to be a tool to help researchers organize their ideas. The project evolved into a research program producing dozens of technical publications, and it produced one of the first hypertext systems. Although this hypertext system never became a product, its features were incorporated into software available to millions of owners of personal computers.[63]

In approximately 1985, the CIA decided to invest in the development of new tools and techniques to support the analysis of data. ORD identified information retrieval as a research topic of importance to the intelligence community that was receiving relatively little government funding. The office sponsored a project that, according to the agency, was so successful in achieving more accurate information retrieval that it was copied and incorporated into several commercial systems for automatic screening and sorting of news wires.[64]

Beginning in 1987, ORD led in the development of image perspective transformation modeling and visualization tools. The system took overhead imagery and, through use of image modeling and rendering tools, warped the images to appear as if the perspective were on the ground. This system proved extremely useful in the civil engineering and urban planning fields to create "what if" scenarios. The operator could artificially insert and visualize new buildings or facilities on empty lots, or place new roads or interstates into a scene to see the impact on local communities.[65] It is also used to familiarize intelligence officers with an area where they will be operating, or arms control inspectors to become familiar with a facility to be inspected.

A joint project conducted by ORD and a component of NSA's research and development directorate developed natural language processing (NLP)—which permitted computer processing of cables arriving at the CIA's Counter-Terrorism Center to weed out irrelevant ones. Cables that took people one to three hours to sort through took a computer a mere ninety seconds. NLP could be used to locate documents containing the type of information the user desired or locate specified information from within a text. It could also be used to automate the construction of databases. By June 1995, it was being used by the Drug Enforcement Administration (DEA).[66]

Facial recognition, another ORD-developed technology, found use outside of the intelligence community by 1995. The facial-recognition program could be used to identify an unknown person against a set of known people. The technology was created to address a problem common to many agencies—databases with large collections of images, sometimes numbering in the millions, and collateral information. ORD wanted to be able to automate the process of identifying individuals using photographs and other existing databases. By mid-1995, users included the Immigration and Naturalization Service, the FBI, the Customs Service, and the DEA. In mid-1995, the INS arrested the first criminal to be identified by facial recognition, a convicted rapist who crossed from Mexico into Texas. The facial-recognition system enabled the INS to obtain positive identification of the individual within thirty minutes.[67]

More important, according to Gene Poteat, was ORD's role in achieving major breakthroughs vital to carrying out the overhead reconnaissance mission. The breakthroughs, which he would not specify in detail, included advances in optics, imagery interpretation, and a unique fusion of collection and analysis. ORD's contributions in that area had often been the work of the office's Applied Physics Division, which was funded through the Reconnaissance Technology budget of the NRO. ORD's accomplishments led Julian Caballero, sometime after he became OD&E head in 1985, to permit ORD to compete with OD&E for funds for proposed reconnaissance technology projects on an equal footing.[68]

David explained that her decision to abolish ORD and establish a small Technology Investment Office (subsequently known as the Investment Program Office, IPO) in its place was based on her belief that because the directorate subcontracted a vast amount of its research and development work (as it had from its inception), with little being done in-house, it did not make sense to maintain a centralized R&D organization. As a result, she decided to distribute ORD's personnel among the offices it supported, while protecting the long-term budget by creating the IPO. The investment office was to ensure that research and development funds were spent on long-term research projects and not shifted by individual offices to cover areas of immediate concern. It was, she acknowledged, a "controversial decision." There were "people who hated it," as well as people thought it a great idea, according to David. Not surprisingly, ORD members hated it, believing it devalued their contribution.[69]

John McMahon noted that the abolition was a "sign of the times" and a reflection that commercial technology was often far ahead of the government's—a dramatic change from 1962. Yet he believed ORD's abolition would "narrow the agency's knowledge into a lot of new technology," and that the agency would still need an organization like ORD. According to Gene Poteat, David did a "great disservice by wiping out the only organization of R&D people who knew the intelligence business."[70]

Both of David's immediate predecessors also questioned her decision to abolish ORD. Evan Hineman called it a "great mistake," but one that would not be noticed for some time. He noted that there was some discussion in the late 1970s and early 1980s about doing away with the office, but the argument that the other offices conduct R&D activities was a false argument. He expressed concern that "today's" activities would take budgetary precedence—which David hoped to prevent through the IPO—and noted that during his tenure, 2.5 percent of the agency's budget was devoted to R&D, but rather than the figure reaching 5 percent as he envisioned, the practice of reserving a specific percentage of the budget for ORD fell victim to budgetary pressure and was ultimately done away with.[71]

James Hirsch also believed the decision was a mistake. He argued that technical experts needed to talk with other technical experts and maintain a certain distance from their customers (the individual offices). He also noted that ORD would usually spend twice its allotted budget, because it received funds from other agencies to manage projects.[72]

The abolition of ORD had a ripple effect, leading to the disestablishment of the Office of Advanced Projects shortly before David left office. According to David, the advanced projects office was no longer needed as a bridge between ORD and its consumers.[73]

11

UNCERTAIN FUTURE

In late June 1998, a CIA press release announced that Ruth David's tenure as Deputy Director for Science and Technology would end that September. She would be departing to become the President and Chief Executive Officer of ANSER, a nonprofit research institute established in 1958 to conduct studies for the Air Force; it subsequently added the Defense Department and other federal agencies to its list of clients.[1]

The press release contained praise from David's boss, DCI George Tenet, who expressed his gratitude for "the wise counsel she has given our intelligence collectors and analysts." He explained that "Dr. David came to the Agency at a time when we needed a leader who could guide the DS&T through major geopolitical transformations that are profoundly affecting how we conduct our mission." The DCI credited her with developing and delivering "the capabilities our collectors and analysts need to do their critical work in this new and fast-changing environment."[2]

Tenet may have been pleased with David's accomplishments, but many in the directorate were not. The controversy over FBIS, the loss of NPIC, and the closure of ORD could not but help hurt morale in at least some segments of the directorate. Many veterans undoubtedly would echo the question of one retired directorate official, who wondered, "How can you have any morale if you keep giving everything away?"[3]

Of course, David came into office with a restructured NRO a fait accompli, and she did not give away NPIC—John Deutch did. In addition, her outsider status, and possibly her gender, made it even more difficult for her to lead the directorate. Perhaps a longtime, well-respected directorate veteran might have made what has been not only a transformation but a decline in its status easier for the rank and file to accept.

It can also be argued that increased attention to information technology, as recommended by one of Jim Hirsch's blue-ribbon panels, should be pursued aggressively in order to cope with the information revolution that has resulted in the availability of an overwhelming volume of data. If the increased emphasis on information technology provides innovative solutions to that problem, it could prove to be at least one significant accomplishment on David's part.

At the same time, there may be merit to the complaints that she did not appreciate the CIA's culture or the DS&T's history. David's decisions with regard to FBIS and ORD clearly rubbed salt in existing wounds. In the view of one former ORD director, she failed to appreciate that there was more to the directorate than "getting into people's computers"—that the directorate involved dozens of specialties.[4]

A SHORT STAY

However much Tenet may have valued David's leadership, the DCI apparently did not consider finding a replacement to be a matter of great urgency. The directorate was left in the hands of an acting deputy director—Joanne Isham, who had served as David's deputy since February 1996, initially focusing on resource management issues. Isham, with a B.A. in government and international studies from Notre Dame, had begun her career at the CIA in 1977. Her assignments included several in the Office of Development and Engineering—as chief of security for the Collection Systems Group, as a reconnaissance program manager, and with the Data Communications Group. She also served as the first head of NRO's public affairs office as well as head of its legislative affairs office. In 1993 and 1994, she was deputy director of resource management for the Community Management Staff. Prior to rejoining the S&T directorate, she served as the CIA's Director of Congressional Affairs.[5]

That Tenet did not consider the DS&T as critical a component as it once was possibly explains why the strategic plan that he introduced in spring 1998 focused on the operations and intelligence directorates. At one point, as the days and weeks and then months dragged on without David's replacement being chosen, Evan Hineman suggested to Tenet that he should either find a new head for the directorate or abolish it.[6]

Tenet chose the first alternative. In late March 1999, the CIA announced that Dr. Gary L. Smith, the recently retired director of the Johns Hopkins University Applied Physics Laboratory (APL), would join the agency later that spring as the new deputy director for science and technology. Smith, who received bachelor's, master's, and doctorate degrees from the University of California at Davis, joined APL in 1970, where he initially was involved in theoretical and experimental research on detecting submerged submarines.[7]

Smith was coming from a position that seemed to provide perfect training for leadership of the science and technology directorate. APL has a staff of about 2,700, over 60 percent of whom are engineers and scientists. The laboratory describes itself as "a technical resource to the Department of Defense . . . for innovative research and development." It designed, for example, the Midcourse Space Experiment (MSX) satellite, which was orbited in April 1996. The MSX carried three sensors whose primary mission was to collect data on ballistic missile signatures.[8]

But Smith's particular background and the CIA press release concerning his appointment suggested that developing collection systems would not be Smith's primary focus. The release noted that in his tenure at APL, Smith had forged "strong ties with the national security community, including operating forces of the military, with senior decisionmakers in a broad range of government agencies, and with Congress." Even more to the point was the praise for Smith's building of "new relationships with commercial and industrial research sponsors" and his role in "commercializing [the lab's] technology breakthroughs."[9]

In the release, Tenet expressed his confidence that Smith would "lead the Directorate of Science and Technology into the next century with equal foresight, boldness and agility" as he displayed at APL. Tenet added that he had no doubt that under Smith's leadership, the directorate "will carry on its proud tradition of putting technology to work enhancing the effectiveness of clandestine collection and all-source analysis."[10]

But Smith would not be leading the directorate into the next century with boldness or any other quality. On January 12, 2000, DCI George Tenet announced that Smith, after only nine months in office, had turned in his resignation. The DCI explained that Smith would "like to continue his interrupted retirement." Tenet told CIA employees that "Gary has facilitated an effective transition . . . I know you all join me in thanking Gary for his contributions." [11]

Smith's sudden departure raised eyebrows both within and outside the CIA, as some wondered if there was something more to the abrupt resignation than a desire to return to retirement—Smith left without either cleaning out his office or submitting a letter of resignation. The story that circulated among a number of present and former CIA personnel is that Smith was never welcomed into the agency's inner circle, and was abruptly fired by DCI George Tenet for pushing him in directions he did not want to go.[12]*

PROMOTION

This time there was no delay in finding a new deputy director. Along with his announcement of Smith's departure, Tenet informed the CIA's employees that Joanne Isham would replace Smith—as deputy director, not acting deputy director. Of Isham, he said, "I have no doubt that under Joanne's leadership, the DS&T will carry on its great tradition of putting technology to work to enhance the effectiveness of clandestine collection and all-source analysis—the key components of our Strategic Direction efforts here at CIA."[13] Significantly, he made no reference to directorate efforts with regard to the development of collection systems or the collection of intelligence—which in the past were the key components of the directorate's activities.

In explaining Isham's selection, a CIA spokesman noted that Tenet was comfortable with her, that she was well-respected, and that she had been "outstanding" as David's deputy. In addition she had both CIA and community experience.[14] Mark Lowenthal, former State Department intelligence official and House intelligence committee staff director, praised the appointment, observing that "she understands collection . . . what the systems are designed to do, and . . . the use to which the intelligence is being put." However, Gordon Oehler, former head of the CIA's Non-Proliferation Center, characterized Tenet as not understanding the importance of science and technology and his appointment of Isham, a nonscientist, as sending the message that he was "no longer interested in S&T." Today, the directorate, Oehler laments, is a "mere shadow of itself."[15]

With Isham moving up to the top job, James Runyan, the director of the Office of Technical Collection, became her associate deputy director. Runyan joined the CIA in January 1997 as deputy director of OTC and became its director in September 1997. Before joining the agency, he had spent thirty years with the National Security Agency, during which time he "developed and deployed collection systems, and managed NSA efforts concerned with field, remote, and special collection responsibilities."[16]

The bureaucratic loser was Dennis Fitzgerald, who served simultaneously as the head of OD&E and the NRO's SIGINT directorate, and whose

*Smith declined to be interviewed for this book.

career had involved the development and operation of collection systems. Fitzgerald had been passed over for the top DS&T job twice in a short period of time—first, in favor of Smith, and then in favor of Isham.[17]

REPRIEVE AND RENEWAL

By the end of September 2000 when one former senior DS&T official spoke to some current employees of the directorate, they expressed the fear that abolition of the directorate might be no more than two weeks away.

It is not clear that abolition was ever a serious possibility. In any case, two weeks later, a letter from Isham to former senior S&T leaders noted that she and her deputy had been assessing the state of the DS&T and that "it has become clear to us that some changes are necessary if we are to operate successfully in tomorrow's dynamic environment."[18]

Those changes focus on achieving "five essential goals" and are to be implemented through some significant organizational changes. The goals include establishing "a single point of entry" into the directorate for new requirements and a central hub for monitoring DS&T responsiveness, combining complementary activities (so as to increase communication and collaboration across organizational lines), integrating information technology activities, revitalizing research and development, and "develop[ing] the work force of the future."[19]

Achieving those goals are the responsibility of several new positions and offices. The Program Analysis and Systems Engineering Staff will receive new requirements and monitor the DS&T's performance. Meanwhile, the Office of Advanced Analytical Tools (AAT) has been supplanted by the Office of Advanced Information Technology (AIT). Unlike the analytical tools office, AIT will not be a joint enterprise with the Directorate of Intelligence. AIT is a combination of AAT, the DS&T Information Services Center, and In-Q-Tel.[20]

In February 2001, Larry Fairchild, the director of AIT, noted that the CIA was not growing at a fast rate, but "the amount of information that comes into this place is growing by leaps and bounds." Among the information tools AIT had under development, Fairchild disclosed, was a computer tool designated "Oasis," which converted audio signals from television and radio broadcasts into text. Oasis can differentiate accented English to produce more accurate transcripts and distinguish between male and female speakers and among different individuals.[21]

Another AIT computer tool is FLUENT, which allows a user to conduct computer searches of documents in a number of foreign languages—including Chinese, Korean, Portuguese, Russian, Serbo-Croatian, and Ukrainian. An analyst can enter English words into the search field and receive relevant foreign-language documents in response. The system then translates the document into English and gives the analyst the option of sending it on to a human translator for more precision.[22]

In-Q-Tel is a nonprofit venture-capital firm that the CIA created in late 1999 and gave $28.5 million in agency funds. It is a legacy of Ruth David, who has recalled that the agency was accustomed to working with large defense contractors but not with the newer, smaller firms involved in information technology innovation. In 2000, In-Q-Tel heard from about 500 vendors who proposed projects that they believed would benefit the agency. Twelve development projects were actually funded.[23]

One In-Q-Tel–assisted project involved a commercial search engine named NetOwl, developed by SRA International in Fairfax, Virginia. NetOwl uses natural-language processing in place of keywords to locate information, and can deduce that a word is a name, an organization, or a place. In-Q-Tel funding has permitted SRA to increase the power of NetOwl—allowing it to identify events and relationships and create structured data from unstructured text. According to SRA's vice-president, Hatte Blejer, it could search the Internet to provide an answer to a question such as "Which high-tech companies were established in northern Virginia last year?"[24]

In-Q-Tel funding was also instrumental in allowing companies to develop the Presidential Intelligence Briefing System (PIDS), which is used to produce the President's Daily Brief (PDB) that only sixteen senior government officials are permitted to read. Previously, CIA analysts had to shuffle hundreds of intelligence cables every day to produce the PDB. The PIDS brings the cables into a Lotus Notes database, performs a variety of search and analysis functions, and then places the brief on a notebook computer. According to Lou Clark, a program manager at In-Q-Tel, PIDS delivers briefs that are more timely because information can easily be added up to the last minute.[25]

A third In-Q-Tel investment may make it easier for the CIA to cover its tracks when collecting information off the Internet. The investment is intended to enhance a piece of software called Triangle Boy, which is produced by SafeWeb of Oakland, California. The commercial version of Triangle Boy allows users who want to examine a website without being detected to go to SafeWeb's website, which acts an intermediary. Anyone monitoring the user's activity would see the traffic between the user and SafeWeb, but not between SafeWeb and the user's ultimate destination. What interested the CIA was the ability of Triangle Boy to permit users to go to any number of innocuous addresses before going on to the actual site of interest. "We want to operate anywhere on the Internet in a way that no one knows the CIA is looking at them," according to a senior CIA official.[26]

SafeWeb also has suggested that the CIA could use the same technology to allow its officers and assets in the field to communicate securely with Langley. Such an application may be part of the CIA's plan, as described by George Tenet, "to take modern Web-based technology and apply it to our business relentlessly."[27]

As another part of the reorganization, most of the responsibilities of the Clandestine Information Technology Office, the joint DS&T-operations directorate office, have been reassigned to the newly created Directorate of Operations Information Operations Center—a center that at one point was going to be assigned to the DS&T. The technical operations element of the CITO was transferred to the DS&T Office of Technical Collection.[28]

The plan to revitalize R&D has resulted in two organizational changes. A chief scientist "will encourage collaboration among the top scientists, engineers, and technologists from across the Intelligence Community, private industry, and academia."[29]

In addition, the Office of Research and Development has been resurrected under a new name—the Office of Advanced Technologies and Programs (ATP). ATP is responsible for overseeing the transfer of new technologies from the drawing board and putting them into operational use. It is to "focus R&D on the CIA's most difficult problems and core mission."[30]

GLORY DAYS

Over the almost forty years of its existence the Directorate of Science and Technology has made an enormous contribution to U.S. intelligence capabilities and national security.

Its development of collection systems, as well as its assorted collection and analysis activities, proved vital to the assessment of Soviet strategic capabilities and intentions during the Cold War. With key assistance from its contractors, the directorate developed and deployed the HEXAGON (KH-9), RHYOLITE, and KENNAN (KH-11) systems and their successors. Each of those systems represented a quantum leap in U.S. intelligence capabilities.

The directorate also guided the development of the A-12/OXCART program. Although that program had a short life, without it there would have been no Air Force SR-71 aircraft, which operated for over two decades and provided valuable intelligence to U.S. national security officials. The agency's efforts in the collection of telemetry intelligence, both from space and ground platforms, were vital to understanding Soviet missile capabilities during some of the darkest days of the Cold War.

Certainly there were missteps—attempting to turn cats into microphones and recruiting psychics are two notable examples. Undoubtedly there were others. But such cases are insignificant compared with the overall accomplishments of the directorate.

The winding down of the Cold War and the emergence of a new world environment have not eliminated the value of the DS&T's contributions. Although the successors to RHYOLITE and the KH-11 are today formally assets of the NRO, they are unmistakably products of the Directorate of Science and Technology. Included are the three advanced KH-11 satellites in orbit, each with greater resolution, area coverage capability, and nighttime capability than those of the first generation. The upgraded version of the MAGNUM/ORION SIGINT satellite, which Bob Kohler fought so hard for and which was temporarily canceled, eventually made it back into the budget and was first launched into its geosynchronous orbit in 1995. Those SIGINT satellites also possess some of the relay capabilities intended to be part of the KODIAK system.

In addition, a number of scientific advances that emerged from the directorate, including its research and development office, not only have augmented U.S. intelligence capabilities but also have aided the work of those outside the national security establishment, including the medical community. Lithium batteries for pacemakers and automatic change recognition applied to the detection of breast cancer are two prominent examples.

It is important to note, both for the sake of history and in charting the directorate's future, that such successes were not simply the result of the directorate carrying out its assigned duties, with the full support of the rest of the agency and intelligence community. Nor were they the result of a cautious, incremental approach.

One element of success was the outside pressure by far-sighted scientists such as James Killian and Edwin Land to develop the agency's scientific capabilities. They were the prime movers in establishing first the Directorate of Research and then the Directorate of Science and Technology.

Another element was the willingness of managers to fight for roles and programs that they believed vital to national security, or to oppose programs they considered useless—even if that meant bureaucratic bloodshed. Had Bud Wheelon not passionately battled Brockway McMillan and the NRO, there would have been no HEXAGON or RHYOLITE. Carl Duckett's lobbying to oppose the Secretary of Defense's choice of FROG was one factor in ensuring that the first KH-11 was launched in 1976 and not 1986.

The DS&T's achievements also required a collection of individuals with advanced technical skills and a sense of adventure—some willing to search for new technical solutions to problems and possibly fail, others willing to man primitive outposts in the Iranian mountains in order to uncover Soviet missile secrets. Leslie Dirks and Lloyd Lauderdale helped bring into being programs that Wheelon and Duckett conceived and fought for.

Another element of success was having an organization that sought to fill important gaps in U.S. collection and analysis capabilities. The DS&T did not try to duplicate what the National Security Agency was doing with regard to COMINT collection, but it did come up with novel ways to provide information that NSA or its military subsidiaries were not collecting—either because of their priorities or their technical approaches to collection problems. As a result, it was the CIA that developed the first telemetry intercept satellite and that deployed personnel to Iran to monitor telemetry from the TACKSMAN sites. Much of the CIA's success resulted from identifying important gaps or shortcomings in other organizations' programs and seeking to fill them.

The directorate's connection to intelligence production—strongest when the agency's nuclear and missile intelligence analysts were part of the directorate, but still strong after their transfer to the intelligence directorate—also helped produce success. The link between satellite developers and analysts that existed at CIA but not at the Air Force Office of Special Projects helped guide the developers' work and motivate them to develop new capabilities that would solve old intelligence problems.

Of course, one factor underlying much of these gains was the presence of a major and very apparent enemy. Despite all the problems that the Soviet political and economic systems imposed on the nation, the USSR was still a formidable military threat—capable of deploying thousands of ICBM warheads and a massive army that could have, at the very least, destroyed Western Europe and the United States as modern civilizations. That threat helped attract many of the best and brightest to service in the CIA.

In addition, during much of the Cold War, CIA science and technology operated at the cutting edge, substantially in advance of what was being done in either the private sector or other parts of the government. For many who liked tough challenges, the CIA was an exciting place to be.

ROAD TO RECOVERY?

How the DS&T will meet the challenges of the future is a chapter of its history yet to be written. It will never be the bureaucratic empire that it was in 1972. Nor should it be. Clearly it is a vastly different world from 1972. The demise of the Soviet Union, the concern about transnational threats including terrorism and the proliferation of weapons of mass destruction to rogue states (with their sophisticated secret police and denial and deception programs), the shift of the development of cutting-edge technologies to the private sector, the deployment of high-resolution commercial imagery satellites, and the shift in the volume and means of international communication mean that priorities and targets have shifted. The volume of information has also increased dramatically, making it harder to find useful information among the flood of data. New collection and processing capabilities have been developed, but much work still needs to be done to enhance collection, processing, and analytical capabilities.

It is clear that the directorate should continue to devote significant attention to how to employ information technology to ease the burden on intelligence analysts. In an April 1999 speech to a technology conference in Raleigh-Durham, North Carolina, Basil Scott, a senior DS&T official, addressed both subjects. He enumerated a number of factors that made it harder to monitor foreign communications—including the spread of fiber-optic systems, the explosion of cellular phones, and encryption. At the same time, he suggested how information technology could be used to help analysts identify biological and chemical weapon activities, although information indicating such activities may be buried in a mass of data. Scott discussed an assortment of data-mining and data-retrieval techniques that could be employed, including clustering techniques that enable analysts to mine the most useful data sets first, link analysis to establish relationships, time-series analysis to identify time trends, and visualization—which lets analysts see "non-traditional presentations of data" that "can help [them] deal with large and complex data sets."[31]

Exploiting information technology will undoubtedly be a key activity for the directorate, but that should not be its only reason for being. Indeed, if the only significant directorate activities were to be information technology and support to clandestine human intelligence operations, there would be little reason for it to exist as a separate directorate—for the offices involved could be placed comfortably in the intelligence and operations directorates.

But outside those activities there remain many potential challenges. Although analysts have a flood of information to deal with, there can also be a paucity of information concerning topics of crucial importance—including foreign weapons of mass destruction programs and terrorism.

As long as the Office of Technical Collection and the Office of Development and Engineering remain part of the directorate, it retains the potential to make a significant contribution to the technical collection of intelligence. With nations adopting increasingly sophisticated denial and deception strategies to foil collection of information by U.S. imagery and signals intelligence satellites, OTC development of emplaced sensor systems to detect nuclear, chemical, and biological weapons activity and OTC participation in the Special Collection Service may prove to be among the directorate's most productive activities.

As previously noted, the Office of Development and Engineering, particularly as a result of the NRO restructuring, serves as a funnel for CIA personnel into the NRO rather than as a separate program element of the reconnaissance office. But the OD&E can ensure that some of the advantages that resulted from the directorate's dual identity as the NRO's Program B not be lost. The office recruited people from the Directorate of Intelligence, particularly the Office of Scientific and Weapons Research; this influx of personnel helped ensure that those developing reconnaissance satellites did not lose touch with the requirements of the analysts. In 1999, former OD&E director Robert Kohler said that the office felt like an "outcast," with the connection to the rest of the agency being a tenuous one. If the CIA were to back away from the OD&E and the NRO, it would be a "huge loss" to the reconnaissance effort, according to Kohler.[32] Likewise, Gordon Oehler, former director of the Non-Proliferation

Center, has complained that "the centralization of the . . . NRO . . . , where the only major pot of development money remains, removed many of the CIA's best technologists from day-to-day contact with operators and analysts in the rest of the CIA."[33] To reverse or limit such disengagement will require leadership from the top of the directorate.

Another factor in determining the extent to which the directorate prospers in the next decade is whether it continues to identify areas where the activities of other CIA and intelligence community components are deficient and moves to fill those gaps. As already noted, the directorate did not rise to empire status by attempting to duplicate what other agencies or CIA components did well.

Of course, people are another vital element in any future directorate successes. Over the almost forty years since it was created, the directorate has employed exceptional managers and scientists—as demonstrated by the directorate personnel named as CIA trailblazers in 1997, including the first four chiefs of the DS&T (Wheelon, Duckett, Dirks, and Hineman) as well as analysts, scientists, and technical service personnel. Recruiting and retaining such people today—when the technological frontier is often found in Silicon Valley and when corporate salaries far exceed government compensation—are far more difficult tasks than in the past.

It will be up to the leadership of the agency and directorate to ensure that the DS&T's mission involves more than helping analysts sort through data, as well as to make talented individuals realize that there are challenges to be met in the directorate that cannot be matched elsewhere. Robert Kohler does see some hope for the directorate. In early 2001, he noted that Joanne Isham was "trying very hard" and boosting morale, and George Tenet seemed to be listening to her. Kohler was "moderately encouraged."[34] It is hoped that in the succeeding years, the reasons to be encouraged will increase, and the next set of wizards will be up to the challenges that will face them.

APPENDIX 1

DS&T Components, 1963–2001

(Items in bold type indicate offices established the previous year)

Date	Components
January 1, 1963	**Office of Special Activities** **Office of Research and Development** **Office of ELINT**
January 1, 1964	Office of Special Activities Office of Research and Development Office of ELINT **Office of Computer Services** **Office of Scientific Intelligence** **Foreign Missile and Space Analysis Center**
January 1, 1966	Office of Special Activities Office of Research and Development Office of ELINT Office of Computer Services Office of Scientific Intelligence **Office of Special Projects** Foreign Missile and Space Analysis Center
January 1, 1974	Office of Special Activities Office of Research and Development Office of ELINT Office of Scientific Intelligence **Office of Development and Engineering** **Office of Technical Service** **Office of Weapons Intelligence** **National Photographic Interpretation Center**
January 1, 1975	Office of Research and Development Office of ELINT Office of Scientific Intelligence Office of Development and Engineering Office of Technical Service Office of Weapons Intelligence National Photographic Interpretation Center
January 1, 1977	Office of Research and Development Office of ELINT Office of Development and Engineering Office of Technical Service **Foreign Broadcast Information Service** National Photographic Interpretation Center

January 1, 1978	Office of Research and Development **Office of SIGINT Operations** Office of Development and Engineering Office of Technical Service Foreign Broadcast Information Service National Photographic Interpretation Center
January 1, 1989	Office of Research and Development Office of SIGINT Operations Office of Development and Engineering Office of Technical Service **Office of Special Projects** Foreign Broadcast Information Service National Photographic Interpretation Center
January 1, 1994	Office of Research and Development **Office of Technical Collection** Office of Development and Engineering Office of Technical Service Foreign Broadcast Information Service National Photographic Interpretation Center
January 1, 1996	Office of Research and Development Office of Technical Collection Office of Development and Engineering Office of Technical Service **Office of Advanced Projects** **Office of Advanced Analytical Tools** **Clandestine Information Technology Office** Foreign Broadcast Information Service National Photographic Interpretation Center
January 1, 1997	Office of Research and Development Office of Technical Collection Office of Development and Engineering Office of Technical Service Office of Advanced Projects Office of Advanced Analytical Tools Clandestine Information Technology Office Foreign Broadcast Information Service
January 1, 1999	Office of Technical Collection Office of Development and Engineering Office of Technical Service Office of Advanced Analytical Tools Clandestine Information Technology Office Foreign Broadcast Information Service **Investment Program Office**
February 1, 2001	Office of Technical Collection Office of Development and Engineering Office of Technical Service Foreign Broadcast Information Service **Office of Advanced Information Technology** **Office of Advanced Technologies and Programs**

APPENDIX 2
DS&T Leadership

Deputy Director for Research

Herbert J. Scoville	April 15, 1962–June 17, 1963

Deputy Director for Science and Technology

Albert D. (Bud) Wheelon	August 5, 1963–September 26, 1966
Carl E. Duckett (Acting)	September 26, 1966–April 20, 1967
Carl E. Duckett	April 20, 1967–June 1, 1976
Leslie C. Dirks	June 1, 1976–July 3, 1982
Richard Evans Hineman	July 3, 1982–September 5, 1989
James V. Hirsch	September 5, 1989–September 5, 1995
Ruth David	September 15, 1995–September 4, 1998
Joanne O. Isham (Acting)	September 5, 1998–April 1, 1999
Gary L. Smith	April 1, 1999–January 10, 2000
Joanne O. Isham	Jan 10, 2000–

Assistant Deputy Director for Research

Col. Edward B. Giller	June 25, 1962–August 5, 1963

Assistant/Associate Deputy Director for Science and Technology

(Title change from Assistant Deputy Director to Associate Deputy Director was effective May 8, 1973)

Col. Edward B. Giller	August 5, 1963–May 4, 1964
Carl Duckett	May 16, 1966–September 26, 1966
Lloyd Lauderdale	June 5, 1967–March 21, 1969
Donald Steininger	November 1, 1969–June 14, 1974
Sayre Stevens	June 14, 1974–May 17, 1976
Ernest J. Zellmer	June 1, 1976–September 24, 1979
James H. Taylor	September 24, 1979–September 27, 1982
James V. Hirsch	May 2, 1983 September 5, 1989
Gary W. Goodrich	October 16, 1989–December 31, 1995
Peter M. Daniher	January 1, 1996–November 12, 1997
Joanne Isham	November 12, 1997–January 10, 2000
James Runyan	January 10, 2000–

Director, Office of Special Activities (OSA)

James A. Cunningham (Acting)	August 1, 1962–September 4, 1962
Brig. Gen. Jack C. Ledford	September 4, 1962–August 1, 1966
Col. Paul N. Bacalis	August 1, 1966–July 12, 1968
Brig. Gen. Donald H. Ross	July 12, 1968–June 1, 1970
Brig. Gen. Harold F. Knowles	June 1, 1970–July 6, 1971
Brig. Gen. Wendell L. Bevan Jr.	July 6, 1971–August 31, 1974
James Cherbonneaux	Nov. 1, 1974–January 1, 1975

Director, Office of Research and Development (ORD)

Col. Edward B. Giller	November 29, 1962–May 4, 1964
Robert M. Chapman (Acting)	May 4, 1964–March 11, 1965
Robert M. Chapman	March 11, 1965–July 1, 1972
Sayre Stevens	July 1, 1972–June 14, 1974
James V. Hirsch	June 14, 1974–September 22, 1975
Donald L. Haas	September 22, 1975–May 23, 1976
Donald L. Reiser (Acting)	May 23, 1976–October 18, 1976
Frank Briglia (Acting)	October 18, 1976–February 27, 1977
Philip K. Eckman	February 27, 1977–April 1, 1989
Robert A. Herd III	April 1, 1989–July 18, 1996
Russell E. Dressell	July 18, 1996–October 1998

Office of Research and Development abolished effective October 1998.

Director, Office of ELINT (OEL)

George C. Miller	July 30, 1962–June 14, 1971
John N. McMahon	June 14, 1971–May 21, 1973
James V. Hirsch (Acting)	May 21, 1973–June 14, 1974
Robert D. Singel	June 14, 1974–September 22, 1975
James V. Hirsch	September 22, 1975–February 14, 1977

Office of ELINT and Division D merged to form Office of Special Operations effective February 14, 1977.

Director, Office of SIGINT Operations (OSO)

Edward Ryan	February 14, 1977–May 30, 1978
D. Barry Kelly	May 30, 1978–September 28, 1981
A. Roy Burks	September 28, 1981–July 15, 1984
M. Corley Wonus	July 15, 1984–March 21, 1989
Joseph B. Castillo	March 21, 1989–August 23, 1993

Office of SIGINT Operations and the Office of Special Projects (1988) were merged to form the Office of Technical Collection effective August 23, 1993.

Director, Office of Computer Services (OCS)

Joseph Becker	September 16, 1963–June 1, 1966
Charles A. Briggs	June 1, 1966–August 18, 1969
W. Douglas Climenson (Acting)	August 18, 1969–September 1, 1970
John D. Iams	September 1, 1970–April 1, 1973

Office of Computer Services transferred to Directorate of Management and Services and renamed Office of Joint Computer Support, effective April 1, 1973.

Director, Office of Scientific Intelligence (OSI)

Donald Chamberlain	August 22, 1963–June 24, 1973
Karl H. Weber	September 20, 1973–November 22, 1976

OSI transferred to the Directorate of Intelligence, effective November 22, 1976.

Director, Foreign Missile and Space Analysis Center (FMSAC)

Carl E. Duckett	November 7, 1963–May 16, 1966
David S. Brandwein	May 16, 1966–September 4, 1973

Foreign Missile and Space Analysis Center merged with component of OSI to form Office of Weapons Intelligence, effective September 4, 1973.

Director, Special Projects Staff (SPS)

Jackson D. Maxey	July 1964–September 1965

Special Projects Staff became Office of Special Projects on September 15, 1965.

Director, Office of Special Projects (OSP)

John J. Crowley	September 15, 1965–November 16, 1970
Harold L. Brownman	November 16, 1970–March 17, 1973

Office of Special Projects abolished and mission assumed by Office of Development and Engineering effective April 23, 1973.

Director, Office of Development and Engineering (OD&E)

Leslie C. Dirks	April 23, 1973–May 23, 1976
Donald L. Haas	May 23, 1976–August 28, 1978
Bert C. Aschenbrenner (Acting)	August 28, 1978–November 20, 1978
Stephens Crosby (Acting)	November 20, 1978–January 22, 1979
Bernard Lubarsky	January 22, 1979–March 8, 1982
Robert J. Kohler	March 8, 1982–August 17, 1985
Julian Caballero Jr.	August 17, 1985–October 3, 1993
Edmund Nowinski	October 3, 1993–October 16, 1995
Dennis Fitzgerald	October 16, 1995–

Director, Office of Weapons Intelligence (OWI)

David S. Brandwein	September 4, 1973–July 29, 1974
R. Evans Hineman	July 29, 1974–January 6, 1975
Ernest J. Zellmer	January 6, 1975–June 7, 1976
R. Evans Hineman	June 7, 1976–October 22, 1979
E. Wayne Boring	October 22, 1979–February 25, 1980

Office of Weapons Intelligence transferred to Directorate of Intelligence, November 22, 1976.

Director, National Photographic Interpretation Center (NPIC)

Arthur Lundahl	May 4, 1973–July 21, 1973
John J. Hicks	July 21, 1973–May 1, 1978
Col. Lorenzo W. Burroughs (Act.)	May 1, 1978–June 29, 1978
Rutledge P. "Hap" Hazard	June 30, 1978–February 20, 1984
R. M. "Rae" Huffstutler	February 20, 1984–January 25, 1988
Frank J. Ruocco	February 15, 1988–January 2, 1991
Leo A. Hazelwood	February 18, 1991–August 30, 1993
Nancy E. Bone	September 7, 1993–October 1, 1996

Director, Office of Technical Service (OTS)

Sidney Gottlieb	May 4, 1973–May 21, 1973
John N. McMahon	May 21, 1973–July 29, 1974
David S. Brandwein	July 29, 1974–June 2, 1980
M. Corley Wonus	June 2, 1980–July 15, 1984
Peter A. Marino	July 15, 1984–December 1, 1986
Joseph R. DeTrani	December 1, 1986–April 17, 1989
Frank R. Anderson	April 17, 1989–May 20, 1991
Robert G. Ruhle	May 20, 1991–February 20, 1994
Robert W. Manners	February 20, 1994–November 14, 1996
James L. Morris	November 14, 1996–April 4, 1997
Patrick L. Meehan	May 2, 1997–

Director, Foreign Broadcast Information Service (FBIS), transferred from DI to DS&T effective November 22, 1976; HN 1–127, November 16 1976.

Don H. Peterson	November 22, 1976–January 7, 1980
John F. Pereira	January 7, 1980–January 25, 1983
John D. Chandlee	January 25, 1983–January 3, 1986
Harrison S. Markham	January 3, 1986–September 28, 1986
Robert W. Manners	September 28, 1986–March 4, 1991
Wayne R. Schreiner	March 19, 1991–January 11, 1996
J. Niles Riddel	January 11, 1996–

Director, Special Projects Staff (SPS)

Gary W. Goodrich	January 18, 1987–October 12, 1987

Director, Office of Special Projects (OSP)

Gary W. Goodrich	October 12,1987–October 16, 1989
Peter M. Daniher	December 4, 1989–August 26, 1993

Director, Office of Technical Collection (OTC), established August 26, 1993, from merger of OSO and OSP (1987).

Peter M. Daniher	August 26, 1993–January 1, 1996
Patrick L. Meehan (Acting)	January 1, 1996–July 18, 1996
Patrick L. Meehan	July 18, 1996–May 1, 1997
James L. Runyan (Acting)	May 5, 1997–September 2, 1997
James L. Runyan	September 3, 1997–January 10, 2000

Director, Office of Advanced Analytical Tools (AAT)

Susan Gordon	July 18, 1996–October 2000

Director, Office of Advanced Projects (OAP)

Richard D. Platte	July 18, 1996–October 1998

Director, Clandestine Information Technology Office (CITO)

James R. Gosler	May 29, 1996–October 2000

CITO was formed from components of the Office of Technical Service (OTS) and the Office of Technical Collection (OTC). Part of CITO was transferred back to OTC in January 2001, and the rest was absorbed by the Directorate of Operations Information Operations Center.

Director, Office of Advanced Information Technology (AIT)

Larry Fairchild	October 2000–

Director, Office of Advanced Technologies and Programs (ATP)

Unknown	October 2000–

ACRONYMS AND ABBREVIATIONS

AAT	Office of Advanced Analytic Tools
ABM	Antiballistic Missile
ACDA	Arms Control and Disarmament Agency
ADSI	Assistant Director for Scientific Intelligence
AEC	Atomic Energy Commission
AFSC	Air Force Systems Command
AIR	American Institutes for Research
AIT	Office of Advanced Information Technology
APL	Applied Physics Laboratory (Johns Hopkins University)
ARDE	Democratic Revolutionary Alliance
ARS	Advanced Reconnaissance System
ATP	Office of Advanced Technologies and Programs
BND	Bundesnachrichtendienst (West German Foreign Intelligence Service)
CCD	Charge-Coupled Device
CIA	Central Intelligence Agency
CIG	Central Intelligence Group
CIO	Central Imagery Office
CITO	Clandestine Information Technology Office
COMINT	Communications Intelligence
COMIREX	Committee on Imagery Requirements and Exploitation
COMOR	Committee on Overhead Reconnaissance
DCI	Director of Central Intelligence
DCID	Director of Central Intelligence Directive
DDI	Deputy Director for Intelligence
DDP	Deputy Directorate for Plans
	Deputy Director for Plans
DDR	Deputy Director for Research
DEFSMAC	Defense Special Missile and Astronautics Center
DIA	Defense Intelligence Agency
DMA	Defense Mapping Agency
DNRO	Director National Reconnaissance Office
DOD	Department of Defense
DPD	Development Projects Division
DPS	Development Projects Staff
DS&T	Directorate of Science and Technology
EARL	Edgewood Arsenal Research Laboratories
ELINT	Electronic Intelligence
ERTS	Earth Resources Technology Satellite
ESO	ELINT Staff Officer
FBIS	Foreign Broadcast Information Service
FMSAC	Foreign Missile and Space Analysis Center

FROG	Film-Readout GAMBIT
FSTC	Foreign Science and Technology Center
FTD	Foreign Technology Division
HALSOL	High-Altitude Solar Energy
HN	Headquarters Notice
ICBM	Intercontinental Ballistic Missile
IDF	Israeli Defense Forces
IEG	Imagery Exploitation Group
INR	Bureau of Intelligence and Research
IPO	Investment Program Office
IRBM	Intermediate-Range Ballistic Missile
JCS	Joint Chiefs of Staff
JPRS	Joint Publications Research Service
JRDB	Joint Research and Development Board
LOROP	Long-Range Oblique Photography
MASINT	Measurement and Signature Intelligence
MIRV	Multiple Independent Reentry Vehicles
MPS	Ministry of Public Security (PRC)
MRBM	Medium-Range Ballistic Missile
MRV	Multiple Reentry Vehicles
MSX	Midcourse Space Experiment
NACA	National Advisory Council on Aeronautics
NARA	National Archives and Records Administration
NASA	National Aeronautics and Space Administration
NEL	National Exploitation Laboratory
NIA	National Imagery Agency
NIA	National Intelligence Authority
NIDL	National Information Display Laboratory
NIMA	National Imagery and Mapping Agency
NIE	National Intelligence Estimate
NORAD	North American Aerospace Defense Command
NPIC	National Photographic Interpretation Center
NRO	National Reconnaissance Office
NRP	National Reconnaissance Program
NRPEC	National Reconnaissance Program Executive Committee
NSA	National Security Agency
NSC	National Security Council
NSCID	National Security Council Intelligence Directive
NURO	National Underwater Reconnaissance Office
NVA	North Vietnamese Army
OAP	Office of Advanced Projects
OCS	Office of Computer Services
OD&E	Office of Development and Engineering
OEL	Office of ELINT
OIA	Office of Imagery Analysis
ORD	Office of Research and Development
ORE	Office of Reports and Estimates
OSA	Office of Special Activities
OSI	Office of Scientific Intelligence
OSO	Office of Special Operations

OSO	Office of SIGINT Operations
OSP	Office of Special Projects
OSR	Office of Strategic Research
OSS	Office of Strategic Services
OTC	Office of Technical Collection
OTH	Over-the-Horizon
OTS	Office of Technical Service
OWI	Office of Weapons Intelligence
PBCFIA	President's Board of Consultants on Foreign Intelligence Activities
PDB	President's Daily Brief
PFIAB	President's Foreign Intelligence Advisory Board
PEG	Priority Exploitation Group, NPIC
PIBS	Presidential Intelligence Briefing System
PIC	Photographic Interpretation Center
PID	Photographic Intelligence Division
PPMS	Power and Pattern Measurement System
PRC	People's Republic of China
PSAC	President's Scientific Advisory Committee
RDD	Radiation Detection Device
RPV	Remotely Piloted Vehicle
SAC	Strategic Air Command
SALT	Strategic Arms Limitation Treaty
SAM	Surface-to-Air Missile
SAVA	Special Assistant for Vietnamese Affairs
SCS	Special Collection Service
SCMC	Shuangchengzi Missile Test Complex
SDS	Satellite Data System
SEATO	Southeast Asia Treaty Organization
SEI	Scientific Engineering Institute
SIC	Scientific Intelligence Committee
SIGINT	Signals Intelligence
SLBM	Submarine-Launched Ballistic Missile
SNA	Somali National Alliance
SNIE	Special National Intelligence Estimate
SOD	Special Operations Division
SOSUS	Sound Surveillance System
SRI	Stanford Research Institute
TCP	Technological Capabilities Panel
TIO	Technology Investment Office
TRW	Thompson-Ramo-Woolridge
TSD	Technical Services Division
TSS	Technical Services Staff
UAV	Unmanned Aerial Vehicle
UCLAs	Unilaterally Controlled Latino Assets
USAF	United States Air Force
USIB	United States Intelligence Board
VC	Vietcong

NOTES

Chapter 1: Unexpected Missions

1. Thomas F. Troy, *Donovan and the CIA: A History of the Establishment of the Central Intelligence Agency* (Frederick, Md.: University Publications of America, 1981), pp. 406–407, 471–472.

2. Ibid., pp. 349, 464–465; Christopher Andrew, *For the President's Eyes Only: Secret Intelligence and the American Presidency from Washington to Bush* (New York: HarperCollins, 1995), pp. 168–169.

3. John Ranelagh, *The Agency: The Rise and Decline of the CIA, from Wild Bill Donovan to William Casey* (New York: Simon & Schuster, 1986), p. 112.

4. Ronald Kessler, *Inside the CIA: Revealing the Secrets of the World's Most Powerful Spy Agency* (New York: Pocket Books, 1992), p. 140; Richard M. Bissell with Jonathan E. Lewis and Francis T. Pudlo, *Reflections of a Cold Warrior: From Yalta to the Bay of Pigs* (New Haven: Yale University Press, 1996), p. 98.

5. Center for the Study of Intelligence, *Declassified National Intelligence Estimates of the Soviet Union and International Communism* (Washington, D.C.: Central Intelligence Agency, 1996), pp. 4, 6.

6. Brig. Gen. E. K. Wright, Deputy Director of Central Intelligence, "Establishment and Functions of the Nuclear Energy Group, Scientific Branch, Office of Reports and Estimates," in C. Thomas Thorne Jr. and David S. Patterson (eds.), *Emergence of the Intelligence Establishment* (Washington, D.C.: U.S. Government Printing Office, 1996), pp. 503–505; Charles A. Zeigler and David Jacobson, *Spying Without Spies: Origins of America's Secret Nuclear Surveillance System* (Westport, Conn.: Praeger, 1995), pp. 60–63; George S. Jackson and Martin P. Clausen, *Organizational History of the Central Intelligence Agency, 1950–1953* (Washington, D.C.: Central Intelligence Agency, 1957), p. 3; interview with Henry S. Lowenhaupt, Springfield, Virginia, April 15, 1999.

7. Lowenhaupt interview; CIA Public Affairs Staff, "'Trailblazers' and Years of CIA Service," www.odci.gov/cia, March 13, 1999.

8. David Z. Beckler, Chief of the Intelligence Section, JRDB, "The Critical Situation in Regard to Atomic Energy Intelligence," December 2, 1947, in Thorne and Patterson (eds.), *Emergence of the Intelligence Establishment*, pp. 820–821.

9. Brig. Gen. E. K. Wright, Deputy Director of Central Intelligence, "Operations-Intelligence Relationship of CIG with JRDB," March 13, 1947, in Thorne and Patterson (eds.), *Emergence of the Intelligence Establishment*, pp. 502–503.

10. Ronald E. Doel and Allan A. Needell, "Science, Scientists, and the CIA: Balancing International Ideals, National Needs, and Professional Opportunities," *Intelligence and National Security* 12, 1 (January 1997): 59–81 at p. 62.

11. Ralph L. Clark, Director of Programs Division, to Dr. Vannevar Bush, Chairman, RDB, "CIA Situation," December 3, 1947, in Thorne and Patterson (eds.), *Emergence of the Intelligence Establishment*, pp. 818–819.

12. Doel and Needell, "Science, Scientists, and the CIA," p. 63.

13. Ibid., pp. 63–65; Jackson and Clausen, *Organizational History of the Central Intelligence Agency*, p. VI-14; Brig. Gen. E. K. Wright, DDCI, Memorandum for Assistant Director for Special Operations et al., Subject: Additional Functions of the Office of Special Operations, March 5, 1948, 2000 CIA Release, National Archives and Records Administration (NARA).

14. Doel and Needell, "Science, Scientists, and the CIA," p. 65.

15. Jackson and Clausen, *Organizational History of the Central Intelligence Agency*, p. 1.

16. Allen W. Dulles, William H. Jackson, and Mathias F. Correa, *The Central Intelligence Agency and National Organization for Intelligence* (Washington, D.C.: National Security Council, January 1, 1949), p. 56.

17. Jackson and Clausen, *Organizational History of the Central Intelligence Agency*, pp. VI-3, VI-16, VI-16 n. 2; Ludwell Lee Montague, *General Walter Bedell Smith as Director of Central Intelligence, October 1950–February 1953* (University Park: Pennsylvania State University Press, 1992), p. 174; Robert Blum to Mathias F. Corea, December 18, 1948, in Thorne and Patterson (eds.), *Emergence of the Intelligence Establishment*, p. 902.

18. Doel and Needell, "Science, Scientists, and the CIA," p. 66.

19. Ibid., p. 67.

20. Willard Machle, Assistant Director for Scientific Intelligence, to Rear Admiral Roscoe Hillenkoetter, Director of Central Intelligence, "Inability of OSI to Accomplish Its Mission," September 29, 1949, in Thorne and Patterson (eds.), *Emergence of the Intelligence Establishment*, pp. 1012–1016; Jackson and Clausen, *Organizational History of the Central Intelligence Agency*, p. VI-19; interview with Karl Weber, Oakton, Virginia, May 5, 1999.

21. Machle, "Inability of OSI to Accomplish Its Mission"; Memorandum for the Record, Subject: Responsibilities of the Office of Scientific Intelligence (Summary of discussion between [deleted], OSI and Mr. Piel [deleted] of Management), November 29, 1951, NARA, RG 263, 1998 CIA, Box 209, Folder 3.

22. Director of Central Intelligence Directive 3/3, "Scientific Intelligence," October 28, 1949; Weber interview.

23. Montague, *General Walter Bedell Smith as Director of Central Intelligence, October 1950–February 1953*, pp. 174–175.

24. Ibid., p. 175; Weber interview.

25. Montague, *General Walter Bedell Smith as Director of Central Intelligence, October 1950–February 1953*, p. 176.

26. Ibid., pp. 177–178; Jackson and Clausen, *Organizational History of the Central Intelligence Agency*, pp. VI-59 to VI-60.

27. Montague, *General Walter Bedell Smith as Director of Central Intelligence, October 1950–February 1953*, pp. 177–178; Ranelagh, *The Agency*, pp. 196–197; Jackson and Clausen, *Organizational History of the Central Intelligence Agency*, p. VI-66.

28. Montague, *General Walter Bedell Smith as Director of Central Intelligence, October 1950–February 1953*, p. 179; Director of Central Intelligence 3/4, "Production of Scientific and Technical Intelligence," August 14, 1952; Jackson and Clausen, *Organizational History of the Central Intelligence Agency*, p. VI-74.

29. Montague, *General Walter Bedell Smith as Director of Central Intelligence, October 1950-February 1953*, p. 180.

30. Ranelagh, *The Agency*, pp. 197, 729–730.

31. Central Intelligence Agency Notice No. 20-191-71, "Announcement of Key Positions," June 28, 1955; Central Intelligence Agency, Memo for Awards Committee, National Civil Service League, November 28, 1958.

32. Director of Central Intelligence Directive No. 3/5, "Production of Scientific and Technical Intelligence," February 3, 1959.

33. Doel and Needell, "Science, Scientists, and the CIA," pp. 70–71.

34. Michael Warner, CIA History Staff, Memorandum for the Record, Subject: The Central Intelligence Agency and Human Radiation Experiments: An Analysis of the Findings, February 14, 1995, p. 11.

35. Jackson and Clausen, *Organizational History of the Central Intelligence Agency*, p. 67 n.49.

36. Intelligence Advisory Committee, NIE 11-3A-54, *Summary: The Soviet Atomic Energy Program to Mid-1957*, February 16, 1954, pp. 1–4.

37. *Allen Welsh Dulles as Director of Central Intelligence, 26 February 1953–29 November 1961, Volume II, Coordination of Intelligence* (Washington, D.C.: CIA, 1973), pp. 42–43; Director of Central Intelligence, NIE 11-6-54, *Soviet Capabilities and Probable Programs in the Guided Missile Field*, October 1954, pp. ii-iii, 1.

38. *Allen Welsh Dulles as Director of Central Intelligence*, pp. 46–47, 51n., 58; Annex D to Director of Central Intelligence Directive 3/4, "Terms of Reference for the Guided Missile Intelligence Committee," January 31, 1956; "Summary Statement of IAC Actions Leading to Consideration of a Guided Missile Intelligence Committee," n.d., NARA, RG 263, 1998 CIA Release, Box 188, Folder 6; interview with Henry Plaster, Vienna, Virginia, September 30, 1999.

39. Avner Cohen, *Israel and the Bomb* (New York: Columbia University Press, 1998), p. 84; Office of Scientific Intelligence, CIA, NIE 38–58, *The Netherlands Nuclear Energy Program*, November 10, 1958; Office of Scientific Intelligence, CIA, *The French Nuclear Weapons Program*, November 13, 1959.

40. Henry S. Lowenhaupt, "The Decryption of a Picture," *Studies in Intelligence* 1, 3 (Summer 1957): 41–53.

41. John Marks, *The Search for the "Manchurian Candidate": The CIA and Mind Control* (New York: Norton, 1991), pp. 59, 79, 80, 83; U.S. Congress, Senate Select Committee to Study Governmental Operations with Respect to Intelligence Activities (hereinafter Senate Select Committee), *Final Report, Book I: Foreign and Military Intelligence* (Washington, D.C.: U.S. Government Printing Office, 1976), pp. 390, 395–397.

42. Tim Weiner, "Sidney Gottlieb, 80, Dies; Took LSD to C.I.A.," *New York Times*, March 10, 1999, p. C22; Marks, *The Search for the "Manchurian Candidate,"* pp. 59–60; Evan Thomas, *The Very Best Men, Four Who Dared: The Early Years of the CIA* (New York: Simon & Schuster, 1995), p. 211.

43. Marks, *The Search for the "Manchurian Candidate,"* pp. 24–25, 27; U.S. Congress, Senate Select Committee, *Final Report, Book I*, p. 387.

44. Marks, *The Search for the "Manchurian Candidate,"* pp. 31–32, 44, p. 59.

45. Ibid., pp. 60–61; U.S. Congress, Senate Select Committee, *Final Report, Book I*, p. 390.

46. Marks, *The Search for the "Manchurian Candidate,"* p. 62.

47. Ibid., pp. 61–62; U.S. Congress, Senate Select Committee, *Final Report, Book I*, p. 389.

48. Marks, *The Search for the "Manchurian Candidate,"* pp. 90, 108; Ranelagh, *The Agency*, p. 207.

49. James R. Killian Jr., *Sputnik, Scientists, and Eisenhower: A Memoir of the First Special Assistant to the President for Science and Technology* (Cambridge: MIT Press, 1982), pp. 67–68.

50. Gregory W. Pedlow and Donald E. Welzenbach, *The Central Intelligence Agency and Overhead Reconnaissance: The U-2 and OXCART Programs, 1954–1974* (Washington, D.C.: CIA, 1992), Preface.

51. Donald E. Welzenbach, "Science and Technology: Origins of a Directorate," *Studies in Intelligence* 30, 2 (Summer 1986): 13–26 at 13–15; Victor K. McElheny, *Insisting on the Impossible: The Life of Edwin Land, Inventor of Instant Photography* (Reading, Mass.: Perseus Books, 1998), p. 294.

52. Killian, *Sputniks, Scientists, and Eisenhower*, p. 79; McElheny, *Insisting on the Impossible*, p. 301.

53. Donald Welzenbach, "Din Land: Patriot from Polaroid," *Optics and Photonics News* 5, 10 (October 1996): 22ff; Attachment 1, Memorandum for: Director of Central Intelligence, Subject: A Unique Opportunity for Comprehensive Intelligence, November 5, 1954.

54. Ranelagh, *The Agency*, p. 314.

55. "A Unique Opportunity for Comprehensive Intelligence—A Summary," attachment, Edwin Land to Allen W. Dulles, November 5, 1954.

56. Pedlow and Welzenbach, *The Central Intelligence Agency and Overhead Reconnaissance*, p. 4; R. Cargill Hall, "Post-War Strategic Reconnaissance and the Genesis of Corona," in Dwayne A. Day, John Logsdon, and Brian Latell (eds.), *Eye in the Sky: The Story of the CORONA Spy Satellites* (Washington, D.C.: Smithsonian, 1998), pp. 86–118 at pp. 87–92.

57. Edwin Land to Allen Dulles, November 5, 1954.

58. Pedlow and Welzenbach, *The Central Intelligence Agency and Overhead Reconnaissance*, pp. 32–35, 40; A. J. Goodpaster, "Memorandum of Conference with the President, 0810, 24 November 1954," November 24, 1954, Ann C. Whitman Diary, November 1954, Box 3, Ann C. Whitman File, DDE Papers as President, Dwight David Eisenhower Library (DDEL); Peter Grose, *Gentleman Spy: The Life of Allen Dulles* (Boston: Houghton Mifflin, 1994), p. 405; Chris Pocock, *Dragon Lady: The History of the U-2 Spyplane* (Shrewsbury, England: Airlife, 1989), p. 26; Oral History Interview with Richard Bissell Jr., Columbia University, 1973, p. 42.

59. Bissell with Lewis and Pudlo, *Reflections of a Cold Warrior*, p. 78; Pedlow and Welzenbach, *The Central Intelligence Agency and Overhead Reconnaissance*, pp. 15–16, 30.

60. Peter Wyden, *The Bay of Pigs: The Untold Story* (New York: Simon & Schuster, 1979), p. 13.

61. Ibid., pp. 12–13.

62. Bissell with Lewis and Pudlo, *Reflections of a Cold Warrior*, pp. 98, 105.

63. Ben R. Rich and Leo Janos, *Skunk Works: A Personal Memoir of My Years at Lockheed* (Boston: Little, Brown, 1994), p. 130.

64. Pedlow and Welzenbach, *The Central Intelligence Agency and Overhead Reconnaissance*, p. 66.

65. Ibid., p. 60; Jonathan E. Lewis, "Tension and Triumph: Civilian and Military Relations and the Birth of the U-2 Program," in Robert A. McDonald (ed.), *CORONA: Between the Sun and the Earth: The First NRO Reconnaissance Eye in Space* (Bethesda, Md.: American Society for Photogrammetry and Remote Sensing, 1997), pp. 13–23 at p. 13. Eisenhower was certainly aware that the Air Force had, for a number of years, been conducting electronic and photographic reconnaissance flights that entered Soviet airspace. But it was expected that the U-2s would fly far deeper into the Soviet Union than the military planes—to reach key missile and nuclear targets that the military flights could not be expected to reach.

66. Pedlow and Welzenbach, *The Central Intelligence Agency and Overhead Reconnaissance*, pp. 94–95, 100; Pocock, *Dragon Lady*, p. 25; William E. Burrows, "That New Black Magic," *Air and Space*, December 1998/January 1999, pp. 29–35.

67. Pedlow and Welzenbach, *The Central Intelligence Agency and Overhead Reconnaissance*, pp. 101, 104.

68. Pocock, *Dragon Lady*, p. 27; Pedlow and Welzenbach, *The Central Intelligence Agency and Overhead Reconnaissance*, pp. 104–105.

69. Pedlow and Welzenbach, *The Central Intelligence Agency and Overhead Reconnaissance*, p. 105; Pocock, *Dragon Lady*, p. 27.

70. Pocock, *Dragon Lady*, p. 28.

71. "Soviet Note No. 23," July 10, 1956, White House Corr., Gen. 1956(3), Box 3, John Foster Dulles Papers, White House Memoranda, DDEL; Pedlow and Welzenbach, *The Central Intelligence Agency and Overhead Reconnaissance*, p. 109.

72. Herbert I. Miller, Memorandum for: Project Director, Subject: Suggestions re Intelligence Value of AQUATONE, July 17, 1956, 2000 CIA Release, NARA.

73. Pedlow and Welzenbach, *The Central Intelligence Agency and Overhead Reconnaissance*, pp. 111, 124.

74. Jay Miller, *Lockheed U-2* (Austin, Tex.: Aerofax, 1983), pp. 27, 30; Pedlow and Welzenbach, *The Central Intelligence Agency and Overhead Reconnaissance*, pp. 135, 139.

75. Pedlow and Welzenbach, *The Central Intelligence Agency and Overhead Reconnaissance*, pp. 135, 139, 143; Henry S. Lowenhaupt, "Mission to Birch Woods," *Studies in Intelligence* 12, 4 (Fall 1968): 1–12 at 3.

76. Pedlow and Welzenbach, *The Central Intelligence Agency and Overhead Reconnaissance*, p. 143.

77. Ibid., p. 165.

78. Ibid., p. 168; CIA, "Situation Estimate for Project CHALICE, Fiscal Years 1961 and 1962," March 14, 1960, 2000 CIA Release, NARA.

79. Pedlow and Welzenbach, *The Central Intelligence Agency and Overhead Reconnaissance,* p. 168.

80. Ibid., pp. 174–176; Chris Pocock, *The U-2 Spyplane: Toward the Unknown* (Atglen, Pa.: Schiffer Books, 2000), p. 165; interview with a former CIA official.

81. Evan Thomas, *The Very Best Men* (New York: Simon & Schuster, 1995), p. 218; Pedlow and Welzenbach, *The Central Intelligence Agency and Overhead Reconnaissance*, p. 176; Transcript, "Debriefing of Francis Gary Powers, Tape #2," February 13, 1962, NARA, RG 263, 1998 CIA Release, Box 230, Folder 3.

82. "Testimony of Allen Dulles," *Executive Sessions of the Senate Foreign Relations Committee (Historical Series), Vol. XII, Eighty-sixth Congress–Second Session, 1960* (Washington, D.C.: U.S. Government Printing Office, 1982), p. 285.

83. Ibid.

84. Seymour M. Hersh, *The Samson Option: Israel's Nuclear Arsenal and American Foreign Policy* (New York: Random House, 1991), p. 52.

85. Pedlow and Welzenbach, *The Central Intelligence Agency and Overhead Reconnaissance*, p. 215; Memorandum for: Director of Central Intelligence, Subject: Identification of Special Projects, August 13, 1958, NARA, RG 263, 1998 CIA Release, Box 42, Folder 5.

86. Central Intelligence Agency, "Future of the Agency's U-2 Capability," July 7, 1960, pp. 4, 10; Miller, *Lockheed U-2*, p. 31; Richard M. Bissell Jr., Deputy Director (Plans), Memorandum for: All Members U.S. Government IDEALIST Community, January 4, 1961, 2000 CIA Release, NARA.

87. Wayne Mutza, *Lockheed P2V Neptune: An Illustrated History* (Atglen, Pa.: Schiffer Military/Aviation History, 1996), pp. 109–110; "Lockheed RB-69A 'Neptune,'" www.wpafb.af.mil/museum/research/bombers/b5/b5-62.htm, July 28, 1999.

88. Mutza, *Lockheed P2V Neptune*, pp. 110, 112–113.

89. Ibid., p. 113; Jay Miller, *Skunk Works: The Official History* (North Branch, Minn.: Specialty Press, 1996), p. 58.

90. Frederic C.E. Oder, James C. Fitzpatrick, and Paul E. Worthman, *The CORONA Story* (Washington, D.C.: National Reconnaissance Office, 1997), p. 123; interview with Albert D. Wheelon, Montecito, California, November 11–12, 1998; interview with John McMahon, Los Altos, California, November 17, 1998; Mutza, *Lockheed P2V Neptune*, pp. 113–114; Miller, *Skunk Works*, p. 58.

91. Pedlow and Welzenbach, *The CIA and Overhead Reconnaissance*, p. 260; Thomas P. McIninch, "The OXCART Story," *Studies in Intelligence* 15, 1 (Winter 1971): 1–34 at 2.

92. McIninch, "The OXCART Story," p. 3.

93. Pedlow and Welzenbach, *The Central Intelligence Agency and Overhead Reconnaissance*, pp. 262–263; John L. Sloop, *Liquid Hydrogen as a Propulsion Fuel* (Washington, D.C.: NASA, 1978), pp. 141–167.

94. Pedlow and Welzenbach, *The Central Intelligence Agency and Overhead Reconnaissance*, p. 263; McIninch, "The OXCART Story," p. 3.

95. McIninch, "The OXCART Story," p. 3; Pedlow and Welzenbach, *The Central Intelligence Agency and Overhead Reconnaissance*, pp. 263, 267.

96. Pedlow and Welzenbach, *The Central Intelligence Agency and Overhead Reconnaissance*, pp. 268–269.

97. Ibid., pp. 270–271, 273; McIninch, "The OXCART Story," p. 3.

98. Pedlow and Welzenbach, *The Central Intelligence Agency and Overhead Reconnaissance*, p. 273; Rich and Janos, *Skunk Works*, p. 200.

99. Pedlow and Welzenbach, *The Central Intelligence Agency and Overhead Reconnaissance*, p. 274.

100. Ibid., pp. 274, 278.

101. Brig. Gen. A. J. Goodpaster, Memorandum for the Record, June 2, 1960, Dwight D. Eisenhower Papers, White House Office: Office of Staff Secretary, Subject Series, alpha sub, b.15, F: "Intel Matters (15)," DDEL.

102. Oder, Fitzpatrick, and Worthman, *The CORONA Story*, p. 18.

103. Jeffrey T. Richelson, *America's Secret Eyes in Space: The U.S. KEYHOLE Spy Satellite Program* (New York: Harper & Row, 1990), p. 27; Bissell with Lewis and Pudlo, *Reflections of a Cold Warrior*, p. 135.

104. Oder, Fitzpatrick, and Worthman, *The CORONA Story*, pp. 10, 15.

105. Kenneth E. Greer, "Corona," *Studies in Intelligence*, Supplement, 17 (Spring 1973), reprinted in Kevin C. Ruffner (ed.), *CORONA: America's First Satellite Program* (Washington, D.C.: Central Intelligence Agency, 1995), pp. 3–39 at p. 5; Hall, "Postwar Strategic Reconnaissance and the Genesis of Corona," p. 113.

106. Central Intelligence Agency/National Reconnaissance Office, "CORONA Pioneers," May 25, 1995; interview with Frank Buzard, Rancho Palos Verdes, California, June 11, 1999; Dwayne A. Day, "Development and Improvement of the Corona Satellite," in Day, Logsdon, and Latell (eds.), *Eye in the Sky*, pp. 48–85 at p. 49; Robert A. McDonald, "Corona's Pioneers," in McDonald (ed.)., *CORONA*, pp. 141–152 at p. 145.

107. Robert A. McDonald, "CORONA: A Success for Space Reconnaissance, a Look into the Cold War, and a Revolution for Intelligence," *Photogrammetric Engineering and Remote Sensing* 51, 6 (June 1995): 689–720 at 693; Central Intelligence Agency/National Reconnaissance Office, "CORONA Pioneers."

108. Dwayne A. Day, "The Development and Improvement of the Corona Satellite," in Day, Logsdon, and Latell (eds.), *Eye in the Sky*, pp. 48–85, at p. 50.

109. Buzard interview.

110. Albert D. Wheelon, "CORONA: A Triumph of American Technology," in Day, Logsdon, and Latell (eds.), *Eye in the Sky*, pp. 29–47 at pp. 34–35; Greer, "Corona," pp. 7–8; Bissell with Lewis and Pudlo, *Reflections of a Cold Warrior*, p. 136.

111. Jonathan McDowell, "Launch Listings," in Day, Logsdon, and Latell (eds.), *Eye in the Sky*, pp. 235–246 at p. 236; Day, "The Development and Improvement of the Corona Satellite," p. 49.

112. Day, "The Development and Improvement of the CORONA Satellite," p. 55.

113. Greer, "Corona," at pp. 16–21; McDowell, "Launch Listings," p. 236; Leonard Mosley, *Dulles: A Biography of Eleanor, Allen, and John Foster and Their Family Network* (New York: Dial Press, 1978), p. 432.

114. "The Origin and Evolution of the Corona System," in Day, Logsdon, and Latell (eds.), *Eye in the Sky*, pp. 181–199 at p. 199.

115. Buzard interview.

116. Richelson, *America's Secret Eyes in Space*, p. 40; Greer, "Corona," pp. 3, 22, 24; Dwayne A. Day, John Logsdon, and Brian Latell, "Introduction," in Day, Logsdon, and Latell (eds.), *Eye in the Sky*, pp. 1–18 at p. 10.

117. Interview with a former CIA official.

118. Ibid.

119. J. Michael Selander, "Image Coverage Models for Declassified Corona, Argon, and Lanyard Satellite Photography: A Technical Explanation," in McDonald (ed.), *CORONA*, pp. 177–188, at p. 177; Greer, "Corona," p. 24; Photographic Interpretation Center, Central Intelligence Agency, *Joint*

Mission Coverage Index, Mission 9009, 18 August 1960, September 1960, pp. 115–125 in Ruffner (ed.), *CORONA*, p. 120.

120. Greer, "Corona," p. 24; McDonald (ed.), *CORONA*, p. 718.

121. McDonald (ed.), *CORONA*, pp. 698–700, 715, 718.

122. Director of Central Intelligence, NIE 11-4-57, "Main Trends in Soviet Capabilities and Policies, 1957–1962," November 12, 1957, pp. 26–27; Lawrence C. McQuade, Memorandum for Mr. Nitze, Subject: But Where Did the Missile Gap Go? (Washington, D.C.: Assistant Secretary of Defense, International Security Affairs, May 31, 1963), pp. 7–8.

123. Director of Central Intelligence, NIE 11-4-59, *Main Trends in Soviet Capabilities and Policies, 1959–1964*, February 9, 1960, pp. 51–52.

124. Desmond Ball, *Politics and Force Levels: The Strategic Missile Program of the Kennedy Administration* (Berkeley: University of California Press, 1980), pp. 10, 15–25, 96.

125. Director of Central Intelligence, NIE 11-4-60, "Main Trends in Soviet Capabilities and Policies, 1960–1965," December 1, 1960, p. 52.

126. Director of Central Intelligence, NIE 11-8-61, *Soviet Capabilities for Long-Range Attack*, June 7, 1961, in Donald P. Steury, *Intentions and Capabilities: Estimates on Soviet Strategic Forces, 1950–1983* (Washington, D.C.: Central Intelligence Agency, 1996), pp. 115–119 at pp. 116–117.

127. Jerrold L. Schechter and Peter S. Deriabin, *The Spy Who Saved the World: How a Soviet Colonel Changed the Course of the Cold War* (New York: Scribner's, 1992), pp. 273–274; Director of Central Intelligence, NIE 11-8/1-61, *Soviet Capabilities for Long-Range Attack*, September 21, 1961, p. 4.

128. Director of Central Intelligence, NIE 11-8/1-61, *Soviet Capabilities for Long-Range Attack*, pp. 2, 10–11, 13.

129. National Security Council, NSCID No. 8, "Photographic Interpretation," January 18, 1961.

130. *The Reminiscences of Arthur C. Lundahl*, Oral History Research Office, Columbia University, 1982, pp. 11, 38, 42.

131. Ibid., pp. 51, 56, 57.

132. Ibid., pp. 182, 187, 197; Jack Anderson, "Getting the Big Picture for the CIA," *Washington Post*, November 28, 1982, p. C7; Dino A. Brugioni and Frederick J. Doyle, "Arthur C. Lundahl: Founder of the Image Exploitation Discipline," pp. 159–168 in McDonald (ed.), *CORONA*, at pp. 160–161.

133. *The Reminiscences of Arthur Lundahl*, p. 221; interview with a former CIA official; Office of the Deputy Director (Intelligence), Notice No. 1-130-5, "Photographic Interpretation Center," August 19, 1958.

134. *The Reminiscences of Arthur C. Lundahl*, pp. 197, 201; John Prados, *The Soviet Estimate: U.S. Intelligence and Russian Military Strength* (New York: Dial, 1982), p. 110; Office of the Deputy Director (Intelligence), Notice No. 1-130-5, "Photographic Interpretation Center."

135. *The Reminiscences of Arthur C. Lundahl*, pp. 197–201, 229.

136. Prados, *The Soviet Estimate*, pp. 122–123.

137. Joint Study Group, *Report on Foreign Intelligence Activities of the United States Government*, December 15, 1960, pp. 1, 2.

138. *The Reminiscences of Arthur Lundahl*, pp. 53, 61.

139. Ibid., pp. 299–300; Marion W. Boggs, Memorandum, Subject: Discussion at the 474th Meeting of the National Security Council, Thursday, January 12, 1961, January 13, 1961, Dwight D. Eisenhower Library, Papers 1953–61, Ann Whitman File, pp. 4–9.

140. Boggs, Memorandum, Subject: Discussion at the 474th Meeting of the National Security Council, Thursday, January 12, 1961, pp. 6–7.

141. Ibid., pp. 7–8.

142. Ibid., pp. 8, 9.

143. Ibid., p. 9; *The Reminiscences of Arthur Lundahl*, pp. 301–302.

144. *Allen Welsh Dulles as Director of Central Intelligence, 26 February 1953–29 November 1961: Volume II, Coordination of Intelligence* (Washington, D.C.: Central Intelligence Agency, July 1973), p. 82.

145. Ibid., p. 81.

146. Ibid., pp. 81–82.

147. Charles A. Kroeger Jr., "ELINT: A Scientific Intelligence System," *Studies in Intelligence* 2, 1 (Winter 1958): 71–83; *Allen Welsh Dulles as Director of Central Intelligence*, p. 94; Richard M. Bissell Jr., Deputy Director (Plans), Memorandum for: Major General J. M. Williams, Assistant Chief of Staff for Intelligence USA, et al., Subject: ELINT Requirements Requiring Sensitive Collection, September 9, 1959, 2000 CIA Release, NARA.

148. Olav Riste, *The Norwegian Intelligence Service, 1945–1970* (London: Frank Cass, 1999), pp. 90, 92, 149–150.

149. Robert P. Berman and John C. Baker, *Soviet Strategic Forces: Requirements and Responses* (Washington, D.C.: Brookings Institution, 1982), pp. 106–107; Riste, *The Norwegian Intelligence Service*, p. 105; interview with a former CIA official.

150. Riste, *The Norwegian Intelligence Service*, pp. 147–148.

151. Ibid., p. 149; Central Intelligence Agency, *Cost Reduction Program: FY 1966-FY 1967*, September 1, 1965, p. 9, NARA, RG 263, Entry 36, HRP 89-2/00443, Box 7, File 713; Rolf Tamnes, *The Cold War in the High North* (Oslo: Ad Notam, 1991), pp. 121–122, 212.

152. Interview with Robert Phillips, Rosslyn, Virginia, June 4, 1999.

153. William H. Nance, "Quality ELINT," *Studies in Intelligence* 12, 2 (Spring 1968): 7–19 at 8.

154. Ibid.

155. William E. Burrows, *Exploring Space: Voyages in the Solar System and Beyond* (New York: Random House, 1990), p. 99.

156. Henry G. Plaster, "Snooping on Space Pictures," *Studies in Intelligence* 8, 4 (Fall 1964): 31–39 at 31.

157. Ibid., pp. 31–32.

158. Ibid., p. 32. NSA went on to design and produce special equipment that would show oscilloscope pictures as a signal was being received, with the first two sent to ELINT sites in Hawaii and Alaska. Video transmissions from *Sputnik 9* and *Sputnik 10,* both launched in March 1961, gave verification that the flights carried canine passengers. More important was the ability of NSA to report, 58 minutes into Yuri Gagarin's 108-minute flight on April 12, 1961, that the Soviets had indeed placed a man into orbit and he was alive. See Plaster, "Snooping on Space Pictures," p. 34.

159. James Burke, "Seven Years to Luna 9," *Studies in Intelligence* 10, 3 (Summer 1966): 1–24 at 4–5, 7; Burrows, *Exploring Space*, p. 420.

160. Burrows, *Exploring Space*, p. 420; Burke, "Seven Years to Luna 9," pp. 7–8.

161. Burke, "Seven Years to Luna 9," pp. 8–9; Burrows, *Exploring Space*, pp. 130–131.

162. David C. Martin, *Wilderness of Mirrors* (New York: Harper & Row, 1980), p. 121; Philip Agee, *Inside the Company: CIA Diary* (San Francisco: Stonehill, 1975), Appendix 3; "CIA Historical Program," January 1971, NARA, RG 263, 1998 CIA Release, Box 4, Folder 3.

163. Agee, *Inside the Company*, p. 351.

164. James Bamford, *The Puzzle Palace: A Report on NSA, America's Most Secret Agency* (Boston: Houghton Mifflin, 1982), p. 142.

165. Memorandum for General Maude, Subject: Proposed U.S./U.K. Cooperation within Area 5 of Technical Cooperation Program, May 4, 1951, NARA, RG 341, Entry 214; Pocock, *Dragon Lady*, p. 47–48.

166. Nicholas R. Garofalo, "Present and Future Capabilities of OTH Radars," *Studies in Intelligence* 13, 2 (Spring 1969): 53–61 at 53–54; [deleted], Assistant Chief, DPD-DD/P, Memorandum for: Acting Deputy Director (Plans), Status of CIA Personnel Staff, Project [deleted], July 22, 1960, 2000 CIA Release, NARA.

167. Ibid., pp. 54–55, 60.

168. Thomas Powers, *The Man Who Kept the Secrets: Richard Helms and the CIA* (London: Weidenfeld and Nicolson, 1979), p. 146; Ranelagh, *The Agency*, p. 211; Kevin Whitelaw, "A Killing in the Congo," *U.S. News and World Report,* July 24–31, 2000, p. 63.

169. Ranelagh, *The Agency*, p. 211.

170. U.S. Congress, Senate Select Committee to Study Governmental Operations with Respect to Intelligence Activities, *Alleged Assassination Plots Involving Foreign Leaders* (Washington, D.C.: U.S. Government Printing Office, 1975), pp. 71, 89.

171. J. S. Earman, Inspector General, CIA, *Report on Plots to Assassinate Fidel Castro* (Washington, D.C.: CIA, 1967), pp. 23–24.

172. Ibid., p. 24; Powers, *The Man Who Kept the Secrets*, p. 148.

173. Powers, *The Man Who Kept the Secrets*, p. 150.

Chapter 2: False Start

1. Allen W. Dulles, Memorandum for: Deputy Secretary of Defense, Special Assistant to the President for Science and Technology, Subject: Proposed Curtailment of Project CORONA, December 4, 1958, in NRO Collection of CORONA, ARGON, LANYARD Records (subsequently CAL Records).

2. John Ranelagh, *The Agency: The Rise and Decline of the CIA, from Wild Bill Donovan to William Casey* (New York: Simon & Schuster, 1986), pp. 410, 730.

3. Donald E. Welzenbach, "Science and Technology: Origins of a Directorate," *Studies in Intelligence* 30, 2 (Summer 1986): 13–26 at 22; CIA, N-120-2, Organization and Functions: Office of the Deputy Director (Plans), Establishment of the Development Projects Division, February 18, 1959, NARA, RG 263, 1998 CIA Release, Box 44, Folder 14.

4. Welzenbach, "Science and Technology," p. 22; Albert D. Wheelon, "Genesis of a Unique National Capability," address at CIA, December 19, 1984, p. 9.

5. U.S. Congress, Senate Select Committee to Study Governmental Operations with Respect to Intelligence Activities, *Final Report, Book IV: Supplementary Detailed Staff Reports on Foreign and Military Intelligence* (Washington, D.C.: U.S. Government Printing Office, 1976), p. 77.

6. Welzenbach, "Science and Technology," p. 22.

7. Ibid.

8. Richard M. Bissell Jr., with Jonathan E. Lewis and Francis T. Pudlo, *Reflections of a Cold Warrior: From Yalta to the Bay of Pigs* (New Haven: Yale University Press, 1996), p. 203.

9. Evan Thomas, *The Very Best Men: Four Who Dared—The Early Years of the CIA* (New York: Simon & Schuster, 1995), p. 272.

10. Letter, Richard M. Bissell to John McCone, February 7, 1962.

11. Ibid.

12. Ibid.

13. Ibid.

14. Ibid.; CIA, HN 1-18, February 14, 1962, NARA, CIA Historical Review Program 89-2 RG 263, NN3-263-94-010, Box 1, HS/HC 706, Folder 7.

15. Welzenbach, "Science and Technology," p. 23.

16. John A. McCone, HN 1-8, February 14, 1962; John A. McCone, HN 1-9, February 16, 1962; information provided by CIA Public Affairs Staff.

17. Lt. Gen. Marshall Carter, DDCI, HN 1-15, "Transfer of Special Projects Branch," April 16, 1962, NARA, CIA HRP 89-2, NN3-263-94-010, Box 5, HS/HC 706, Box 7.

18. "Reconsideration of the Missions and Functions of the Deputy Director (Research)," July 3, 1962, 2000 CIA Release.

19. Lt. Gen. Marshall Carter, Deputy Director, HN 1-23, "Deputy Director (Research)," July 30, 1962.

20. Ibid.; Col. Stanley W. Beerli, Assistant Director for Special Activities, Office of Special Activities, OSA HQS Notice No. 1-16, June 20, 1962.

21. Interview with Albert Wheelon, Montecito, California, November 11–12, 1998.

22. Ray S. Cline, *Secrets, Spies, and Scholars: The Essential CIA* (Washington, D.C.: Acropolis, 1976), pp. 4, 54–55, 105, 120, 123, 133, 149, 172, 194; Welzenbach, "Science and Technology," p. 23.

23. Welzenbach, "Science and Technology," pp. 22–23; Cline, *Secrets, Spies, and Scholars*, p. 200.

24. "Reconsideration of the Missions and Functions of the Deputy Director (Research)." Helms did not object to the DDR's conducting "agent-oriented" research that would be useful to the Plans directorate. (John A. Bross, Memorandum for: Deputy Director of Central Intelligence, Subject: [Deleted], December 21, 1962, NARA, RG 263, 1998 CIA Release, Box 47, Folder 15.)

25. Telephone interview with Edward Giller, June 29, 1999; Wheelon interview.

26. "ORD Milestones," September 1966, NARA, TRB, RG 263, 1998 CIA Release, Box 66, Folder 5; "Missions and Responsibilities of the Office of Research and Development," September 26, 1962, NARA, RG 263, 1998 CIA Release, Box 66, Folder 4.

27. "Missions and Responsibilities of the Office of Research and Development."

28. John Marks, *The Search for the "Manchurian Candidate": The CIA and Mind Control* (New York: Norton, 1991), pp. 210, 224; telephone conversation with Bud Wheelon, January 28, 2000.

29. Marks, *The Search for the "Manchurian Candidate,"* pp. 224–225.

30. Ibid., p. 225.

31. Ibid., pp. 225–226.

32. Henry G. Plaster, "Snooping on Space Pictures," *Studies in Intelligence* 8, 4 (Fall 1964): 31–39 at 34; Peter A. Gorin, "ZENIT: The Response to CORONA," in Dwayne A. Day, John M. Logsdon, and Brian Latell (eds.), *Eye in the Sky: The Story of the CORONA Spy Satellites* (Washington, D.C.: Smithsonian, 1998), pp. 157–170 at p. 162.

33. Donald C. Brown, "On the Trail of Hen House and Hen Roost," *Studies in Intelligence* 13, 2 (Spring 1969): 11–19 at 11; Chris Pocock, *The U-2 Spyplane: Toward the Unknown* (Atglen, Pa.: Schiffer Books, 2000), pp. 172–174.

34. Brown, "On the Trail of Hen House and Hen Roost," p. 12.

35. Ibid., pp. 12–13.

36. Gene Poteat, "Stealth, Countermeasures, and ELINT, 1960–1975," *Studies in Intelligence* 42, 1 (1998): 51–59 at 53.

37. Ibid.

38. Ibid.

39. Ibid., p. 55.

40. Ibid.

41. Ibid.

42. Ibid.

43. Ibid.

44. Ibid., pp. 55–56.

45. Ibid., p. 56.

46. Ibid.

47. Robert A. McDonald, "CORONA: Success for Space Reconnaissance, a Look into the Cold War, and a Revolution in Intelligence," *Photogrammetric Engineering and Remote Sensing* 60, 6 (June 1995): 689–720 at 715–716.

48. Gregory W. Pedlow and Donald E. Welzenbach, *The Central Intelligence Agency and Overhead Reconnaissance: The U-2 and OXCART Programs, 1954–1974* (Washington, D.C.: CIA, 1992), p. 200.

49. Ibid., pp. 200–201.

50. Dino Brugioni, *Eyeball to Eyeball: The Inside Story of the Cuban Missile Crisis* (New York: Random House, 1991), p. 105.

51. Pedlow and Welzenbach, *The Central Intelligence Agency and Overhead Reconnaissance*, p. 205.

52. Ibid., p. 206.

53. Ibid., pp. 206–207.

54. Interview with Jack C. Ledford, Arlington, Virginia, October 7, 1999.

55. Ibid.; United States Air Force, Biography: Brigadier General Jack C. Ledford, n.d.

56. Pedlow and Welzenbach, *The Central Intelligence Agency and Overhead Reconnaissance*, p. 207.

57. Ibid.; *Office of Special Projects, 1965–1970, Volume One, Chapters I-II* (Washington, D.C.: CIA, 1973), p. 100; Ledford interview.

58. Pedlow and Welzenbach, *The Central Intelligence Agency and Overhead Reconnaissance*, pp. 207–208.

59. Capt. Sanders A. Laubenthal, *The Missiles in Cuba, 1962: The Role of SAC Intelligence* (Offutt AFB, Nebr.: Strategic Air Command, 1984), pp. 22–26.

60. Pedlow and Welzenbach, *The Central Intelligence Agency and Overhead Reconnaissance*, pp. 208–209.

61. McDonald, "CORONA," p. 700; Director of Central Intelligence, SNIE 13-2-63, "Communist China's Advanced Weapons Program," July 24, 1963, pp. 4, 5–6; National Photographic Interpretation Center, CIA, "Search for Uranium Mining in the Vicinity of A-Ko-Su, China," August 1963, in Kevin Ruffner (ed.), *CORONA: America's First Satellite* (Washington, D.C.: CIA, 1995), pp. 175–183 at p. 176.

62. National Photographic Interpretation Center, CIA, "Chronological Developments of the Kapustin Yar/Vladimirovka and Tyuratam Missile Test Centers, USSR, 1957 Through 1963," November 1963, in Ruffner (ed.), *CORONA*, pp. 191–196 at pp. 192–193; National Photographic Interpretation Center, CIA, "Suspect CW Agent Production Plants—Dzerzhinsk USSR, Changes Since 1962," August 1963, in Ruffner (ed.), *CORONA*, pp. 185–189; National Photographic Interpretation Center, CIA, "Probable Solid Propellants Testing Facilities and Associated Explosives Plants in the USSR," December 1963, in Ruffner (ed.), *CORONA*, pp. 197–214 at pp. 199, 213.

63. Pedlow and Welzenbach, *The Central Intelligence Agency and Overhead Reconnaissance*, p. 289.

64. Thomas P. McIninch, "The OXCART Story," *Studies in Intelligence* 15, 1 (Winter 1971): 1–34 at 11–12.

65. Ibid., pp. 12–13.

66. Ibid., p. 13.

67. Ibid., pp. 13–14; telephone conversation with Albert Wheelon, January 28, 2000.

68. Dwayne A. Day, "The Development and Improvement of the CORONA Satellite," in Dwayne A. Day, John M. Logsdon, and Brian Latell (eds.), *Eye in the Sky: The Story of the CORONA Spy Satellites* (1998), pp. 48–85 at pp. 75–77; McDonald, "CORONA," p. 695.

69. Interview with a former CIA official; Welzenbach, "Science and Technology," p. 24.

70. Dwayne A. Day, "A Failed Phoenix: The KH-6 LANYARD Reconnaissance Satellite," *Spaceflight* 39, 5 (May 1997): 170–174, McDonald, "CORONA," p. 694.

71. Day, "A Failed Phoenix."

72. Frederic C.E. Oder, James C. Fitzpatrick, and Paul E. Worthman, *The CORONA Story* (Washington, D.C.: NRO, 1987), p. 92; Welzenbach, "Science and Technology," p. 26; Herbert Scoville Jr., letter to John A. McCone, April 25, 1963.

73. Herbert Scoville Jr., letter to John A. McCone, April 25, 1963.

74. Roswell Gilpatric, Deputy Secretary of Defense, to Allen W. Dulles, Director of Central Intelligence, September 6, 1961.

75. Robert Perry, *A History of Satellite Reconnaissance, Volume 5: Management of the National Reconnaissance Program, 1960–1965* (Washington, D.C.: NRO, 1969), pp. 42, 47, 51.

76. Ibid., p. 49.

77. Ibid., pp. 49–50; interview with Joseph V. Charyk, June 1, 1999; Herbert R. Scoville Jr., Deputy Director (Research), Memorandum for Dr. Charyk, Subject: SecDef-DCI Agreement on NRO, April 20, 1962.

78. "Agreement Between Secretary of Defense and the Director of Central Intelligence on Responsibilities of the National Reconnaissance Office," May 2, 1962; *Office of Special Projects, 1965–1970, Volume Four: Appendixes B, C, & D & Annex I* (Washington, D.C.: CIA, 1973), p. 6 in CAL Records 2/A/0077; Perry, *A History of Satellite Reconnaissance, Volume 5*, pp. 51–52.

79. Joseph V. Charyk, Memorandum for: NRO Program Directors, NRO Staff, Subject: (S) Organization and Functions of the NRO, July 23, 1962; Gerald K. Haines, *The National Reconnaissance Office: Its Origins, Creation, and Early Years* (Washington, D.C.: NRO, 1997), p. 22; Martin interview; Secretary of the Air Force/Public Affairs, "Biography: Major General John L. Martin, Jr."; telephone interview with Albert Wheelon, May 19, 1997; interview with a former CIA official; Jeffrey T. Richelson, "The Wizards of Langley: The CIA's Directorate of Science and Technology, 1962–1996," *Intelligence and National Security* 12, 1 (January 1997): 82–103; Organization Chart, Office of Special Activities, July 1962; *GRAB: Galactic RAdiation and Background* (Washington, D.C.: NRL, 1997); Dwayne A. Day, "Listening from Above: The First Signals Intelligence Satellite," *Spaceflight* 41, 8 (August 1999): 339–346.

80. Col. John L. Martin Jr., Memorandum for the Record, Subject: 22–23 May Conference on NRO, May 24, 1962; Perry, *A History of Satellite Reconnaissance, Volume 5*, p. 53.

81. Perry, *A History of Satellite Reconnaissance, Volume 5*, p. 61.

82. Ibid., pp. 61, 63–64.

83. Herbert Scoville Jr., Memorandum for: Director, National Reconnaissance Office, Subject: Comments on Organization and Functions of NRO, August 29, 1962.

84. Wheelon interview; interview with John McMahon, Los Altos, California, November 17, 1998.

85. Wheelon interview; McMahon interview.

86. Interview with Edward Giller, June 29, 1999; Wheelon, "Genesis of a Unique National Capability."

87. Scoville, Comments on Organization and Functions of NRO.

88. Perry, *A History of Satellite Reconnaissance, Volume 5*, p. 67.

89. Ibid., pp. 67, 73.

90. Ibid., pp. 71–73.

91. Ibid., p. 73–74.

92. Ibid., p. 74; Wheelon, "Genesis of a Unique National Capability."

93. Perry, *A History of Satellite Reconnaissance, Volume 5*, p. 75.

94. Ibid.

95. National Security Council Intelligence Directive No. 5, "U.S. Espionage and Counterintelligence Activities Abroad," January 18, 1961.

96. Oder, Kirkpatrick, and Worthman, *The CORONA Story*, pp. 90–91; telephone interview with Brockway McMillan, September 15, 1999; Buzard interview.

97. Perry, *A History of Satellite Reconnaissance, Volume 5*, p. 78.

98. Ibid., p. 91; Joseph Charyk, "A Summary Review of the National Reconnaissance Office," February 25, 1963.

99. Perry, *A History of Satellite Reconnaissance,* pp. 93, 96–97.

100. l. Edward Giller, Assistant Deputy Director, Research, Memorandum for the Record, Subject: Meeting Between Mr. McCone and Dr. McMillan–21 March 1963, March 22, 1963, NRO CAL Records, 1/E/0011. Perhaps McCone believed the agreement was more workable because he did not see it as significantly limiting his authority over the DNRO. Thus, in the same meeting, he also voiced his displeasure to Charyk's successor about the state of the satellite reconnaissance program. He also wanted to know if certain instructions he had given to the DNRO had been carried out, obtained a promise from the DNRO to produce a new launch schedule for presentation to the USIB, and instructed him to involve the NRO in the aerial portion of the NRP.

101. John A. McCone, Director of Central Intelligence, and Roswell Gilpatric, "Agreement between the Secretary of Defense and the Director of Central Intelligence on Management of the National Reconnaissance Program," March 13, 1963, p. 1.
102. Ibid., pp. 1–2.
103. Ibid., pp. 3–4.
104. Perry, *A History of Satellite Reconnaissance, Volume 5*, pp. 93–96.
105. Oder, Fitzpatrick, and Worthman, *The CORONA Story*, p. 92; Buzard interview.
106. Oder, Fitzpatrick, and Worthman, *The CORONA Story*, p. 92.
107. Ibid.
108. Ibid.
109. Interview with Herbert Scoville, McLean, Virginia, 1983.
110. Giller interview.

Chapter 3: A New Beginning

1. Donald E. Welzenbach, "Science and Technology: Origins of a Directorate," *Studies in Intelligence* 30, 2 (Summer 1986): 13–26 at 24; interview with John McMahon, Los Altos, California, November 17, 1998.
2. Welzenbach, "Science and Technology," p. 24.
3. Ibid., pp. 24–25.
4. Ibid., pp. 25–26.
5. Ibid., p. 26; Albert D. Wheelon, "Genesis of a Unique National Capability," December 19, 1984, address at CIA, p. 12; CIA, HN 20-49, "Announcement of Assignment to Key Position Deputy Director (Intelligence)," June 4, 1962.
6. Central Intelligence Agency, *R. V. Jones Intelligence Award Ceremony Honoring Dr. Albert Wheelon*, December 13, 1994; Central Intelligence Agency, "Biographic Profile, Albert Dewell Wheelon," May 10, 1966; interview with Albert Wheelon, Montecito, California, November 11–12, 1998; Robert P. Crease and Charles C. Mann, *The Second Creation: Makers of the Revolution in 20th-Century Physics* (New York: Macmillan, 1986), p. 175.
7. Vita, Albert D. Wheelon, April 10, 1999.
8. Wheelon interview; Wheelon, "Genesis of a Unique National Capability," pp. 7–8.
9. Wheelon interview; Wheelon, "Genesis of a Unique National Capability," pp. 8–9; telephone conversation with Bud Wheelon, January 28, 2000.
10. Wheelon interview; telephone conversation with Albert Wheelon, September 16, 1999; Wheelon telephone conversation, January 28, 2000.
11. MSC [Marshall S. Carter], Memorandum for the Director, February 22, 1963.
12. Welzenbach, "Science and Technology," p. 26; Wheelon, "Genesis of a Unique National Capability," p. 12; Wheelon interview; interview with Albert Wheelon, Montecito, California, June 14, 1999.
13. Wheelon interview, June 14, 1999.
14. Ibid.
15. Ibid.
16. Ibid.
17. Ibid.
18. Wheelon, "Genesis of a Unique National Capability," pp. 12–13; Wheelon interview, June 14, 1999; Welzenbach, "Science and Technology," p. 26.
19. Lt. Gen. Marshall S. Carter, Acting DCI, HN 1-36, August 5, 1963, NARA, CIA HRP 89-2, RG 263, NN3-263-94-010, Box 5, HS/HC 706, Folder 7; Diary Notes for Colonel White, August 6, 1963, 2000 CIA Release.

20. Interview with Brig. Gen. Jack C. Ledford, Arlington, Virginia, October 7, 1999.

21. Lt. Gen. Marshall S. Carter, Acting DCI, HN 1-36, August 5, 1963.

22. Wheelon interview, May 11–12, 1998.

23. Telephone interview with Albert Wheelon, April 2, 1997; Wheelon interview, June 14, 1999; interview with Karl Weber, Oakton, Virginia, May 5, 1999.

24. John Ranelagh, *The Agency: The Rise and Decline of the CIA, from Wild Bill Donovan to William Casey* (New York: Simon & Schuster, 1986), p. 491; interview with Albert Wheelon, Montecito, California, March 21, 2000.

25. Ray S. Cline, *Secrets, Spies, and Scholars: Blueprint of the Essential CIA* (Washington, D.C.: Acropolis Books, 1976), pp. 199–200. The battle over OSI was the most important but not the only dispute between Cline and Wheelon. They also clashed over the role of Cline's Collection Guidance Staff and the related issues of the location of the Special Intelligence Staff and the intelligence directorate's access to information about DS&T reconnaissance activities. Wheelon described the conflict over the Collection Guidance Staff as one of Cline's "petty bureaucratic gambits." Of more concern to Wheelon was Cline's drafting of an OSI analyst to help produce an assessment in October 1963 of the significance of Soviet leader Nikita Khrushchev's remarks on abandoning the race to the moon. In a memo to OSI chief Donald Chamberlain, Wheelon noted that Cline had not consulted him (Wheelon) or his deputy (Carl Duckett), nor had he shown Wheelon a copy of the assessment before it was distributed. In his memo, Wheelon noted that "I raised this with Cline yesterday and told him this would have to stop." He instructed Chamberlain to inform everyone in OSI not to take any assignments from Cline unless "you . . . or your designated officer, are in the loop."One battle that was not joined was an attempt to transfer NPIC from Cline's directorate to the DS&T. A December 1963 memo to Wheelon asked him if he had "given thought to . . . Indian wrestling Ray Cline for control of NPIC." The justification offered was NPIC's inactivity in the research and development area. However, Wheelon felt that he already "had enough trouble with Cline," and fighting for NPIC would not be worth a "bruising fight." The best thing the DS&T could do for NPIC, Wheelon believed, was to "give them really good pictures." (Ray S. Cline, Memorandum for: Deputy Director of Central Intelligence, Subject: Rationale for a Central Collection Guidance Function, February 28, 1964; Ray S. Cline [DDI], Memorandum for: Director of Central Intelligence, Subject: Differences of Opinion Regarding Collection Guidance Staff [CGS], March 13, 1964; interview with Albert Wheelon, Montecito, California, November 11–12, 1998; Albert D. Wheelon, Deputy Director for Science and Technology, Memorandum for: Assistant Director/Scientific Intelligence, Subject: Coordination with DD/I, October 31, 1963, 2000 CIA Release; [Deleted], Acting Assistant Director, Special Activities, Memorandum for: Deputy Director (Science and Technology), Subject: National Photographic Interpretation Center, December 31, 1963, 2000 CIA Release; telephone conversation with Albert Wheelon, March 5, 2001.)

26. Systems Analysis Staff, Directorate of Science and Technology, CIA, *A Report on DS&T Intelligence Collection Requirements*, July 12, 1966, p. 7; China Task Force, Central Intelligence Agency, "The Production Effort," July 1965–June 1967, p. 20, NARA, RG 263, CIA HRP 89-2, NN3-263-94-010, Box 9, File HS/HC 735, Folder 2.

27. Wheelon telephone conversations, September 16, 1999, and June 16, 2000.

28. Office of Scientific Intelligence, CIA, *Japanese Nuclear Energy Program*, OSI-SR/65-55, November 1964; Office of Scientific Intelligence, CIA, *Indian Nuclear Energy Program,* November 6, 1964; Office of Scientific Intelligence, Central Intelligence Agency, *Soviet Nuclear Research Reactors*, OSI-SR/64-41, September 22, 1964.

29. Director of Central Intelligence, NIE 11-2-64, *The Soviet Atomic Energy Program*, July 16, 1964, p. 3; Director of Central Intelligence, NIE 11-2A-65, *The Soviet Atomic Energy Program*, May 19, 1965.

30. Donald F. Chamberlain, Director of Scientific Intelligence, Memorandum for: Mr. Charles E. Johnson, Staff Member, National Security Council, Subject: The Nuclear Weapons Capability, October 18, 1965.

31. Weber interview.

32. George McGhee to Secretary of State Dean Rusk, "Anticipatory Action Pending Chinese Demonstration of a Nuclear Capability," September 13, 1961, NARA, RG 59, Records of Policy Planning Staff, 1957–1961; "Telegram from State Department to Embassy in Soviet Union," July 15, 1963, in David M. Mabon and David S. Patterson (eds.), *Foreign Relations of the United States [FRUS], 1961–1963, Volume VII: Arms Control and Disarmament* (Washington, D.C.: Government Printing Office, 1996), p. 801; "Telegram from Embassy in Soviet Union to State Department," July 27, 1963, in Mabon and Patterson (eds.), *FRUS, 1961–1963, Volume VII*, p. 860. Rusk's rejection of the McGhee proposal is noted in handwritten comments that appear on the document.

33. Director of Central Intelligence, SNIE 13-2-63, *Communist China's Advanced Weapons Program*, July 24, 1963, p. 1.

34. John Wilson Lewis and Xue Litai, *China Builds the Bomb* (Stanford, Calif.: Stanford University Press, 1988), p. 114; Joel Ullom, "Enriched Uranium Versus Plutonium: Proliferant Preferences in the Choice of Fissile Material," *Nonproliferation Review* 2, 1 (Fall 1994): 1–15 at 1, 5.

35. Director of Central Intelligence, SNIE 13-2-63, *Communist China's Advanced Weapons Program*, p. 1.

36. Ibid., pp. 2, 4; Lewis and Xue, *China Builds the Bomb*, pp. 134–135.

37. SNIE 13-2-63, *Communist China's Advanced Weapons Program*, p. 2.

38. Gen. Maxwell Taylor, Memorandum for General LeMay et al., "Chinese Nuclear Development," November 18, 1963, NARA, RG 218, Taylor Papers, Box 1.

39. Johnson's study remains classified but is concisely summarized in George W. Rathjens, "Destruction of Chinese Nuclear Weapons Capabilities," December 14, 1964. The paper was produced by Rathjens while he was a staff member of the Arms Control and Disarmament Agency.

40. Robert S. Norris, Andrew S. Burrows, and Richard W. Fieldhouse, *Nuclear Weapons Databook Volume V: British, French, and Chinese Nuclear Weapons* (Boulder, Colo.: Westview, 1994), p. 333.

41. Director of Central Intelligence, SNIE 13-4-64, *The Chances of an Imminent Communist Chinese Nuclear Explosion*, August 26, 1964, p. 1.

42. Ibid., p. 2.

43. Interview with Albert Wheelon, Washington, D.C., April 9, 1997.

44. Interview by William Burr with Allen S. Whiting, Crystal City, Virginia, December 13, 1996; interview with former CIA official, April 7, 1997.

45. "Transcript of Daily Press Briefing, Tuesday, September 29, 1964," RG 59, Records of Special Assistant to Undersecretary for Political Affairs, 1963–1965, Box 2, Psychological Preparations of Chinese Test, October 16, 1964.

46. Donald Chamberlain, AD/SI to DDCI, Subject: Estimated Imminence of a Chinese Nuclear Test, October 15, 1964, in Harriet Dashiell Schwar (ed.), *Foreign Relations of the United States 1964–1968, Volume XXX, China*, (Washington, D.C.: U.S. Government Printing Office, 1998), pp. 107–108.

47. Ibid.

48. Glenn T. Seaborg with Benjamin S. Loeb, *Stemming the Tide: Arms Control in the Johnson Years* (Lexington, Mass.: Lexington Books, 1986), p. 116; V. Gupta and D. Rich, "Locating the Detonation of China's First Nuclear Explosive Test on 16 October 1964," *International Journal of Remote Sensing* 17, 10 (October 1996): 1969–1974.

49. Norris, Burrows, and Fieldhouse, *Nuclear Weapons Databook, Volume V*, p. 345; Willis Armstrong, William Leonhart, William J. McCaffrey, and Herbert C. Rothenberg, "The Hazards of Single-Outcome Forecasting," *Studies in Intelligence* 28, 3 (Fall 1984): 57–70, reprinted in H. Bradford Westerfield (ed.), *Inside the CIA's Private World: Declassified Articles from the Agency's Internal Journal 1955–1992* (New Haven: Yale University Press, 1995), pp. 238–254 at p. 246; Wheelon interview, April 9, 1997.

50. Letter, B. A. Schriever, Commander, Air Force Systems Command, to General Curtis E. LeMay, December 26, 1963.

51. Office of Computer Services, Directorate of Science and Technology, CIA, *OCS Computer System Planning Report*, June 1, 1965. FMSAC's work was aided by help from outside specialists—from contractors as well as the national labs that analyzed the radar signatures and telemetry of satellites and missiles. Telemetry of Soviet reconnaissance satellites was analyzed in an attempt to determine their targets. Another group, at Lawrence Livermore National Laboratory, analyzed Soviet and Chinese nuclear weapons programs. (Albert D. Wheelon, Memorandum for: Director, BPAM, Subject: Replies for Questions by Bureau of the Budget Examiners, November 19, 1964; interview with Albert Wheelon, Montecito, California, November 11–12, 1998.)

52. Albert D. Wheelon and Sidney N. Graybeal, "Intelligence for the Space Race," *Studies in Intelligence* 7, 4 (Fall 1963): 1–13 at 1.

53. Ibid., p. 3.

54. Telephone interview with Edward Proctor, March 16, 1999; Wheelon interview, June 14, 1999; Wheelon interview, November 11–12, 1998.

55. Interview with R. Evans Hineman, Chantilly, Virginia, February 17, 1999; Wheelon interview, April 9, 1997.

56. David S. Brandwein, "The SS-8 Controversy," *Studies in Intelligence* 13, 3 (Summer 1969): 27–35.

57. Ibid.; Director of Central Intelligence, NIE 11-8-63, *Soviet Capabilities for Strategic Attack*, October 18, 1963, p. 12.

58. Wheelon interview, November 11–12, 1998.

59. Interview with former CIA official.

60. Ibid.; Wheelon telephone conversation, September 16, 1999.

61. Wheelon interview, April 9, 1997; telephone conversation with Albert Wheelon, November 29, 1998.

62. Hineman interview.

63. Ibid.

64. Letter, Schriever to LeMay.

65. Ibid.

66. Ibid.

67. Jack E. Thomas, Assistant Chief of Staff, Intelligence, Subject: CIA Foreign Missile and Space Analysis Center, January 2, 1964.

68. Draft of Letter, Gen. Curtis E. LeMay to Gen. B. A. Schriever, AFSC, January 7, 1964.

69. Department of Defense Directive S-5100.43, "Defense Special Missile and Astronautics Center (Defense/SMAC)," April 27, 1964; Richard L. Bernard, "The Defense Special Missile and Astronautics Center," *Cryptologic Spectrum*, Fall 1981, pp. 30–33; Mark Clesh, "Dedication of New Operations Center for DEFSMAC," *Communiqué*, March/April 1998, pp. 42–43.

70. Clesh, "Dedication of New Operations Center for DEFSMAC"; National Security Agency, *A Historical Perspective of DefSMAC with Charles Tevis and Max Mitchell*, 1980 (video); Hineman interview.

71. Nicholas L. Johnson, *Soviet Military Strategy in Space* (London: Jane's, 1987), p. 51; James Harford, *Korolev: How One Man Masterminded the Soviet Drive to Beat America to the Moon* (New York: John Wiley, 1997), pp. 190–200; Director of Central Intelligence, NIE 11-1-65, *The Soviet Space Program*, n.d., pp. 23–24, 28; Director of Central Intelligence, NIE 11-1-67, *The Soviet Space Program*, March 2, 1967, pp. 6–7.

72. Director of Central Intelligence, NIE 11-1-65, *The Soviet Space Program*, p. 27; Director of Central Intelligence, NIE 11-1-67, *The Soviet Space Program*, p. 5.

73. Director of Central Intelligence, NIE 11-1-67, *The Soviet Space Program*, pp. 5–6, 34–35; Harford, *Korolev*, pp. 155–156; William E. Burrows, *Exploring Space: Voyages in the Solar System and Beyond* (New York: Random House, 1990), p. 162.

74. Director of Central Intelligence, NIE 11-1-67, *The Soviet Space Program*, pp. 6, 34–35; Harford, *Korolev*, p. 154; Burrows, *Exploring Space*, p. 134.

75. Hineman interview.

76. Wheelon and Graybeal, "Intelligence for the Space Race," p. 5.

77. Ibid., pp. 4–5.

78. Harford, *Korolev*, p. 152.

79. Frank A. Whitmire and Edward G. Correll, "The Failure of Cosmos 57," *Studies in Intelligence* 10, 3 (Summer 1966): 25–29.

80. Ibid.

81. Ibid.; Director of Central Intelligence, NIE 11-1-67, *The Soviet Space Program*, p. 33.

82. James Burke, "Seven Years to Luna 9," *Studies in Intelligence* 10, 2 (Summer 1966): 1–24 at 20.

83. Ibid.; Burrows, *Exploring Space*, pp. 162–163.

84. Robert C. Berman and John P. Baker, *Soviet Strategic Forces: Requirements and Responses* (Washington, D.C.: Brookings Institution, 1982), p. 104; "Soviets Step Up Testing of First-Line ICBM Systems," *EUCOM Intelligence Report*, April 13, 1966, p. 1.

85. Jerold H. Klaimon, "Reentry Vehicle Analysis," *Studies in Intelligence* 12, 3 (Summer 1968): 23–33.

86. Ibid., p. 24.

87. David S. Brandwein, "Telemetry Analysis," *Studies in Intelligence* 8, 4 (Fall 1964): 21–29 at 23–24.

88. Ibid., p. 24.

89. Ibid., pp. 26–27; Klaimon, "Reentry Vehicle Analysis," p. 28.

90. Director of Central Intelligence, NIE 11-8-64, *Soviet Capabilities for Strategic Attack*, October 8, 1964, p. 41.

91. Central Intelligence Agency, *Cost Reduction Program FY 1966-FY 1967*, September 1, 1965, p. 9, NARA, RG 263, HRP 89-2, Box 7, File HS/HC 713.

92. Olav Riste, *The Norwegian Intelligence Service, 1945–1970* (London: Frank Cass, 1999), pp. 149, 158; Rolf Tamnes, *The United States and the Cold War in the High North* (Oslo: Ad Notam, 1991), pp. 211–212.

93. McMahon interview.

94. Hedrick Smith, "U.S. Aides Say Loss of Post in Iran Impairs Missile-Monitoring Ability," *New York Times*, March 2, 1979, pp. A1, A8; Wheelon interview, April 9, 1997.

95. Interview with William H. Nance, Bethesda, Maryland, May 4, 1999.

96. Smith, "U.S. Aides Say Loss of Post in Iran Impairs Missile-Monitoring Ability."

97. Interview with Robert Phillips, Rosslyn, Virginia, June 4, 1999; Nance interview.

98. Nance interview; U.S. Congress, Senate Foreign Relations Committee, *Fiscal Year 1980 International Security Assistance Authorization* (Washington, D.C.: U.S. Government Printing Office, 1979), p. 366; Wheelon interview, April 9, 1997; Phillips interview.

99. Director of Central Intelligence, NIE 11-8-67, *Soviet Capabilities for Strategic Attack*, October 26, 1967, p. 10; Berman and Baker, *Soviet Strategic Forces*, p. 104; Director of Central Intelligence, NIE 11-8-64, *Soviet Capabilities for Strategic Attack*, October 8, 1964, p. 13.

100. "Soviets Step Up Testing of First-Line ICBM Systems," *EUCOM Intelligence Report*, April 13, 1966; "Soviets Maintaining High Launch Rate for Major ICBM's; SS-11 Crew Training May Be Under Way," *EUCOM Intelligence Report*, August 18, 1966; "Series of SS-11 ICBM Tests to Pacific Impact Area Concluded," *EUCOM Intelligence Report*, September 7, 1966.

101. Frank Eliot, "Moon Bounce Elint," *Studies in Intelligence* 11, 2 (Spring 1967): 59–65 at 64.

102. Ibid., p. 60.

103. N. C. Gerson, "SIGINT in Space," *Studies in Intelligence* 28, 2 (Summer 1984): 41–48 at 47; Directorate of Collection, Office, ACS/Intelligence, U.S. Air Force, *History: Directorate of Collection, Office, ACS/Intelligence 1 July 31–December 1962*, n.d., p. 3; Eliot, "Moon Bounce Elint," pp. 60–61.

104. Eliot, "Moon Bounce Elint," pp. 63–64; Donald C. Brown, "On the Trail of Hen House and Hen Roost," *Studies in Intelligence* 13, 2 (Spring 1969): 11–19 at 13.

105. Brown, "On the Trail of Hen House and Hen Roost," pp. 13–14, 19.

106. Eliot, "Moon Bounce Elint," pp. 61, 64.

107. Ibid., pp. 64–65.

108. William H. Nance, "Quality ELINT," *Studies in Intelligence* 12, 2 (Spring 1968): 7–19 at 7–8; Gene Poteat, "Stealth, Countermeasures, and ELINT, 1960–1975," *Studies in Intelligence* 42, 1 (Spring 1998): 51–59 at 54–55. The specific technical characteristics that fall in the power and coverage categories are maximum beam power, total radiated power, antenna gain, and variation in gain (side and back lobe distribution) (Nance, "Quality ELINT," pp. 7–19 at 10.)

109. Nance, "Quality ELINT," p. 15.

110. Ibid., pp. 16–17.

111. Nicholas R. Garofalo, "Present and Future Capabilities of OTH Radars," *Studies in Intelligence* 13, 2 (Spring 1969): 53–61 at 55.

112. Ibid.; "Telegram from the Department of State to the Embassy in Iran," August 25, 1965, in Nina D. Howland (ed.), *Foreign Relations of the United States, 1964–1968, Volume XXII: Iran* (Washington, D.C.: U.S. Government Printing Office, 1999), pp. 166–167.

113. "The Indian Connection," *India Today*, December 31, 1983, p. 10; Wheelon interview, November 11–12, 1998. "The Indian Connection" and other sources have reported this device to be aimed at monitoring Chinese nuclear tests. Wheelon and McMahon recalled that the Himalaya project was to monitor telemetry.

114. Interview with a former CIA official; Wheelon interview, November 11–12, 1998.

115. Interview with a former CIA official; Ben R. Rich and Leo Janos, *Skunk Works: A Personal Memoir of My Years at Lockheed* (Boston: Little, Brown, 1994), p. 182.

116. Interview with Richard Bissell, Farmington, Connecticut, March 16, 1984.

117. Chris Pocock, *Dragon Lady: The History of the U-2 Spyplane* (Shrewsbury, England: Airlife, 1989), p. 98.

118. Ibid.

119. Ibid., p. 100; Gregory W. Pedlow and Donald E. Welzenbach, *The Central Intelligence Agency and Overhead Reconnaissance: The U-2 and OXCART Programs, 1954–1974* (Washington, D.C.: CIA, 1992), p. 282.

120. Pedlow and Welzenbach, *The Central Intelligence Agency and Overhead Reconnaissance*, p. 282; Pocock, *Dragon Lady*, p. 100.

121. Pocock, *Dragon Lady*, p. 100.

122. Ibid., pp. 100–101; R. E. Lawrence and Harry W. Woo, "Infrared Imagery in Overhead Reconnaissance," *Studies in Intelligence* 11, 3 (Summer 1967): 17–40 at 23.

123. Pocock, *Dragon Lady*, p. 111.

124. Ibid., pp. 102–103, 111; Wheelon interview, November 11–12, 1998.

125. Ledford interview. An undated, but clearly pre-1963, "Inspector General's Survey of Air Activities: Summary of Recommendations" (NARA, RG 263, 1998 CIA Release, Box 45, Folder 5), contained the recommendation that the CIA explore "with the U.S. Navy the feasibility and arrangements necessary for staging of missions from aircraft carriers whenever the target lies beyond the range of U.S.-based U-2s."

126. Ledford interview; Pedlow and Welzenbach, *The Central Intelligence Agency and Overhead Reconnaissance*, pp. 247–248.

127. Pocock, *Dragon Lady*, pp. 107–109; Norris, Burrows, and Fieldhouse, *Nuclear Weapons Databook, Volume V*, p. 407; interview with a former CIA official.

128. Wheelon interview, November 11–12, 1998.

129. David Reade, *The Age of Orion: Lockheed P-3, an Illustrated History* (Atglen, Pa.: Schiffer Military/Aviation History, 1998), p. 104; interview with Robert Singel, Great Falls, Virginia, February 25, 1999.

130. Singel interview; Reade, *The Age of Orion*, p. 105; Wheelon interview, June 14, 1999.

131. Reade, *The Age of Orion*, p. 105.

132. Ibid., p. 106.

133. McMahon interview; Wayne Mutza, *Lockheed P2V Neptune: An Illustrated History* (Atglen, Pa.: Schiffer Military/Aviation History, 1996), p. 115; Wheelon interview, November 11–12, 1998; telephone conversation with Albert Wheelon, January 28, 2000.

134. Singel interview; Wheelon interview, June 14, 1999.

135. Reade, *The Age of Orion*, p. 106. By November 1965, the CIA was involved in another program to modify P-2V7 aircraft for intelligence purposes. That month, representatives from ORD and OSA visited E-Systems at Greenville, Texas, to explore the possibility of using the planes as multisensor platforms. A memo noted that the CIA would likely be able to use such an aircraft for reconnaissance of undefended areas where conventional photography was limited because of dense foliage. A March 1966 memo noted that ORD had been directed to run the program and that "the continuation of any OSA program to achieve a low-altitude multi-sensor capability depends directly on the success or failure of this [effort]."The reference to dense foliage and the fact that the NRO was not providing funds for the program suggest that its primary focus was reconnaissance of Southeast Asian territory in support of CIA covert operations. ("Memorandum for the Record, Subject: Visit to [deleted], Project [deleted], November 22, 1965; Memorandum for: see Distribution, Subject: [deleted] Meetings, March 23, 1966, NARA, RG 263, 1998 CIA Release RG 263, Box 45, Folder 5 [both memos]).

136. Wheelon interview, November 11–12, 1998; Wheelon interview, March 21, 2000.

137. Wheelon interview, November 11–12, 1998.

138. Thomas P. McIninch, "The OXCART Story," *Studies in Intelligence* 15 (Winter 1971): 1–34 at 17.

139. Ibid.

140. Ibid., p. 19.

141. Ibid., p. 20; Pedlow and Welzenbach, *The Central Intelligence Agency and Overhead Reconnaissance*, pp. 300–301.

142. McIninch, *The OXCART Story*, p. 20.

143. Ibid., p. 21.

144. Ibid.

145. Ibid., p. 23.

146. Ibid.; Pedlow and Welzenbach, *The Central Intelligence Agency and Overhead Reconnaissance*, pp. 301–302.

147. Pedlow and Welzenbach, *The Central Intelligence Agency and Overhead Reconnaissance*, p. 302.

148. Ibid., p. 307.

149. Ibid.

150. Wheelon interview, November 11–12, 1998.

151. Interview with a former CIA official.

Chapter 4: Space Reconnaissance Wars

1. Interview with a former CIA official.

2. Interview with Albert Wheelon, Washington, D.C., April 9, 1997.

3. Interview with Albert Wheelon, Montecito, California, November 11–12, 1998; Robert Perry, *A History of Satellite Reconnaissance, Volume 5: Management of the National Reconnaissance Program, 1960–1965* (Washington, D.C.: NRO, 1969), pp. 123–124n. in NRO CAL Records, 2/A/0066.

4. Lt. Gen. Marshall S. Carter, DDCI, Memorandum for the Record, Subject: Meeting with Dr. Brockway McMillan, July 23, 1963.

5. Perry, *A History of Satellite Reconnaissance, Volume 5*, p. 120.

6. Office of Public Affairs, Secretary of the Air Force, "General Lew Allen Jr.," September 1981; interview with Gen. Lew Allen Jr., Pasadena, California, June 10, 1999.

7. General Lew Allen Jr. interview.

8. Roswell Gilpatric, Memorandum for the Record, Subject: Mr. McCone's Concerns Regarding NRO, August 22, 1963.

9. *Office of Special Projects, 1965–1970, Volume One, Chapters I-II* (Washington, D.C.: CIA, 1973), pp. 105–106.

10. Letter, Albert D. Wheelon, June 17, 1999.

11. Jonathan McDowell, "Launch Listings," in Dwayne A. Day, John M. Logsdon, and Brian Latell (eds.), *Eye in the Sky: The Story of the CORONA Spy Satellites* (Washington, D.C.: Smithsonian Institution Press, 1998), pp. 235–246 at p. 238.

12. Robert S. McNamara, Secretary of Defense, Memorandum for the Director, National Reconnaissance Office, Subject: Policy Guidance on Management Control over Reconnaissance Programs, October 22, 1963, NRO CAL Records, 1/A/0043.

13. Brockway McMillan, Memorandum for the Director of Central Intelligence, Subject: Management of the CORONA Project, October 28, 1963, NRO CAL Records, 1/A/0044.

14. Wheelon letter.

15. John A. McCone, Memorandum for: General Carter, Dr. Wheelon, September 20, 1963.

16. Brockway McMillan, Director, National Reconnaissance Office, Memorandum for Director of Central Intelligence, Subject: Management of CORONA Project, December 10, 1963, NRO CAL Records, 1/C/0062; Brockway McMillan, Director, National Reconnaissance Office, Memorandum for Director, NRO Program A, Director, NRO Program B, Subject: Responsibility for Operating Management of the CORONA Project, December 10, 1963, NRO CAL Archives, 1/A/0045.

17. Perry, *A History of Satellite Reconnaissance, Volume 5*, p. 134.

18. John A. McCone, Director, to Dr. Brockway McMillan, Director, National Reconnaissance Office, December 13, 1963, NRO CAL Records, 1/A/0047.

19. Albert D. Wheelon, Deputy Director (Science and Technology), Memorandum for: Director of Central Intelligence, Subject: Recommendation re Fubini's proposal, February 3, 1964, NRO CAL Records, 1/C/0067.

20. Brockway McMillan, Director, National Reconnaissance Office, to John McCone, February 4, 1964.

21. Albert D. Wheelon, Deputy Director (Science and Technology), Memorandum for: DCI, DDCI, Subject: Dissolution of CORONA Project Office, March 13, 1964, NRO CAL Records 1/C/0070.

22. Cyrus Vance, Deputy Secretary of Defense, to Lt. Gen. Marshall S. Carter, DDCI, August 28, 1964, NRO CAL Records 1/A/0063.

23. Cyrus R. Vance to John McCone, October 15, 1964, NRO CAL Records; [Deleted] to Albert Wheelon, October 22, 1964, NRO CAL Records, 1/C/0064.

24. Brig. Gen. Jack Ledford, USAF Assistant Director, Special Activities, Memorandum for the Record, Subject: Unsolved Management and Relationship, November 9, 1964, NRO CAL Records, 1/C/0087.

25. John A. McCone, Memorandum for: Honorable Cyrus R. Vance, Deputy Secretary of Defense, Subject: CIA Program B Participation in CORONA, November 17, 1964, NRO CAL Records, 1/A/0079.

26. Lt. Gen. Marshall S. Carter, Deputy Director, to Dr. Brockway McMillan, Director, National Reconnaissance Office, November 17, 1964, NRO CAL Records, 1/A/0080.

27. Directorate of Science and Technology, CIA, *CORONA Program History, Volume II: Governmental Activities*, May 19, 1976, pp. 1–19, in NRO CAL Records, 2/A/0089.

28. Brockway McMillan to [Deleted], June 14, 1965, NRO CAL Records, 1/A/0010.

29. "Examples of the Air Force Impacts on the CORONA Program," March 31, 1965, NRO CAL Records, 1/C/0010.

30. Marshall S. Carter, Lt. Gen. USA, Deputy Director, Memorandum for the Record, Subject: Meeting with Mr. Vance and Dr. McMillan, on Thursday, 25 March, March 26, 1965, NRO CAL Records, 1/A/0096.

31. Ibid.; Jackson D. Maxey, Chief, Special Projects Staff, Memorandum for the Record, Subject: Fact Sheet Regarding the Allegation That Since August 1964 CIA Has Been Withholding Payload Data from the Air Force in the CORONA Program, March 25, 1965, in NRO CAL Records, 1/C/0099.

32. Carter, Memorandum for the Record, Subject: Meeting Mr. Vance and Dr. McMillan.

33. Ibid.

34. "Robert Harry Mathams—Hands-on Intelligence Analyst," n.d.

35. Wheelon interview, November 11–12, 1998.

36. Ibid.

37. Interview with Roy Burks, North Potomac, Maryland, May 10, 1999; Sayre Stevens, "The Soviet BMD Program," in Ashton B. Carter and David N. Schwartz (eds.), *Ballistic Missile Defense* (Washington, D.C.: Brookings Institution, 1984), pp. 182–220 at 192.

38. *United States of America, Plaintiff v. William Peter Kampiles, Defendant,* United States District Court, Northern District of Indiana, Hammond Division, Testimony of Leslie Dirks, November 13, 1978, p. 4.

39. Burks interview; Wheelon interview, November 11–12, 1998.

40. Public Affairs Staff, "Biographical Information on William J. Perry," April 15, 1999; Wheelon interview, November 11–12, 1998; CIA Public Affairs Staff, "DCI Tenet Presents Dr. William J. Perry with Prestigious R. V. Jones Intelligence Award," April 15, 1999. In presenting him with the award, DCI George Tenet noted Perry's "leadership in promoting, modifying, and upgrading our national SIGINT capabilities are legendary." (CIA Public Affairs Staff, "DCI Tenet Presents Dr. William J. Perry with Prestigious R. V. Jones Intelligence Award," April 15, 1999.)

41. Wheelon interview, November 11–12, 1998; Desmond Ball, *Pine Gap: Australia and the U.S. Geostationary SIGINT Satellite Program* (Sydney: Allen & Unwin, 1988), p. 13; Desmond Ball, *A Suitable Piece of Real Estate: American Installations in Australia* (Sydney: Hale & Iremonger, 1980), p. 73; Philip Klass, "U.S. Monitoring Capability Impaired," *Aviation Week and Space Technology*, May 14, 1979, p. 18; telephone conversation with Albert Wheelon, February 8, 2000. Wheelon later recalled how some subordinates told him they were going to establish a committee to pick a code name for the project. Wheelon told them that by the time the name was chosen, the system would be built. Wheelon later noted that he was "impatient, intolerant" with regard to such "traditional time wasters." (Albert Wheelon, Washington, D.C., April 9, 1997.)

42. Wheelon interview, June 14, 1999.

43. McMillan interview; Wheelon interview, November 11–12, 1998, Christopher Anson Pike, "CANYON, RHYOLITE, and AQUACADE: U.S. Signals Intelligence Satellites in the 1970s," *Spaceflight* 37, 11 (November 1995): 381–383; Wheelon telephone interview, April 2, 1997; interview with John McMahon, Los Altos, California, November 17, 1998; Brockway McMillan, Memorandum for the Secretary of Defense, Subject: Comments on NRO and NRP, September 30, 1965, pp. 8–9. Both CANYON and RHYOLITE satellites were to orbit the earth once every twenty-four hours—which is what made them geosynchronous. RHYOLITE, but not CANYON, was geostationary because with virtually a zero-degree inclination, it essentially hovered over a single point at an altitude of 22,300 miles, whereas CANYONs traced a figure eight—drifting from about ten degrees below the equator to ten degrees above. In addition, the perigee and apogee of the orbit were approximately 19,000 and 24,000 miles.

44. Buzard interview.

45. Desmond Ball, *Pine Gap*, p. 55; interview with a former CIA official.

46. Desmond Ball, *Pine Gap*, p. 56.

47. Wheelon interview, April 9, 1997; telephone conversation with Albert Wheelon, October 12, 1999.

48. President's Foreign Intelligence Advisory Board, Memorandum for the President, Subject: National Reconnaissance Program, May 2, 1964, p.2, NRO CAL Records, 6/B/0044.

49. Ibid., p. 2.

50. Ibid., p. 3.

51. Cyrus Vance, Memorandum for McGeorge Bundy, Subject: Memorandum for the President, by the President's Foreign Intelligence Advisory Board, re National Reconnaissance Program, June 2, 1964, LBJ Library, National Security File, Intelligence File, NRO, Box 9.

52. J. Patrick Coyne, Memorandum for Mr. Bundy, Subject: National Reconnaissance Program, June 15, 1964, LBJ Library, National Security File, Intelligence File, "NRO," Box 9.

53. Spurgeon M. Keeny Jr., Memorandum for Mr. Bundy, July 2, 1964, LBJ Library, National Security File, Intelligence File, "NRO," Box 9; telephone interview with Spurgeon Keeny, July 10, 2000; Peter Jessup, "Some Borborygmous Rumblings from the Innards of the NRO," n.d., LBJ Library, National Security File, Intelligence File, "NRO," Box 9. Jessup also noted that the CIA-appointed NRO deputy director, Eugene Kiefer, "is even excluded from the NRO communications routing. When the Air Force has wind that McCone will issue a blast at a USIB meeting, McMillan absents himself and sends Kiefer. The tragicomedy then ensues of McCone blasting his own man."

54. McGeorge Bundy, Memorandum for the Secretary of Defense, the Director of Central Intelligence, Subject: National Reconnaissance Program, n. d., LBJ Library, Intelligence File, NRO, Box 9.

55. John A. McCone, Memorandum for the Record, Subject: Discussion at the NRO Executive Meeting, Attended by McCone, Vance, Fubini, and McMillan, August 12, 1964, NRO CAL Records, 1/A/0062.

56. Directorate of Science and Technology, *CORONA Program History, Volume II: Governmental Activities*, p. 1–18; NRO, *Program Directors of the NRO: ABC&D* (Chantilly, Va.: NRO, 1999), n.p.; Wheelon interview, April 2, 1997. Wheelon recalled that he established the SPS in fall 1963, shortly after he became Deputy Director for Science and Technology. A CIA listing of DS&T staff and office heads gives July 1964 as the official beginning of the staff. The *CORONA Program History* cites September 1 as when the existence of SPS became official.

57. Albert D. Wheelon, Deputy Director for Science and Technology, Memorandum for: Deputy Director of Central Intelligence, Subject: Establishment of a Satellite Office Within the Science and Technology Directorate, February 26, 1965, NRO CAL Records, 2/A/0078.

58. Ibid.

59. Ibid.

60. *Office of Special Projects, 1965–1970, Volume One, Chapters I-II* (Washington, D.C.: CIA, 1973), p. 116.

61. Ibid., p. 118.

62. Perry, *A History of Satellite Reconnaissance, Volume 5*, pp. 186–187.

63. Ibid., p. 187.

64. Ibid., p. 188.

65. Ibid.

66. Ibid., p. 189.

67. Ibid., pp. 174–175, 189.

68. Wheelon letter.

69. John Ranelagh, *The Agency: The Rise and Decline of the CIA, from Wild Bill Donovan to William Casey* (New York: Simon & Schuster, 1986), pp. 413n, 730–731; *Office of Special Projects, 1965–1970, Volume One, Chapters I-II*, p. 120.

70. *Office of Special Projects, 1965–1970, Volume One, Chapters I-II*, p. 6.

71. Albert D. Wheelon, "A Summary of the National Reconnaissance Problem," May 13, 1965, p. 5, NRO CAL Records, 1/D/0008.

72. Ibid., pp. 5–6.

73. Ibid., p. 6.

74. Ibid., pp. 7–10.
75. Ibid., pp. 19–21.
76. Ibid., p. 21.
77. Ibid., pp. 21–22.
78. Ibid., pp. 22–23.
79. Perry, *A History of Satellite Reconnaissance, Volume 5*, p. 195; W. F. Raborn, Director, to Honorable Cyrus R. Vance, Deputy Secretary of Defense, August 13, 1965, NRO CAL Records, 2/A/0078.
80. Cyrus Vance, Deputy Secretary of Defense, and William F. Raborn, Director of Central Intelligence (signatories), "Agreement for Reorganization of the National Reconnaissance Program," August 13, 1965.
81. Ibid.
82. Ibid.; W. F. Raborn, Director of Central Intelligence, to Honorable Cyrus R. Vance, Deputy Secretary of Defense, August 13, 1965, NRO CAL Records, 2/A/0078.
83. Raborn to Vance, August 13, 1965.
84. Ibid.
85. Ibid.; *Office of Special Projects, 1965–1970, Volume One, Chapters I-II*, p. 122.
86. McMillan interview; telephone interview with Albert Wheelon, May 19, 1997; letter from Frank Buzard to author, January 16, 1997; Brockway McMillan, Memorandum for the Secretary of Defense, Subject: Comments on NRO and NRP, pp. 4–5.
87. Directorate of Science and Technology, *CORONA Program History, Volume II, Governmental Activities*, p. 1–20; Frederic C.E. Oder, James C. Fitzpatrick, and Paul E. Worthman, *The CORONA Story* (Washington, D.C.: NRO, November 1987), p. 108; Burks interview.
88. Oder, Fitzpatrick, and Worthman, *The CORONA Story*, pp. 103, 105; Ludwell Lee Montague, *General Walter Bedell Smith as Director of Central Intelligence, October 1950-February 1953* (University Park: Pennsylvania State University Press, 1992), pp. 168–169; Wheelon interview, November 11–12, 1998. Sheldon died in 1987 as part of a suicide pact with his wife Alice, a prominent science fiction writer who used the pseudonym James Triptree Jr. He was bedridden and blind at the time. (Patricia Davis, "Bullets End 2 'Fragile' Lives," *Washington Post*, May 20, 1987, pp. A1, A14.)
89. McDowell, "Launch Listings," p. 238; "Appendix A," in Day, Logsdon, and Latell (eds.), *Eye in the Sky*, pp. 231–233 at p. 233.
90. Oder, Fitzpatrick, and Worthman, *The CORONA Story*, p. 109; "Appendix A," in Day, Logsdon, and Latell (eds.), *Eye in the Sky*, p. 233.
91. Buzard letter to author.
92. Perry, *A History of Satellite Reconnaissance, Volume 5*, p. 106; "Actions Under Way Responsive to Purcell Panel Report Recommendations," attachment to Brockway McMillan, Memorandum for the Director, CIA, Subject: Implementation of the Purcell Panel Recommendations, September 11, 1963; Brockway McMillan, Memorandum for the Director, CIA, Subject: Implementation of the Purcell Panel Recommendations, September 11, 1963.
93. John N. McMahon, Memorandum for [Deleted], Subject: References to the Purcell Panel, December 14, 1964; Perry, *A History of Satellite Reconnaissance, Volume 5*, p. 106; "Actions Under Way Responsive to Purcell Panel Report Recommendations," attachment to Brockway McMillan, Memorandum for the Director, CIA, Subject: Implementation of the Purcell Panel Recommendations, September 11, 1963.
94. Purcell Panel Report, p. 3.
95. Interview with a former CIA official; *Office of Special Projects, 1965–1970, Volume One, Chapters I-II*, p. 2.
96. Wheelon interview, April 9, 1997; Wheelon interview, November 11–12, 1998.
97. Perry, *A History of Satellite Reconnaissance, Volume 5*, pp. 130–131; Albert D. Wheelon, Deputy Director (Science and Technology), to Dr. Brockway McMillan, Director, National Recon-

naissance Office, November 5, 1963; telephone conversation with Albert Wheelon, December 26, 1999.

98. Wheelon to McMillan, November 5, 1963; Brockway McMillan, Director, National Reconnaissance Office, to Dr. Albert D. Wheelon, Deputy Director (Science and Technology), November 18, 1963. The picture of this episode as described in an NRO history is significantly different from that indicated by the memos described here. The history claims that by late November, McMillan had become aware of and annoyed about the Drell group's activities, and his reaction was a barbed comment that he would appreciate receiving more advance notice of such activities affecting NRO's mission. Further, he objected to several of Wheelon's concepts as well as the scope of the group's task and therefore would provide no funds for the project. (Perry, *A History of Satellite Reconnaissance, Volume 5*, pp. 131, 206 n.77.)

99. Wheelon interview, November 11–12, 1998; Wheelon interview, April 9, 1997.

100. Ibid.; Wheelon interview, November 11–12, 1998.

101. Wheelon letter.

102. Ibid.; *Office of Special Projects, 1965–1970, Volume I, Chapters I-II*, pp. 2–3; interview with John McMahon, Los Altos, California, November 17, 1998.

103. *Office of Special Projects, 1965–1970, Volume One, Chapters I-II*, pp. 2–3; McMahon interview.

104. Perry, *A History of Satellite Reconnaissance, Volume 5*, pp. 156, 159.

105. Ibid., pp. 159–160.

106. Ibid., p. 160.

107. Ibid., p. 161.

108. Ibid.

109. Ibid., pp. 162, 176; Wheelon letter.

110. John N. McMahon, Memorandum for: [Deleted], Subject: References to the Purcell Panel, December 14, 1964. Not everyone in the CIA involved in CORONA believed it was necessary to build a new search system. Roy Burks, the field technical director for CORONA at the time, questioned whether it would be possible to replace both the CORONA and GAMBIT systems with a single high-resolution search system. Technical intelligence analysts would not be satisfied, and the difference in going from a resolution of four feet to three feet was hundreds of millions of dollars. If the intelligence community was going to retain the high-resolution system in any event, he believed it made sense to keep down the cost of the search system by extending the focal length of CORONA and staying with the Thor booster. He feared that two very expensive systems would not be affordable. (Interview with Roy Burks, North Potomac, Maryland, May 10, 1999.)

111. Telephone interview with Walter Levison, September 17, 1999; McMillan interview; Perry, *A History of Satellite Reconnaissance, Volume 5*, p. 177. McMillan later recalled that MATCHBOX was proposed by someone from IBM. The promise of attaining high resolution with a smaller optical system would permit smaller and less expensive boosters—which greatly appealed to the Pentagon's Office of Systems Analysis. However, according to McMillan, the physics was "crazy." (Interview with Brockway McMillan, September 15, 1999.)

112. Perry, *A History of Satellite Reconnaissance, Volume 5*, pp. 176, 180; Wheelon interview, November 11–12, 1998.

113. Levison interview.

114. Interview with a former CIA official; Levison interview; telephone interview with Frank Madden, November 3, 2000.

115. Col. Paul Worthman, Memorandum for the Record, Subject: Telephone Conversation with Representatives of the Itek Corporation, February 24, 1965.

116. Col. Paul E. Worthman, Memorandum for the Record, Subject: Itek Discussions with Dr. McMillan and Mr. Land, February 25, 1965.

117. McMahon interview; Burks interview; Wheelon interview, November 11–12, 1998; Perry, *A History of Satellite Reconnaissance, Volume 5*, p. 179; McMillan interview, Levison interview; interview with a former CIA official; Brockway McMillan, Memorandum for Mr. Vance, February 25, 1965.

118. McMahon interview.

119. Telephone conversation with Albert Wheelon, April 13, 2000.

120. Wheelon interview, November 11–12, 1998; telephone conversation with Albert Wheelon, February 8, 2000; McMillan interview; Wheelon telephone conversation, April 13, 2000.

121. Perry, *A History of Satellite Reconnaissance, Volume 5*, p. 195.

122. Ibid., pp. 196–197.

123. Ibid., p. 198.

124. Ibid., p. 194.

125. McMahon interview; John N. McMahon, Memorandum for the Record, Subject: Meeting with Mr. Reber [Deleted] re NRO Problems and Issues, Subject: Participation by [Deleted] and [Deleted], 13 September 1965, 1/E/0045.

126. Burks interview.

127. Perry, *A History of Satellite Reconnaissance, Volume 1: CORONA* (Washington, D.C.: NRO, 1969), p. 162. A former CIA official believes AQUILINE was the initial code name, but it was replaced when officials discovered it had been assigned to another project.

128. Albert Wheelon to Richard Helms, August 2, 1966, CIA 2000 Release.

129. Interview with a former CIA official.

Chapter 5: Change of Command

1. Central Intelligence Agency, The R. V. Jones Intelligence Award Ceremony honoring Dr. Albert D. Wheelon, December 13, 1994.

2. Information provided by CIA Public Affairs Staff.

3. Telephone interview with Albert Wheelon, October 12, 1999.

4. Ibid.

5. Telephone interview with Dino Brugioni, May 21, 1996.

6. Telephone interview with Robert Kohler, July 6, 1999.

7. Interview with Robert Singel, Great Falls, Virginia, February 25, 1999.

8. Interview with a former CIA official.

9. Sherry Sontag and Christopher Drew with Annette Lawrence Drew, *Blind Man's Bluff: The Untold Story of American Submarine Espionage* (New York: Public Affairs, 1998), p. 77; Robert P. Berman and John C. Baker, *Soviet Strategic Forces: Requirements and Responses* (Washington, D.C.: Brookings Institution, 1982), pp. 106–108; William J. Broad, *The Universe Below: Discovering the Secrets of the Deep Sea* (New York: Simon & Schuster, 1997), p. 72; Roy Varner and Wayne Collier, *A Matter of Risk: The Incredible Inside Story of the CIA's Hughes* Glomar Explorer *Mission to Raise a Russian Submarine* (New York: Random House, 1978), pp. 11, 15–16; William J. Broad, "Russia Says U.S. Got Sub's Atom Arms," *New York Times*, June 20, 1993, p. 4; Clyde W. Burleson, *The Jennifer Project* (College Station: Texas A&M, 1997), pp. 19–22.

10. Broad, *The Universe Below*, pp. 72–73; Sontag and Drew, *Blind Man's Bluff*, p. 75.

11. Sontag and Drew, *Blind Man's Bluff*, pp. 76–77, 79; Broad, *The Universe Below*, p. 73; "The Great Submarine Snatch," *Time*, March 31, 1975, pp. 20–27; Burleson, *Jennifer Project*, p. 18.

12. Sontag and Drew, *Blind Man's Bluff*, p. 77.

13. Ibid., pp. 52–53; Broad, *The Universe Below*, p. 63.

14. Broad, *The Universe Below*, p. 74; Sontag and Drew, *Blind Man's Bluff*, pp. 80–81.

15. Sontag and Drew, *Blind Man's Bluff*, p. 81; Broad, *The Universe Below*, p. 74.

16. Burleson, *Jennifer Project*, p. 33; "The Great Submarine Snatch."

17. Burleson, *Jennifer Project*, p. 33; "The Great Submarine Snatch."

18. Sontag and Drew, *Blind Man's Bluff*, p. 82.

19. Ibid., p. 84; John Ranelagh, *The Agency: The Rise and Decline of the CIA* (New York: Simon and Schuster, 1986), p. 601.

20. "The Great Submarine Snatch"; Seymour Hersh, "Human Error Is Cited in '74 Glomar Failure," *New York Times*, December 9, 1976, pp. 1, 55.

21. Sontag and Drew, *Blind Man's Bluff*, p. 83.

22. United States Air Force, "Biography: Brigadier General Jack C. Ledford," n.d.; United States Air Force, "Biography: Major General Paul N. Bacalis," n.d.

23. Telephone interview with Gen. Paul N. Bacalis, December 1, 1999.

24. Gregory W. Pedlow and Donald E. Welzenbach, *The Central Intelligence Agency and Overhead Reconnaissance: The U-2 and OXCART Programs, 1954–1974* (Washington, D.C.: CIA, 1992), pp. 251–253; Chris Pocock, *Dragon Lady: The History of the U-2 Spyplane* (Shrewsbury, England: Airlife Publishing, 1989), p. 115.

25. Memorandum for Record, Subject: Resume of C216C, December 12, 1966, 2000 CIA Release.

26. Pocock, *Dragon Lady*, pp. 112–113.

27. Translation of portion of Colonel Li-Liang, *Piercing the Bamboo Curtain from the Sky*, provided by Joe Donoghue.

28. Pocock, *Dragon Lady*, p. 115; Pedlow and Welzenbach, *The Central Intelligence Agency and Overhead Reconnaissance*, p. 253.

29. Pocock, *Dragon Lady*, p. 115.

30. Interview with John McLucas, Washington, D.C., May 25, 1995.

31. Letter, David Packard to Richard M. Helms, December 9, 1969; David Packard, Memorandum for: Dr. McLucas, Subject: Consolidation of CIA and SAC U-2 Fleet (TS), December 8, 1969.

32. Donald H. Ross to [deleted], December 25, 1969, 2000 CIA Release; Col. Charles P. Wilson, *Strategic and Tactical Aerial Reconnaissance in the Near East* (Washington, D.C.: Washington Institute for Near East Policy, 1999), p. 58.

33. Pedlow and Welzenbach, *The Central Intelligence Agency and Overhead Reconnaissance*, p. 256.

34. Pedlow and Welzenbach, *The Central Intelligence Agency and Overhead Reconnaissance*, p. 256; Wilson, *Strategic and Tactical Reconnaissance in the Near East*, p. 58.

35. Pedlow and Welzenbach, *The Central Intelligence Agency and Overhead Reconnaissance*, p. 256; Wilson, *Strategic and Tactical Reconnaissance in the Near East*, p. 58.

36. Pedlow and Welzenbach, *The Central Intelligence Agency and Overhead Reconnaissance*, p. 310; Thomas P. McIninch, "The OXCART Story," *Studies in Intelligence* 15, 1 (Winter 1971): 1–34 at 30; Brig. Gen. Jack C. Ledford, Director (Special Activities), Briefing Note for the Director of Central Intelligence, Subject: Bureau of the Budget Recommendations for the OXCART Program, November 16, 1965.

37. Pedlow and Welzenbach, *The Central Intelligence Agency and Overhead Reconnaissance*, p. 310; McIninch, "The OXCART Story," p. 30; [Deleted] Assistant for Programs, Research and Development, Special Activities, Memorandum for: Director of Special Activities, Subject: Comments to W. R. Thomas III Memorandum to the Director, BOB, July 27, 1966, Draft, 2000 CIA Release.

38. McIninch, "The OXCART Story," p. 23.

39. Pedlow and Welzenbach, *The Central Intelligence Agency and Overhead Reconnaissance*, p. 310; McIninch, "The OXCART Story," p. 31.

40. McIninch, "The OXCART Story," p. 31; Pedlow and Welzenbach, *The Central Intelligence Agency and Overhead Reconnaissance*, p. 309.

41. Pedlow and Welzenbach, *The Central Intelligence Agency and Overhead Reconnaissance*, p. 309.

42. Walter Rostow, Memorandum for the President, December 27, 1966; "OXCART/SR-71 Background Papers," Attachment to Col. Abbot C. Greenleaf, Memorandum for Dr. Foster, Dr. Enthoven, Dr. Flax, Gen. Carroll, Gen. Steakley, January 1968; Pedlow and Welzenbach, *The Central Intelligence Agency and Overhead Reconnaissance*, p. 310; McIninch, "The OXCART Story," p. 31.

43. Pedlow and Welzenbach, *The Central Intelligence Agency and Overhead Reconnaissance*, pp. 302–303, 310.

44. Ibid., pp. 302–303.

45. Director of Central Intelligence, NIE 11-3-67, *Soviet Strategic Air and Missile Defenses*, November 9, 1967, pp. 1, 9, 20–21.

46. Pedlow and Welzenbach, *The Central Intelligence Agency and Overhead Reconnaissance*, p. 303.

47. Ibid.

48. Ibid.

49. Ibid., pp. 303–304.

50. Ibid., pp. 304–305; McIninch, "The OXCART Story," p. 25.

51. Pedlow and Welzenbach, *The Central Intelligence Agency and Overhead Reconnaissance*, p. 305; McIninch, "The OXCART Story," p. 27.

52. Bacalis interview.

53. Paul F. Crickmore, *Lockheed SR-71: The Secret Missions Exposed* (London: Osprey, 1993), pp. 26–28; Pedlow and Welzenbach, *The Central Intelligence Agency and Overhead Reconnaissance*, p. 305; McIninch, "The OXCART Story," p. 27; NPIC, *Black Shield Mission X-001, 31 May 1967,* June 1967, 2000 CIA Release.

54. Pedlow and Welzenbach, *The Central Intelligence Agency and Overhead Reconnaissance*, p. 306; McIninch, "The OXCART Story," pp. 27–28; NPIC, *Black Shield Mission BX-6705, 20 June 1967,* June 1967, 2000 CIA Release; NPIC, *Black Shield Mission BX-6706, 30 June 1967,* July 1967, 2000 CIA Release.

55. Pedlow and Welzenbach, *The Central Intelligence Agency and Overhead Reconnaissance*, p. 307; Crickmore, *Lockheed SR-71,* pp. 30–31.

56. NPIC, *Black Shield Mission BX-6723, 17 September 1967,* November 1967, p. 1, 2000 CIA Release; NPIC, *Black Shield Mission BX-6725, 4 October 1967,* December 1967, pp. 1–2, 2000 CIA Release; NPIC, *Black Shield Mission BX-6732, 28 October 1967,* December 1967, p. 1, 2000 CIA Release.

57. Pedlow and Welzenbach, *The Central Intelligence Agency and Overhead Reconnaissance*, pp. 310–311.

58. 9th SRW, *History of the 9th Strategic Reconnaissance Wing, 1 October–31 December 1967,* n.d., pp. 43–44; Pedlow and Welzenbach, *The Central Intelligence Agency and Overhead Reconnaissance*, p. 310.

59. Pedlow and Welzenbach, *The Central Intelligence Agency and Overhead Reconnaissance*, pp. 310–311.

60. Ibid., p. 311.

61. Paul H. Nitze, Deputy Secretary of Defense, Memorandum for Director, National Reconnaissance Office, Chairman, Joint Chiefs of Staff, Subject: OXCART and SR-71 Operations, December 29, 1967.

62. Pedlow and Welzenbach, *The Central Intelligence Agency and Overhead Reconnaissance*, p. 307; McIninch, "The OXCART Story," p. 28.

63. Crickmore, *Lockheed SR-71*, pp. 32–33.

64. Pedlow and Welzenbach, *The Central Intelligence Agency and Overhead Reconnaissance*, pp. 307, 309; Lt. Gen. Joseph F. Carroll, Director, DIA, Memorandum for the Chairman, Joint Chiefs of Staff, Subject: Requirement for a Second BLACK SHIELD Mission over North Korea, January 29, 1968, LBJ Library, National Security File, Intelligence File, "NRO," Box 9.

65. McIninch, "The OXCART Story," p. 32.

66. Ibid.

67. Ibid., pp. 32–33; Pedlow and Welzenbach, *The Central Intelligence Agency and Overhead Reconnaissance*, p. 313.

68. L. K. White, Deputy Director for Support, "Announcement of Assignment to Key Position, Office of the Deputy Director for Science and Technology," HN 20-115, September 13, 1963; "ORD Milestones," n.d.; Albert D. Wheelon, Deputy Director for Science and Technology, General Notice No. 12, May 5, 1964; L. K. White, Deputy Director for Support, "Announcement of Assignment to Key Position, Office of the Deputy Director for Science and Technology, Office of Research and Development," HN 20-197, March 19, 1965. All NARA, RG 263, 1998 CIA Release, Box 66, Folder 5.

69. John Marks, *The Search for the "Manchurian Candidate": The CIA and Mind Control* (New York: Norton, 1991), p. 227.

70. Michael Warner, CIA History Staff, Memorandum for the Record, Subject: The Central Intelligence Agency and Human Radiation Experiments: An Analysis of the Findings, February 14, 1995, pp. 7–8; Memorandum for: Director of Research and Development, Subject: Transfer of Funds to EARL for Follow-Up Study of Medical Volunteers, February 17, 1971. CIA, congressional, and DOD investigators subsequently could not determine whether such tests ever took place.

71. Interview with Victor Marchetti, October 12, 1999.

72. Ibid.; John Ranelagh, *The Agency*, p. 208.

73. Ranelagh, *The Agency*, p. 208.

74. Memorandum for: [Deleted], [Deleted] Views on Trained Cats [Deleted] for [Deleted] Use, n.d.

75. Interview with a former CIA official.

76. Ibid.

77. Ibid.

78. Ibid.

79. Ibid.; Marchetti interview.

80. Interview with a former CIA official.

81. Kirsten Lundberg, "The SS-9 Controversy: Intelligence as Political Football," Kennedy School of Government, C16-89-884.0, Case Program, 1989, p. 1; William Beecher, "Soviet Missile Deployment Puzzles Top U.S. Analysts," *New York Times*, April 14, 1969, pp. 1, 39.

82. Lundberg, "The SS-9 Controversy," p. 2; John Prados, *The Soviet Estimate: U.S. Intelligence Analysis and Russian Military Strength* (New York: Dial Press, 1982), p. 210; John Newhouse, *War and Peace in the Nuclear Age* (New York: Knopf, 1989), p. 215.

83. Lundberg, "The SS-9 Controversy," p. 2; Prados, *The Soviet Estimate*, pp. 209–210.

84. Lundberg, "The SS-9 Controversy," p. 3; Anne Hessing Cahn, *Killing Détente: The Right Attacks the CIA* (University Park: Pennsylvania State University Press, 1998), p. 93; Prados, *The Soviet Estimate*, p. 208.

85. Director of Central Intelligence, NIE 11-8-68, *Soviet Strategic Attack Forces*, in Donald P. Steury (ed.), *Intentions and Capabilities: Estimates on Soviet Strategic Forces, 1950–1953* (Washington, D.C.: CIA, 1996), pp. 239–251 at pp. 249–250.

86. Lundberg, "The SS-9 Controversy," p. 5.

87. Prados, *The Soviet Estimate*, p. 208.

88. Extracts from David S. Brandwein's Personal Notebook, provided to author.

89. Ibid.

90. Lundberg, "The SS-9 Controversy," pp. 5–6.

91. Ibid., p. 7.

92. Ibid., pp. 7, 11.

93. Ibid., p. 13; Cahn, *Killing Détente*, pp. 93–96.

94. Extract from Brandwein diary, June 6, 1969.

95. Peter Grose, "U.S. Intelligence Doubts First-Strike Goal," *New York Times*, June 19, 1969, pp. 1, 10.

96. Extract from Brandwein diary.

97. Cahn, *Killing Détente*, p. 97; U.S. Congress, Senate Select Committee to Study Governmental Operations with Respect to Intelligence Activities, *Final Report, Book I: Foreign and Military Intelligence* (Washington, D.C.: U.S. Government Printing Office, 1976), p. 78; extract from Brandwein diary. Helms, however, dropped a paragraph from the memo that reemphasized the view that the Soviet Union was not seeking a first-strike capability. An assistant to Laird objected to the paragraph, noting that it was a direct contradiction of Laird's position and he was about to make a speech claiming that an ABM system was essential. Helms complied by dropping the paragraph from the main text, only to have it restored as a footnote by the director of the State Department's Bureau of Intelligence and Research. (Russell Jack Smith, *The Unknown CIA: My Three Decades with the Agency* [New York: Berkley, 1992], p. 243; U.S. Congress, Senate Select Committee to Study Governmental Operations with Respect to Intelligence Activities, *Final Report, Book I: Foreign and Military Intelligence*, p. 78.)

98. Lundberg, "The SS-9 Controversy," p. 13.

99. Ibid., p. 14.

100. "Statement by the Director, Senate Foreign Relations Committee," June 23, 1969, NARA, RG 263, 1998 CIA Release, Box 182, Folder 8.

101. U.S. Congress, Senate Committee on Foreign Relations, *Intelligence and the ABM* (Washington, D.C.: U.S. Government Printing Office, 1969), pp. 3, 13; Lundberg, "The SS-9 Controversy," pp. 16–17.

102. Extract from Brandwein diary.

103. Lundberg, "The SS-9 Controversy," pp. 17–18.

104. Ibid. p. 18; Cahn, *Killing Détente*, p. 98.

105. Nicholas R. Garafalo, "Present and Future Capabilities of OTH Radars," *Studies in Intelligence* 13, 1 (Spring 1969): 53–61 at 55.

106. Ibid., p. 56.

107. Ibid.; Robert S. Norris, Andrew S. Burrows, and Richard W. Fieldhouse, *Nuclear Weapons Databook, Volume V: British, French, and Chinese Nuclear Weapons* (Boulder, Colo.: Westview, 1994), p. 362.

108. Desmond Ball, *Pine Gap: Australia and the U.S. Geostationary Signals Intelligence Satellite Program* (Sydney: Allen & Unwin, 1988), p. 57.

109. Interview with Roy Burks, North Potomac, Maryland, May 10, 1999; interview with John McMahon, Los Altos, California, November 17, 1998.

110. Ball, *Pine Gap*, pp. 57–58, 61.

111. John Noble Wilford, "A Secret Payload Is Orbited by U.S.," *New York Times*, August 7, 1968, p. 7; Air Force Eastern Test Range, *Eastern Test Range Index of Missile Launchings, July 1968–June 1969* (Patrick AFB, Fla.: AFETR, 1969), p. 3; Christopher Anson Pike, "CANYON, RHYOLITE, and AQUACADE," *Spaceflight* 37, 11 (November 1995): 381–383.

112. Pike, "CANYON, RHYOLITE, and AQUACADE"; interview with a former CIA official; Ball, *Pine Gap*, p. 18; Philip J. Klass, "U.S. Monitoring Capability Impaired," *Aviation Week and Space Technology*, May 14, 1979, p. 18.

113. Ball, *Pine Gap*, p. 16.

114. Interview with a former CIA official.

115. Ibid.

116. Interview with Henry Plaster, Vienna, Virginia, September 30, 1999.

117. Interview with a former CIA official.

118. Ibid. A third camera was carried on five HEXAGON missions. The film of this twelve-inch mapping camera was fed into the final film capsule and returned at the end of the mission. A secondary experimental system was used on some early missions to transmit pictures by radio signals—essentially

the same system that had failed when it operated on SAMOS. The results were no better this time, and the system was eventually jettisoned.

119. Ibid.; "Space Reconnaissance Dwindles," *Aviation Week and Space Technology*, October 6, 1980, pp. 18–20.

120. Interview with a former CIA official.

121. Curtis Peebles, "The Guardians," *Spaceflight*, November 1978, pp. 381ff.

122. William Burrows, *Deep Black: Space Espionage and National Security* (New York: Random House, 1986), p. 239.

123. Warren F. Carey and Myles Maxfield, "Intelligence Implications of Disease," *Studies in Intelligence* 16, 1 (Spring 1972): 71–78 at 71.

124. Ibid., pp. 71–72.

125. Ibid., pp. 74, 76.

126. Ibid., p. 76.

127. Ibid., pp. 76–77.

128. Ibid., p. 77.

129. Ibid.

Chapter 6: Empire

1. "Introduction: Producing National Intelligence Estimates," in Donald P. Steury (ed.), *Intentions and Capabilities: Estimates on Soviet Strategic Forces, 1950–1983* (Washington, D.C.: Central Intelligence Agency, 1996), p. xvi.

2. Telephone conversation with Sayre Stevens, November 11, 1998; undated, untitled, CIA summary of functions of selected offices, circa 1975.

3. *The Reminiscences of Arthur C. Lundahl*, Columbia University, Oral History Research Office, 1982, p. 302.

4. Ibid.. p. 303.

5. Ibid., p. 305.

6. Telephone interview with Dino Brugioni, May 21, 1996.

7. Ibid.

8. Interview with R. M. Huffstutler, Falls Church, Virginia, March 23, 1999; Brugioni interview; telephone interview with Edward Proctor, March 16, 1999. According to R. M. "Rae" Huffstutler, there was some opposition to the transfer of NPIC. Dino Brugioni recalled that this opposition included Edward Proctor, the Deputy Director for Intelligence. Proctor recalled that he recommended the transfer.

9. John Ranelagh, *The Agency: The Rise and Decline of the CIA, from Wild Bill Donovan to William Casey* (New York: Simon & Schuster, 1986), pp. 545–546, 732; William Colby and Peter Forbath, *Honorable Men: My Life in the CIA* (New York: Simon & Schuster, 1978), p. 332.

10. Colby and Forbath, *Honorable Men*, pp. 333, 335–336.

11. Interview with John McMahon, Los Altos, California, November 17, 1998; U.S. Congress, Senate Select Committee on Intelligence, *Nomination of John N. McMahon* (Washington, D.C.: U.S. Government Printing Office, 1982), p. 18.

12. McMahon interview.

13. Ibid.

14. Fred Emery, *Watergate: The Corruption of American Politics and the Fall of Richard Nixon* (New York: Times Books, 1994), pp. 52–53; Thomas Powers, *The Man Who Kept the Secrets: Richard Helms and the CIA* (London: Weidenfeld and Nicolson, 1979), p. 253.

15. McMahon interview; Ranelagh, *The Agency*, pp. 552–553.

16. McMahon interview.

17. H. Keith Melton, *CIA Special Weapons and Equipment: Spy Devices of the Cold War* (New York: Sterling Publishing, 1994), pp. 16, 21, 28, 30, 48.

18. Ibid., pp. 64, 66, 68, 70, 72–77, 78–79, 87, 92–93, 96–97.

19. Ibid., pp. 107–109, 110–111. Not all CIA officers were enthralled by every creation of the technical services unit. John Stockwell recalled being handed a slender notebook that included a pad of soluble rice paper, which he could supposedly gobble down if captured. He wrote that "like many OTS gimmicks this was a classroom toy which had little use in the field," explaining that a case officer would not want to make irreplaceable notes on a pad that would dissolve "at the slightest touch of rain or sweat." (John Stockwell, *In Search of Enemies: A CIA Story* [New York: Norton, 1978], p. 98.)

20. U.S. Congress, House Select Committee on Intelligence, *U.S. Intelligence Agencies and Activities: Intelligence Costs and Fiscal Procedures, Part 1* (Washington, D.C.: U.S. Government Printing Office, 1975), p. 543; Memorandum for: Deputy Director for Science and Technology, Subject: Functional Relationships Between the Office of Research and Development and the Office of Development and Engineering, July 18, 1973, NARA, RG 263, 1998 CIA Release, Box 66, Folder 4.

21. *United States of America v. Christopher John Boyce,* Reporter's Transcript, Volume 5, District Court, Central District of California, Hon. Robert J. Kelleher, CR-77-131-RJK, April 20, 1977, pp. 971–972; U.S. Congress, Senate Select Committee on Intelligence, *Nomination of John N. McMahon*, p. 18.

22. Jonathan McDowell, "US Reconnaissance Satellite Programs, Part I: Photoreconnaissance," *Quest* 4, 2 (Summer 1995): 22–31 at 31.

23. Director of Central Intelligence, NIE 11-8-71, *Soviet Forces for Intercontinental Attack*, October 21, 1971, p. 10; Director of Central Intelligence, NIE 11-8-70, *Soviet Forces for Intercontinental Attack*, November 24, 1970, pp. 4–5; Director of Central Intelligence, NIE 11-8-72, *Soviet Forces for Intercontinental Attack*, October 26, 1972, p. 22; Robert P. Berman and John C. Baker, *Soviet Strategic Forces: Requirements and Responses* (Washington, D.C.: Brookings Institution, 1982), pp. 106–107.

24. Philip J. Klass, "U.S. Monitoring Capability Impaired," *Aviation Week and Space Technology*, May 14, 1979, p. 18.

25. Ibid.

26. [James Cunnningham], DD/OSA, Memorandum for: Deputy for Technology/OSA, Subject: A Covert Reconnaissance Satellite, April 17, 1963.

27. Ibid.

28. Interview with a former CIA official.

29. Merton E. Davies and William R. Harris, *RAND's Role in the Evolution of Balloon and Satellite Observation Systems and Related U.S. Space Technology* (Santa Monica, Calif.: RAND, 1988), p. 75.

30. Interview with Albert Wheelon, Montecito, California, March 21, 2000.

31. Interview with a former CIA official; telephone conversation with Albert Wheelon, February 12, 2000.

32. Joint Chiefs of Staff, "Point Paper for Luncheon with President's Foreign Intelligence Advisory Board," June 5, 1970.

33. Donald Neff, *Warriors for Jerusalem: The Six Days That Changed the Middle East* (New York: Simon & Schuster, 1984), pp. 201–202; Ze'ev Schiff, *A History of the Israeli Army: 1874 to the Present* (New York: Macmillan, 1985), pp. 127, 130.

34. Schiff, *A History of the Israeli Army*, pp.133, 134.

35. Neff, *Warriors for Jerusalem*, pp. 203–204; Schiff, *A History of the Israeli Army*, p. 140.

36. Interview with a former CIA official; interview with Robert McNamara, January 20, 1989, Washington, D.C.

37. [Leslie Dirks], Chief, Design and Analysis Division, Office of Special Projects, Subject: Briefing to General Maxwell Taylor on Photographic Satellite Support to Middle East Crisis, 31 August 1967, September 8, 1967.

38. [Leslie Dirks], Chief, Design and Analysis Division, Office of Special Projects, Memorandum for: Director, NRO Staff, Subject: General Maxwell Taylor's Inquiries Concerning the Application of Photographic Satellites in Crisis Situations," September 5, 1967.

39. John N. McMahon, Acting Director of Special Projects, Memorandum for: Director for Science and Technology, Subject: Assessment of KH Information in Light of the Soviet Invasion of Czechoslovakia, August 30, 1968.

40. Interview with a former CIA official; Cynthia Grabo, "The Watch Committee and the National Indications Center: The Evolution of U.S. Strategic Warning," *International Journal of Intelligence and Counterintelligence* 3, 3 (Fall 1989): 363–386.

41. Interview with a former CIA official.

42. Roland S. Inlow, "How the Cold War and Its Intelligence Problems Influenced CORONA Operations," in Robert A. McDonald (ed.), *CORONA: Between the Sun and the Earth, the First NRO Reconnaissance Eye in Space* (Bethesda, Md.: American Society for Photogrammetry and Remote Sensing, 1997), pp. 221–229 at p. 228; remarks of W. Y. Smith at Conference on "Piercing the Curtain: CORONA and the Revolution in Intelligence," May 23–24, 1995, George Washington University, Washington, D.C.

43. Interview with a former CIA official. A dissenting view came from the Office of Strategic Research of the Directorate of Intelligence. OSR was asked to assess what its analysts would have predicted if they had access to the photography throughout the period leading up to the invasion. According to OSR, even access to photography on a daily basis from July 1 to August 19 would not have enabled them to say "with any reasonable certainty that the Soviets were going to invade." (John N. McMahon, Acting Director of Special Projects, Memorandum for: Director for Science and Technology, Subject: Assessment of KH Information in Light of the Soviet Invasion of Czechoslovakia, August 30, 1968.)

44. Ibid.

45. Ibid.

46. Ibid.

47. Bruce C. Clarke Jr., Special Assistant to the DDI for Special Projects, Memorandum for: Mr. Borel et al., Subject: DDI Requirements in Connection with New Reconnaissance System, August 11, 1966; interview with Albert Wheelon, Montecito, California, June 14, 1999.

48. Interview with a former CIA official.

49. Ibid.

50. Ibid.

51. Ibid.; Memorandum for President's File, Subject: President's Foreign Intelligence Advisory Board, Meeting with the President, June 4, 1971.

52. Interview with a former CIA official.

53. Gregory W. Pedlow and Donald E. Welzenbach, *The Central Intelligence Agency and Overhead Reconnaissance: The U-2 and OXCART Programs, 1954–1974* (Washington, D.C.: CIA, 1992), p. 257.

54. U.S. Air Force, "Biography, Brigadier General Wendell L. Bevan Jr.," July 15, 1970, with updates.

55. Secretary of Defense, Memorandum for Director of Central Intelligence, Subject: Management of the U-2R Fleet, n.d.; Pedlow and Welzenbach, *The Central Intelligence Agency and Overhead Reconnaissance*, p. 257.

56. Pedlow and Welzenbach, *The Central Intelligence Agency and Overhead Reconnaissance*, p. 256; Chris Pocock, *Dragon Lady: The History of the U-2 Spyplane* (Shrewsbury, England: Airlife, 1989), p. 119.

57. Pedlow and Welzenbach, *The Central Intelligence Agency and Overhead Reconnaissance*, p. 257; Pocock, *Dragon Lady*, p. 120.

58. Pedlow and Welzenbach, *The Central Intelligence Agency and Overhead Reconnaissance*, p. 257; Pocock, *Dragon Lady*, p. 120; Memo B/Gen Wendell L. Bevan to [deleted], June 26, 1974.

59. CIA Inspector General, *Inspector General's Survey of the Office of Research and Development*, October 1972, pp. 5–6, 74, NARA, RG 263, 1998 CIA Release, Box 66, Folder 2; Sayre Stevens remarks, "DS&T 35th Anniversary: Celebrating 50 Years of CIA History," July 24, 1997, videotape.

60. CIA Inspector General, *Inspector General's Survey of the Office of Research and Development*, pp. 16, 42.

61. Interview with Sayre Stevens, Springfield, Virginia, March 18, 1999; interview with James Hirsch, Fairfax, Virginia, February 12, 1999; Sayre Stevens remarks, "DS&T 35th Anniversary." Not everyone saw the approach of Stevens's predecessor as sterile. Gene Poteat noted that research is always controversial, especially if it is not directed—that is, not targeted on fulfilling a requirement specified by a consumer. But in his view, ORD's search for technological breakthroughs before identifying specific customers led to important discoveries, such as large-scale integrated circuits. (Interview with Gene Poteat, McLean, Virginia, April 25, 2000.)

62. Hirsch interview; Stevens interview; National Foreign Assessment Center, CIA, *The Soviet Earth Resources Satellite Program*, June 1980, p. 8; "Project UPSTREET," CIA Public Affairs Fact Sheet, n.d.

63. Hirsch interview.

64. Stevens interview; Bob Preston, *Plowshares and Power: The Military Use of Civil Space* (Washington, D.C.: National Defense University Press, 1994), pp. 55–56; James B. Campbell, *Introduction to Remote Sensing* (New York: Guilford, 1987), pp. 118–122.

65. Campbell, *Introduction to Remote Sensing*, p. 135.

66. Stevens interview; "Project UPSTREET"; "History Biological Sciences Division—1963 Through 1968," NARA, RG 263, 1998 CIA Release, Box 66, Folder 5.

67. National Foreign Assessment Center, CIA, *The Soviet Earth Resources Satellite Program*, p. 8; "Project UPSTREET."

68. Hirsch interview.

69. Ibid.

70. Stevens interview; CIA Inspector General, *Inspector General's Survey of the Office of Research and Development*, p. 80.

71. Stevens interview, March 18, 1999.

72. Jim Schnabel, *Remote Viewers: The Secret History of America's Psychic Spies* (New York: Dell, 1997), pp. 86, 120; "Harold E. Puthoff," www.firedocs.com/remoteviewing/oooh/people/puthoff.html; "Russell Targ," www.firedocs.com/remoteviewing/oooh/people/targ.html; Martin Gardner, "Distant Healing and Elizabeth Targ," *Skeptical Inquirer,* March/April 2001, pp. 12–14.

73. Schnabel, *Remote Viewers*, p. 87.

74. Martin Gardner, "Zero-Point Energy and Harold Puthoff," *Skeptical Inquirer*, May/June 1998, pp. 13–15, 60; Harold Puthoff, "To Whom It May Concern," May 31, 1970.

75. Kenneth A. Kress, "Parapsychology In Intelligence: A Personal Review and Conclusions," *Studies in Intelligence* 21, 4 (Winter 1977): 7–17 at 8.

76. Ibid.; H. E. Puthoff, "CIA-Initiated Remote Viewing at Stanford Research Institute," *Journal of Scientific Exploration* 10, 1 (1996): 63–76 at 64–65.

77. Schnabel, *Remote Viewers*, p. 97.

78. John D. La Mothe, *Controlled Offensive Behavior—USSR (U)*, (Washington, D.C.: DIA, July 1972). The paper was actually authored by a member of the Medical Intelligence Office, Office of the Surgeon General, Department of the Army, and approved and issued by DIA. La Mothe clearly believed in paranormal phenomena, considered the *National Enquirer* a legitimate research resource and felt it worth quoting the opinion of astrologer Sybil Leek that "there is great danger that within the next ten years the Soviets will be able to steal our top secrets by using out-of-body spies." (p. 30.; also see P. T. Van Dyke and M. L. Juncosa, *Paranormal Phenomena: Briefing on a Net Assessment Study* [Santa Monica, Calif.: RAND, January 1973]).

79. Puthoff, "CIA-Initiated Remote Viewing," pp. 65–66; Kress, "Parapsychology in Intelligence," pp. 8–9; Schnabel, *Remote Viewers*, p. 108.

80. Kress, "Parapsychology in Intelligence," p. 9.

81. Puthoff, "CIA-Initiated Remote Viewing," p. 68.

82. Interview with John McMahon, Los Altos, California, November 17, 1998.

83. Schnabel, *Remote Viewers*, pp. 106, 111.

84. Ibid., pp. 107–108; Harold E. Puthoff and Russell Targ, *Perceptual Augmentation Techniques: Final Report (Covering the Period January 1974 through February 1975,) Part Two—Research Project* (Menlo Park, Calif.: Stanford Research Institute, December 1, 1975), p. 4.

85. Puthoff and Targ, *Perceptual Augmentation Techniques: Final Report*, pp. 6–7.

86. Ibid., p. 7.

87. Kress, "Parapsychology in Intelligence," p. 10; Schnabel, *Remote Viewers*, p. 111.

88. Kress, "Parapsychology in Intelligence," p. 10; Schnabel, *Remote Viewers*, p. 112; James Bamford, *The Puzzle Palace: A Report on NSA, America's Most Secret Agency* (Boston: Houghton Mifflin, 1982), p. 169.

89. Harold E. Puthoff and Russell Targ, *Perceptual Augmentation Techniques, Part One—Technical Proposal,* SRI No. ISH 73–146, October 1, 1973; Memorandum for the Record, Subject: Verification of Remote Viewing Experiments at Stanford Research Institute, November 9, 1973, pp. 2–3.

90. Memorandum for the Record, Subject: Verification of Remote Viewing Experiments at Stanford Research Institute, p. 4.

91. Schnabel, *Remote Viewers*, pp. 112–113.

92. Memorandum for the Record, Subject: Verification of Remote Viewing Experiments at Stanford Research Institute, p. 5.

93. Schnabel, *Remote Viewers*, p. 120.

94. Memorandum for the Record, Subject: Verification of Remote Viewing Experiments at Stanford Research Institute, pp. 6–7.

95. Ibid., p. 8.

96. Ibid., p. 9.

97. Bamford, *The Puzzle Palace*, p. 408; Schnabel, *Remote Viewers*, p. 97.

98. Kress, "Parapsychology in Intelligence," p. 10; telephone conversation with Sayre Stevens, November 11, 1999; interview with Sayre Stevens, Springfield, Virginia, March 18, 1999.

99. Kress, "Parapsychology in Intelligence," p. 10.

100. Russell Targ and Harold Puthoff, "Information Transmission Under Conditions of Sensory Shielding," *Nature*, October 18, 1974, pp. 602–607; "Investigating the Paranormal," *Nature*, October 18, 1974, pp. 559–560. A subsequent note challenged the validity of Puthoff and Targ's research. See David Marks and Richard Kammann, "Information Transmission in Remote Viewing Experiments," *Nature*, August 17, 1978, pp. 680–681. Also see David Marks and Richard Kammann, *The Psychology of the Psychic* (Buffalo, N.Y.: Prometheus Books, 1980).

101. Kress, "Parapsychology in Intelligence," p. 11; U.S. Congress, Senate Select Committee on Intelligence, *Nomination of John N. McMahon*, p. 19; McMahon interview; information provided by the CIA Public Affairs Staff; interview with James V. Hirsch, Fairfax, Virginia, February 12, 1999.

102. D. Stillman, "An Analysis of a Remote-Viewing Experiment of URDF-3," Los Alamos Scientific Laboratory, December 4, 1975, p. 4; Schnabel, *Remote Viewers*, p. 120.

103. Schnabel, *Remote Viewers*, p. 120; Michael Dobbs, "Deconstructing the Death Ray," *Washington Post*, October 17, 1999, pp. F1, F4.

104. Stillman, "An Analysis of Remote-Viewing Experiment of URDF-3," p. 5.

105. Ibid., p. 11.

106. Ibid., p. 12.

107. Ibid., pp. 13–14, 17, 18.

108. Ibid., p. 18.

109. Ibid., p. 25.

110. Ibid., p.27.

111. Ibid., p. 28.

112. Dobbs, "Reconstructing the Death Ray."

113. Puthoff and Targ, *Perceptual Augmentation Techniques: Final Report*, p. 9; Kress, "Parapsychology in Intelligence," p. 14.

114. Kress, "Parapsychology in Intelligence"; Schnabel, *Remote Viewers*, pp. 177–178.

115. Kress, "Parapsychology in Intelligence," p. 14.

116. Ibid.; Hirsch interview.

117. Kress, "Parapsychology in Intelligence," p. 15.

118. Ibid.

119. Ibid., pp. 15–16; Schnabel, *Remote Viewers*, passim; Jeremiah O'Leary, "Turner Says U.S. Didn't Bug Park," *Washington Times*, August 9, 1977, pp. A1, A6. The *Post* article was John L. Wilhelm, "Psychic Spying?" *Washington Post*, August 7, 1977, pp. B1, B5; interview with Gene Poteat, McLean, Virginia, April 25, 2000.

120. Joseph E. Perisco, *Piercing the Reich: The Penetration of Nazi Germany by American Secret Agents During World War II* (New York: Ballantine Books, 1979), pp. 201–203.

121. Interview with a former CIA official.

122. McMahon interview.

123. Jeffrey M. Lenorovitz, "CIA Satellite Data Link Study Revealed," *Aviation Week and Space Technology*, May 2, 1977, pp. 25–26.

124. Testimony of Leslie Dirks, *United States of America v. Christopher John Boyce (CR-77-131-RJK),* Reporter's Transcript, *Volume 5*, District Court, Central District of California, April 20, 1977, pp. 976, 983; Robert Lindsey, *The Falcon and the Snowman: A True Story of Friendship and Espionage* (New York: Simon & Schuster, 1979), p. 215.

125. Testimony of Leslie Dirks, pp. 984–986.

126. Lindsey, *The Falcon and the Snowman*, p. 214.

127. Testimony of Leslie Dirks, pp. 1001–1002; Lindsey, *The Falcon and the Snowman*, p. 218.

128. Lenorovitz, "CIA Satellite Data Link Study Revealed."

129. Lindsey, *The Falcon and the Snowman*, p. 218; testimony of Leslie Dirks, p. 994.

130. "The Great Submarine Snatch," *Time*, March 31, 1975, pp. 20–27; Roy Varner and Wayne Collier, *A Matter of Risk: The Incredible Inside Story of the CIA's Hughes* Glomar Explorer *Mission to Raise a Russian Submarine* (New York: Random House, 1978), p. 134; William Broad, *The Universe Below: Discovering the Secrets of the Deep Sea*, (New York: Simon & Schuster, 1997), pp. 255–256.

131. William Colby and Peter Forbath, *Honorable Men: My Life in the CIA* (New York: Simon & Schuster, 1978), pp. 389, 413.

132. "The Great Submarine Snatch"; Varner and Collier, *A Matter of Risk*, p. 144.

133. Seymour Hersh, "Human Error Is Cited in '74 Glomar Failure," *New York Times*, December 9, 1976, pp. 1, 55; Clyde W. Burleson, *The Jennifer Project* (College Station: Texas A&M, 1997), pp. 112, 133; Sherry Sontag and Christopher Drew with Annette Lawrence Drew, *Blind Man's Bluff: The Untold Story of American Submarine Espionage* (New York: Public Affairs, 1998), pp. 191, 196; Broad, *The Universe Below*, p. 79. A June 1993 report issued by a panel of experts under the office of Russian president Boris Yeltsin claimed that the United States had recovered two warheads. The amount of radiation the panel suggested was removed from the sub would be consistent with that contained by two nuclear torpedoes. The panel's claim was said to be made on the basis of Russian information, not Western press accounts—perhaps indicating that the Soviet navy had used minisubs to investigate the wreckage subsequent to U.S. press reports of the recovery operation. (William J. Broad, "Russia Says U.S. Got Sub's Atom Arms," *New York Times*, June 20, 1993, p. 4; "CIA Raising USSR Sub Raises Questions," *FBIS-SOV-92-145*, July 28, 1992, pp. 15–16.)

134. Hersh, "Human Error Cited in '74 Glomar Failure."

135. "CIA Raising USSR Sub Raises Questions," *FBIS-SOV-92-145*, July 28, 1992, pp. 15–16; CIA, "Burial at Sea," videotape, September 4, 1974.

136. Colby and Forbath, *Honorable Men*, pp. 414–417. According to one account, the sunken sub would not have had anything worth recovering. In late 1974, the USS *Seawolf* was sent back to the site. Its reconnaissance showed, according to a high-ranking naval official, that "It dissolved just like that, like an Alka-Seltzer in water. . . . It spread all over acres on the ocean floor. According to another official, "there was no possibility to recover anything more." (Sontag and Drew, *Blind Man's Bluff*, p. 197.)

137. Ranelagh, *The Agency*, pp. 624–625; Colby, *Honorable Men*, pp. 7–10.

138. Stevens interview, March 18, 1999.

139. Interview with a former CIA official.

140. Seymour M. Hersh, *The Samson Option: Israel's Nuclear Arsenal and American Foreign Policy* (New York: Random House, 1991), p. 240.

141. Ibid., p. 239.

142. Ibid.; Arthur Kranish, "CIA: Israel Has 10–20 Weapons," *Washington Post*, March 15, 1976, p. A2.

143. Kranish, "CIA: Israel Has 10–20 Weapons."

144. Andrew and Leslie Cockburn, *Dangerous Liaison: The Inside Story of the U.S.-Israeli Covert Relationship* (New York: HarperCollins, 1991), p. 94.

Chapter 7: Cracks in the Empire

1. Information provided by CIA Public Affairs Staff.

2. Robert Lindsey, *The Falcon and the Snowman: A True Story of Friendship and Espionage* (New York: Simon & Schuster, 1979), p. 287.

3. Interview with Robert Phillips, Rosslyn, Virginia, June 4, 1999.

4. Interview with Philip Eckman, Alexandria, Virginia, May 16, 2000.

5. Telephone interview with Sayre Stevens, May 29, 1996; interview with Sayre Stevens, Springfield, Virginia, March 18, 1999.

6. Stevens telephone interview; Stevens interview.

7. Interview with R. Evans Hineman, Chantilly, Virginia, February 17, 1999.

8. Interview with R. M. (Rae) Huffstutler, Falls Church, Virginia, March 23, 1999; Stevens telephone interview.

9. Interview with a former CIA official; Stevens interview; Huffstutler interview.

10. Interview with Henry Plaster, Vienna, Virginia, September 30, 1999; Eckman interview.

11. Interview with Philip Eckman, Alexandria, Virginia, May 16, 2000.

12. Ibid.; Philip Eckman, "Some Random Thoughts and Musings on ORD," n.d.

13. Eckman, "Some Random Thoughts and Musings on ORD."

14. Ibid.

15. Anthony Kenden, "U.S. Reconnaissance Satellite Programs," *Spaceflight*, July 1978, pp. 243ff.

16. William E. Burrows, *Deep Black: Space Espionage and National Security* (New York: Random House, 1986), p. 227.

17. Interview with a former CIA official; Jeffrey T. Richelson, *America's Secret Eyes in Space* (New York: Harper & Row, 1990), p. 362.

18. John Noble Wilford, "Spy Satellite Reportedly Aided in Shuttle Flight," *New York Times*, October 20, 1981, p. C4.

19. James Janesick and Morley Blouke, "Sky on a Chip: The Fabulous CCD," *Sky and Telescope*, September 1987, pp. 238–242; Burrows, *Deep Black*, p. 244.

20. James R. Janesick and Morley M. Blouke, "Introduction to Charged Couple Device Imaging Sensors," in Kosta Tsipis (ed.), *Arms Control Verification: The Technologies That Make It Possible* (New

York: Pergamon-Brassey's, 1985), p. 104; Curtis Peebles, *Guardians: Strategic Reconnaissance Satellites* (Novato, Calif.: Presidio Press, 1987), pp. 118–119.

21. Burrows, *Deep Black*, p. 244.

22. Ibid., p.247; interview with a former CIA official.

23. Interview with a former CIA official.

24. Jeffrey Richelson, "The Satellite Data System," *Journal of the British Interplanetary Society* 37, 5 (1984): 226–228.

25. Ibid.; telephone conversation with Albert Wheelon, February 15, 2000.

26. John Pike, "Reagan Prepares for War in Outer Space," *CounterSpy* 7, 1 (September-November 1982): 17–22; James Bamford, "America's Supersecret Eyes in Space," *New York Times Magazine*, January 13, 1985, pp. 39ff.

27. Richelson, *America's Secret Eyes in Space*, p. 362.

28. Interview with a former CIA official.

29. Ibid.

30. E. H. Knoche, Deputy Director of Central Intelligence, Memorandum for the Record, Subject: Meeting with National Security Adviser Brzezinski, December 30, 1976.

31. Burrows, *Deep Black*, p. 226.

32. Ibid.

33. Ibid.

34. Ibid., pp. 228–229; interview with a former CIA official.

35. Interview with a former CIA official.

36. Lindsey, *The Falcon and the Snowman*, pp. 49, 54.

37. Ibid., pp. 54–63; James Bamford, *The Puzzle Palace: A Report on NSA, America's Most Secret Agency* (Boston: Houghton Mifflin, 1982), pp. 512–514.

38. Harry Rostizke, *KGB: The Eyes of Russia* (New York: Doubleday, 1981), p. 203; Bamford, *The Puzzle Palace*, p. 514; Lindsey, *The Falcon and the Snowman*, pp. 164–168.

39. Rositze, *KGB*, pp. 203–204; Bamford, *The Puzzle Palace*, pp. 520–521.

40. Rositze, *KGB*, p. 204; Bamford, *The Puzzle Palace*, p. 521.

41. *United States of America v. Christopher John Boyce, CR-77-131-RJK,* United States District Court, Central District of California, Volume 5, Reporter's Transcript of Proceedings, April 20, 1977, pp. 957–1008.

42. Lindsey, *The Falcon and the Snowman*, p. 287.

43. *United States of America v. Christopher John Boyce, CR-77-131-RJK,* pp. 1008–1009, 1012.

44. Ibid., p. 1013; Lindsey, *The Falcon and the Snowman*, p. 287.

45. Bamford, *The Puzzle Palace*, pp. 521–522; Philip J. Klass, "U.S. Monitoring Capability Impaired," *Aviation Week and Space Technology*, May 14, 1979, p. 18; Burrows, *Deep Black*, p. 192; interview with Bernard Lubarsky, May 9, 2000.

46. Andrew Tully, *Inside the FBI* (New York: Dell, 1987), p. 45; George Lardner Jr., "Spy Rings of One," *Washington Post Magazine*, December 4, 1983, pp. 60–65.

47. Henry Hurt, "CIA in Crisis: The Kampiles Case," *Reader's Digest*, June 1979, pp. 65–72.

48. Tully, *Inside the FBI*, p. 45; Lardner, "Spy Rings of One"; Stansfield Turner, *Secrecy and Democracy: The CIA in Transition* (Boston: Houghton Mifflin, 1985), p. 65; interview with a former CIA official; Arthur S. Hulnick, *Fixing the Spy Machine: Preparing American Intelligence for the Twenty-first Century* (Westport, Conn.: Praeger, 1999), p. 104 n.14.

49. Turner, *Secrecy and Democracy*, p. 69.

50. Lardner, "Spy Rings of One"; Peebles, *Guardians*, p. 120; *United States of America v. William Peter Kampiles*, United States District Court, Northern District of Indiana, November 6, 1978, Direct Testimony of Donald E. Stukey, pp. 804–808.

51. *United States of America v. William Peter Kampiles*, Direct Testimony of Donald E. Stukey, p. 809; *United States of America v. William Peter Kampiles*, Direct Testimony of Vivian Psachos, p. 259;

Lardner, "Spy Rings of One"; Tully, *Inside the FBI*, p. 42–43; Griffin Bell, *Taking Care of the Law* (New York: William Morrow, 1982), p. 119.

52. Tully, *Inside the FBI*, pp. 43–44; Hurt, "CIA in Crisis"; Thomas O'Toole and Charles Babcock, "CIA 'Big Bird' Satellite Manual Was Allegedly Sold to the Soviets," *Washington Post*, August 23, 1978, pp. A1, A16; Michael Ledeen, "A Mole in Our Midst," *New York*, October 2, 1978, pp. 55–57; James Ott, "Espionage Trial Highlights CIA Problems," *Aviation Week and Space Technology*, November 27, 1978, pp. 21–23; David Wise, "The Spy Who Wouldn't Die," *GQ*, July 1998, pp. 148ff.

53. Tully, *Inside the FBI*, p. 52; *United States of America v. William Kampiles,* Direct Testimony of James Murphy, p. 352.

54. Bell, *Taking Care of the Law*, p. 121.

55. Ott, "Espionage Trial Highlights CIA Problems."

56. *United States of America v. William Peter Kampiles,* Direct Testimony of Leslie Dirks, pp. 6, 8.

57. Ibid., pp. 10, 12.

58. Ibid., p. 13.

59. Ott, "Espionage Trial Highlights CIA Problems."

60. Ibid.

61. Tully, *Inside the FBI*, pp. 48, 55.

62. Ibid., p. 56.

63. Interview with Roy Burks, North Potomac, Maryland, May 10, 1999.

64. Interview with Robert Singel, Great Falls, Virginia, February 25, 1999; Burks interview.

65. Michael E. Ruane, "Ex-CIA Employee Has Saluted Tiny Paper Soldiers Since '20s," *Dallas Morning News*, February 28, 1999, p. 9F; "Appointment of Eight Special Assistants to the President for National Security Affairs," White House, February 11, 1987; private information.

66. Phillips interview.

67. Ibid.; Burks interview.

68. Bob Woodward, *VEIL: The Secret Wars of the CIA, 1981–1987* (New York: Simon & Schuster, 1987), p. 313.

69. Burks interview.

70. Laurence Stern, "U.S. Tapped Top Russians' Car Phones," *Washington Post*, December 5, 1973, pp. A1, A16; Ernest Volkman, "U.S. Spies Lend an Ear to Soviets," *Newsday*, July 12, 1977, p. 7; Michael Frost and Michel Gratton, *Spyworld: Inside the Canadian and American Intelligence Establishments* (Toronto: Doubleday Canada, 1994), p. 60.

71. Stern, "U.S. Tapped Top Russians' Car Phones"; Volkman, "U.S. Spies Lend an Ear to Soviets"; Bill Gertz, "CIA Upset Because Perle Detailed Eavesdropping," *Washington Times*, April 15, 1987, p. 2A.

72. Jack Anderson, "CIA Eavesdrops on Kremlin Chiefs," *Washington Post*, September 16, 1971, p. F7.

73. Patrick Tyler, *A Great Wall: Six Presidents and China—An Investigative History* (New York: Public Affairs, 1999), pp. 83–84, 157.

74. Burks interview; Phillips interview.

75. Burks interview.

76. Ibid.

77. Woodward, *VEIL*, p. 314.

78. NRO, *Deputy Directors of the NRO*, 1997, n.p.; "Office of Development and Engineering," no date, portion of CIA document obtained under the Freedom of Information Act (FOIA); "Office of Research and Development," no date, portion of CIA document obtained under the FOIA.

79. Lubarsky interview.

80. Ibid.; "Office of Development and Engineering."

81. Biography, Jeffrey K. Harris; private information.

82. NRO, "Biography: Dennis Fitzgerald," 1997.

83. NRO, "David A. Kier, National Reconnaissance, Technical Director," April 1997; private information.

84. Interview with former CIA officials.

85. Lubarsky interview; private information.

86. Dial Torgeson, "U.S. Spy Devices Still Running at Iran Post," *International Herald Tribune*, March 7, 1979, pp. A1, A8.

87. Hedrick Smith, "U.S. Aides Say Loss of Post in Iran Impairs Missile-Monitoring Ability," *New York Times*, March 2, 1979, pp. A1, A8.

88. William Sullivan, *Mission to Iran* (New York: W. W. Norton, 1981), pp. 21–22.

89. U.S. Congress, House Permanent Select Committee on Intelligence, *Iran: Evaluation of U.S. Intelligence Performance Prior to November 1978* (Washington, D.C.: U.S. Government Printing Office, 1979), pp. 6, 7; Central Intelligence Agency, *Iran in the 1980s* (Washington, D.C.: CIA, August 1977), p. iii.

90. Interview with a former CIA official.

91. Torgeson, "U.S. Spy Devices Still Running at Iran Post."

92. Desmond Ball, *Pine Gap: Australia and the U.S. Geostationary Signals Intelligence Program* (Sydney: Allen & Unwin, 1988), pp. 58–59.

93. Torgeson, "U.S. Spy Devices Still Running at Iran Post."

94. Ibid.; Cyrus Vance, *Hard Choices: Critical Years in America's Foreign Policy* (New York: Simon & Schuster, 1983), p. 342; William Branigan, "Iran's Airmen Keep U.S. Listening Posts Intact and Whirring," *Washington Post*, May 20, 1979, p. A20.

95. Smith, "U.S. Aides Say Loss of Post in Iran Impairs Missile-Monitoring Ability."

96. Vance, *Hard Choices*, pp. 354–355.

97. Burks interview. On Teal Amber, see L. F. Dean, C. R. Johnson, and H. J. Strasler, "Teal Amber I," *Journal of Defense Research*, Special Issue 78-3, 1978, pp. 151–170.

98. Interview with William H. Nance, Bethesda, Maryland, May 4, 1999.

99. Ibid.

100. John Newhouse, *War and Peace in the Nuclear Age* (New York: Knopf, 1989), p. 224; Robert S. Ross, *Negotiating Cooperation: The United States and China, 1969–1989* (Stanford, Calif.: Stanford University Press, 1995), p. 45; William Burr (ed.), *The Kissinger Transcripts: The Top-Secret Talks with Beijing and Moscow* (New York: New Press, 1999), pp. 50–51, 170–171, 204; Tyler, *A Great Wall,* p. 98.

101. Nance interview.

102. Ibid.

103. Tyler, *A Great Wall*, pp. 205–207.

104. Ibid., pp. 277–278.

105. Philip Taubman, "U.S. and Peking Jointly Monitor Russian Missiles," *New York Times*, June 18, 1981, pp. A1, A14; Murrey Marder, "Monitoring: Not-So-Secret-Secret," *Washington Post*, June 19, 1981, p. 10.

106. Tyler, *A Great Wall*, p. 284.

107. Nance interview.

108. Robert Gates, *From the Shadows: The Ultimate Insider's Account of Five Presidents and How They Won the Cold War* (New York: Simon & Schuster, 1996), p. 123.

109. David Bonavia, "Radar Post Leak May Be Warning to Soviet Union," *The Times* (London), June 20, 1981, p. 5; Tyler, *A Great Wall*, p. 284.

110. Tyler, *A Great Wall*, pp. 278, 285; "Spying on Russia, with China's Help," *U.S. News & World Report*, June 29, 1981, p. 10; Taubman, "U.S. and Peking Joint Monitor Russian Missiles"; Robert C. Toth, "U.S., China Jointly Track Firings of Soviet Missiles," *Los Angeles Times*, June 19, 1981, pp. 1, 9; Walter Pincus, "U.S. Seeks A-Test Monitoring Facility," *Washington Post*, March 19, 1986, p. A8.

111. Communication from former CIA officer.

112. Antonio J. Mendez with Malcolm McConnell, *The Master of Disguise: My Secret Life in the CIA* (New York: Morrow, 1999), p. 269.

113. Ibid.; Jean Pelletier and Claude Adams, *The Canadian Caper* (New York: William Morrow, 1981), pp. 59–60, 79, 196.

114. Mendez with McConnell, *The Master of Disguise*, p. 267; CIA Public Affairs Staff, "'Trailblazers' and Years of CIA Service," 1997.

115. Mendez with McConnell, *The Master of Disguise,* pp. 270, 272–273.

116. Ibid., pp. 275–276.

117. Antonio J. Mendez, "A Classic Case of Deception," *Studies in Intelligence*, Winter 1999–2000, pp. 1–16 at pp. 2–3.

118. Ibid., p. 3.

119. Ibid., p. 3; Mendez with McConnell, *The Master of Disguise*, pp. 128, 277–278.

120. Mendez with McConnell, *The Master of Disguise*, p. 278.

121. Ibid., pp. 280–282; Mendez, "A Classic Case of Deception," p. 4; Michael E. Ruane, "Seeing Is Deceiving," *Washington Post*, February 15, 2000, pp. C1, C8.

122. Mendez with McConnell, *The Master of Disguise*, pp. 284–286; Ruane, "Seeing Is Deceiving."

123. Mendez, "A Classic Case of Deception."

124. Mendez with McConnell, *The Master of Disguise*, pp. 296, 298; Mendez, "A Classic Case of Deception," p. 6.

125. Mendez with McConnell, *The Master of Disguise*, pp. 298, 301–305; Ruane, "Seeing Is Deceiving"; Mendez, "A Classic Case of Deception," p. 7.

126. Mendez with McConnell, *The Master of Disguise*, pp. 339–340; Ruane, "Seeing Is Deceiving."

Chapter 8: Breaking Down Barriers

1. Interview with R. Evans Hineman, Chantilly, Virginia, February 17, 1999; *United States of America, Plaintiff v. Samuel L. Morison, Defendant, Case No. Y-84-00455*, United States District Court, District of Maryland, Baltimore, October 15, 1985, Transcript of Trial Before the Honorable Joseph H. Young, pp. 443–444; "DS&T Leadership History," n.d., provided by CIA Public Affairs Staff.

2. Interview with James V. Hirsch, Fairfax, Virginia, February 12, 1999; telephone interview with Robert Kohler, July 6, 1999; "DS&T Leadership History."

3. *DS&T 35th Anniversary: Celebrating 50 Years of CIA History*, July 24, 1997, video.

4. Ibid.; Hineman interview.

5. "DS&T Leadership History"; Hineman interview.

6. "DS&T 35th Anniversary"; Hineman interview.

7. A phone interview with Thomas Twetten, March 12, 2001.

8. Warren E. Leary, "The Dream of Eternal Flight Begins to Take Wing," *New York Times*, January 12, 1999, pp. D1, D6; Stuart F. Brown, "The Eternal Airplane," *Popular Science*, April 1994, pp. 70, 100; interview with Philip Eckman, Alexandria, Virginia, May 16, 2000; interview with a former CIA official.

9. Brown, "The Eternal Airplane"; David A. Fulghum, "Solar-Powered UAV to Fly at Edwards," *Aviation Week and Space Technology*, October 4, 1993, p. 27; "Environmental Research Aircraft and Sensor Technology: Pathfinder, Past Flight Information," www.dfrc.nasa.gov/Projects/erast/Projects/Pathfinder/pastinfo.html, November 1, 1998.

10. Leary, "The Dream of Eternal Flight"; "Environmental Research Aircraft and Sensor Technology: Pathfinder," www.dfrc.nasa.gov/Projects/erast/Projects/Pathfinder/pastfltinfo.html, November 1, 1998. In November 1998, a successor to PATHFINDER, with a 206-foot wingspan and the designation CENTURION, made its debut, flying at just over 80,000 feet and able to stay aloft for

fourteen to fifteen hours during daylight. It is expected to be capable of flying at over 100,000 feet. Scientists hope the vehicle will provide data to help in the development of another advanced UAV, HELIOS, which is expected to be able to remain over a target for months using an energy storage system to power the aircraft at night. Projected possible uses for the aircraft include monitoring the upper atmosphere, long-term monitoring of ocean storms, and forest and crop monitoring.

11. John Boatman, "USA Planned Stealthy UAV to Replace SR-71," *Jane's Defence Weekly*, December 17, 1994, pp. 1, 3; David A. Fulghum and Peter A. Wall, "Long-Hidden Research Spawns Black UAV," *Aviation and Space Technology,* September 25, 2000, pp. 28–29; private information.

12. Fulghum and Wall, "Long-Hidden Research Spawns Black UAV"; Boatman, "USA Planned Stealthy UAV to Replace SR–71."

13. Fulghum and Wall, "Long-Hidden Research Spawns Black UAV"; Boatman, "USA Planned Stealthy UAV to Replace SR–71"; private information.

14. Fulghum and Wall, "Long-Hidden Research Spawns Black UAV"; Boatman, "USA Planned Stealthy UAV to Replace SR–71"; U.S. Congress, Senate Committee on Armed Services, *Department of Defense Authorization for Appropriations for Fiscal Year 1994 and the Future Years Defense Program* (Washington, D.C.: U.S. Government Printing Office, 1993), p. 477.

15. Peter Kornbluh, *Nicaragua: The Price of Intervention, Reagan's War Against the Sandinistas* (Washington, D.C.: Institute for Policy Studies, 1987), pp. 18–20.

16. James Le Moyne, "The Secret War Boils Over," *Newsweek*, April 11, 1983, pp. 46–50; Joanne Omang, "Historical Background to the CIA's Nicaraguan Manual," in *Psychological Operations in Guerrilla Warfare* (New York: Vintage, 1985), pp. 15, 22; "A Secret War for Nicaragua," *Newsweek*, November 8, 1982, pp. 42–53; Kornbluh, *Nicaragua*, pp. 22–23; Robert C. Toth, "CIA Covert Action Punishes Nicaragua for Salvador Aid," *New York Times*, April 18, 1984, pp. A1, A12.

17. Ronald Reagan, National Security Decision Directive 17, "National Security Directive on Cuba and Central America," January 4, 1982. Top Secret.

18. LeMoyne, "Secret War Boils Over"; Kornbluh, *Nicaragua*, pp. 23–24, 40.

19. "The CIA Blows an Asset," *Newsweek*, September 3, 1984, pp. 48–49.

20. Kornbluh, *Nicaragua*, p. 48; Philip Taubman, "U.S. Officials Say C.I.A. Helped Nicaraguan Rebels Plan Attacks," *New York Times*, October 16, 1984, pp. 1, 22; "Oct. 10 Assault on Nicaraguans Is Laid to C.I.A.," *New York Times*, April 18, 1994, pp. A1, A12.

21. Kornbluh, *Nicaragua*, p. 48; Taubman, "U.S. Officials Say C.I.A. Helped Nicaraguan Rebels Plan Attacks"; "Oct. 10 Assault on Nicaraguans Is Laid to C.I.A."; John Prados, *President's Secret Wars: CIA and Pentagon Covert Operations from World War II Through the Persian Gulf* (Chicago: Ivan R. Dee, 1996), p. 415; Capt. James M. Martin, "Sea Mines in Nicaragua," *Proceedings of the U.S. Naval Institute* 116, 9 (September 1990): 111–116.

22. Kornbluh, *Nicaragua*, pp. 48–50; Hedrick Smith, "Britain Criticizes Mining of Harbors Around Nicaragua," *New York Times*, April 7, 1984, pp. 1, 4; Fred Hiatt and Joanne Omang, "CIA Helped to Mine Ports in Nicaragua," *Washington Post*, April 7, 1984, p. 1; Philip Taubman, "Americans on Ship Said to Supervise Nicaragua Mining," *New York Times*, April 8, 1984, pp. 1, 12; Martin, "Sea Mines in Nicaragua."

23. Prados, *President's Secret Wars*, p. 413; Memorandum for Robert C. MacFarlane, From: Oliver L. North, Constantine Menges, Subject: Special Activities in Nicaragua, March 2, 1984, in National Security Archive, *Nicaragua: The Making of U.S. Policy, 1978–1990* (Alexandria, Va.: Chadwyck-Healey, 1991), Document No. 01994.

24. Kornbluh, *Nicaragua*, pp. 48–50; Smith, "Britain Criticizes Mining of Harbors Around Nicaragua"; Hiatt and Omang, "CIA Helped to Mine Ports in Nicaragua"; Taubman, "Americans on Ship Said to Supervise Nicaragua Mining"; American Embassy Managua to Secretary of State, Washington, D.C., Subject: Soviet Ship Damaged by Mine at Puerto Sandino, 211755 March 1984 in National Security Archive, *Nicaragua: The Making of U.S. Policy*, Document No. 02017.

25. Duane R. Claridge, *A Spy for All Seasons: My Life in the CIA* (New York: Scribner's, 1996), p. 205; Leslie H. Gelb, "Officials Say CIA Made Mines with Navy Help," *New York Times*, June 1, 1984, p. A4; Claridge, *A Spy for All Seasons*, p. 386.

26. *United States of America, Plaintiff v. Samuel L. Morison*, pp. 1022–1024.

27. Interview with Robert M. Huffstutler, Falls Church, Virginia, March 23, 1999; Résumé, Robert M. Huffstutler, n.d.

28. Hineman interview; Huffstutler interview; John J. Hicks, Director, National Photographic Interpretation Center, Memorandum for: Deputy Director for Science and Technology, Subject: Use of Photointerpreter and Supporting Resources, July 25, 1975. The problem persists to this day. In fall 1999, Congress threatened to cut the funding for the next generation of imagery satellites unless the administration came up with sufficient funds to pay for a processing and exploitation capability to match the new generation's collection capability. (Vernon Loeb and Walter Pincus, "New Spy Satellites at Risk Because Funding Is Uncertain, Pentagon Told," *Washington Post*, November 12, 1999, p. A7.)

29. Hineman interview.

30. Huffstutler interview.

31. Ibid.

32. Ibid.

33. Ibid.

34. Hineman interview; Huffstutler interview.

35. Huffstutler interview.

36. Ibid.

37. Ibid.

38. Ibid.

39. Nigel Hawkes, Geoffrey Lean, David Leigh, Robin McKie, Peter Pringle, and Andrew Wilson, *Chernobyl: The End of the Nuclear Dream* (New York: Vintage, 1986), pp. 99–103.

40. Stephen Engelberg, "U.S. Says Intelligence Units Did Not Detect the Accident," *New York Times*, May 2, 1986, p. A9.

41. Hawkes, Lean, Leigh McKie, Pringle, and Wilson, *Chernobyl*, p. 122; Huffstutler interview.

42. "Meltdown," *Newsweek*, May 12, 1986, pp. 20–35; Boyce Rensberg, "Explosion: Graphite Fire Suspected," *Washington Post*, April 30,1986, pp.A1, A17; Carl M. Cannon and Mark Thompson, "Threat to Soviets Grows, U.S. Spy Photos Indicate," *Miami Herald*, April 30, 1986, pp.1A, 14A.

43. "Meltdown."

44. Robert C. Toth, "Satellites Keep Eye on Reactor," *Los Angeles Times*, May 2, 1986, p. 22.

45. "Meltdown"; Bernard Gwertzman, "Fire in Reactor May Be Out, New U.S. Pictures Indicate; Soviet Says Fallout Is Cut," *New York Times*, May 2, 1986, pp.A1, A8.

46. Philip M. Boffey, "U.S. Panel Calls the Disaster in the Ukraine the Worst Ever," *New York Times*, May 4, 1986, pp. 1, 20.

47. Serge Schemann, "Soviet Mobilizes a Vast Operation to Overcome the Disaster," *New York Times*, May 19, 1986, p. A8.

48. Walter Pincus and Mary Thornton, "U.S. to Orbit 'Sigint' Craft from Shuttle," *Washington Post*, December 19, 1984, pp.A1, A8-A9.

49. Edward H. Kolcum, "Night Launch of Discovery Boosts Secret Military Satellite into Orbit," *Aviation Week and Space Technology*, November 27, 1989, p. 29; private information.

50. James Gerstenzang, "Shuttle Lifts Off with Spy Cargo," *Los Angeles Times*, January 25, 1985, pp. 1, 11; "Final Launch Preparations Under Way for Signal Intelligence Satellite Mission," *Aviation Week and Space Technology*, November 6, 1989, p. 24; interview with Bernard Lubarsky, Alexandria, Virginia, May 9, 2000; interview with a former CIA official.

51. Kohler interview.

52. Lubarsky interview; telephone conversation with Albert Wheelon, November 15, 1999; Kohler interview, July 6, 1999.

53. Kohler interview.
54. Ibid.
55. Ibid.
56. Ibid.
57. Ibid.
58. Ibid.
59. Ibid.; Wheelon telephone conversation; telephone conversation with Albert Wheelon, February 15, 2000.
60. Wheelon telephone conversation, November 15, 1999; Wheelon telephone conversation, February 15, 2000.
61. Kohler interview.
62. List of Directors, Office of Development and Engineering, n.d.
63. Interview with a former CIA official.
64. Lubarsky interview; Jeffrey T. Richelson, *America's Space Sentinels: DSP Satellites and National Security* (Lawrence: University Press of Kansas, 1999), pp. 131–136.
65. Richelson, *America's Space Sentinels,* pp. 131–136.
66. Ruth Marcus and Joe Pichirallo, "Chin Believed Planted in U.S. as Spy," *Washington Post*, December 6, 1985, pp. A1, A22; Philip Shenon, "Former C.I.A. Analyst Is Arrested and Accused of Spying for China," *New York Times*, November 24, 1985, pp. 1, 31; Joe Pichirallo, "Ex-CIA Analyst Gave Secrets to China for 30 Years, FBI Says," *Washington Post*, November 24, 1985, pp. A1, A24.
67. Pichirallo, "Ex-CIA Analyst"; Stephen Engelberg, "30 Years of Spying for China Is Charged," *New York Times*, November 27, 1985, p. B8.
68. Pichirallo, "Ex-CIA Analyst"; "A Chinese Agent in the CIA?" *Newsweek*, December 2, 1985, p. 49.
69. Marcus and Pichirallo, "Chin Believed Planted in U.S. as Spy"; Philip Shenon, "U.S. Says Spy Suspect Had Access to Highly Classified Data," *New York Times*, January 3, 1986, p. A12; Michael Wines, "Bigger Role Laid to Suspected Spy," *Los Angeles Times*, November 28, 1985, pp. 1, 10; *United States of America v. Larry Wu Tai Chin aka Chin Wu-Tai*, United States District Court for the Eastern District of Virginia, Alexandria Division, Criminal No. 85-00263-A, January 2, 1986, pp. 2–3, 14.
70. Joe Pichirallo, "Retiree Kept Close CIA Ties," *Washington Post*, November 27, 1985, pp. A1, A10; Robin Toner, "Bail Denied Ex-CIA Worker in China Spy Case," *New York Times*, November 28, 1985, p. B8; Joe Pichirallo, "Ex-CIA Analyst Gave Secrets to China," *Washington Post*, November 24, 1985, pp. A1, A24.
71. "'Ministry of State Security' Set Up on Mainland China," *Issues and Studies*, July 1983, pp. 5–8; Nicholas Eftimiades, "China's Ministry of State Security: Coming of Age in the International Arena," *Intelligence and National Security* 8, 1 (January 1993): 23–43; "Chinese Official Said Exposer of CIA Turncoat," *Washington Post*, September 5, 1986, p. A18; Michael Wines, "Spy Reportedly Unmasked by China Defector," *Los Angeles Times*, September 5, 1986, pp. 1, 12; Daniel Southerland, "China Silent on Reported Defection of Intelligence Official," *Washington Post*, September 4, 1986, p. A30.
72. "Chinese Official Said to Be Exposer of CIA Turncoat"; Wines, "Spy Reportedly Unmasked by China Defector"; Thomas Allen and Norman Polmar, *Merchants of Treason: America's Secrets for Sale from the* Pueblo *to the Present* (New York: Delacorte, 1988), p. 302.
73. Ronald Kessler, *Spy vs. Spy: Stalking Soviet Spies in America* (New York: Scribner's, 1988), pp. 202–203.
74. Remarks by William O. Studeman, Deputy Director of Central Intelligence, at the Symposium on "National Security and National Competitiveness: Open Source Solutions," December 1, 1992, McLean, Va., p. 4; Robert Pear, "Radio Broadcasts Report Protests Erupting All over China," *New York Times*, May 23, 1989, p. A14.

75. Bob Woodward, *VEIL: The Secret Wars of the CIA, 1981–1987* (New York: Simon & Schuster, 1987), p. 32; NBC, *Inside the KGB: Narration and Shooting Script*, May 1993, p. 39.

76. Peter Earley, *Confessions of a Spy: The Real Story of Aldrich Ames* (New York: Putnam, 1997), p. 117.

77. Ibid., p. 118.

78. Ibid.

79. Ibid., pp. 118–119, 197.

80. Interview; "Seismic Sensors," *Intelligence Newsletter*, January 17, 1990, p. 2.

81. Hineman interview.

82. John O. Koehler, *STASI: The Untold Story of the East German Secret Police* (Boulder, Colo.: Westview Press, 1998), p. 295.

83. Hineman interview.

84. Ibid.

85. Ibid.; CIA document fragment, "Office of Special Projects," July 22, 1988.

86. Interview with Robert Phillips, Rosslyn, Virginia, June 4, 1999.

87. Ibid.

Chapter 9: A New World

1. Benjamin B. Fischer (ed.), *At Cold War's End: U.S. Intelligence on the Soviet Union and Eastern Europe 1989–1991* (Washington, D.C.: Central Intelligence Agency, 1999), p. xi.

2. Ibid.

3. Interview with James V. Hirsch, Fairfax, Virginia, February 12, 1999; remarks of James V. Hirsch, "DS&T 35th Anniversary: Celebrating 50 Years of CIA History," July 24, 1997, videotape.

4. Remarks of James V. Hirsch, "DS&T 35th Anniversary,."

5. Ibid.

6. Hirsch interview.

7. Ibid.

8. Bob Woodward, *The Commanders* (New York: Simon & Schuster, 1991), p. 206.

9. Ibid.

10. Ibid., p. 207; Michael R. Gordon and Bernard Trainor, *The General's War: The Inside Story of The Conflict in the Gulf* (Boston: Little, Brown, 1994), pp. 9–10.

11. U.S. News & World Report, *Triumph Without Victory: The Unreported History of the Persian Gulf War* (New York: Times Books, 1992), pp. 21–22.

12. Ibid., p. 32.

13. Gordon and Trainor, *The General's War*, p. 25.

14. Ibid., pp. 24–25; Woodward, *The Commanders*, pp. 208, 216, 218–219.

15. U.S. News & World Report, *Triumph Without Victory*, pp. 7–9; George Bush, National Security Directive 45, "U.S. Policy in Response to the Iraqi Invasion of Kuwait," August 20, 1990, p. 2.

16. Richard Hallion, *Storm over Iraq: Air Power and the Gulf War* (Washington, D.C.: Smithsonian Institution, 1992), p. 159; George Bush, National Security Directive 54, "Responding to Iraqi Aggression in the Gulf," January 15, 1991.

17. Doug Waller, *The Commandos: The Inside Story of America's Secret Soldiers* (New York: Simon & Schuster, 1994), p. 243; U.S. News & World Report, *Triumph Without Victory*, p. 212.

18. Bill Gertz, "New Spy Satellite, Needed to Monitor Treaty, Sits on Ground," *Washington Times*, October 20, 1987, p. A5; Bob Woodward, *Veil: The Secret Wars of the CIA 1981–1987* (New York: Simon & Schuster, 1987), p. 221; private information.

19. Douglas Isbell and Vincent Kiernan, "Long-Delayed Atlantis Flight Orbits Military Spy Satellite," *Space News*, March 5–11, 1990, p. 12; Edward H. Kolcum, "Atlantis Lofts AFP-731 Recon-

naissance Satellite," *Aviation Week and Space Technology*, March 5, 1990, p. 22; Warren E. Leary, "Problems Are Reported with New Spy Satellite," *New York Times*, March 18, 1990, p. 20; Patrick E. Tyler, "Satellite Fails," *Washington Post*, March 17, 1990, pp. A1, A11.

20. Warren E. Leary, "Debris from Secret U.S. Satellite Is Burning Up in Fall from Space," *New York Times*, March 22, 1990, p. A24; "Soviets Claim Reconnaissance Satellite Launched by Atlantis Has Failed," *Aviation Week and Space Technology*, March 26, 1990, p. 23; "Shuttle Spy Satellite Has Not Reentered," *Spaceflight*, January 1991, p. 4; private information.

21. Private information.

22. Ibid.

23. Ibid.

24. Ibid.

25. Ibid.

26. Douglas G. Armstrong, "The Gulf War's Patched-Together Air Intelligence," *Naval Institute Proceedings*, November 1992, pp. 109–111; Desmond Ball, *Intelligence in the Gulf War* (Canberra, Australia: SDSC, Australian National University, 1991), pp. 32, 34.

27. Craig Covault, "Space Recon of Iraq Taxes CIA Operations," *Aviation Week and Space Technology*, September 3, 1990, pp. 30–31.

28. Interview with Patrick Eddington, Centerville, Virginia, April 12, 1999.

29. Ibid.

30. Covault, "Space Recon of Iraq Taxes CIA Operations; U.S. News & World Report, *Triumph Without Victory*, p. 277; Thomas Christie et al., *Desert Storm SCUD Campaign* (Arlington, Va.: Institute for Defense Analyses, 1992), p. IV-6.

31. Department of Defense, *Conduct of the Persian Gulf War, Final Report to Congress* (Washington, D.C: DOD, April 1992), C-14 to C-15; Rick Atkinson, *Crusade: The Untold Story of the Persian Gulf War* (Boston: Houghton Mifflin, 1993), p. 265.

32. E. C. Aldridge Jr., Director, NRO, to David L. Boren, Chairman, Senate Select Committee on Intelligence, November 21, 1988.

33. Ibid.

34. Ibid.; Rear Adm. Robert K. Geiger and D. Barry Kelly, *NRO Restructure Study, Final Report, Volume II* (Washington, D.C.: NRO, 1989).

35. Kelly and Geiger, *NRO Restructure Study, Final Report, Volume II*, p. 16.

36. Letter, Secretary of Defense Richard Cheney and Director of Central Intelligence William Webster to Senator David Boren, Chairman, Senate Select Committee on Intelligence.

37. Ibid.

38. U.S. Congress, Senate Select Committee on Intelligence, *NRO Headquarters Project* (Washington, D.C.: U.S. Government Printing Office, 1995), p. 37; U.S. Congress, House Permanent Select Committee on Intelligence, *NRO Headquarters Facility* (Washington, D.C.: U.S. Government Printing Office, 1995), p. 2.

39. U.S. Congress, House Permanent Select Committee on Intelligence, *NRO Headquarters Facility*, p. 19; U.S. Congress, Senate Select Committee on Intelligence, *NRO Headquarters Project*, p. 52; Letter from Mary Jo Kingsley, Chief Information Access and Release Center, NRO, to author, August 9, 1996.

40. Martin C. Faga, Memorandum for the Secretary of Defense, Subject: DCI Task Force on the NRO-INFORMATION MEMORANDUM," May 19, 1992; George Bush, National Security Directive 67, "Intelligence Capabilities, 1992–2005," March 30, 1992.

41. DCI Task Force on the National Reconnaissance Office, *Report to the Director of Central Intelligence, DCI Task Force on the National Reconnaissance Office, Final Report*, April 1992, p. 2.

42. Ibid., p. 6.

43. U.S. Congress, Senate Select Committee on Intelligence and House Permanent Select Committee on Intelligence, *S. 2198 and S. 421 to Reorganize the United States Intelligence Community* (Washington, D.C.: U.S. Government Printing Office, 1993), p. 18.

44. Ralph Vartabedian, "Air Force Spy Satellite Unit Leaving California," *Los Angeles Times* (Washington ed.), October 16, 1992, pp. A1, A5; Ralph Vartabedian, "Air Force Spy Satellite Unit Leaving Southland," *Los Angeles Times*, October 16, 1992, pp. A1, A12; Vincent Kiernan, "NRO Streamlines to Cut Intelligence Bureaucracy," *Space News*, December 7–13, 1992, pp. 1, 29.

45. Ronald Kessler, *Inside the CIA: Revealing the Secrets of the World's Most Powerful Spy Agency* (New York: Pocket Books, 1992), pp. 77–78; CIA document fragment, July 22, 1988.

46. Interview with a former CIA official.

47. Interview with Robert Phillips, Rosslyn, Virginia, June 4, 1999.

48. Hirsch interview.

49. Vernon Loeb, "After-Action Report," *Washington Post Magazine*, February 27, 2000, pp. 7ff.

50. Ibid.

51. Ibid.

52. Ibid.

53. R. Jeffrey Smith, "Tracking Aideed Hampered by Intelligence Failures," *Washington Post*, October 8, 1993, p. A19.

54. Loeb, "After-Action Report."

55. Ibid.

56. Ibid.

57. Ibid.

58. CIA, "DCI Speech on New Frontiers in Breast Cancer Screening," October 11, 1994.

59. Sam Grant and Peter C. Oleson, "Breast Cancer Detection Research," *Studies in Intelligence*, Semiannual Unclassified Edition, No. 1, 1997, pp. 27–34 at pp. 27–28.

60. Grant and Oleson, "Breast Cancer Detection Research."

61. Ibid.

62. Tom Bowman and Scott Shane, "Espionage from the Front Lines," *Baltimore Sun*, December 8, 1995, pp. 1A, 20A–21A.

63. Ibid.; Howard Kurtz, "Pollard: Top Israelis Backed Spy Ring," *Washington Post*, February 28, 1987, p. A8.

64. Seymour Hersh, "The Wild East," *Atlantic Monthly*, June 1994, pp. 61–86.

65. Bowman and Shane, "Espionage from the Front Lines."

66. Ibid.

67. Ibid.

68. Ibid.

69. Ibid.; Seymour Hersh, *"The Target Is Destroyed": What Really Happened to Flight 007 and What America Knew About It* (New York: Random House, 1986), p. 4.

70. Bowman and Shane, "Espionage from the Front Lines."

71. Ibid.

72. Ibid.

73. Ibid. By mid-1994, individuals from the military services were being seconded to work for the SCS, after cover problems had been overcome. Four Air Intelligence Agency (AIA) candidates were selected to participate in the program, designated SENSOR SILVER. (Joyce M. Hons, Juan R. Jimenez, Gabriell G. Marshall, and Johnny D. Ford, *History of the Air Intelligence Agency, 1 January–31 December 1994, Volume I* [San Antonio, Tex.: AIA, December 1995], p. 39.)

74. R. Jeffrey Smith, "Pentagon Has Spent Millions on Tips from Trio of Psychics," *Washington Post*, November 29, 1995, pp. A1, A18; "U.S. Agencies Used Psychics for Years for 'Remote Viewing,'" *Washington Times*, November 30, 1995, p. A12; Steven Emerson, *Secret Warriors: Inside the Covert Military Operations of the Reagan Era* (New York: Putnam, 1988), pp. 65–66.

75. Smith, "Pentagon Has Spent Millions on Tips from Trio of Psychics"; R. Jeffrey Smith and Curt Suplee, "'Psychic Arms Race' Had Several Funding Channels," *Washington Post*, November 30, 1995, pp. A1, A13; "U.S. Agencies Used Psychics for Years for 'Remote Viewing.'"

76. Smith and Suplee, "'Psychic Arms Race' Had Several Funding Channels."

77. Douglas Waller, "The Vision Thing," *Time*, December 11, 1995, p. 48; Martin Gardner, "Claiborne Pell: The Senator from Outer Space," *Skeptical Inquirer,* March/April 1996, pp. 12–15.

78. Hirsch interview; Office of Public Affairs, "CIA Statement on 'Remote Viewing,'" September 6, 1995.

79. Information about AIR is accessible from its web site: www.air-dc.org.

80. Michael D. Mumford, Andrew M. Rose, and David M. Goslin, *An Evaluation of Remote Viewing: Research and Applications* (Washington, D.C.: American Institutes for Research, September 29, 1995), pp. 1–3 to 1–4.

81. Ibid., pp. 1–4 to 1–5.

82. Ibid., p. E-1; Ray Hyman, "Evaluation of the Military's Twenty-Year Program on Psychic Spying," *Skeptical Inquirer*, March/April 1996, pp. 24–26; Ray Hyman, "Parapsychological Research: A Tutorial Review and Critical Appraisal," *Proceedings of the IEEE* 74, 6 (June 1986): 823–849; Smith, "Pentagon Has Spent Millions on Tips from Trio of Psychics"; Mumford, Rose, and Goslin, *An Evaluation of Remote Viewing*, p. E-2.

83. Mumford, Rose, and Goslin, *An Evaluation of Remote Viewing*, p. E-3.

84. Ibid., p. E-4.

85. Ibid. For a critique of the AIR report's conclusions as well as claims of bias in its preparation, see Edwin C. May, "The American Institutes for Research Review of the Department of Defense's STAR GATE Program: A Commentary," *Journal of Scientific Exploration* 10, 1 (1996): 89–107.

86. Hirsch interview.

Chapter 10: Agile Intelligence

1. Telephone interview with James Hirsch, April 11, 2000.

2. Ibid.; interview with Steven Koonin, Pasadena, California, March 22, 2000.

3. Vita, Steven E. Koonin, n.d.; Koonin interview.

4. Hirsch telephone interview.

5. Interview with Ruth David, Arlington, Virginia, February 22, 1999; CIA, Public Affairs, "Ruth A. David, Deputy Director of Science and Technology, Central Intelligence Agency," n.d.

6. CIA, Public Affairs, "Ruth A. David, Deputy Director of Science and Technology, Central Intelligence Agency"; "Meet the CEO," www.anser.org/aboutanser/meetceo.html; David interview.

7. CIA, Public Affairs, "Ruth A. David, Deputy Director for Science and Technology, Central Intelligence Agency."

8. Ibid.; CIA Public Affairs, "DS&T Leadership History," n.d.; interview with Robert Phillips, Rosslyn, Virginia, June 4, 1999.

9. David interview.

10. Ibid.; Ruth David, "Prologue," to Frederick Thomas Martin, *Top Secret Intranet: How U.S. Intelligence Built INTELINK-The World's Largest, Most Secure Network* (Upper Saddle River, N.J.: Prentice-Hall PTR, 1998), p. xix.

11. David interview.

12. David, "Prologue," to Martin, *Top Secret Intranet*, p. xx; Ruth David, speech to Armed Forces Communications Electronics Association, January 1998, p. 7.

13. David, speech to Armed Forces Communications Electronics Association, p. 8.

14. Ibid., pp. 14–15.

15. Ibid., pp. 10, 14.

16. CIA Office of Public Affairs, "Restructuring in the DS&T," 1996.

17. "Computer Scientists,(AAT)," www.cia.gov/cia/employment/jobpostings/comsciad.htm.

18. Clarence A. Robinson, "Intelligence Agency Adjusts as Mission Possible Unfolds," *Signal*, October 1998.

19. Ibid.

20. Ibid.

21. David interview; CIA Public Affairs, "Restructuring in the DS&T."

22. Jeffrey T. Richelson, "CIA's Science and Technology Gurus Get New Look, Roles," *Defense Week*, August 19, 1996, p. 6.

23. CIA Public Affairs, "Restructuring in the DS&T"; private information.

24. Phillips interview.

25. Phillips interview; interview with Philip Eckman, Alexandria, Virginia, May 16, 2000; "Public Support Swells for CIA's FBIS Program," *Secrecy and Government Bulletin*, July 1996; "Costly Cuts?" *Newsweek*, November 25, 1996, p. 6. As of February 1995, FBIS had fourteen foreign bureaus located in Abidjan, Ivory Coast; Amman, Jordan; Asunción, Paraguay; Bangkok, Thailand; Chiva Chiva, Panama; Hong Kong; Islamabad, Pakistan; London, UK; Mbabane, Swaziland; Nicosia, Cyprus; Okinawa, Japan; Seoul, Republic of Korea; Tel Aviv, Israel; and Vienna, Austria. Domestically, in addition to its Reston, Virginia, headquarters, FBIS operated a bureau in Key West.

26. FBIS, "Overview for CNC Conference," n.d.

27. Phillips interview.

28. Ibid.

29. "Public Support Swells for CIA's FBIS Program."

30. U.S. Congress, House of Representatives, House Permanent Select Committee on Intelligence, *Intelligence Authorization Act for Fiscal Year 1998, Report 105-135, Part 1* (Washington, D.C.: U.S. Government Printing Office, 1997), pp. 23–24.

31. Stephen Barr, "Monitoring Service Spared in Latest Crisis," *Washington Post*, February 6, 1997, p. A21. In 1997, FBIS did complete a transition, started in 1995, from the production of hard-copy reports—including the FBIS Daily Report and the Joint Publications Research Service translations—as a step toward purely electronic transmission. (FBIS, "Overview for CNC Conference, n.d., Slide 5.)

32. U.S. Congress, House of Representatives, House Permanent Select Committee on Intelligence, *Intelligence Authorization Act for Fiscal Year 1998*, p. 24.

33. Ibid.

34. Peter Maass, "From His Bed, CIA's Best Makes His Breakthroughs," *Washington Post*, April 21, 1996, pp. A1, A20; CIA, "'Trailblazers' and Years of CIA Service," 1997.

35. Maass, "From His Bed, CIA's Best Makes His Breakthroughs."

36. Ibid.

37. Ibid.

38. Ibid.

39. Ibid.

40. Robert M. Gates, Director of Central Intelligence, *Statement on Change in CIA and the Intelligence Community*, April 1, 1992, p. 28.

41. H.R. 4165, "National Security Act of 1992," 1992; S. 2198, "Intelligence Reorganization Act of 1992," 1992.

42. Robert M. Gates, Director of Central Intelligence, *Statement on Change in CIA and the Intelligence Community*, April 1, 1992, p. 28; telephone conversation with R. Evans Hineman, February 24, 2000.

43. Central Imagery Office, *Briefing Slides*, 1992.

44. Department of Defense Directive 5105.26, "Central Imagery Office," May 6, 1992; Central Imagery Office, *Briefing Slides*, pp. 2–3; Director of Central Intelligence Directive 2/9, "Management of National Imagery Intelligence," June 1, 1992.

45. Central Imagery Office, *Briefing Slides*, p. 2.

46. Statement of John Deutch before Senate Select Committee on Intelligence, April 26, 1995, pp. 8–9.

47. "DCI Plans a National Imagery Agency," *Communiqué*, August 1995, pp. 1, 8; DCI, "Terms of Reference for National Imagery Agency," circa May 1995.

48. Central Intelligence Agency, "National Imagery and Mapping Agency Proposed to Congress," November 28, 1995.

49. Ibid.

50. Interview with John N. McMahon, Los Altos, California, November 17, 1998.

51. Interview with James V. Hirsch, Fairfax, Virginia, February 12, 1999; CIA, Office of Public Affairs, "Unclassified Imagery Analysis Presentation," n.d.

52. Hirsch interview.

53. Ibid. Until 1994, OIA and NPIC were two distinct organizations. In 1994, NPIC assumed responsibility for staffing and managing OIA. At the same time, a number of OIA managers moved into positions at NPIC. The change, according to Patrick Eddington, was not one that he or others at NPIC felt was beneficial. He noted that NPIC, in the Navy Yard, lived a separate life from the CIA and that there were different cultures. In his view, NPIC was more independent and felt no obligation to support the intelligence directorate's conclusions, had a more exacting standard in its analysis of imagery, offered more extensive training to its analysts, and had a broader customer base—which included State, Defense, the Federal Emergency Management Agency, and Commerce. Whereas OIA never maintained an extensive database, the NPIC's National Data System was available to the entire intelligence community. The reorganization, according to Eddington, threw NPIC into "a state of turmoil" and made it "a less exciting and rewarding place to work." (Interview with Patrick Eddington, Centreville, Virginia, April 12, 1999. Also see Patrick Eddington, *Gassed in the Gulf: The Inside Story of the Pentagon-CIA Cover-Up of Gulf War Syndrome* ([Washington, D.C.: Insignia, 1997], p. 25.)

54. Interview with R. Evans Hineman, Chantilly, Virginia, February 17, 1999.

55. Interview with Patrick Eddington, Centreville, Virginia, April 12, 1999.

56. Eddington, *Gassed in the Gulf*, p. 151.

57. U.S. Congress, Senate Select Committee on Intelligence, *Special Report of the Senate Select Committee on Intelligence, United States Senate, January 4, 1995 to October 3, 1996* (Washington, D.C.: U.S. Government Printing Office, 1997), pp. 7–8. There was also some concern about the proposed merger from Defense Mapping Agency officials, who feared that their formal inclusion in the intelligence community might have a negative impact on the relationship with foreign nations who provide mapping information.

58. NIMA, "National Imagery and Mapping Agency Established," October 1, 1996.

59. First "Announced NRO Payload," *Spaceflight* 39, 3 (March 1997): 77. In 1995, the NRO and CIA had acknowledged the launch dates associated with the CORONA, ARGON, and LANYARD programs, the last of which was in May 1972.

60. Vincent Kiernan, "Titan 4 Launches Spy Satellite from Vandenberg AFB," *Space News*, December 7–13, 1992, p. 26; Craig Covault, "Advanced KH-11 Broadens U.S. Recon Capability," *Aviation Week and Space Technology*, January 6, 1997, pp. 24–25; Craig Covault, "New Intelligence Ops Debut in Iraqi Strikes," *Aviation Week and Space Technology*, December 21–28, 1998, pp. 124–125; William Harwood, "Titan Boosts Military Payload for Ninth Consecutive Success," *Space News*, December 11–17, 1995, p. 26; private information.

61. Interview with Bernard Lubarsky, Alexandria, Virginia, May 16, 2000; private information.

62. Barbara Crosette, "U.S. Seeks to Prove Mass Killings," *New York Times*, August 11, 1995, p. A3; Bill Gertz, "New Chinese Missiles Target All of East Asia," *Washington Times*, July 10, 1997, pp. A1, A16; Tim Weiner, "U.S. Suspects India Prepares for Nuclear Test," *New York Times*, December 15, 1995, p. A6; Elaine Sciolino, "U.S. Says It's Won Votes to Maintain Sanctions on Iraq," *New York Times*, March 5, 1995, pp. 1, 9; Bill Gertz, "Libyans Stop Work on Chemical Plant," *Washington Times*, June 24, 1996, p. A4; Joseph S. Bermudez Jr., "North Korea Set for More Ballistic Missile Tests," *Jane's Defence Weekly*, October 23, 1996, p. 5.

63. CIA Office of Public Affairs, "Hypertext Systems," n.d.

64. CIA, Office of Public Affairs, "Information Retrieval," n.d.

65. CIA, Office of Public Affairs, "Image Perspective Transformation Modeling and Visualization," n.d. circa 1996.

66. CIA Public Affairs, "Dual-Use Technology Projects: Law Enforcement and the Environment," 1996.

67. Ibid.; "Once-Secret Technology Assists Cancer Detection," *Signal*, June 1995, pp. 66–67; CIA, Public Affairs, "Facial Recognition Program," n.d.

68. Interview with Gene Poteat, McLean, Virginia, April 25, 2000; Philip Eckman, "Some Random Thoughts and Musings on ORD," n.d. Previously, according to former ORD director Philip Eckman, OD&E competed with ORD for funds and also was the agency's executive authority for decisions on funding reconnaissance projects, making it both "judge and jury." According to Eckman, that had been a sore point for many years, "since it was generally acknowledged that ORD had the lion's share of innovative proposals each year, yet never received more than about 20% of the funds." (Philip Eckman, "Some Random Thoughts and Musings on ORD," n.d.)

69. David interview.

70. McMahon interview; Poteat interview.

71. Hineman interview.

72. Hirsch interview.

73. David interview.

Chapter 11: Uncertain Future

1. CIA, "CIA's Deputy Director for Science and Technology to Become CEO of Public Service Research Institute," June 22, 1998; "History," www.anser.org/aboutanser/history.html.

2. CIA, "CIA's Deputy Director for Science and Technology to Become CEO of Public Service Research Institute."

3. Interview with Robert Singel, Great Falls, Virginia, February 25, 1999.

4. Interview with Philip Eckman, Alexandria, Virginia, May 16, 2000.

5. "Joanne Isham," www.odci.gov/cia, 1998; CIA Public Affairs, "DCI Tenet Announces Appointment of Deputy Directors for Science and Technology," January 12, 2000; CIA Public Affairs, "Joanne O. Isham, Deputy Director for Science and Technology," January 13, 2000.

6. Vernon Loeb, "Inside Information," www.washingtonpost.com, January 10, 2000; interview with R. Evans Hineman, Chantilly, Virginia, February 17, 1999.

7. CIA, "Director of Central Intelligence Appoints Dr. Gary L. Smith, Deputy Director for Science and Technology," March 24, 1999.

8. "Profile of APL," www.jhuapl.edu/profile/profile.htm; "MSX Satellite Passes Rocket Tracking Test," *Space News*, April 24–30, 1997, p. 10.

9. CIA, "Director of Central Intelligence Appoints Dr. Gary L. Smith, Deputy Director for Science and Technology."

10. Ibid.

11. CIA Public Affairs, "DCI Tenet Announces Appointment of Deputy Director for Science and Technology," January 12, 2000.

12. Vernon Loeb, "CIA Science Chief Quits; Deputy Named," *Washington Post*, January 14, 2000, p. A25; private information.

13. CIA Public Affairs, "DCI Tenet Announces Appointment of Deputy Director for Science and Technology."

14. Telephone conversation with CIA spokesman, January 21, 2000.

15. Loeb, "CIA Science Chief Quits; Deputy Named"; telephone interview with Gordon Oehler, October 5, 2000.

16. CIA Public Affairs, "James L. Runyan, Associate Deputy Director for Science and Technology," January 2000.

17. Private information.

18. Letter, Joanne O. Isham to Albert Wheelon, October 13, 2000.

19. CIA, "DS&T Realignment Overview," n.d.

20. Ibid.; CIA, "DS&T Response to Author's Questions," February 9, 2001.

21. Tabassum Zakaria, "CIA Using 'Data Mining' Technology to Find Nuggets," Reuters, March 2, 2001.

22. Ibid.

23. Gary H. Anthes, "Cloak & Dagger IT," www.computerworld.com, accessed February 6, 2001; Rick E. Yannuzzi, "In-Q-Tel: A New Partnership Between the CIA and the Private Sector," *Defense Intelligence Journal* 9, 1 (Winter 2000).

24. Anthes, "Cloak & Dagger IT."

25. Ibid.

26. Neil King Jr., "Small Start-Up Helps the CIA to Mask Its Moves on the Web," *Wall Street Journal,* February 12, 2001, pp. B1, Bb.

27. Ibid.

28. CIA, "DS&T Response to Author's Questions"; private information.

29. CIA, "DS&T Realignment Overview."

30. Ibid.

31. Basil H. Scott, "A 21st Century CIA—Meeting Challenges, Realizing Opportunities," April 4, 1999, www.odci.gov/dst.

32. Telephone interview with Robert Kohler, July 6, 1999.

33. Gordon Oehler, "Warning and Detection," in Sidney D. Drell, Abraham D. Sofaer, and George D. Wilson, *The New Terror: Facing the Threat of Biological and Chemical Weapons* (Stanford, Calif.: Hoover Institution Press, 1999), pp. 138–151 at p. 143.

34. Telephone interview with Robert Kohler, February 1, 2001.

SOURCES

Interviews (Dates without locations indicate a telephone interview)

Lew Allen: Pasadena, California, June 10, 1999.
Paul Bacalis: December 1, 1999.
Richard Bissell: Farmington, Connecticut, January 6, 1984; Farmington, Connecticut, March 16, 1984.
Dino Brugioni: May 21, 1996.
Roy Burks: North Potomac, Maryland, May 10, 1999.
Frank Buzard: Rancho Palos Verdes, California, June 11, 1999.
Joseph Charyk: June 1, 1999.
Ruth David: Arlington, Virginia, February 22, 1999.
Philip Eckman: Alexandria, Virginia, May 16, 2000.
Patrick Eddington: Centreville, Virginia, April 12, 1999.
Edward Giller: June 29, 1999.
R. Evans Hineman: Chantilly, Virginia, February 17, 1999.
James V. Hirsch: Fairfax, Virginia, February 12, 1999.
R. M. Huffstutler: Falls Church, Virginia, March 23, 1999.
Robert Kohler: July 6, 1999; February 1, 2001.
Steven Koonin: Pasadena, California, March 22, 2000.
Jack C. Ledford: Arlington, Virginia, October 7, 1999.
Walter Levison: September 17, 1999.
Henry S. Lowenhaupt: Springfield, Virginia, April 15, 1999.
Bernard Lubarsky: Alexandria, Virginia, May 9, 2000.
Arthur Lundahl: October 19, 1988; July 27, 1989.
Frank Madden: November 3, 2000.
Victor Marchetti: October 12, 1999.
John Martin: September 7, 1996.
John McMahon: Los Altos, California, November 17, 1998.
Brockway McMillan: September 15, 1999.
William H. Nance: Bethesda, Maryland, May 4, 1999.
Gordon Oehler: October 5, 2000.
Robert Phillips: Rosslyn, Virginia, June 4, 1999.
Henry Plaster: Vienna, Virginia, September 30, 1999.
Gene Poteat: McLean, Virginia, April 25, 2000.
Edward Proctor: March 10, 1999.
Robert Singel: Great Falls, Virginia, February 25, 1999.
Sayre Stevens: May 29, 1996; Springfield, Virginia, March 18, 1999.

Thomas Twetten: March 12, 2001.
Karl Weber: Oakton, Virginia, May 5, 1999.
Albert Wheelon: April 2, 1997; Washington, D.C., April 9, 1997; May 19, 1997; Montecito, California, May 11–12, 1998; November 29, 1998; Montecito, June 14, 1999; Montecito, March 21, 2000.

Government/Contractor Documents, Publications, and Videos (excluding memos, letters, and press releases)

"Agreement Between Secretary of Defense and the Director of Central Intelligence on Responsibilities of the National Reconnaissance Office." May 2, 1962.

Air Force Eastern Test Range, *Eastern Test Range Index of Missile Launchings, July 1968–June 1969.* Patrick AFB, Fla.: AFETR, 1969.

Allen Welsh Dulles as Director of Central Intelligence, 26 February 1953–29 November 1961, Volume II, Coordination of Central Intelligence. Washington, D.C.: Central Intelligence Agency, 1973.

Armstrong, Willis, William Leonhart, William J. McCaffrey, and Herbert C. Rothenberg. "The Hazards of Single-Outcome Forecasting." *Studies in Intelligence* 28, 3 (Fall 1984): 57–70.

Bernard, Richard L. "The Defense Special Missile and Astronautics Center." *Cryptologic Spectrum*, Fall 1983, pp. 30–33.

Brandwein, David S. "Telemetry Analysis." *Studies in Intelligence* 8, 4 (Fall 1964): 21–29.

______. "The SS-8 Controversy." *Studies in Intelligence* 13, 3 (Summer 1969): 27–35.

Brown, Donald C. "On the Trail of Hen House and Hen Roost." *Studies in Intelligence* 13, 2 (Spring 1969): 11–19.

Burke, James. "Seven Years to Luna 9." *Studies in Intelligence* 10, 3 (Summer 1966): 1–24.

Bush, George. National Security Directive 45. "U.S. Policy in Response to the Iraqi Invasion of Kuwait," August 20, 1990.

______. National Security Directive 54. "Responding to Iraqi Aggression in the Gulf," January 15, 1991.

Carey, Warren F., and Myles Maxfield. "Intelligence Implications of Disease." *Studies in Intelligence* 16, 1 (Spring 1972): 71–78.

Center for the Study of Intelligence. *Declassified National Intelligence Estimates of the Soviet Union and International Communism.* Washington, D.C.: Central Intelligence Agency, 1996.

Central Imagery Office. *Briefing Slides,* 1992.

Central Intelligence Agency. *The French Nuclear Energy Weapons Program*, November 13, 1959.

______. "Future of the Agency's U-2 Capability," July 7, 1960.

______. *Cost Reduction Program FY 1966–FY 1967*, September 1, 1965, NARA/CP, TRB, RG 263, Entry 36, HRP 89-2/00443, Box 7, File 713.

______. "Biographic Profile, Albert Dewell Wheelon," May 10, 1966, NARA, MRB, RG 263.

______. *Burial at Sea*, September 4, 1974. Videotape.

______. *Iran in the 1980s*, August 1977.

______. *R. V. Jones Intelligence Award Ceremony Honoring Dr. Albert Wheelon*, December 13, 1994.

______. *DS&T 35th Anniversary: Celebrating 50 Years of CIA History*, July 24, 1997. Videotape.

Central Intelligence Agency and National Reconnaissance Office. "CORONA Pioneers," May 25, 1995.

Central Intelligence Agency, Photographic Interpretation Center. *Joint Mission Coverage Index, Mission 9009, 18 August 1960*, September 1960. In Kevin C. Ruffner (ed.), *CORONA: America's First Satellite Program.* Washington, D.C.: Central Intelligence Agency, 1995.

Charyk, Joseph. "A Summary Review of the National Reconnaissance Office," February 25, 1963.

China Task Force, Central Intelligence Agency. "The Production Effort," July 1965–June 1967, NARA, RG 263, CIA HRP 89-2, NN3-263-94-010, Box 9, File HS/HC 735, Folder 2.
"CIA Raising USSR Sub Raises Questions." *FBIS-SOV-92-145*, July 28, 1992, pp. 15–16.
Clesh, Mark. "Dedication of New Operations Center for DEFSMAC," *Communiqué*, March/April 1998, pp. 42–43.
David, Ruth. Speech to Armed Forces Communications Electronics Association, January 1998.
Davies, Merton, and William R. Harris. *RAND's Role in the Evolution of Balloon and Satellite Observation Systems and Related U.S. Space Technology.* Santa Monica, Calif.: RAND, 1988.
"DCI Plans a National Imagery Agency." *Communiqué*, August 1995, pp. 1, 8.
DCI Task Force on the National Reconnaissance Office. *Report to the Director of Central Intelligence, DCI Task Force on the National Reconnaissance Office, Final Report*, April 1992.
Dean, L. E., C. R. Johnson, and H. J. Strasler. "Teal Amber I." *Journal of Defense Research*, Special Issue 78-3, 1978, pp. 151–170.
"Debriefing of Francis Gary Powers, Tape #2." February 13, 1962, NARA, RG 263, 1998 CIA release, Box 230, Folder 3.
Department of Defense. DOD Directive S-5100.43, "Defense Special Missile and Astronautics Center (Defense/SMAC)," April 27, 1964.
______. *Conduct of the Persian Gulf War, Final Report to Congress.* Washington, D.C.: Department of Defense, April 1992.
______. DOD Directive 5105.26, "Central Imagery Office," May 6, 1992.
Department of State. "Transcript of Daily Press Briefing, Tuesday, September 29, 1964."
Deutch, John. Statement before Senate Select Committee on Intelligence, April 26, 1995.
Director of Central Intelligence. NIE 11-6-54, *Soviet Capabilities and Probable Programs in the Guided Missile Field*, October 1954.
______. NIE 11-4-57, *Main Trends in Soviet Capabilities and Policies, 1957–1962*, November 12, 1957.
______. NIE 11-4-59, *Main Trends in Soviet Capabilities and Policies, 1959–1964*, February 9, 1960.
______. NIE 11-4-60, *Main Trends in Soviet Capabilities and Policies, 1956–1965*, December 1, 1960.
______. NIE 11-8-61, *Soviet Capabilities for Long Range Attack*, June 7, 1961.
______. NIE 11-8/1-61, *Soviet Capabilities for Long Range Attack*, September 21, 1961.
______. SNIE 13-2-63, *Communist China's Advanced Weapons Program*, July 24, 1963.
______. NIE 11-8-63, *Soviet Capabilities for Strategic Attack*, October 18, 1963.
______. NIE 11-2-64, *The Soviet Atomic Energy Program*, July 16, 1964.
______. SNIE 13-4-64. *The Chances of an Imminent Communist Chinese Nuclear Explosion*, August 26, 1964.
______. NIE 11-8-64, *Soviet Capabilities for Strategic Attack*, October 8, 1964.
______. NIE 11-1-65. *The Soviet Space Program*, 1965.
______. NIE 11-2A-65, *The Soviet Atomic Energy Program*, May 19, 1965.
______. NIE 11-1-67, *The Soviet Space Program*, March 2, 1967.
______. NIE 11-8-67, *Soviet Capabilities for Strategic Attack*, October 26, 1967.
______. NIE 11-3-67, *Soviet Strategic Air and Missile Defenses*, November 9, 1967.
______. NIE 11-8-70, *Soviet Forces for Intercontinental Attack*, November 24, 1970.
______. NIE 11-8-71, *Soviet Forces for Intercontinental Attack*, October 21, 1971.
______. NIE 11-8-72, *Soviet Forces for Intercontinental Attack*, October 26, 1972.
______. DCID 3/3, "Scientific Intelligence," October 28, 1949.
______. DCID 3/4, "Production of Scientific and Technical Intelligence," August 14, 1952.
______. DCID 3/5, "Production of Scientific and Technical Intelligence," February 3, 1959.
______. DCID 2/9, "Management of National Imagery Intelligence," June 1, 1992.

Directorate of Collection, Office, ACS/Intelligence, Air Force. *History: Directorate of Collection, Office, ACS/Intelligence 1 July–31 December 1962*, n.d.

Directorate of Science and Technology, CIA. *CORONA Program History, Volume II: Governmental Activities*, May 1976.

Dulles, Allen W., William H. Jackson, and Mathias F. Correa. *The Central Intelligence Agency and National Organization for Intelligence.* Washington, D.C.: National Security Council, 1949.

Earman, J. S., Inspector General, CIA. *Report on Plots to Assassinate Fidel Castro.* Washington, D.C.: CIA, 1967.

Eliot, Frank. "Moon Bounce Elint." *Studies in Intelligence* 11, 2 (Spring 1967): 59–65.

Fischer, Benjamin B. (ed.) *At Cold War's End: U.S. Intelligence on the Soviet Union and Eastern Europe 1989–1991.* Washington, D.C.: Central Intelligence Agency, 1999.

Foreign Broadcast Information Service. "Overview for CNC Conference," n.d.

Garofalo, Nicholas R. "Present and Future Capabilities of OTH Radars." *Studies in Intelligence* 13, 2 (Spring 1969): 53–61.

Gates, Robert M. *Statement on Change in CIA and the Intelligence Community*, April 1, 1992.

Geiger, Rear Adm. Robert, and D. Barry Kelly. *NRO Restructure Study, Final Report, Volume II.* Washington, D.C.: NRO, 1989.

Gerson, N. C. "SIGINT in Space." *Studies in Intelligence* 28, 2 (Summer 1984): 41–48.

GRAB: Galactic Radiation and Background. Washington, D.C.: Naval Research Laboratory, 1997.

Grant, Sam, and Peter C. Oleson. "Breast Cancer Detection Research." *Studies in Intelligence*, Semiannual Unclassified Edition No. 1, 1997, pp. 27–34.

Greer, Kenneth E. "Corona." *Studies in Intelligence*, Supplement, 17 (Spring 1973).

Haines, Gerald K. *The National Reconnaissance Office: Its Origins, Creation, and Early Years.* Washington, D.C.: NRO, 1997.

Hons, Joyce M., Juan R. Jimenez, Gabriell G. Marshall, and Johnny D. Ford. *History of the Air Intelligence Agency, 1 January–31 December 1994, Volume I.* San Antonio, Tex.: AIA, 1995.

Howland, Nina D. (ed.). *Foreign Relations of the United States, 1964–1968, Volume XXII: Iran.* Washington, D.C.: U.S. Government Printing Office, 1999.

Inspector General, CIA. *Inspector General's Survey of the Office of Research and Development*, October 1972.

"Inspector General's Survey of Air Activities: Summary of Recommendations," circa 1962.

Intelligence Advisory Committee. NIE 11-3A-54, *Summary: The Soviet Atomic Energy Program to Mid-1957*, February 16, 1954.

Jackson, George S., and Martin F. Clausen. *Organizational History of the Central Intelligence Agency, 1950–1953.* Washington, D.C.: Central Intelligence Agency, 1957.

Joint Study Group. *Report on Foreign Intelligence Activities of the United States Government*, December 15, 1960.

Klaimon, Jerold H. "Reentry Vehicle Analysis." *Studies in Intelligence* 12, 3 (Summer 1968): 23–33.

Kress, Kenneth A. "Parapsychology in Intelligence: A Personal Review and Conclusions." *Studies in Intelligence* 21, 4 (Winter 1977): 7–17.

Kroeger, Charles A., Jr. "ELINT: A Scientific Intelligence System." *Studies in Intelligence* 2, 1 (Winter 1958): 71–83.

LaMothe, John D. *Controlled Offensive Behavior–USSR (U).* Washington, D.C.: DIA, 1972.

Laubenthal, Capt. Sanders A. *The Missiles in Cuba, 1962: The Role of SAC Intelligence.* Offutt AFB, Nebr.: Strategic Air Command, 1984.

Lawrence, R. E., and Harry W. Woo. "Infrared Imagery in Overhead Reconnaissance." *Studies in Intelligence* 11, 3 (Summer 1967): 17–40.

Lowenhaupt, Henry S. "The Decryption of a Picture." *Studies in Intelligence* 1, 3 (Summer 1957).

______. "Mission to Birch Woods." *Studies in Intelligence* 12, 4 (Fall 1968): 1–12.

Mabon, David M., and David S. Patterson (eds.). *Foreign Relations of the United States, 1961–1963, Volume VII: Arms Control and Disarmament.* Washington, D.C.: U.S. Government Printing Office, 1996.

McCone, John A., Director of Central Intelligence, and Roswell Gilpatric, Deputy Secretary of Defense. "Agreement Between the Secretary of Defense and the Director of Central Intelligence on Management of the National Reconnaissance Program," March 13, 1963.

McIninch, Thomas P. "The OXCART Story." *Studies in Intelligence* 15, 1 (Winter 1971): 1–34.

Mendez, Antonio. "A Classic Case of Deception." *Studies in Intelligence*, Unclassified Edition, Winter 1999–2000, pp. 1–16.

Montague, Ludwell Lee. *General Walter Bedell Smith as Director of Central Intelligence, October 1950–February 1953.* University Park: Pennsylvania State University Press, 1992.

Mumford, Michael D., Andrew D. Rose, and David M. Goslin. *An Evaluation of Remote Viewing: Research and Applications.* Washington, D.C.: American Institutes for Research, September 29, 1995.

Nance, William H. "Quality ELINT." *Studies in Intelligence* 12, 2 (Spring 1968): 7–19.

National Foreign Assessment Center, CIA. *The Soviet Earth Resources Satellite Program*, June 1980.

National Photographic Interpretation Center, CIA. "Search for Uranium Mining in the Vicinity of A-Ko-Su, China," August 1963. In Kevin C. Ruffner (ed.), *CORONA: America's First Satellite Program.* Washington, D.C.: Central Intelligence Agency, 1995, pp. 175–183.

______."Suspect CW Agent Production Plants—Dzerzhinsk USSR, Changes Since 1962," August 1963. In Kevin C. Ruffner (ed.), *CORONA: America's First Satellite Program.* Washington, D.C.: Central Intelligence Agency, 1995, pp. 185–189.

______. "Chronological Developments of the Kapustin Yar/Vladimirovka and Tyuratam Missile Test Centers, USSR, 1957 Through 1963," November 1963. In Kevin C. Ruffner (ed.), *CORONA: America's First Satellite Program.* Washington, D.C.: Central Intelligence Agency, 1995, pp. 191–196.

______. "Probable Solid Propellants Testing Facilities and Associated Explosives Plants in the USSR," December 1963. In Kevin C. Ruffner (ed.), *CORONA: America's First Satellite Program.* Washington, D.C.: Central Intelligence Agency, 1995, pp. 197–214.

______*Black Shield Mission X–001, 31 May 1967,* June 1967.

______*Black Shield Mission BX–6705, 20 June 1967,* June 1967.

______*Black Shield Mission BX–6706, 30 June 1967,* July 1967.

______*Black Shield Mission BX–6723, 17 September 1967,* November 1967.

______*Black Shield Mission BX–6725, 4 October 1967,* December 1967.

______*Black Shield Mission BX–6732, 28 October 1967,* December 1967.

National Reconnaissance Office. *Deputy Directors of the NRO.* Chantilly, Va.: NRO, 1997.

______. "Biography: Dennis Fitzgerald." Chantilly, Va.: NRO, 1997.

______. *Program Directors of the NRO: ABC&D.* Chantilly, Va.: NRO, 1999.

National Security Agency. *A Historical Perspective of DefSMAC with Charles Tevis and Max Mitchell*, 1980. Video.

National Security Council. NSCID No. 5, "U.S. Espionage and Counterintelligence Activities Abroad," January 18, 1961.

______. NSCID No. 8, "Photographic Interpretation," January 18, 1961.

9th Strategic Reconnaissance Wing. *History of the 9th Strategic Reconnaissance Wing, 1 October–31 December 1967*, n.d.

Oder, Frederic C.E., James C. Fitzpatrick, and Paul E. Worthman. *The CORONA Story.* Washington, D.C.: National Reconnaissance Office, 1997.

Office of Computer Services, Directorate of Science and Technology, CIA. *OCS Computer System Planning Report*, June 1, 1965.

Office of Scientific Intelligence, Central Intelligence Agency. *Indian Nuclear Energy Program,* November 6, 1964.

______. *Japanese Nuclear Energy Program,* OSI-SR/65-55, November 1964.

______. *Soviet Nuclear Research Reactors*, OSI-SR/64-41, September 22, 1964.

Office of Special Projects, 1965–1970, Volume One, Chapters I-II. Washington, D.C.: CIA, 1973.

Office of Special Projects, 1965–1970, Volume Four: Appendixes B, C, and D. Washington, D.C.: CIA, 1973.

"ORD Milestones," September 1966, NARA, TRB, RG 263, 1998 CIA Release, Box 66, Folder 5.

Pedlow, Gregory W., and Donald E. Welzenbach. *The Central Intelligence Agency and Overhead Reconnaissance: The U-2 and OXCART Programs, 1954–1974.* Washington, D.C.: CIA, 1992.

Pekel, Kent. "Integrity, Ethics, and the CIA," *Studies in Intelligence*, Unclassified Edition, Spring 1998, pp. 85–94.

Perry, Robert. *A History of Satellite Reconnaissance, Volume 5: Management of the National Reconnaissance Program, 1960–1965.* Washington, D.C.: NRO, 1969.

Plaster, Henry G. "Snooping on Space Pictures." *Studies in Intelligence* 8, 4 (Fall 1964): 31–39.

Poteat, Gene. "Stealth, Countermeasures, and ELINT, 1960–1975." *Studies in Intelligence* 42, 1 (1998): 51–59.

Psychological Operations in Guerrilla Warfare. New York: Vintage, 1985.

Puthoff, Harold E., and Russell Targ. *Perceptual Augmentation Techniques, Part One—Technical Proposal.* SRI No. ISH 73–146, October 1, 1973.

______. *Perceptual Augmentation Techniques: Final Report (Covering the Period January 1974 through February 1975, Part Two—Research Project).* Menlo Park, Calif.: Stanford Research Institute, December 1, 1975.

Rathjens, George W. "Destruction of Chinese Nuclear Weapons Capabilities." ACDA, December 14, 1964.

Reagan, Ronald. National Security Decision Directive 17, "National Security Directive on Cuba and Central America," January 4, 1982.

Ruffner, Kevin C. (ed.). *CORONA: America's First Satellite Program.* Washington, D.C.: CIA, 1995.

Schwar, Harriet Dashiell (ed.). *Foreign Relations of the United States, 1964–1968, Volume 30: China.* Washington, D.C.: U.S. Government Printing Office, 1998.

Scott, Basil H. "A 21st Century CIA—Meeting Challenges, Realizing Opportunities," April 4, 1999. www. odci.gov/dst.

Secretary of the Air Force/Public Affairs. "Biography: Major General John L. Martin Jr.," n.d.

______. "Biography: General Lew Allen Jr.," September 1981.

"Series of SS-11 ICBM Tests to Pacific Impact Area Concluded." *EUCOM Intelligence Report*, September 7, 1966.

Sloop, John L. *Liquid Hydrogen as a Propulsion Fuel.* Washington, D.C.: NASA, 1978.

"Soviets Maintaining High Launch Rate for Major ICBMs: SS-11 Crew Training May Be Under Way." *EUCOM Intelligence Report*, August 18, 1966.

"Soviets Step Up Testing of First-Line ICBM Systems." *EUCOM Intelligence Report*, April 13, 1966.

"Statement by the Director, Senate Foreign Relations Committee," June 23, 1969.

Steury, Donald P. (ed.). *Intentions and Capabilities: Estimates on Soviet Strategic Forces, 1950–1983.* Washington, D.C.: CIA, 1996.

Stillman, D., "An Analysis of a Remote-Viewing Experiment of URDF-3." Los Alamos, Los Alamos Scientific Laboratory, December 4, 1975, p. 4.

Studeman, William O., Deputy Director of Central Intelligence. Remarks at Symposium on "National Security and National Competitiveness: Open Source Solutions," December 1, 1992, McLean, Va.

Systems Analysis Staff, Directorate of Science and Technology, CIA. *A Report on DS&T Intelligence Collection Requirements*, July 12, 1966.

"Testimony of Allen Dulles." *Executive Sessions of the Senate Foreign Relations Committee (Historical Series), Vol. XII, Eighty-sixth Congress–Second Session, 1960.* Washington, D.C.: U.S. Government Printing Office, 1982.

Thorne, C. Thomas, Jr., and David S. Patterson (eds.). *Emergence of the Intelligence Establishment.* Washington, D.C.: U.S. Government Printing Office, 1996.

United States Air Force, "Biography: Major General Paul N. Bacalis," n.d.

______. "Biography: Brigadier General Jack C. Ledford, n.d.

______. "Biography: Brigadier General Wendell L. Bevan Jr., July 15, 1970, with updates.

United States of America v. Christopher John Boyce. Reporter's Transcript, District Court, Central District of California, Hon. Robert J. Kelleher, CR-77-131-RJK, April 20, 1977.

United States of America v. Larry Wu Tai Chin aka Chin Wu-Tai. United States District Court, Eastern District of Virginia, Alexandria Division, Criminal No. 85-00263-A, January 2, 1986.

United States of America v. William Kampiles. United States District Court, Northern District of Indiana, November 6, 1978.

U.S. Congress, House Permanent Select Committee on Intelligence. *Iran: Evaluation of U.S. Intelligence Performance Prior to November 1978.* Washington, D.C.: U.S. Government Printing Office, 1979.

______. *NRO Headquarters Facility.* Washington, D.C.: U.S. Government Printing Office, 1995.

______. *Intelligence Authorization Act for Fiscal Year 1998, Report 105–135, Part 1.* Washington, D.C.: U.S. Government Printing Office, 1997.

U.S. Congress, House Select Committee on Intelligence. *U.S. Intelligence Agencies and Activities: Intelligence Costs and Fiscal Procedures, Part 1.* Washington, D.C.: U.S. Government Printing Office, 1975.

U.S. Congress, Senate Committee on Armed Services. *Department of Defense Authorization for Appropriations for Fiscal Year 1994 and the Future Years Defense Program.* Washington, D.C.: U.S. Government Printing Office, 1993.

U.S. Congress, Senate Foreign Relations Committee. *Intelligence and the ABM.* Washington, D.C.: U.S. Government Printing Office, 1969.

______. *Fiscal Year 1980 International Security Assistance Authorization.* Washington, D.C.: U.S. Government Printing Office, 1979.

U.S. Congress, Senate Select Committee on Intelligence. *Nomination of John McMahon.* Washington, D.C.: U.S. Government Printing Office, 1982.

______. *S. 2198 and S. 421 to Reorganize the United States Intelligence Community.* Washington, D.C.: U.S. Government Printing Office, 1993.

______. *NRO Headquarters Project.* Washington, D.C.: U.S. Government Printing Office, 1995.

______. *Special Report of the Senate Select Committee on Intelligence, United States Senate, January 4, 1995 to October 3, 1996.* Washington, D.C.: U.S. Government Printing Office, 1997.

U.S. Congress, Senate Select Committee to Study Governmental Operations with Respect to Intelligence Activities. *Alleged Assassination Plots Involving Foreign Leaders.* Washington, D.C.: U.S. Government Printing Office, 1975.

______. *Final Report, Book I: Foreign and Military Intelligence.* Washington, D.C.: U.S. Government Printing Office, 1976.

______. *Final Report, Book IV: Supplementary Detailed Staff Reports on Foreign and Military Intelligence.* Washington, D.C.: U.S. Government Printing Office, 1976.

Welzenbach, Donald E. "Science and Technology: Origins of a Directorate." *Studies in Intelligence* 30, 2 (Summer 1986): 13–26.

Wheelon, Albert D,. and Sidney Graybeal. "Intelligence for the Space Race." *Studies in Intelligence* 7, 4 (Fall 1963): 1–13.

Whitmire, Frank A., and Edward G. Correll. "The Failure of Cosmos 57." *Studies in Intelligence* 10, 3 (Summer 1966): 25–29.

Books and Monographs

Agee, Philip. *Inside the Company: CIA Diary.* San Francisco: Stonehill, 1975.

Allen, Thomas, and Norman Polmar. *Merchants of Treason: America's Secrets for Sale from the* Pueblo *to the Present.* New York: Delacorte, 1988.

Andrew, Christopher. *For the President's Eyes Only: Secret Intelligence and the American Presidency from Washington to Bush.* New York: HarperCollins, 1995.

Atkinson, Rick. *Crusade: The Untold Story of the Persian Gulf War.* Boston: Houghton Mifflin, 1993.

Ball, Desmond. *Politics and Force Levels: The Strategic Missile Program of the Kennedy Administration.* Berkeley: University of California Press, 1980.

______. *A Suitable Piece of Real Estate: American Installations in Australia.* Sydney: Hale & Iremonger, 1980.

______. *Pine Gap: Australia and the U.S. Geostationary SIGINT Satellite Program.* Sydney: Allen & Unwin, 1988.

______. *Intelligence in the Gulf War.* Canberra, Australia: SDSC, Australian National University, 1991.

Bamford, James. *The Puzzle Palace: A Report on NSA, America's Most Secret Agency.* Boston: Houghton Mifflin, 1982.

Beck, Melvin C. *Secret Contenders: The Myth of Cold War Counterintelligence.* New York: Sheridan Square, 1984.

Bell, Griffin. *Taking Care of the Law.* New York: William Morrow, 1982.

Berman, Robert P., and John C. Baker. *Soviet Strategic Forces: Requirements and Responses.* Washington, D.C.: Brookings Institution, 1982.

Bissell, Richard M., with Jonathan E. Lewis and Francis T. Pudlo. *Reflections of a Cold Warrior.* New Haven: Yale University Press, 1996.

Broad, William. *The Universe Below: Discovering the Secrets of the Deep Sea.* New York: Simon & Schuster, 1997.

Brugioni, Dino. *Eyeball to Eyeball: The Inside Story of the Cuban Missile Crisis.* New York: Random House, 1991.

Burleson, Clyde W. *The Jennifer Project.* College Station, Tex.: Texas A&M, 1997.

Burr, William (ed.). *The Kissinger Transcripts: The Top-Secret Talks with Beijing and Moscow.* New York: New Press, 1998.

Burrows, William E. *Deep Black: Space Espionage and National Security.* New York: Random House, 1986.

______. *Exploring Space: Voyages in the Solar System and Beyond.* New York: Random House, 1990.

Cahn, Anne Hessing. *Killing Détente: The Right Attacks the CIA.* University Park: Pennsylvania State University Press, 1998.

Campbell, James B. *Introduction to Remote Sensing.* New York: Guilford, 1987.

Claridge, Duane R. *A Spy for All Seasons: My Life in the CIA.* New York: Scribner's, 1996.

Cline, Ray S. *Secrets, Spies, and Scholars: Blueprint of the Essential CIA.* Washington, D.C.: Acropolis, 1976.

Cockburn, Andrew, and Leslie Cockburn. *Dangerous Liaison: The Inside Story of the U.S.-Israeli Covert Relationship.* New York: HarperCollins, 1991.

Cohen, Avner. *Israel and the Bomb.* New York: Columbia University Press, 1998.

Colby, William, with Peter Forbath. *Honorable Men: My Life in the CIA.* New York: Simon & Schuster, 1978.

Crease, Robert P. and Charles C. Mann. *The Second Creation: Makers of the Revolution in 20th-Century Physics.* New York: Macmillan, 1986.

Crickmore, Paul F. *Lockheed SR-71: The Secret Missions Exposed.* London: Osprey, 1993.

Day, Dwayne A., John Logsdon, and Brian Latell (eds.). *Eye in the Sky: The Story of the CORONA Spy Satellites*. Washington, D.C.: Smithsonian, 1998.

Drell, Sidney, Abraham D. Sofaer, and George D. Wilson (eds.). *The New Terror: Facing the Threat of Biological and Chemical Weapons*. Stanford, Calif.: Hoover Institution Press, 1999.

Earley, Peter. *Confessions of a Spy: The Real Story of Aldrich Ames*. New York: Putnam, 1997.

Eddington, Patrick G. *Gassed in the Gulf: The Inside Story of the Pentagon-CIA Cover-Up of Gulf War Syndrome*. Washington, D.C.: Insignia, 1997.

Emerson, Steven. *Secret Warriors: Inside the Covert Military Operations of the Reagan Era*. New York: Putnam, 1988.

Emery, Fred. *Watergate: The Corruption of American Politics and the Fall of Richard Nixon*. New York: Times Books, 1994.

Frost, Michael, and Michel Gratton. *Spyworld: Inside the Canadian and American Intelligence Establishments*. Toronto: Doubleday Canada, 1994.

Gates, Robert. *From the Shadows: The Ultimate Insider's Account of Five Presidents and How They Won the Cold War*. New York: Simon & Schuster, 1996.

Gordon, Michael, and Bernard Trainor. *The General's War: The Inside Story of the Conflict in the Gulf*. Boston: Little, Brown, 1994.

Grose, Peter. *Gentleman Spy: The Life of Allen Dulles*. Boston: Houghton Mifflin, 1994.

Hallion, Richard. *Storm over Iraq: Air Power and the Gulf War*. Washington, D.C.: Smithsonian Institution, 1992.

Harford, James. *Korolev: How One Man Masterminded the Soviet Drive to Beat America to the Moon*. New York: John Wiley, 1997.

Hawkes, Nigel, Geoffrey Lean, David Leigh, Robin McKie, Peter Pringle, and Andrew Wilson. *Chernobyl: The End of the Nuclear Dream*. New York: Vintage, 1986.

Hersh, Seymour H. *"The Target is Destroyed": What Really Happened to Flight 007 and What America Knew About It*. New York: Random House, 1986.

______. *The Samson Option: Israel's Nuclear Arsenal and American Foreign Policy*. New York: Random House, 1991.

Hulnick, Arthur S. *Fixing the Spy Machine: Preparing American Intelligence for the Twenty-first Century*. Westport, Conn.: Praeger, 1999.

Johnson, Nicholas L. *Soviet Military Strategy in Space*. London: Jane's, 1987.

Kessler, Ronald. *Spy vs. Spy: Stalking Soviet Spies in America*. New York: Scribner's, 1988.

______. *Inside the CIA: Revealing the Secrets of the World's Most Powerful Spy Agency*. New York: Pocket Books, 1992.

Killian, James R., Jr. *Sputnik, Scientists, and Eisenhower: A Memoir of the First Special Assistant to the President for Science and Technology*. Cambridge: MIT Press, 1982.

Koehler, John O. *STASI: The Untold Story of the East German Secret Police*. Boulder, Colo.: Westview Press, 1998.

Kornbluh, Peter. *Nicaragua: The Price of Intervention, Reagan's War Against the Sandinistas*. Washington, D.C.: Institute for Policy Studies, 1987.

Lewis, John Wilson, and Xue Litai. *China Builds the Bomb*. Stanford, Calif.: Stanford University Press, 1988.

Lindsay, Robert. *The Falcon and the Snowman: A True Story of Friendship and Espionage*. New York: Simon & Schuster, 1979.

Marks, David, and Richard Kammann. *The Psychology of the Psychic*. Buffalo, N.Y.: Prometheus Books, 1980.

Marks, John. *The Search for the "Manchurian Candidate": The CIA and Mind Control*. New York: Norton, 1991.

Martin, David C. *Wilderness of Mirrors*. New York: Harper & Row, 1980.

Martin, Frederick Thomas Martin. *Top-Secret Intranet: How U.S. Intelligence Built INTELINK–The World's Largest, Most Secure Network*. Upper Saddle River, N.J.: Prentice-Hall PTR, 1998.

McDonald, Robert A. (ed.). *CORONA: Between the Sun and the Earth, the First NRO Reconnaissance Eye in Space*. Bethesda, Md.: American Society for Photogrammetry and Remote Sensing, 1997.

McElheny, Victor K. *Insisting on the Impossible: The Life of Edwin Land, Inventor of Instant Photography*. Reading, Mass.: Perseus Books, 1998.

Melton, Keith. *CIA Special Weapons and Equipment: Spy Devices of the Cold War*. New York: Sterling Publishing, 1994.

Mendez, Antonio, with Malcolm McConnell. *The Master of Disguise: My Secret Life in the CIA*. New York: Morrow, 1999.

Miller, Jay. *Lockheed U-2*. Austin, Tex.: Aerofax, 1983.

______. *Skunk Works: The Official History*. North Branch, Minn.: Specialty Press, 1996.

Mosley, Leonard. *Dulles: A Biography of Eleanor, Allen, and John Foster and Their Family Network*. New York: Dial Press, 1978.

Mutza, Wayne. *Lockheed P2V Neptune: An Illustrated History*. Atglen, Pa.: Schiffer Military/Aviation History, 1996.

Neff, Donald. *Warriors for Jerusalem: The Six Days That Changed the Middle East*. New York: Simon & Schuster, 1984.

Newhouse, John. *War and Peace in the Nuclear Age*. New York: Knopf, 1989.

Norris, Robert S., Andrew S. Burrows, and Richard W. Fieldhouse. *Nuclear Weapons Databook Volume V: British, French, and Chinese Nuclear Weapons*. Boulder, Colo.: Westview, 1994.

Peebles, Curtis. *Guardians: Strategic Reconnaissance Satellites*. Novato, Calif.: Presidio Press, 1987.

Pelletier, Jean, and Claude Adams. *The Canadian Caper*. New York: William Morrow, 1981.

Perisco, Joseph E. *Piercing the Reich: The Penetration of Nazi Germany by American Secret Agents During World War II*. New York: Ballantine Books, 1979.

Pocock, Chris. *Dragon Lady: The History of the U-2 Spyplane*. Shrewsbury, England: Airlife, 1989.

______. *The U-2 Spyplane: Toward the Unknown*. Atglen, Pa.: Schiffer Books, 2000.

Powers, Thomas. *The Man Who Kept the Secrets: Richard Helms and the CIA*. London: Weidenfeld and Nicolson, 1979.

Prados, John. *The Soviet Estimate: U.S. Intelligence and Russian Military Strength*. New York: Dial, 1982.

______. *Presidents' Secret Wars: CIA and Pentagon Covert Operations from World War II Through the Persian Gulf*. Chicago: Elephant Paperbacks, 1996.

Preston, Bob. *Plowshares and Power: The Military Use of Civil Space*. Washington, D.C.: National Defense University Press, 1994.

Ranelagh, John. *The Agency: The Rise and Decline of the CIA, from Wild Bill Donovan to William Casey*. New York: Simon & Schuster, 1986.

Reade, David. *The Age of Orion: Lockheed P-3, an Illustrated History*. Atglen, Pa.: Schiffer Military/Aviation History, 1998.

Rich, Ben R., and Leo Janos. *Skunk Works: A Personal Memoir of My Years at Lockheed*. Boston: Little, Brown, 1994.

Richelson, Jeffrey T. *America's Secret Eyes in Space: The U.S. KEYHOLE Spy Satellite Program*. New York: Harper & Row, 1990.

______. *America's Space Sentinels: DSP Satellites and National Security*. Lawrence: University Press of Kansas, 1999.

Riste, Olav. *The Norwegian Intelligence Service, 1945–1970*. London: Frank Cass, 1999.

Ross, Robert S. *Negotiating Cooperation: The United States and China, 1969–1989*. Stanford, Calif.: Stanford University Press, 1995.

Rostizke, Harry. *KGB: The Eyes of Russia*. New York: Doubleday, 1981.
Schechter, Jerrold L., and Peter S. Deriabin. *The Spy Who Saved the World: How a Soviet Colonel Changed the Course of the Cold War.* New York: Scribner's 1992.
Schiff, Ze'ev. *A History of the Israeli Army: 1874 to the Present*. New York: Macmillan, 1985.
Schnabel, Jim. *Remote Viewers: The Secret History of America's Psychic Spies*. New York: Dell, 1997.
Seaborg, Glenn T., with Benjamin S. Loeb. *Stemming the Tide: Arms Control in the Johnson Years*. Lexington, Mass.: Lexington Books, 1986.
Smith, Russell Jack. *The Unknown CIA: My Three Decades with the Agency*. New York: Berkley, 1992.
Sontag, Sherry, and Christopher Drew, with Annette Lawrence Drew. *Blind Man's Bluff: The Untold Story of American Submarine Espionage*. New York: Public Affairs, 1998.
Stockwell, John. *In Search of Enemies: A CIA Story*. New York: Norton, 1978.
Sullivan, William. *Mission to Iran*. New York: W. W. Norton, 1981.
Tamnes, Rolf. *The Cold War in the High North*. Oslo: Ad Notam, 1991.
Thomas, Evan. *The Very Best Men: Four Who Dared: The Early Years of the CIA*. New York: Simon & Schuster, 1995.
Troy, Thomas F. *Donovan and the CIA: A History of the Establishment of the Central Intelligence Agency*. Frederick, Md.: University Publications of America, 1981.
Tsipis, Kosta (ed.). *Arms Control Verification: The Technologies That Make It Possible*. New York: Pergamon-Brassey's, 1985.
Tully, Andrew. *Inside the FBI*. New York: Dell, 1987.
Turner, Stansfield. *Secrecy and Democracy: The CIA in Transition*. Boston: Houghton Mifflin, 1985.
Tyler, Patrick. *A Great Wall: Six Presidents and China—An Investigative History*. New York: Public Affairs, 1999.
U.S. News and World Report. *Triumph Without Victory: The Unreported History of the Persian Gulf War*. New York: Times Books, 1992.
Vance, Cyrus. *Hard Choices: Critical Years in America's Foreign Policy*. New York: Simon & Schuster, 1983.
Varner, Roy, and Wayne Collier. *A Matter of Risk: The Incredible Inside Story of the CIA's Glomar Explorer Mission to Raise a Russian Submarine*. New York: Random House, 1978.
Waller, Doug. *The Commandos: The Inside Story of America's Secret Soldiers*. New York: Simon & Schuster, 1994.
Westerfield, H. Bradford (ed.). *Inside the CIA's Private World: Declassified Articles from the Agency's Internal Journal, 1955–1992*. New Haven: Yale University Press, 1995.
Wilson, Col. Charles P. *Strategic and Tactical Aerial Reconnaissance in the Near East*. Washington, D.C.: Washington Institute for Near East Policy, 1999.
Woodward, Bob. *VEIL: The Secret Wars of the CIA, 1981–1987*. New York: Simon & Schuster, 1987.
______. *The Commanders*. New York: Simon & Schuster, 1991.
Wyden, Peter. *The Bay of Pigs: The Untold Story*. New York: Simon & Schuster, 1979.
Ziegler, Charles A., and David Jacobson. *Spying Without Spies: Origins of America's Secret Nuclear Surveillance System*. Westport, Conn.: Praeger, 1995.

Articles and Book Chapters

Anderson, Jack. "CIA Eavesdrops on Kremlin Chiefs." *Washington Post*, September 16, 1971, p. F7.
______. "Getting the Big Picture for the CIA." *Washington Post*, November 28, 1982.
Armstrong, Douglas G. "The Gulf War's Patched-Together Air Intelligence." *Naval Institute Proceedings*, November 1992, pp. 109–111.

Bamford, James. "America's Supersecret Eyes in Space." *New York Times Magazine*, January 13, 1985, pp. 39ff.

Barr, Stephen. "Monitoring Service Spared in Latest Crisis." *Washington Post*, February 6, 1997, p. A21.

Beecher, William. "Soviet Missile Deployment Puzzles Top U.S. Analysts." *New York Times*, April 14, 1969.

Bermudez, Joseph S., Jr. "North Korea Set for More Ballistic Missile Tests." *Jane's Defence Weekly*, October 23, 1996, p. 5.

Boatman, John. "USA Planned Stealth UAV to Replace SR-71." *Jane's Defence Weekly*, December 17, 1994, pp. 1, 3.

Boffey, Philip M. "U.S. Panel Calls the Disaster in the Ukraine the Worst Ever." *New York Times*, May 4, 1986, pp. 1, 20.

Bonavia, David. "Radar Post Leak May Be Warning to Soviet Union." *The Times* (London), June 20, 1981, p. 5.

Bowman, Tom, and Scott Shane. "Espionage from the Front Lines." *Baltimore Sun*, December 8, 1995, pp. 1A, 20A–21A.

Branigan, William. "Iran's Airmen Keep U.S. Listening Posts Intact and Whirring." *Washington Post*, May 20, 1979, p. A20.

Broad, William J. "Russia Says U.S. Got Sub's Atom Arms." *New York Times*, June 20, 1993, p. 4.

Brown, Stuart F. "The Eternal Airplane." *Popular Science*, April 1994, pp. 70, 100.

Brugioni, Dino, and Frederick J. Doyle. "Arthur C. Lundahl: Founder of the Image Exploitation Discipline." In Robert A. McDonald (ed.), *CORONA: Between the Sun and the Earth: The First NRO Reconnaissance Eye in Space*. Bethesda, Md.: American Society for Photogrammetry and Remote Sensing, 1997, pp. 159–168.

Burrows, William E. "That New Black Magic." *Air and Space*, December 1998/January 1999, pp. 29–35.

Cannon, Carl M., and Mark Thompson. "Threat to Soviets Grows, U.S. Spy Photos Indicate." *Miami Herald*, April 30, 1986, pp. 1A, 14A.

"A Chinese Agent in the CIA?" *Newsweek*, December 2, 1985, p. 49.

"Chinese Official Said Exposer of CIA Turncoat." *Washington Post*, September 5, 1986, p. A18.

"The CIA Blows an Asset." *Newsweek*, September 3, 1984, pp. 48–49.

"Costly Cuts?" *Newsweek*, November 25, 1996, p. 6.

Covault, Craig. "Space Recon of Iraq Taxes CIA Operations." *Aviation Week and Space Technology*, September 3, 1990, pp. 30–31.

______. "Advanced KH-11 Broadens U.S. Recon Capability." *Aviation Week and Space Technology*, January 6, 1997, pp. 24–25.

______. "New Intelligence Ops Debut in Iraqi Strikes." *Aviation Week and Space Technology*, December 21–28, 1998, pp. 124–125.

Crosette, Barbara. "U.S. Seeks to Prove Mass Killings." *New York Times*, August 11, 1995, p. A3.

Day, Dwayne A. "A Failed Phoenix: The KH-6 LANYARD Reconnaissance Satellite." *Spaceflight* 39, 5 (May 1997): 170–174.

______. "The Development and Improvement of the Corona Satellite." In Dwayne A. Day, John Logsdon, and Brian Latell (eds.), *Eye in the Sky: The Story of the CORONA Spy Satellites*. Washington, D.C.: Smithsonian, 1998, pp. 48–85.

______. "Listening from Above: The First Signals Intelligence Satellite." *Spaceflight*, 41, 8 (August 1999): 339–346.

Dobbs, Michael. "Deconstructing the Death Ray." *Washington Post*, October 17, 1999, pp. F1, F4.

Doel, Ronald E., and Allan A. Needell. "Science, Scientists, and the CIA: Balancing International Ideals, National Needs, and Professional Opportunities." *Intelligence and National Security* 12, 1 (January 1997): 59–81.

Eftimiades, Nicholas. "China's Ministry of State Security: Coming of Age in the International Arena." *Intelligence and National Security* 8, 1 (January 1993): 23–43.
Engelberg, Stephen. "30 Years of Spying for China Is Charged." *New York Times*, November 27, 1985, p. B8.
______. "U.S. Says Intelligence Units Did Not Detect the Accident." *New York Times*, May 2, 1986, p. A9.
"Final Launch Preparations Under Way for Signal Intelligence Satellite Mission." *Aviation Week and Space Technology*, November 6, 1989, p. 24.
Fulghum, David A. "Solar-Powered UAV to Fly at Edwards." *Aviation Week and Space Technology*, October 4, 1993, p. 27.
Fulghum, David A., and Robert A. Wall. "Long-Hidden Research Spawns Black UCAV." *Aviation Week and Space Technology,* September 25, 2000, pp. 28–29.
Gardner, Martin. "Claiborne Pell: The Senator from Outer Space." *Skeptical Inquirer* 20, 2 (March/April 1996), pp. 12–15.
______. "Zero-Point Energy and Harold Puthoff." *Skeptical Inquirer*, May/June 1998, pp. 13–15.
______. "Distant Healing and Elizabeth Targ." *Skeptical Inquirer,* March/April 2001, pp. 12–14.
Gelb, Leslie H. "Officials Say CIA Made Mines with Navy Help." *New York Times*, June 1, 1984, p. A4.
Gerstenzang, James. "Shuttle Lifts Off with Spy Cargo." *Los Angeles Times*, January 25, 1985, pp. 1, 11.
Gertz, Bill. "CIA Upset Because Perle Detailed Eavesdropping." *Washington Times*, April 15, 1987, p. 2A.
______. "New Spy Satellite, Needed to Monitor Treaty, Sits on Ground." *Washington Times*, October 20, 1987, p. A5.
______. "Libyans Stop Work on Chemical Plant." *Washington Times*, June 24, 1996, p. A4.
______. "New Chinese Missiles Target All of East Asia." *Washington Times*, July 10, 1997, pp. A1, A16.
Gorin, Peter A. "ZENIT: The Response to CORONA." In Dwayne A. Day, John Logsdon, and Brian Latell (eds.), *Eye in the Sky: The Story of the CORONA Spy Satellites*. Washington, D.C.: Smithsonian, 1998, pp. 157–170.
Grabo, Cynthia. "The Evolution of U.S. Strategic Warning." *International Journal of Intelligence and Counterintelligence* 3, 3 (Fall 1989): 363–386.
"The Great Submarine Snatch." *Time*, March 31, 1975, pp. 20–27.
Grose, Peter. "U.S. Intelligence Doubts First-Strike Goal." *New York Times*, June 19, 1969.
Gupta, V., and D. Rich. "Locating the Detonation of China's First Nuclear Explosive Test on 16 October 1964." *International Journal of Remote Sensing* 17, 10 (October 1996): 1969–1974.
Gwertzman, Bernard. "Fire in Reactor May Be Out, New U.S. Pictures Indicate; Soviet Says Fallout Is Cut." *New York Times*, May 2, 1986, pp. A1, A8.
Hall, Cargill. "Post-War Strategic Reconnaissance and the Genesis of Corona." In Dwayne A. Day, John Logsdon, and Brian Latell (eds.), *Eye in the Sky: The Story of the CORONA Spy Satellites.* Washington, D.C.: Smithsonian, 1998, pp. 86–118.
Harwood, William. "Titan Boosts Military Payload for Ninth Consecutive Success." *Space News*, December 11–17, 1995, p. 26.
Hersh, Seymour. "Human Error Is Cited in '74 Glomar Failure." *New York Times*, December 9, 1976, pp. 1, 55.
______. "The Wild East." *Atlantic Monthly*, June 1994, pp. 61–86.
Hiatt, Fred, and Joanne Omang. "CIA Helped to Mine Ports in Nicaragua." *Washington Post*, April 7, 1984, p. 1.
Hurt, Henry. "CIA in Crisis: The Kampiles Case." *Reader's Digest*, June 1979, pp. 65–72.

Hyman, Ray. "Parapsychological Research: A Tutorial Review and Critical Appraisal." *Proceedings of the IEEE* 74, 6 (June 1986): 823–849.

______. "Evaluation of the Military's Twenty-Year Program on Psychic Spying." *Skeptical Inquirer*, March/April 1996, pp. 24–26.

"The Indian Connection." *India Today*, December 31, 1983, p. 10.

Inlow, Roland. "How the Cold War and Its Intelligence Problems Influenced CORONA Operations." In Robert A. McDonald (ed.), *CORONA: Between the Sun and the Earth: The First NRO Reconnaissance Eye in Space*. Bethesda, Md.: American Society for Photogrammetry and Remote Sensing, 1997, pp. 221–229.

"Investigating the Paranormal." *Nature*, October 18, 1974, pp. 559–560.

Isbell, Doug, and Vincent Kiernan. "Long-Delayed Atlantis Flight Orbits Military Spy Satellite." *Space News*, March 5–11, 1990, p. 12.

Janesick, James, and Morley Blouke. "Introduction to Charge-Coupled Devices Imaging Sensors." In Kosta Tsipis (ed.), *Arms Control Verification: The Technologies That Make It Possible*. New York: Pergamon-Brassey's, 1985.

______. "Sky on a Chip: The Fabulous CCD." *Sky and Telescope*, September 1987, pp. 238–242.

Kenden, Anthony. "U.S. Reconnaissance Satellite Programmes." *Spaceflight*, July 1978, pp. 243ff.

Kiernan, Vincent. "NRO Streamlines to Cut Intelligence Bureaucracy." *Space News*, December 7–13, 1992, pp. 1, 29.

______. "Titan 4 Launches Spy Satellite from Vandenberg AFB." *Space News*, December 7–13, 1992, p. 26.

King, Neil, Jr. "Small Start-Up Helps the CIA to Mask Its Moves on the Web." *Wall Street Journal,* February 12, 2001.

Klass, Philip. "U.S. Monitoring Capability Impaired." *Aviation Week and Space Technology*, May 14, 1979.

Kolcum, Edward H. "Night Launch of Discovery Boosts Secret Military Satellite into Orbit." *Aviation Week and Space Technology*, November 27, 1989, p. 29.

______. "Atlantis Lofts AFP-731 Reconnaissance Satellite." *Aviation Week and Space Technology*, March 5, 1990, p. 22.

Kranish, Arthur. "CIA: Israel Has 10–20 Weapons." *Washington Post*, March 15, 1976, p. A2.

Kurtz, Howard. "Pollard: Top Israelis Backed Spy Ring." *Washington Post*, February 28, 1987, p. A8.

Lardner, George. "Spy Rings of One." *Washington Post Magazine*, December 4, 1983, pp. 60–65.

Leary, Warren E. "Problems Are Reported with New Spy Satellite." *New York Times*, March 18, 1990, p. 20.

______. "Debris from Secret U.S. Satellite Is Burning Up in Fall from Space." *New York Times*, March 22, 1990, p. A24.

______. "The Dream of Eternal Flight Begins to Take Wing." *New York Times*, January 12, 1999, pp. D1, D6.

Ledeen, Michael. "A Mole in Our Midst." *New York*, October 2, 1978, pp. 55–57.

Le Moyne, James. "The Secret War Boils Over." *Newsweek*, April 11, 1983, pp. 46–50.

Lenorovitz, Jeffrey M. "CIA Satellite Data Link Study Revealed." *Aviation Week and Space Technology*, May 2, 1977, pp. 25–26.

Lewis, Jonathan E. "Tension and Triumph: Civilian and Military Relations and the Birth of the U-2 Program. In Robert A. McDonald (ed.), *CORONA: Between the Sun and the Earth, the First NRO Reconnaissance Eye in Space*. Bethesda, Md.: American Society for Photogrammetry and Remote Sensing, 1997.

Loeb, Vernon. "New Spy Satellites at Risk Because Funding Is Uncertain, Pentagon Told." *Washington Post*, November 12, 1999, p. A7.

______. "CIA Science Chief Quits, Deputy Named." *Washington Post*, January 14, 2000, p. A25.

______. "After-Action Report." *Washington Post Magazine*, February 27, 2000, pp. 7ff.

Lundberg, Kirsten. "The SS-9 Controversy: Intelligence as Political Football." Kennedy School of Government, C16-89-884.0, Case Program, 1989.

Maass, Peter. "From His Bed, CIA's Best Makes His Breakthroughs." *Washington Post*, April 21, 1996, pp. A1, A20.

Marcus, Ruth, and Joe Pichirallo. "Chin Believed Planted in U.S. as Spy." *Washington Post*, December 6, 1985, pp. A1, A22.

Marder, Murrey. "Monitoring: Not-So-Secret-Secret." *Washington Post*, June 19, 1981, p. 10.

Marks, David, and Richard Kammann. "Information Transmission in Remote Viewing Experiments." *Nature*, August 17, 1978, pp. 680–681.

Martin, Capt. James M. "Sea Mines in Nicaragua." *Proceedings of the U.S. Naval Institute* 116, 9 (September 1990): 111–116.

May, Edwin C. "The American Institutes for Research Review of the Department of Defense's STAR GATE Program: A Commentary." *Journal of Scientific Exploration* 10, 1 (1996): 89–107.

McDonald, Robert A. "CORONA: A Success for Space Reconnaissance, a Look into the Cold War, and a Revolution for Intelligence." *Photogrammetric Engineering and Remote Sensing* 61, 6 (June 1995): 689–720.

McDowell, Jonathan. "U.S. Reconnaissance Satellite Programs, Part I: Photoreconnaissance." *Quest* 4, 2 (Summer 1995): 22–31.

______. "Launch Listings." In Dwayne A. Day, John Logsdon, and Brian Latell (eds.), *Eye in the Sky: The Story of the CORONA Spy Satellites*. Washington, D.C.: Smithsonian, 1998.

"Meltdown." *Newsweek*, May 12, 1986, pp. 20–35.

"'Ministry of State Security' Set Up on Mainland China." *Issues and Studies*, July 1983, pp. 5–8.

"MSX Satellite Passes Rocket Tracking Test." *Space News*, April 24–30, 1997, p. 10.

"Oct. 10 Assault on Nicaraguans Is Laid to C.I.A.." *New York Times*, April 18, 1994, pp. A1, A12.

Oehler, Gordon. "Warning and Detection." In Sidney Drell, Abraham D. Sofaer, and George D. Wilson (eds.), *The New Terror: Facing the Threat of Biological and Chemical Weapons*. Stanford, Calif.: Hoover Institution Press, 1999.

O'Leary, Jeremiah. "Turner Says U.S. Didn't Bug Park." *Washington Times*, August 9, 1977, pp. A1, A6.

Omang, Joanne. "Historical Background to the CIA's Nicaraguan Manual." In *Psychological Operations in Guerrilla Warfare*. New York: Vintage, 1985.

"Once-Secret Technology Assists Cancer Detection." *Signal*, June 1995, pp. 66–67.

O'Toole, Thomas, and Charles Babcock. "CIA 'Big Bird' Satellite Manual Was Allegedly Sold to the Soviets." *Washington Post*, August 23, 1978, pp. A1, A16.

Ott, James. "Espionage Trial Highlights CIA Problems." *Aviation Week and Space Technology*, November 27, 1978, pp. 21–23.

Pear, Robert. "Radio Broadcasts Report Protests Erupting All over China." *New York Times*, May 23, 1989, p. A14.

Peebles, Curtis. "The Guardians." *Spaceflight*, November 1978, pp. 381 ff.

Pichirallo, Joe. "Ex-CIA Analyst Gave Secrets to China for 30 Years, FBI Says." *Washington Post*, November 24, 1985, pp. A1, A24.

______. "Retiree Kept Close CIA Ties." *Washington Post*, November 27, 1985, pp. A1, A10.

Pike, Christopher Anson. "CANYON, RHYOLITE, and AQUACADE: U.S. Signals Intelligence Satellites in the 1970s." *Spaceflight* 37, 11 (November 1995): 381–383.

Pike, John. "Reagan Prepares for War in Outer Space." *CounterSpy* 7, 1 (September–November 1982), pp. 17–22.

Pincus, Walter. "U.S. Seeks A-Test Monitoring Facility." *Washington Post*, March 19, 1986, p. A8.

Pincus, Walter, and Mary Thornton. "U.S. to Orbit 'Sigint' Craft from Shuttle." *Washington Post*, December 19, 1984, pp. A1, A8–A9.

"Public Support Swells for CIA's FBIS Program." *Secrecy and Government Bulletin*, July 1996.

Puthoff, Harold E. "CIA-Initiated Remote Viewing at Stanford Research Institute." *Journal of Scientific Exploration* 10, 1 (Spring, 1996): 63–76.

Rensberg, Boyce. "Explosion: Graphite Fire Suspected." *Washington Post*, April 30, 1986, pp. A1, A17.

Richelson, Jeffrey. "The Satellite Data System." *Journal of the British Interplanetary Society* 37, 5 (1984): 226–228.

______. "CIA's Science and Technology Gurus Get New Look, Roles." *Defense Week*, August 19, 1996, p. 6.

______. "The Wizards of Langley: The CIA's Directorate of Science and Technology, 1962–1996." *Intelligence and National Security* 12, 1 (January 1997): 82–103.

Robinson, Clarence A. "Intelligence Agency Adjusts as Mission Possible Unfolds." *Signal*, October 1998.

Ruane, Michael E. "Ex-CIA Employee Has Saluted Tiny Paper Soldiers Since '20s." *Dallas Morning News*, February 28, 1999, p. 9F.

______. "Seeing Is Deceiving." *Washington Post*, February 15, 2000, pp. C1, C8.

Schemann, Serge. "Soviet Mobilizes a Vast Operation to Overcome the Disaster." *New York Times*, May 19, 1986, p. A8.

"A Secret War for Nicaragua." *Newsweek*, November 8, 1992, pp. 42–53.

"Seismic Sensors." *Intelligence Newsletter*, January 17, 1990, p. 2.

Selander, J. Michael. "Image Coverage Models for Declassified Corona, Argon, and Lanyard Satellite Photography–a Technical Explanation." In Robert A. McDonald (ed.), *CORONA: Between the Sun and the Earth, the First NRO Reconnaissance Eye in Space*. Bethesda, Md.: American Society for Photogrammetry and Remote Sensing, 1997.

Shenon, Philip. "Former C.I.A. Analyst Is Arrested and Accused of Spying for China." *New York Times*, November 24, 1985, pp. 1, 31.

______. "U.S. Says Spy Suspect Had Access to Highly Classified Data." *New York Times*, January 3, 1986, p. A12.

"Shuttle Spy Satellite Has Not Reentered." *Spaceflight*, January 1991, p. 4.

Smith, Hedrick. "U.S. Aides Say Loss of Post in Iran Impairs Missile-Monitoring Ability." *New York Times*, March 2, 1979, pp. A1, A8.

______. "Britain Criticizes Mining of Harbors Around Nicaragua." *New York Times*, April 7, 1984, pp. 1, 4.

Smith, R. Jeffrey. "Tracking Aideed Hampered by Intelligence Failures." *Washington Post*, October 8, 1993, p. A19.

______. "Pentagon Has Spent Millions on Tips from Trio of Psychics." *Washington Post*, November 29, 1995, pp. A1, A18.

Smith, R. Jeffrey, and Curt Suplee. "'Psychic Arms Race' Had Several Funding Channels." *Washington Post*, November 30, 1995, pp. A1, A13.

Southerland, Daniel. "China Silent on Reported Defection of Intelligence Official." *Washington Post*, September 4, 1986, p. A30.

"Soviets Claim Reconnaissance Satellite Launched by Atlantis Has Failed." *Aviation Week and Space Technology*, March 26, 1990, p. 23.

"Space Reconnaissance Dwindles." *Aviation Week and Space Technology*, October 6, 1980, pp. 18–20.

"Spying on Russia, with China's Help." *U.S. News and World Report*, June 29, 1981, p. 10.

Stern, Laurence,. "U.S. Taped Top Russians' Car Phones." *Washington Post*, December 5, 1973, pp. A1, A16.

Stevens, Sayre. "The Soviet BMD Program." In Ashton D. Carter and David N. Schwartz (eds.), *Ballistic Missile Defense*. Washington, D.C.: Brookings Institution, 1984, pp. 182–220.

Targ, Russell. "Remote Viewing at Stanford Research Institute in the 1970s: A Memoir." *Journal of Scientific Exploration* 10, 1 (Spring 1996): 77–88.

Targ, Russell, and Harold Puthoff. "Information Transmission Under Conditions of Sensory Shielding." *Nature*, October 18, 1974, pp. 602–607.

Taubman, Philip. "U.S. and Peking Jointly Monitor Russian Missiles." *New York Times*, June 18, 1981, pp. A1, A14.

______. "Americans on Ship Said to Supervise Nicaragua Mining." *New York Times*, April 8, 1984, pp. 1, 12.

______. "U.S. Officials Say C.I.A. Helped Nicaraguan Rebels Plan Attacks." *New York Times*, October 16, 1984, pp. 1, 22.

Toner, Robin. "Bail Denied Ex-CIA Worker in China Spy Case." *New York Times*, November 28, 1985, p. B8.

Torgeson, Dial. "U.S. Spy Devices Still Running at Iran Post." *International Herald Tribune*, March 7, 1979, pp. A1, A8.

Toth, Robert C. "U.S., China Jointly Track Firings of Soviet Missiles." *Los Angeles Times*, June 19, 1981, pp. 1, 9.

______. "CIA Covert Action Punishes Nicaragua for Salvador Aid." *New York Times*, April 18, 1984, pp. A1, A12.

______. "Satellites Keep Eye on Reactor." *Los Angeles Times*, May 2, 1986, p. 22.

Tyler, Patrick. "Satellite Fails." *Washington Post*, March 17, 1990, pp. A1, A11.

Ullom, Joel. "Enriched Uranium Versus Plutonium: Proliferant Preferences in the Choice of Fissile Material." *Nonproliferation Review* 2, 1 (Fall 1994): 1–15.

"U.S. Agencies Used Psychics for Years for 'Remote Viewing.'" *Washington Times*, November 30, 1995, p. A12.

Vartabedian, Ralph. "Air Force Spy Satellite Unit Leaving California." *Los Angeles Times* (Washington ed.), October 16, 1992, pp. A1, A5.

______. "Air Force Spy Satellite Unit Leaving Southland." *Los Angeles Times*, October 16, 1992, pp. A1, A12.

Volkman, Ernest. "U.S. Spies Lend an Ear to Soviets." *Newsday*, July 12, 1977, p. 7.

Waller, Douglas. "The Vision Thing." *Time*, December 11, 1995, p. 48.

Weiner, Tim. "U.S. Suspects India Prepares for Nuclear Test." *New York Times*, March 5, 1995, pp. 1, 9.

______. "Sidney Gottlieb, 80, Dies: Took LSD to C.I.A.." *New York Times*, March 10, 1999.

Welzenbach, Donald. "Din Land: Patriot from Polaroid." *Optics and Photonics News* 5, 10 (October 1996): 22ff.

Wheelon, Albert D. "Genesis of a Unique National Capability." Address at CIA, December 19, 1985.

______. "CORONA: A Triumph of American Technology." In Dwayne A. Day, John Logsdon, and Brian Latell (eds.), *Eye in the Sky: The Story of the CORONA Spy Satellites*. Washington, D.C.: Smithsonian, 1998.

Whitelaw, Kevin. "A Killing in the Congo." *U.S. News and World Report,* July 24–31, 2000, p. 63.

Wilford, John Noble. "A Secret Payload Is Orbited by U.S." *New York Times*, August 7, 1968, p. 7.

______. "Spy Satellite Reportedly Aided in Shuttle Flight." *New York Times*, October 20, 1981, p. C4.

Wilhelm, John L. "Psychic Spying?" *Washington Post*, August 7, 1977, pp. B1, B5.

Wines, Michael. "Bigger Role Laid to Suspected Spy." *Los Angeles Times*, November 28, 1985, pp. 1, 10.

______. "Spy Reportedly Unmasked by China Defector." *Los Angeles Times*, September 5, 1986, pp. 1, 12.

Wise, David. "The Spy Who Wouldn't Die." *GQ*, July 1998, pp. 148ff.

Yannuzzi, Rick E. "In-Q-Tel: A New Partnership Between the CIA and the Private Sector." *Defense Intelligence Journal* 9, 1 (Winter 2000).

Zakaria, Tabassum. "CIA Using 'Data Mining' Technology to Find Nuggets." Reuters, March 2, 2001.

Internet

Anthes, Gary H. "Cloak and Dagger IT." www.computerworld.com, accessed February 6, 20001.
"Environmental Research Aircraft and Sensor Technology: Pathfinder, Past Flight Information." www.dfrc.nasa.gov/Projects/erast/Projects/Pathfinder/pastinfo.html.
"Harold E. Puthoff." www.firedocs.com/remoteviewing/oooh/people/puthoff.html.
"Lockheed RB-69A 'Neptune.'" www.wpafb.af.mil/museum/research/bombers/b5/b5-62.htm.
Loeb, Vernon. "Inside Information." www.washingtonpost.com, accessed January 10, 2000.
"Meet the CEO." www.anser.org/aboutanser/meetceo.html.
"Profile of APL." www.jhuapl.edu/profile/profile.htm.
"Russell Targ." www.firedocs.com/remoteviewing/oooh/people/targ/html.

Other

NBC. *Inside the KGB: Narration and Shooting Script*, May 1993.
Oral History Interview with Richard Bissell Jr., Columbia University, 1973.
The Reminiscences of Arthur C. Lundahl. Oral History Research Office, Columbia University, 1982.

INDEX